AF822793

Policy, Program and Project Evaluation

Anwar Shah
Editor

Policy, Program and Project Evaluation

A Toolkit for Economic Analysis in a Changing World

palgrave
macmillan

Editor
Anwar Shah
Governance Studies
Brookings Institution
Washington, DC, USA

ISBN 978-3-030-48566-5 ISBN 978-3-030-48567-2 (eBook)
https://doi.org/10.1007/978-3-030-48567-2

© The Editor(s) (if applicable) and The Author(s), under exclusive licence to Springer Nature Switzerland AG 2020
This work is subject to copyright. All rights are solely and exclusively licensed by the Publisher, whether the whole or part of the material is concerned, specifically the rights of translation, reprinting, reuse of illustrations, recitation, broadcasting, reproduction on microfilms or in any other physical way, and transmission or information storage and retrieval, electronic adaptation, computer software, or by similar or dissimilar methodology now known or hereafter developed.
The use of general descriptive names, registered names, trademarks, service marks, etc. in this publication does not imply, even in the absence of a specific statement, that such names are exempt from the relevant protective laws and regulations and therefore free for general use.
The publisher, the authors and the editors are safe to assume that the advice and information in this book are believed to be true and accurate at the date of publication. Neither the publisher nor the authors or the editors give a warranty, expressed or implied, with respect to the material contained herein or for any errors or omissions that may have been made. The publisher remains neutral with regard to jurisdictional claims in published maps and institutional affiliations.

This Palgrave Macmillan imprint is published by the registered company Springer Nature Switzerland AG.
The registered company address is: Gewerbestrasse 11, 6330 Cham, Switzerland

Preface

In recent decades, evaluation as a discipline has progressed from a tool for post-evaluation to current operational management. Because of this, the evaluation techniques have come into widespread use both in public and private sector operations. The practice of this discipline has leapfrogged the available guidance from the existing literature creating a wide vacuum especially in evaluating the design and impact of policies, policy analysis, and advice. This book attempts to fill this void by providing a primer on both traditional and newer evaluation techniques. The book presents easily comprehensible and comprehensive tools of economic analysis that are currently used in the evaluation literature to evaluate public projects, programs, policies, and policy analysis and advice. It is hoped that the book would appeal to a wide range of readers interested in this subject such as scholars, researchers, students, evaluation professionals and practitioners, policymakers and public managers.

Washington, DC, USA Anwar Shah

Acknowledgements

This project took a long time from inception to fruition. The editor is grateful to the authors for their patience and perseverance. Hopefully, their patience will be rewarded by the potential impact of this book in fostering the better design of public policies and programs globally to advance the public interest.

Contents

List of Figures

List of Tables

List of Boxes

Notes on Contributors

Robin Boadway is Emeritus Professor of Economics at Queen's University, Canada. He is past Editor of the *Journal of Public Economics* and *Canadian Journal of Economics*, and past President of the International Institute of Public Finance and Canadian Economics Association. He was Distinguished Fellow of the Centre for Economic Studies at the University of Munich. His research interests are in public economics and policy, and fiscal federalism. He works on fiscal federalism, cost–benefit analysis and tax policy. His recent books include *Fiscal Federalism: Principles and Practice of Multiorder Governance* (2009) with Anwar Shah, and *From Optimal Tax Theory to Tax Policy: Retrospective and Prospective Views, The Munich Lectures* (2012).

Bev Dahlby is Research Director and Distinguished Fellow at The School of Public Policy at University of Calgary, Canada. Dahlby attended St. Peter's College, the University of Saskatchewan, Queen's University, and the London School of Economics. Dahlby has published extensively on tax policy and fiscal federalism, including his book *The Marginal Cost of Public Funds: Theory and Applications* (2008). He has served as a policy advisor to the Canadian federal and provincial governments. He was a member of Statistics Canada's advisory council from 2005 to 2012. Dahlby was a member of the Expert Panel on Federal Support to Research and Development in 2010–2011 and the Ecofiscal Commission from 2014 to 2019. In 2016, he chaired the British Columbia Commission on Tax Competitiveness. In 2019, Dahlby served on the Blue Ribbon Panel appointed by the Government of Alberta to review the province's finances. His international experience includes advisory work on tax reform for the IMF in Malawi, for the Thailand Development Research Institute, and for the World Bank in Brazil and Mexico.

Saubhik Deb is Economist and Independent Consultant with over 20 years of experience in policy research and evaluation. He has worked with organizations such as the World Bank, Indian Council for Research on International Economic Relations (ICRIER), and PwC on various projects relating to evaluation of public sector programs. He specializes in impact evaluations using experimental and quasi-experimental designs. His recent areas of interest include rural water supply and sanitation, child health, nutrition, and education and he has several books and journal publications to his credit. Deb holds a PhD in Economics from Rutgers University, USA and an MA and MPhil in Economics from Jawaharlal Nehru University, India.

Jeff Huther is Senior Project Manager for the LIBOR transition at the Federal Reserve Board, USA. His past work at the Fed includes co-leading the section that assesses money market conditions and the Fed's balance sheet projections, overseeing the section that provides analyses of money and reserves, and providing analyses of money market conditions to the FOMC. He has also served as Assistant Vice President within the Markets Group at the Federal Reserve Bank of New York. Prior to his work at the Federal Reserve, Huther was Vice President for Financial Engineering at Freddie Mac. He also worked for six years at the US Treasury's Office of Debt Management including three years as Director. Earlier postgraduate work included two years as Senior Analyst at the New Zealand Treasury. He holds a PhD from Georgetown University, an MA from Boston University, and a BS in Chemistry from St. Lawrence University.

Stuart Landon is Professor Emeritus of Economics at the University of Alberta, Canada. He holds degrees in economics from Queen's University (PhD), the University of British Columbia (MA) and McGill University (BA Honors), and has been a visiting academic at the Australian National University and Victoria University of Wellington. He has published papers on a wide variety of topics in Canadian, US, European and Australian economics and finance journals and was awarded the Canadian Economics Association's Vanderkamp Prize (along with three coauthors) and the University of Alberta's Rutherford Award for Excellence in Undergraduate Teaching. He served in numerous administrative positions at the University of Alberta and co-chaired the working group that designed the new revenue allocation model for the University.

Melville McMillan is Professor Emeritus in the Department of Economics and a Fellow of the Institute of Public Economics at the University of Alberta, Canada. McMillan's research and teaching interests are in public economics, particularly urban and local economics, fiscal federalism, and the demand/supply of public goods and services. He has published in these areas and has advised governments and organizations nationally and internationally (e.g., the World Bank). Although "retired," McMillan remains actively involved in academic and policy matters.

Anwar Shah is Non-Resident Senior Fellow at the Brookings Institution, USA. He is also an advisor/consultant to the World Bank and Distinguished Visiting Professor of Economics at Southwestern University of Finance and Economics, China. He has previously served the World Bank, Government of Canada (Ministry of Finance), the Government of Alberta, and the UN Intergovernmental Panel on Climate Change. He has published more than two dozen books in English, Spanish, Chinese, Vietnamese and Russian languages and numerous articles in leading economic journals on governance, public management reforms, budget reform, federalism, local governance, fiscal reforms and global climate change issues.

Ewa Tomaszewska is Principal Economist at HDR, Canada. She has over 20 years of consulting experience in economic analysis of infrastructure projects, regulatory proposals, policies and programs for private and public sector clients in the United States and Canada. She has extensive experience across a wide range of economic assessments supporting client needs with a major focus on cost–benefit analysis studies to support applications for funding from higher-order governments, strategic planning and decisions, or regulatory submissions; economic and social impacts studies to support stakeholder and community relations; and economic policy research and analysis to inform and support strategic planning, policy decisions, and best practices development. Tomaszewska holds a PhD in Economics from the University of Alberta.

CHAPTER 1

Introduction

Anwar Shah

Evaluation as a discipline, in recent decades, has progressed from providing answers to questions like economic viability, cost-effectiveness, and efficiency to questions that are critical for effective planning, financing, design, implementation, and success of a program. Today evaluation can provide valuable assistance in defining a problem, identifying program targets, designing of interventions, identifying winners and losers and organizational strengths and weaknesses, assessing the quality of interventions and performance of program delivery and its impact, suggesting modifications and alterations, and ultimately guiding a program or project to its successful end. Evaluation is no longer just a tool for program or project appraisals but also an important tool in operational management. It is not just a snapshot of the end; it is also the means to the end (see also Williams and Giardina 1993). This book provides an easily comprehensible and comprehensive survey of tools of analysis that are used in the evaluation literature to evaluate public projects, programs, policies, and policy analysis and advice. The following paragraphs provide an overview of the book.

Chapter 2 by Deb and Shah provides a brief survey of the program evaluation methods, their objectives, strengths, and weaknesses. The

A. Shah (✉)
Governance Studies, Brookings Institution, Washington, DC, USA

© The Author(s) 2020

A. Shah (ed.), *Policy, Program and Project Evaluation*,
https://doi.org/10.1007/978-3-030-48567-2_1

methods have been presented in a manner that reflects the changes in outlook towards public programs and the changing role of evaluation. Accordingly, we have first presented methods like cost-benefit analysis, cost effectiveness analysis, the social marginal cost of funds analysis, and data envelopment analysis that are appropriate for guiding efficient allocation and utilization of resources. This is followed by a discussion on multiple-objective evaluation, which is much more holistic. Apart from efficiency, it addresses issues like the relevance of a program, effectiveness of a program in achieving its objectives and sustainability of the program benefits. Newer multi-criteria approaches such as the Iron Triangle, Alternate Service Delivery Framework (ASDF), and the Results-Oriented Management and Evaluation (ROME) are briefly sketched. The Iron Triangle notes three important constraints faced by public managers—time, cost, and quality. The ASDF brings into sharper focus the role of government as a catalyst in managing and coordinating service delivery by government and beyond government providers. ROME is particularly noteworthy for recognizing the role of citizens as the principals and various orders of governments as their agents. It provides an integrated approach to managing for results, citizens-based evaluation of those results, and the processes to hold the government to account by citizens. Finally, the authors outline the theory-based evaluation approach. It is a relatively new concept in evaluation literature where the focus is not just on whether a program succeeds or fails but also on how and why a program succeeds or fails.

The chapter concludes that the methods discussed serve different purposes. Methods like cost-benefit analysis, cost-effectiveness analysis, and data envelopment analysis address the question of efficiency in the allocation and utilization of funds. In multiple-objective evaluation, the emphasis is more on accountability in public sector programs, the effectiveness of programs, and the sustainability of program benefits. The evaluation is concerned with issues like identification of program beneficiaries, assessing their requirements, tailoring of interventions to meet those requirements, monitoring of interventions to ensure that the appropriate interventions are being delivered to the participants, and finally the overall effectiveness of the interventions in achieving the program objectives. So, a multiple-objectives evaluation plays a big role in program planning, design, and implementation. A theory-based evaluation assigns an even bigger role to an evaluation in public programs. It goes deeper into the mechanism through which the interventions bring about the desired effects. It analyzes the causal links between interventions and outcomes. So, instead of passing a summative judgment on whether a program succeeded or failed in achieving its objectives, the theory-based evaluation shows *why* it succeeded or failed. Thus, it contributes to the development of more effective programs in the future.

The authors argue that evaluation is different from other social research in the sense that it derives its questions from policymakers, program sponsors, program managers, and stakeholders. So, the applicability of any specific evaluation method depends on the questions that the evaluator has been asked to address. When the evaluation question is deciding upon alternative interventions aimed at producing similar effects, cost-effectiveness analysis might be more suitable. But it is not useful at all when the problem is prioritizing among different programs addressing different problems. A cost-benefit analysis will be more appropriate in that case. Similarly, data envelopment analysis might not have the valuation problems associated with the cost-benefit or cost-effectiveness analysis. But its applicability is limited to comparing efficiencies of similar programs only. For programs whose efficacies have already been established, multiple objective evaluations might be enough for performance evaluations. However, for pilot studies or for programs that have not been tested before, a theory-based evaluation is much more desirable. But it is also more time consuming and more expensive than any other evaluation methods. So, the choice of the evaluation method would also depend upon the availability of time and resources.

Chapter 3 by Robin Boadway summarizes the principles used to evaluate projects (such as individual investment projects, general expenditure programs, and the implementation of government policies) from an economic point of view. Following the principles of welfare economics, the objective of project evaluation is to measure the costs and benefits to individuals in society. The chapter begins with some theoretical perspectives on cost-benefit analysis and then proceeds to discuss the difficulties of implementing such an analysis and practical ways of dealing with these problems. He describes project evaluation as "an art, though one with scientific underpinnings."

Broadly, the measurement of costs and benefits amounts to a measurement of individuals' "willingness to pay." Two methods that have been developed in the theoretical literature are "compensating variation" and "equivalent variation," depending on whether one wishes to use final or initial prices (respectively) for goods affected by the project. In addition, one must consider that projects that have costs and benefits spread over time must use a common set of prices to adjust for inflation and the time value of money. Policymakers may also wish to add distributive weights—in other words weighting more heavily improvements in the incomes of the poorest. Once the discounted stream of costs and benefits is summed (yielding the Net Present Value, or NPV), the decision rule for project approval is simply determined by a (positive) sign of the NPV. Finally, the risk and uncertainty of outcomes should also be included. Other, similar techniques for project evaluation include the benefit-cost ratio and the internal rate of return methods. However, these alternative measures have some problems and may rank projects differently than the NPV criterion.

While the NPV method is in principle the same as is used by the private sector to guide the choice of investment decisions, the implementation of this procedure differs in some important ways when applied to the public sector. This is because the public sector must take into consideration: the marginal social values or shadow prices (rather than just market prices, since markets may be distorted) of inputs including labor, capital, and foreign exchange, and the impact of externalities such as pollution, general equilibrium effects of the project, valuation of intangible benefits and costs (such as time saved due to public transport), excess burden of public financing (due to distortions of the tax system—the so-called marginal cost of public funds, or MCF), the social discount rate, and social considerations (such as equity or protection of special groups). Each of these issues is considered in turn in this chapter.

Chapter 4 by Bev Dahlby probes more deeply into an evaluation tool that received brief treatment in Chaps. 1 and 2—the Marginal Cost of Public Funds (MCF), or the loss to consumers and producers caused by raising an additional dollar of tax revenue. Taxes impose a cost on the economy if they alter taxpayers' consumption, production, and asset allocation decisions, leading to a less-efficient allocation of resources. Raising an additional dollar of tax revenue costs the private sector more than a dollar if the allocation of resources in the economy becomes more distorted. The marginal cost of public funds, MCF, is a measure of the cost imposed on the private sector in raising an additional dollar of tax revenue. Dahlby argues that the marginal cost of public funds should be used in evaluating the opportunity cost of financing public sector expenditures. It also provides a guide for tax reform by revealing which taxes impose the greatest welfare losses in generating additional revenues. The MCF can also be used to measure the gains from tax reforms that shift the burden from the high-cost tax bases to ones with lower costs.

In this chapter, Dahlby introduces the concept of the marginal cost of public funds (MCF), examples of how the MCFs can be measured, and examples of how they can be applied to guide tax reform and public expenditure policies. In keeping with the theme of this volume, the emphasis is on using the MCF as a tool for public policy analysis. Two practical examples demonstrate the use of this evaluation tool in public policy analysis and evaluation. The first is an assessment of the gains from a tax reform that shifts some of the tax burdens from corporate to the personal income tax base in Alberta, Canada. The second example illustrates how the MCF can be used to derive optimal matching rates for intergovernmental infrastructure grants in a federation. In presenting these applications, the author makes a convincing case of the critical importance of the MCF as a tool for the evaluation of tax and expenditure policies.

Theory-based evaluation traces the factors that contributed to a specific outcome for the project. This a challenging task for project evaluation as it requires establishing a causal chain based upon theoretical considerations and analyzing data on various links in this causal chain. Ewa Tomaszewska in Chap. 5 provides a guidebook for those interested in conducting case studies in project evaluation determining the impact of various projects in combating corruption. The author provides a conceptual framework and data requirements for such evaluation case studies for privation programs, judicial and legal reforms, civil service reforms, trade liberalization, tax administration reforms, and direct anticorruption activities (anti-corruption agencies), the Office of Ombudsman, transparency rules and decentralization.

The impact of corruption on public service delivery performance and poverty alleviation is widely recognized. A wide consensus has also recently emerged that corruption is a symptom of failed governance and hence curtailing corruption requires addressing the causes of misgovernance. Nevertheless, the menu of potential actions to curtail corruption is very large so a framework is needed that provides guidance on ordering potential actions. Prioritization of various actions depends on both the conceptual and empirical views of what works and what does not work in the context of particular countries. Such a framework is also needed for evaluating country anti-corruption programs and policies. Chapter 6 by Huther and Shah proposes a framework for such evaluations. The chapter concludes that path dependency is critical in determining the relative efficacy of various anti-corruption programs. For example, in a largely corruption-free environment, anti-corruption agencies, ethics offices, and ombudsmen serve to enhance the standards of accountability. In countries with endemic corruption, the same institutions serve a function in form only and not in substance. Under a best-case scenario, these institutions might be helpful, but the more likely outcome is that they help to preserve the existing system of social injustice. Successful anti-corruption programs are those which address the underlying governance failures, resulting in lower opportunities for gain and a greater likelihood of sanctions. Thus, programs must be targeted to a country's existing quality of governance. Past experiences of the industrialized world confirm these conclusions since, without exception, these countries did not achieve a reduction in corruption by introducing technocratic solutions but, rather, by encouraging a sense of public duty among officials through accountability for results. Such an accountability culture came about by empowering people and by decentralizing decision making. These conclusions suggest the following stylized presentation of anti-corruption measures based on the existing quality of governance. Addressing the governance failures which distort officials' cost-benefit assessment is likely to be the only route to success in countries with high levels of corruption and poor governance since direct dialogue on corruption is likely to be counter-productive (resulting in simply another level of corrupt officials under the name of anti-corruption offices). In countries with poor governance quality, external advice can promote economic liberalization, judicial reform, and greater public participation in public expenditure decisions without explicitly raising contentious issues of corruption and, one hopes, without threatening their existing relationships. In countries with modest levels of corruption and governance quality, where the existing governance structure has the capacity to reform, it is an important focus on improvements in readily identifiable output indicators rather than uncertain measures of corruption as measures of success. In countries with high governance quality, explicit efforts to reduce corruption are likely to be successful—commissions on corruption, ombudsmen, ethics offices, and the like can rely on an infrastructure of public accountability and transparency to ensure that their findings result in lower incentives to commit corrupt acts.

Public Expenditure Review (PER) is a widely used tool by the development assistance community to develop advice on budgetary institutions and allocations. This tool has also been used by both industrial and developing countries as an aid to public sector reforms. The most common format of PERs begins with a presentation of an overall picture of the country's fiscal situation. This picture typically focuses on the country's expenditure trends. This presentation provides the background, and frequently the justification, for the specific issues addressed by the review. The picture of the fiscal situation is frequently followed by an analysis of the budget process which typically provides the foil for recommendations made in the PER. In some cases, providing a picture of the country's fiscal situation and outlining the budget process may be the only tasks undertaken in the PER. In other cases, PERs review selected inter- and intra-sectoral issues. Almost all formal, and many informal, reviews also include extensive data on a country's expenditures. Chapter 7 by Huther and Shah presents a framework for evaluating the quality and timeliness of PERs as well as conducting a review of their impact. They highlight specific elements to consider and to rate in such an analysis and how to develop final cost-efficiency and benefit-cost ratings.

Given that the empirical evidence on the relationship between government expenditures and economic growth is inconclusive, Stuart Landon in Chap. 8 asks if the composition of expenditures and design of programs is a better determinant of the effectiveness of government expenditures than the size of the public sector. Although there are no universal rules, he suggests that a review of the empirical evidence drawn from a broad number of countries can help to identify the sectors that should generally receive the highest priority in government budgets.

In theory, government intervention can improve welfare in the presence of market failure (such as insufficient competition and incomplete markets arising from public goods and asymmetric information). However, the nature and magnitude of the market failure must be known when designing the program to ensure that the costs of intervention are justified and that the government has the capacity to successfully carry it out. In states with weak capacity, government intervention may be more harmful than the market failure that the program was intended to address. Given that state capacity is a critical input for the successful implementation of government programs (and therefore the effectiveness of public expenditures generally), it is worthwhile to invest in the capacity of public administration and reduce the size while improving the quality of the civil service (though this may be politically difficult) and developing a system to monitor expenditure effectiveness. Incentives for improved public sector performance may be created by increasing wages and reducing wage compression when coupled with mechanisms that create accountability for performance. Other tools for improving the public sector include subjecting the public sector to greater competition, involving the private sector for provision, implementing user fees.

Landon also deals with sector-specific issues, including law and security, military spending, infrastructure, transportation, operation and maintenance expenditures, education, health, redistribution, regulation, financial markets, state-owned enterprises, and industrial subsidies. For each of these, he discusses whether the sector should be a priority in the public budget as well as ways to make expenditures in each area more effective. He also considers the efficiency and equity effects of expenditures in addition to the likely re-distributional consequences. Based on a review of the literature, Landon assigns a low priority to subsidies to many state-owned enterprises and private industry, poorly targeted consumption subsidies, infrastructure that could be undertaken by the private sector, social security programs, tertiary education and hospital care, military spending, and extensive regulatory regimes. High priority should be assigned to develop an effective legal system to protect and enforce property rights, effective financial regulation, maintenance of existing infrastructure, and transportation, communications, and electricity infrastructure. Spending priority should also be given to improvements in the quality and quantity of primary education and basic health care, water and sanitation, and well-targeted consumption subsidy programs for the very poor.

Governments are becoming more decentralized. Political power and public decision making in many countries around the world have, to varying degrees, shifted away from central governments, particularly over the past quarter-century. This movement has been attributed to various forces; for example, the growing number of democracies, urbanization, increasing literacy, rising incomes, a growing middle class, and the failures of central governments. The World Bank has been involved in this transition in developing countries. Given the extent of the movement occurring and the Bank's initiatives, there is a natural wish to assess the Bank's activities regarding decentralization. A comprehensive evaluation of the Bank's undertakings in this area creates the opportunity to understand better the potential for and limitations of decentralization, to identify the strengths and weaknesses of Bank activities and practices relating to decentralization, and to assist in refining Bank policies concerning decentralization. Essentially, an evaluation is to generate information that will help the Bank's decentralization policies, programs, and practices to be more successful. Chapter 9 by McMillan outlines an approach in evaluating the Bank's decentralization initiatives. The basic methodology for evaluating individual decentralization projects is outlined with elaboration components of decentralization and steps to be taken in the evaluation. The method for extending the evaluation across many projects follows. The problem of selecting or sampling the projects to be evaluated is discussed. Special treatment is given to projects on community-driven development. The chapter also presents thoughts on bringing the various analyses and the analysis of a rather diverse set of projects together and putting the results into perspective.

Chapter 10 by Shah evaluates the conditionality of development assistance in terms of its intended and unintended consequences. Development assistance is motivated by altruistic, economic, political, military, and humanitarian considerations. It is used to advance wide-ranging objectives such as minimizing risks for loan repayment, efficiency, equity of the public sector, overcoming infrastructure deficiencies, promoting growth, facilitating poverty alleviation and good governance, combating terrorism, support for a specific ideology, influence peddling, and economic and political imperialism. The provision of such assistance is often conditional as even unconditional assistance almost always carries some explicit preconditions and implicit conditions. Conditions are imposed as part of lending or grant assistance unilaterally or by mutual agreement of the donor and the recipient. These conditions form the contractual terms of such assistance which bind the recipient to expected actions or results as a quid pro quo for receiving such financial assistance. These conditions can vary from being very vague to extremely clear and precise. They may impose formal binding requirements or simply indicate informal non-binding expectations. The chapter provides conceptual perspectives from game theory, public choice, fiscal federalism, political economy, new institutional economics, and New Public Management literature on the design of external assistance and its potential impacts. It shows how the neglect of these conceptual considerations can result in a lack of effectiveness of aid conditionality and waste of such assistance. It provides an overview of the historical evolution of perspectives on donor-recipient relations and on the conditionality of external assistance. It highlights the developing consensus by the development assistance community on both the instruments of development finance and associated conditions. It also briefly notes progress, or lack thereof, for practice to conform to emerging consensus. It cites examples where the inappropriate design of conditionality led to adverse consequences for project and program outcomes. The chapter provides lessons on major issues in the conditionality of development assistance.

Reference

Williams, Alan, and Emilio Giardina. 1993. *Efficiency in the Public Sector: The Theory and Practice of Cost-Benefit Analysis*. Brookfield: Edward Elgar.

CHAPTER 2

A Primer on Public Sector Evaluations

Saubhik Deb and Anwar Shah

Introduction

Program evaluation has undergone major changes over the years at both a conceptual and a functional level. It has transformed from a tool designed mainly to assess the efficient allocation of resources to a full-grown discipline concerned with the all-round development of a program. The multitude of social and economic problems and the constraint on available resources require prioritization among both problems and programs directed at addressing those problems. As a result, assessment of the cost efficiency of public interventions still occupies a prominent role in evaluation research. However, a heightened awareness of the potentials and perils of public problems both at the national and international arena and the need for proactive measures have brought forth issues like efficacy and accountability in the parlance of program evaluation. Consequently, evaluation as a discipline has transgressed from providing answers to questions like economic viability and efficiency to questions that are critical for effective planning, design, implementation, and success of a program. Today evaluation can provide valuable assistance in defining a problem,

S. Deb (✉)
Kolkata, India

A. Shah
Governance Studies, Brookings Institution, Washington, DC, USA

© The Author(s) 2020

A. Shah (ed.), *Policy, Program and Project Evaluation*,
https://doi.org/10.1007/978-3-030-48567-2_2

identifying program targets, designing interventions, identifying organizational strengths and weaknesses, assessing the quality of interventions and performance of program delivery, suggesting modifications and alterations and ultimately guiding a program to its successful end. Evaluation is no longer just a tool for program appraisals or a snapshot of the end of a project or program. It also serves as a means to an end.

This chapter provides a brief survey of the program evaluation methods, their objectives, strengths, and weaknesses. The methods have been presented in a manner that reflects the changes in outlook towards public programs and the changing role of evaluation. Accordingly, we have first presented methods like cost-benefit analysis, cost-effectiveness analysis, the social marginal cost of funds analysis, and data envelopment analysis that are appropriate for guiding efficient allocation and utilization of resources. This is followed by a discussion on multi-criteria or multiple-objectives evaluation (MCE/MOE), which is much more holistic in nature. Apart from efficiency, it addresses issues like the relevance of a program, effectiveness of a program in achieving its objectives and sustainability of the program benefits. Newer approaches such as the Iron Triangle, Alternate Service Delivery Framework, and the Results-Oriented Management and Evaluation (ROME) are briefly sketched. Finally, we discuss theory-based evaluation. It is a relatively new concept in evaluation literature where the focus is not just on whether or not a program succeeds or fails but also on how and why a program succeeds or fails. This is followed by the conclusion. An annex to this chapter provides a brief overview of the evaluation approach used by the World Bank.

Leading Approaches to Evaluation

In the following sub-sections, leading approaches to public sector evaluations are highlighted.

Cost-Benefit Analysis

Cost-benefit analysis is one of the earliest methods of program evaluation. It analyzes the economic viability of programs by comparing their total benefits with the total costs. When resources are limited and different programs need to be pitted against one another for allocation of funds, cost-benefit analysis can be used for prioritization of programs based on their net worth.

Cost-benefit analysis estimates the net present value of a program by comparing the benefits of the program with the associated costs. The notion of benefits and costs typically depends on the evaluation perspective. Costs and benefits calculated from program sponsors' perspective would be very different from those calculated from the perspective of program beneficiaries and would lead to very different conclusions regarding feasibility of programs. For public sector projects, cost-benefit analysis should be conducted from a social perspective. In other words, all costs and benefits for the community or the society as a whole should be taken into consideration rather than restricting attention to program beneficiaries only. Such benefits and costs can be both direct and indirect. For example, in an irrigation project, the direct costs are the capital and operational costs of the project and the compensation costs for the loss of land due to construction or inundation. The direct benefits are regeneration of degraded lands, enhanced crop yields, higher agricultural income and employment, a decline in the variability of agricultural production and increased sense of livelihood security. The indirect benefits include employment generation for the irrigation project and improvement in the quality of life, whereas indirect costs might include the loss in bio-diversity and the sufferings of people displaced from their lands.

The analysis requires determination of the length of the program—the number of years over which benefits and costs of the program are to be evaluated. Monetary values are then assigned to all benefits and costs. Since benefits and costs materialize over different periods, for comparison purpose, all current and future streams of benefits and costs are converted to their present values by using an appropriate discount factor. Net present value of a program is calculated as the difference between the present value of its benefits and the present value of its costs. A program is feasible only when its net present value is positive. Net present value can be used as a criterion for allocating funds among competing programs. Alternatively, benefit-cost ratios can also be used. Benefit-cost ratio is the ratio of present value of benefits to present value of costs. However, for mutually exclusive programs where implementation of one program precludes the possibility of others, the comparison of programs based on benefit-cost ratios can be misleading. In those cases, net present value should be used instead.

One of the important aspects of social cost-benefit analysis is the choice of the appropriate discount rate (Department of Finance 1987). The discount rate reflects the opportunity cost of capital (the rate of return that could have been earned through alternative investment of the funds). For public programs, the interest rate on government borrowing can be used for discounting future benefits and costs. However, if public investment displaces private investment, such an interest rate will not reflect the true opportunity cost of capital. In that case, the appropriate discount rate should be the social opportunity cost rate. The social opportunity cost rate is the return on private sector investment that has been displaced by the public project. Another alternative is to use the social time preference rate. It represents society's preference between current and future consumption. Social time preference rate is the required additional future consumption that is necessary to compensate for the loss of one unit of present consumption. Unfortunately, there is no authoritative way of choosing a discount rate. But the outcome of the cost-benefit analysis crucially depends on the choice of the discount rate. A lower discount rate puts relatively more emphasis on future costs and benefits whereas a higher discount rate puts more emphasis on short-term benefits and costs. Accordingly, as the discount rate increases, the net present value of a project decreases. So, depending on the choice of the discount rate, the net present value of a project can be positive or negative, thereby making or breaking the project. A sensitivity analysis (i.e., repeating the same cost-benefit analysis for different discount rates) is required for checking the robustness of results. Alternatively, the internal rate of return (IRR) of a project can be reported. IRR is the discount rate at which the net present value of a program is zero. So, it gives the decision makers a measure of risk associated with the project. However, IRR is not a criterion for program selection.

Another important aspect of cost-benefit analysis is the estimation and valuation of social benefits and costs. The analysis involves the estimation of incremental benefits and incremental costs that can be assigned solely to the project. So it is important to construct the counterfactual, i.e., what would happen or would have happened without the project. Incremental values can then be calculated by comparing the benefits and costs with and without the project. In *ex post* analysis, the problem is constructing the counterfactual. For *ex ante* analysis, the problem is not only constructing the counterfactual but also forecasting the expected benefits and costs of the project. So, there is a certain amount of uncertainty involved in the estimation of benefits and costs. Once the benefits and costs have been estimated, the next step is to assign monetary values by using prices that would reflect their true opportunity costs. When markets are perfectly competitive, the market prices represent the opportunity costs of goods and services. However, a perfectly competitive market seldom exists. There are always market distortions in the form of monopolies, taxes, and subsidies. In such cases shadow prices are used. Shadow prices are derived prices that would mimic the prices under perfect competition (Squire and van der Tak 1975). For non-marketed goods, marginal costs are used as shadow prices. For marketed goods, shadow prices are calculated by multiplying the market prices with appropriate conversion factors. However, the problem arises in the valuation of intangibles that cannot be quantified and for which no market exists. In an irrigation project, increased sense of livelihood security, loss in bio-diversity, sufferings of the displaced people are examples of intangibles. In the absence of market prices, there are indirect ways of assigning monetary values to these benefits and costs (Pearce et al. 2006). For example, the costs of pollution can be measured using depreciation of housing prices (hedonic pricing method). Alternatively, the project beneficiaries and/or people affected by the project can be asked directly to assign monetary values to these intangibles (contingent valuation method). However, such valuations can always be subject to criticisms.

Cost-benefit analysis can be useful for evaluation when it is relatively easy to assign monetary values to benefits and costs. For industrial and technical projects, cost-benefit analysis resembles a private profitability analysis (Rossi and Freeman 1993) and gives valuable information on economic viability of projects. Moreover, when resources are limited, it provides a framework for allocation of resources among different programs.

However, the problem arises when cost-benefit analysis is extended to evaluation of public sector programs. Many of these programs like construction of dams for irrigation purposes have negative spillover effects. Cost-benefit analysis evaluates programs on the basis of their overall gains and losses. So it fails to take into account such adverse distributional consequences. A possible remedy is to undertake separate cost-benefit analysis for different subgroups of the population. This would facilitate a better understanding of the distributional effects of the program. Moreover, assigning monetary values to benefits and costs of some programs can be very complicated and controversial. For example, when the programs involved are health campaigns and family planning, the problem boils down to assigning monetary values to human life—a life saved or a life prevented. So for projects where intangibles are important, the outcomes of cost-benefit analyses should be used with caution.

Cost-Effectiveness Analysis

Cost-benefit analyses of many public programs are often viewed with skepticism due to the inherent difficulty and subjectivity involved in monetary valuation of outcomes for which market prices seldom exist. But such valuations of program outcomes are redundant and can be avoided when the decision problem is to choose among alternative programs to attain similar goals. Cost-effectiveness analysis (CEA) can provide useful information on cost efficiency of those alternatives. In programs where it is difficult, if not impossible, to assign a monetary value to the program objectives, like the benefits of saving a life or raising the educational achievement levels of students, cost-effectiveness analysis can help the decision makers in making judicious allocation of resources. As a result, it has been used extensively for evaluations of health, educational, and environmental programs.

The basic purpose of cost-effectiveness analysis is to identify programs that can attain specific objectives at the lowest cost (Levin 1983). The analysis involves identification of the alternatives, an estimation of their costs, and an assessment of their effectiveness. Cost estimation takes into account both the direct and indirect costs of the intervention. While direct costs are the costs of inputs, like personnel, equipment, materials, utilities, etc., indirect costs are the externalities or 'spillover' effects associated with the intervention and should be included in the cost calculation. Many programs use volunteers and other donated resources. The cost of these resources would typically be omitted in normal cost accounting. But they do represent a cost from the society's perspective. So the appropriate notion of cost to use is the opportunity cost, which would reflect the true cost of a resource to the society. When markets are functioning efficiently, market prices reflect the opportunity cost and, hence, should be used for cost calculation. If market prices are not available, appropriate proxies need to be used (Levin 1983).

The cost-effectiveness of a program is measured using either the cost-effectiveness ratio or the incremental cost-effectiveness ratio (ICER). Cost-effectiveness ratio is the ratio of the cost of a program to the effects produced. For independent programs, programs that can be implemented simultaneously, cost-effectiveness ratios for each of the alternatives are calculated and ranked in ascending order. The project with the lowest cost-effectiveness ratio is the most cost efficient and gets the highest priority. For example, if the program objective is to increase the life expectancy of a targeted population, the possible program alternatives can be provision of drinking water, provision of health care, or a health awareness campaign. A cost-effectiveness analysis would involve estimation and ranking of costs per life-year gained for each of these alternatives. The programs can then be implemented based on their priority rankings and the availability of funds.

However, for mutually exclusive programs where the implementation of one program precludes the implementation of another, incremental cost-effectiveness ratios are used for comparison. ICER is the ratio of the difference in costs to the difference in effects between two alternative programs. For cost-effectiveness comparison, the programs are ranked based on their effectiveness. If a program is more expensive and less effective than the alternative, the program is dominated by the alternative, and hence not considered for implementation. This is called the principle of strong dominance. Once the dominated programs are eliminated, ICERs are calculated for the remaining alternatives. The principle of extended dominance rules out any program that has a higher ICER compared to a more effective intervention. Finally, the programs are selected based on the availability of funds or the society's willingness to pay. For example, it has been observed that the US healthcare system rejects any intervention with an ICER (compared to the existing system) higher than $50,000 per quality-adjusted life-year (Owens 1998).

The appeal of cost-effectiveness analysis arises from its operational simplicity. Since cost estimations are very often straightforward and require much less value judgment, cost-effectiveness analyses are likely to be more accurate or less inaccurate than their cost-benefit counterparts. Apart from measuring cost-effectiveness of outcomes, it can also be used for measuring cost economy of program activities and cost efficiency of program outputs. So, cost-effectiveness analysis can serve as a very useful tool for program appraisal, planning, and implementation.

The problems of cost-effectiveness analysis are very similar to the ones associated with the cost-benefit analysis. If the costs and effects of a program are distributed over the years, the future costs and effects need to be discounted for comparison. The choice of the discount rate might affect the outcome of the analysis. Moreover, if there are qualitative differences in the outcomes of alternative programs, the differences in quality are added as costs to the deficient program. A cost-effectiveness analysis, in such cases, would require a valuation of benefits. So, it would encounter the same types of problems that it tries to avoid. However, the most serious problem with this type of *ex ante* evaluation is the uncertainty about the future. As Quade aptly pointed out (Quade 1967, p. 11): "While one may be able to forecast coming events in the sense of mapping out possible futures, there is no satisfactory way to predict a single future in terms of which to work out the best system or determine the optimum policy. Consequently, it becomes necessary to consider a range of possible futures or contingencies. In any one of these futures, it may be possible to designate a preferred course of action, but there is no way to determine one for the entire range of possibilities." To capture the uncertainty surrounding such measures, in simulation-based studies like health interventions, the focus of research in recent years has been to attach a probabilistic measure to the incremental cost-effectiveness ratio (Van Hout et al. 1994; Briggs and Fenn 1998; O'Brien and Briggs 2002). The cost-effectiveness acceptability curve (CEAC) is one such measure that indicates the probability that a program is cost-effective in comparison to the alternative for a given value of the maximum socially acceptable cost-effectiveness ratio. However, it is difficult to incorporate such measures in survey-based evaluation studies. In such cases, it is important to carry out sensitivity analysis, especially when the measures of cost-effectiveness of the alternative programs are not very different from each other.

Social Marginal Cost of Funds Analysis

This approach argues that to evaluate public expenditure programs, the social benefits from the program should be compared with the social costs of the program and at the margin, marginal social benefits (MSB) should equal marginal social costs (MSC). Marginal social cost is the marginal cost of funds (MCF) interpreted as the loss of consumer and producer surplus per dollar of additional tax revenue raised to finance public goods (see Chap. 4 by Dahlby, this volume). Note that depending upon the tax instrument used, additional financing may have implications for government revenues from other sources or the revenues of other orders of governments and these impacts must be quantified to determine the MCF. Also there are special considerations that need to be taken into account when attempting to measure the MCF when non-tax distortions such as monopoly and externalities also exist. Under monopoly, the degree of tax shifting (how the tax affects the final good price) is a major determinant of the MCF. In the case of externalities, taxing goods with positive externalities raises the MCF beyond what it would be in the absence of spillovers. On the other hand, taxing negative-externality-producing goods (such as pollutants) instead of non-externality-producing goods creates a 'double dividend.'

Data Envelopment Analysis

Data Envelopment Analysis (DEA) is a non-parametric, linear-programming-based approach to performance evaluation within organizational units. It is a technique to determine the relative efficiency of a set of homogeneous units like schools, hospitals, banks etc. DEA was originally developed as a tool for better evaluation and management of public sector activities (Charnes et al. 1978, 1979). But over the years, it has been applied in a wide range of areas like agriculture, mining, fisheries, energy, banking, health care, education, housing, transportation, market research, retail outlets, organizational effectiveness, and benchmarking (Charnes et al. 1994).

For an organizational unit, efficiency can be measured as a ratio of output to input. But in the presence of multiple inputs or multiple outputs, such a measure can be inadequate unless the inputs and outputs can be aggregated to form a weighted sum of inputs and outputs. However, such aggregation requires the inputs and outputs to be expressed in a common unit of measurement and also a choice of weights for each input and output indicating their relative importance. While a priori choice of weights is at best subjective, the inputs and outputs are very often measured in different units. They can be non-marketable, intangible, or qualitative in nature for which prices might not exist. In such cases, DEA provides a feasible alternative.

In DEA, an organizational unit is efficient if it is not possible to increase any output without increasing any input and without decreasing any other output, or if it is not possible to decrease any input without increasing any other input and without decreasing any output (Charnes et al. 1978, 1981). So, the efficient units are Pareto optimal. The DEA identifies the efficient organizational units that are the best-practice units and they form the extreme points or the efficiency frontier. Similarly, a combination of the efficient organizational units can be calculated to form an efficient composite unit with composite inputs and composite outputs. These efficient composite units (also called virtual producers) along with the best-practice units constitute the entire efficient frontier and receive a relative efficiency score of one. The inefficient units that are inside the frontier are compared with their respective reference efficient units or the virtual units to determine their relative efficiency.

So for each organizational unit, the central problem in DEA is to identify the best-practicing unit or the best 'virtual producer' with which it is to be compared. This can be formulated as a linear programming problem. The solution to the linear programming problem determines the weights, and the relative technical efficiency is calculated as a ratio of the weighted sum of outputs to the weighted sum of inputs. The DEA assigns the weight in such a manner so that the maximum weight is placed on the favorable variables and the minimum weight is placed on the variable where the unit compares unfavorably. In other words, the weights are chosen in a way that gives the evaluation unit the maximum relative efficiency score.

Apart from identifying inefficient units, DEA can also identify the sources and level of inefficiency for each of the inputs and outputs and can assign targets so as to maximize output. So it can be used for identification of improvement priorities.

One of the main advantages of DEA is the non-parametric nature of the analysis. It doesn't require the specification of any functional form. In parametric approach like regression analysis, a pre-specified production function relating inputs to outputs is estimated using the data. The estimated regression equation applies to all the organizational units. DEA in contrast optimizes on each organizational unit. So, in DEA the focus is on each evaluation unit and how it compares to a reference unit rather than the entire population average. DEA also avoids the usual valuation problems associated with cost-benefit and cost-effectiveness analysis. It can handle multiple inputs and multiple outputs and it does not require the inputs and outputs to have the same unit of measurement. DEA overcomes another shortcoming of cost-benefit and cost-effectiveness analysis. It can incorporate exogenous factors in evaluation (Banker and Morey 1986a). This is done by treating these variables either as inputs or outputs. It can also handle categorical variables (Banker and Morey 1986b).

As an evaluation method, DEA can be used for identification of inefficient units, reallocation of resources for efficient utilization, and also for setting targets for inefficient units to improve performance (Kittelsen and Førsund 1992; Tulkens 1993). For multi-criteria evaluation, i.e., when the observational units are evaluated based on multiple criteria, DEA can also be used to aggregate these criteria to construct a single index of performance.

However, the main problem with DEA is that it relies on the authenticity of the data. It uses the extreme point method to estimate the efficiency frontier. So, any error in the data can create significant problems. For example, the presence of outliers in the sample can have a significant effect on forming the frontier and can jeopardize the relative efficiency estimations. Moreover, DEA estimates the relative efficiency, efficiency relative to the best-practice units. But the best-practice units can themselves be inefficient. Since the efficiency estimates are bounded within zero and one, DEA cannot capture the differences among organizational units with an efficiency score of one.

Multiple-Criteria Evaluation (MCE)/Multiple-Objectives Evaluation (MOE)

Public sector programs emerge out of society's awareness of the deficiencies in the existing social structure and its attempt to rectify these problems through mitigating interventions. Since social problems are innumerous and resources are scarce, cost efficiency is an important criterion in program evaluation. However, it is equally important to ensure that the program interventions are translated into positive outcomes, contributing to the well-being of the program targets. So, apart from cost efficiency, issues like relevance, the consistency of the program objectives with the requirements of its beneficiaries, efficacy, the extent to which the program is successful in achieving its objectives, and sustainability, the continuation of program benefits even after completion of the program, are crucial from an evaluation perspective. A multiple-objective evaluation is an all-round assessment of a program in terms of its relevance, efficacy, efficiency, sustainability, and its contribution towards development of institutions necessary for design, delivery, and implementation of successful programs in future. The World Bank uses a multiple-criteria evaluation approach in evaluating the impact of its programs and projects (see the Annex for details).

A program, from its inception to its end can be divided into the following stages: conceptualization, design, implementation, and outcome. At the conceptualization stage, the problem is specified and defined as precisely as possible to facilitate selection of the target group, design of appropriate interventions, and later evaluation of the program. Designing a program is developing a set of interventions or treatments that would be delivered to the target group and would eventually help in achieving the program objectives. At the implementation stage, the inputs are used to generate activities that are delivered to the program participants. The activities produce a set of outputs. The outputs in turn are translated into outcomes that are the ultimate goals or objectives of the program.

Multiple-objectives evaluation can be used at different stages of a program. Depending on its nature and purpose, it can be broadly categorized as formative or summative (Scriven 1967). Formative evaluation plays a very critical role in the overall development of a program. It has two components—a diagnostic evaluation and a process evaluation. Diagnostic evaluations are carried out at the planning and design stage of a program. It involves specification of program objectives, identification of target groups, and an assessment of their needs. It also contributes to the design of program activities by examining the extent to which the interventions are consistent with the needs. A process evaluation, on the other hand, is concerned with the monitoring of program activities and operations—examining program deliveries, organizational strengths and weaknesses, quality of the interventions, and consistency of the implementations with the original design of the program. It provides the program staff continuous feedback on the performance of program activities, uncovering any obstacle that might emerge and suggesting modifications to ensure the success of the program. So, a formative evaluation assists in the development of a program. Summative evaluation, in contrast, assesses the efficacy of a program in terms of achievement or non-achievement of program objectives. Summative evaluation includes both outcome evaluation and impact assessment. An outcome evaluation studies the usefulness of a program in delivering its stated objectives. Impact assessment, in contrast, not only evaluates a program on the basis of its stated objectives but also looks into the indirect and unintended effects of the program.

The difference between formative and summative evaluation is the difference in purpose: "When the cook tastes the soup, that's formative; when the guests taste the soup, that's summative" (Robert Stake, quoted in Scriven 1991, p. 169). However, in spite of their differences, it is important to recognize the complementarities between the two. A summative evaluation is unwarranted and a waste of time, effort, and resources unless it is possible to ensure that a program has measurable goals, has been well implemented, and the activities have been delivered to the appropriate targets. Moreover, with a growing emphasis on result-based monitoring, formative evaluation includes assessment of early outcome measures that are linked to the final objectives of the program.

Diagnostic Evaluation

A program conceived at a political, community, or administrative level contains in it a broad definition of the problem and a list of goals that are equally broad in nature. However, the planning, implementation, and evaluation of a program require much more precise and operational definitions that are clear, measurable, economical, and adequate. One of the main purposes of diagnostic evaluation is to identify and define the problem. A usable definition is important for understanding the prevalence and the magnitude of the problem, identification of the target groups and their specific needs, and the design of interventions to meet the requirements of the program targets. For example, in a poverty alleviation program, the identification of people who are in need of assistance requires a definition of poverty. Poverty can be defined either in terms of annual household income or daily calorie intake. Once the thresholds on income or calorie intakes are established, only then is it possible to identify the target population. It is the group that falls below the threshold. So thresholds or boundaries are rules determining the eligibility to participate in a program. If the rules are too stringent, the target population might shrink to the level of non-existence. If the rules are too lax, the target population might be too large and too diverse to design any effective intervention strategy, and the program might become prohibitively expensive. Target definitions should also be feasible to apply based on observable and measurable characteristics for which data are readily available (Rossi and Freeman 1993).

It is also important to collect information on the magnitude of the problem and the geographic distribution of the target population. Understanding the magnitude of the problem is necessary because target populations are hardly homogenous in terms of their degree of deprivations. A family that goes without food for several days at a stretch and a family that eats one meal a day might be both eligible in a poverty alleviation program. But their needs are very different and accordingly they might require very different types of assistance. Moreover, in programs where funds are insufficient to cover the entire target population, such characterization based on need helps to identify the groups who are the worst affected. Information on geographical distribution is important for feasibility of the program and the subsequent outcome evaluations. If the target population is sparsely located across a geographic region, it might be difficult and expensive to administer an effective program. And if the target group becomes too small, it might be impossible to do any outcome evaluation. For example, an evaluation study of a tobacco use prevention and cessation project in Southern California found no effect of the program in changing the attitude of the students towards smoking (Flay et al. 1995). The researchers concluded that the target group of the seventh graders had strong anti-tobacco feelings and very low rates of smoking, making it impossible to find any effect of the program. The problem with the program was that it failed to define an appropriate target group.

For appropriate identification of target population, concepts like prevalence rate, incidence rate, and population at risk can be very useful. The prevalence rate defined for a given area over a specified period of time is the ratio of the number of existing cases to the total population at risk. The population at risk refers to the people who are most likely to develop a particular problem. For health programs, the characterization might include the incidence rate. Incidence rate is the ratio of number of new cases of a particular problem in a given area over a specified period of time to the total population at risk. These rates can also be estimated by age group, sex, language, religion, ethnicity, and economic status. A detailed characterization of the target population is essential for identification of the appropriate target groups and tailoring of interventions to the particular characteristics of the groups.

Another important aspect of diagnostic evaluation is the specification of program objectives in terms of measurable outcomes. In defining the outcome measure, it is often best to take a collaborative approach (Weiss 1998). Discussions with the program sponsors, staff, and stakeholders can reveal important evaluation questions. Moreover, in the formulation of outcome measures, it is important to take into account the opinions of the sponsors and other stakeholders to ensure that the outcome measures are close approximations of the program objectives and reflect the views, needs, and concerns of the major stakeholders.

In recent years, there is a growing emphasis on greater accountability in public sector programs. Consequently, there is a shift in paradigm from monitoring of activities and implementations to result-based monitoring. Under result-based monitoring, the emphasis is more on whether the program inputs, activities, and outputs are contributing towards the achievement of the program objectives (Kusek and Rist 2004). So, it is imperative to develop indicators not only for performance measurement of program activities, outputs, and outcomes but also for interim markers of progress towards achievement of these outcomes.

The fruitfulness of an evaluation, be it a process evaluation or an outcome evaluation, depends crucially on the development of appropriate performance indicators. The indicators might be either quantitative or qualitative. The outputs of a program might be quantifiable for which quantitative indicators would suffice. But the outcomes are very often less tangible and might require qualitative indicators. In developing the indicators the C.R.E.A.M criteria can be used. The C.R.E.A.M criteria require the indicators to be clear, relevant, economic, adequate, and monitorable (Kusek and Rist 2004). In other words, a good indictor should be precise and unambiguous, adequate and reliable in measuring the relevant variable, available readily at reasonable cost, and can be validated independently.

Process Evaluation

The main objective of process evaluation is to provide a systematic assessment of program performance to facilitate progress towards achievement of program objectives. The focus of traditional monitoring of programs is concerned with the assessment of inputs, activities, and outputs. A process evaluation, in contrast, is an evaluation strategy that tries to ensure that the activities and outputs contribute to the achievement of program objectives. So, a process evaluation is an integral part of a result-based monitoring system. It provides crucial information on program coverage, quality, and propriety of interventions and effectiveness of the interventions in producing the desired effects. So it constitutes a feedback mechanism that promotes informed decision making, better decision making, improved performance, and greater accountability.

The success of a program depends on its ability to reach the appropriate targets and the degree to which the targets actually participate in a program. Program coverage measures the extent of actual target participation in comparison to the desired level. Since the effectiveness and approval of a program depends on its coverage, the objective of any program is to maximize coverage given its budget constraint. Two related concepts in this regard are under-coverage and over-coverage. Under-coverage of a program can be measured as the ratio of the number served who are in need of the program to total number in need. Over-coverage is the ratio of the number served who are not in need of the program to the total number served. The difference between these two ratios indicates a program's coverage efficiency. The higher a program's coverage efficiency, the more successful the program is in reaching its desired targets. So, coverage efficiency is a very useful indicator of target participation that can be used for modifying target definitions. Higher coverage efficiency can also help program managers to gain the approval and support of program sponsors and other stakeholders.

Another problem in public programs is the bias in target participation. The bias refers to the degree to which different subgroups of target population participate differently in the program (Rossi and Freeman 1993). Such biases might occur due to implementation failure. All participants might not have equal access to the program. Infrequent participation might also reflect participants' dissatisfaction with the program. Some participants might be more motivated and find the program more useful. The program staff can also contribute to the bias by treating participants differently. The participants who are more likely to succeed might be treated favorably whereas the participants who are likely to fail might be encouraged to drop out. As discussed later, the presence of such biases in coverage can seriously jeopardize the validity of subsequent outcome evaluations. So, regular evaluation of participants' satisfaction with a program is necessary not only to reduce such biases but also to modify interventions for better participation.

It is also important to monitor the delivery of the program and the quantity and quality of interventions. A delivery is the procedure used to provide treatments to the program participants. A failure in the delivery system occurs when the interventions fail to meet the requirements of the program beneficiaries. This can be either due to a failure to reach the program beneficiaries or due to a failure to provide them with the appropriate interventions. Different participants might receive different levels of interventions, wrong interventions, or no interventions due to lack of commitment on the part of program staff or failure of the program to standardize the interventions or both. Such deficiencies in program delivery can also result in participation biases. Evaluation of the actual delivery of interventions can identify these deficiencies in implementation and suggest corrective measures. Qualitative methods like observing the program in operation and informal interviews with the program participants can provide valuable insights into actual program delivery (Weiss 1998).

Another aspect of process evaluation is to identify the interim markers of progress and evaluate the effectiveness of the interventions in achieving them. Interim markers are the short-term objectives of a program that are causally linked to the overall objectives of the program. A failure to achieve the interim objectives would also imply an eventual failure in achieving the goals of the program. An interim evaluation is essential for the performance evaluation of the program interventions. Based on the findings of such evaluations, interventions can be modified or replaced altogether.

A process evaluation is important because it provides information that is crucial for the success of a program. An outcome evaluation is meaningless unless a program successfully delivers the appropriate interventions to the appropriate targets. A process evaluation provides program managers timely feedback on performance of different elements of the program and identifies elements and areas that require improvement or modification. So it helps program managers to make informed decisions. Process evaluation can also be used for measuring cost economy of inputs in providing the interventions and the cost efficiency of interventions to produce the program outputs. It provides information on program coverage and the effectiveness of the program in achieving its short-term objectives. All these factors are essential elements of accountability, which is an important issue in public sector programs.

Outcome Evaluation

Outcome evaluations study the effectiveness of programs in delivering the program objectives, which can be both short term and long term. Since process evaluation includes evaluations of program based on short-term objectives (the interim markers of progress), outcome evaluations can be used for both formative and summative evaluations.

The basic idea of an outcome evaluation is to study the net effect of an intervention on participants or beneficiaries in terms of the outcome variables. The net effect refers to the changes in the outcome measures that can be attributed solely to the intervention. In other words, it is the difference between the outcome measures after participation in the program and the counterfactual, the outcome measures that would have been observed had they not participated in the program. This is not the same as differences in outcome measures before and after participation in the program because there might be many other factors or events apart from the program treatments which might directly or indirectly influence the outcomes. The objective of an outcome evaluation is to establish causality between the treatments offered and the outcomes produced by filtering out the effects produced by all these external factors.

The prerequisite for any outcome assessment is to establish a set of well-defined outcome measures and to recognize the factors apart from the treatments that might influence these outcomes. The credibility of an outcome evaluation crucially depends on the reliability and validity of the outcome measures. Reliability of measures refers to the authenticity of the data and the validity implies the extent to which the measures represent the stated objectives of the program. It is also important to recognize and control for the external factors and processes that might influence the outcomes. Such external factors include endogenous factors specific to the participants; short-term and long-term trends at the local, regional, or national level; maturational factors; biases in the selection of the participants; and the program design effects. Endogenous factors refer to the naturally occurring events. For example, in clinical trials, the participants might recover from an illness naturally due to the inherent defense mechanism of the body. The purpose of outcome assessments in such cases is to study whether the medicines fasten the recovery process. Similarly, overall economic conditions like expansions or recessions will affect the outcomes of a job-training program or an income enhancement program. Maturational factors related to naturally occurring changes due to the passage of time might also influence the effects of a program. With age, people might get smarter, wiser, and more experienced. This will cause behavioral changes or changes in receptive capability that cannot be attributed to the program. Maturational effects are very relevant in the evaluations of educational programs for the young and also in juvenile justice programs.

The presence of the program itself can influence the behavior of the participants and in turn affect the program outcomes. This is known as the design effect and it is an integral part of any program. A classic example is the evaluation study of the effect of intensity of illumination on workers' productivity conducted at the Hawthorne Works of the Western Electric Company in the 1930s (Weiss 1998). It was observed that the productivity of the workers in the study group increased irrespective of the intensity of illumination. The fact that they were getting more attention resulted in higher efforts on the part of the workers. This is known as the 'Hawthorne Effect' and it can be part of any program involving human subjects.

Another major problem associated with outcome evaluations is the presence of selection biases (Barnow et al. 1980). Selection biases arise when the program participants are characteristically different from the non-participants in a way that might affect the program outcomes. The differences might be due to differences in observable characteristics and/or due to differences in unobservable characteristics. Very often in public sector programs there is 'creaming' in the selection of targets. The participants might be selected based on observable characteristics that also make them more likely to succeed. There is also the possibility of self-selection. In voluntary programs, the participants might be individuals who are more likely to gain from the program and are more motivated, a factor that can itself contribute to the outcome. For example, in evaluation studies of the effects of job training programs on employment, the participants might be more motivated to find a job than the non-participants, and hence they are more likely to find a job even in the absence of the program. Similarly, in the evaluations of the effects of job training program on wage rate, the participants might be individuals with lower skills than the non-participants and accordingly their salary gains might be relatively smaller. De-selection or attrition bias is also a common phenomenon in public programs (Heckman et al. 2000). Participants drop out in the middle of the programs. The dropout process is seldom random. It might happen that the participants who decided to leave found the program undesirable and benefited the least from the program while participants who completed the program did so because they found the program rewarding. So an outcome assessment based on the participants who completed the program would overestimate the impact of the program.

Outcome Evaluation Designs

An appropriate outcome evaluation design should control for all possible external factors and biases that might influence outcomes. The available evaluation designs in social research can be broadly classified into two categories—randomized experimental designs, and non-experimental designs.

Randomized Experimental Designs

Causal impact of a program on its beneficiaries is the change in the desired outcome of the program that can be solely attributed to the program interventions. So, theoretically, it can be easily estimated if we can observe the outcome among the beneficiaries with and without the program. However, the counterfactual does not exist. An alternative would be to construct a control group—a group of individuals who would be similar to the program beneficiaries in all possible aspects but would not receive the program interventions. We would then be able to estimate the impact of the program by comparing the post-intervention outcomes among the program beneficiaries (the treatment group) and the non-beneficiaries (the control group). A problem with this approach is that the presence of selection biases would make it difficult to disentangle the impact of the interventions from the factors that drove selection. The program participants would be very different from the non-participants and the differences in outcome between the participants and non-participants would be not only due to the program interventions but also due to pre-existing differences that can potentially affect the outcome.

In randomized experimental designs, the selection problem is addressed through random assignment. The target population, i.e., all subjects who are eligible to participate in the program are randomly assigned to a treatment group and a control group. The treatment group constitutes of subjects who would receive the intervention under evaluation. The control group receives no intervention. The random assignment ensures that each of the eligible participants has an equal probability of being selected either in the treatment group or in the control group. So, it removes the biases that might arise from selection because even the most motivated target has equal chances of being selected either in the treatment group or in the control group. Since both treatment and control groups face equal exposure to the external factors that can affect outcome, the net effect of the intervention can be estimated as the difference in outcome between the treatment and control groups post intervention. In a linear regression framework, the causal impact can be estimated using ordinary least square regressions. In regression framework, often pre-treatment values of variables that have a large effect on outcome are used as control variables. Using pre-treatment data can greatly reduce the sample size requirement and hence the cost of randomized trials. However, using control variables that are affected by the treatment would lead to inaccurate estimates of the impact because these variables would capture part of the impact. Similarly, controlling for variables that have little or no impact on outcome can reduce precision of the estimates. So control variables need to be selected carefully and preferably at the design stage of the evaluation to avoid data mining.

There are many different variations of randomized experiments (Boruch 1997; Shadish et al. 2001; Duflo et al. 2007). Cluster randomization can be used when the program is delivered at the cluster level and not at the individual level. For example, sanitation programs like construction of sewerage system can be delivered at village level and all the inhabitants of the village will benefit from the program. In this case, randomization can only be done at the village level. Randomized block designs can be used when sample sizes are relatively small, threatening the equivalence of the treatment and the control groups. It incorporates randomizations in selection as well as matching. The target population is matched and grouped based on variables that might affect the program outcomes. Once the groups are formed, the subjects in each group can be randomly assigned to a treatment and a control group. Groupings are also done when a program has more than one intervention and the evaluator wants to estimate the separate effects of each intervention as well as the interaction effects of different interventions. This is called the factorial design.

Randomized experimental designs are one of the most powerful methods of outcome evaluation. A rigorous and carefully implemented randomized design can establish causality about the effects of a program. However, it has some serious limitations as well. Such evaluations cannot be conducted at the early stage of a program when the interventions are regularly modified for program improvement. They can neither be readily used in full-coverage programs where the entire target population receives the intervention because it is not possible to construct a control group. However, for many full-coverage public sector programs, the implementing agency seldom has the capacity to implement the program in one go. Instead the program is rolled out in phases. The phased nature of implementation can be used to construct a phase-in randomization design, where treatment and control groups are randomly selected and the program is withheld in the control group until the outcomes have matured in the treatment group and the post-intervention data has been collected. This can be problematic when outcomes take long to mature. It might not be feasible to withhold program delivery in the control group for such a long time. Another problem is the ethical issues related to the purposeful denial of services to the members of target groups who are in as much in need of assistance as the program participants. However, a counter-argument might be that the evaluation requirement implies that the effectiveness of the program interventions has not been fully tested. So it is not a denial of benefits, because the benefits of the interventions are not known with certainty. Even then a truly random selection might be difficult to implement because of the pressures from the stakeholders. It is not possible to ignore their views and preferences because the success of many public programs requires involvement and co-operation of the stakeholders.

A well-run randomized experimental design can effectively take into account the influences of external factors and selection biases. However, they are susceptible to the biases that might arise from the presence of externality, partial compliance, and attrition. The presence of externalities or spillover effects can lead to inaccurate estimates of a program's impact. A spillover effect exists when delivery of the program to the treatment group also affects the outcome in the control group. For example, in deworming programs, children receiving the deworming tablets will remain protected against the worms and since they will no longer be transmitting the worms, children from the control group who they are in contact with will also be benefitted because of fewer infections. In the presence of spillover effects, randomized trials would underestimate or overestimate the impact of the program depending on whether these effects are positive or negative. Partial compliance to the program might also jeopardize the results of randomized trials. Partial compliance happens when the interventions are not delivered equally to all members of the treatment group and/or some members of the control group also receive the interventions. In such cases, dropping observations from analysis would violate the random assignment and lead to erroneous results. An intention-to-treat analysis estimates the causal impact based on the original treatment and control assignment, ignoring who finally received the program and who did not. So, it estimates the effectiveness of an intervention policy and not of a specific treatment. For most public sector programs, an intention-to-treat estimate is viable because policymakers are interested in the effectiveness of a policy that can be scaled up. For example, if the objective is to evaluate the effectiveness of a universal school-based deworming program, an intention-to-treat estimate would be accurate. There will always be some students who will be absent from school on the day of the treatment. Partial compliance does not invalidate the intention-to-treat estimate. However, the same will not be true if the objective is to study the effectiveness of deworming tablets. Intention-to-treat analysis will not be able to estimate the true effect because some students did not take the pill. Attrition or dropouts from control and treatment groups might also lead to inaccurate estimates of the impact of the program. An intention-to-treat analysis will not be possible in this case because there is no post-treatment data of individuals who dropped out or went missing. A solution to the problem is to collect data at regular intervals and do repeated evaluations. This will also strengthen the reliability of evaluation findings.

Non-experimental Designs

Non-experimental designs (McClendon 1994; Shadish et al. 2001; Todd 2007) can be used when random assignment of target population is not feasible. In contrast to experimental designs, in a non-experimental setup, an evaluator has no control over the treatment assignment. Non-experimental evaluations try to address the selection bias by creating a control group that might be used as a valid counterfactual if certain assumptions are fulfilled. However, these assumptions are not testable. Here we are going to discuss briefly some of the most frequently used non-experimental designs in program evaluations.

Matched Control Designs

In matched control designs, the treatment group is selected by the program administrator. Once the treatment group has been selected, the control group is constructed from the non-participants by matching them with the program beneficiaries in such characteristics that might potentially affect the outcome variables. The idea is to construct a control group that resembles the program participants as closely as possible so that the differences in outcome measures between them can be attributed to the program. Matching can be done either on an individual basis or on an aggregate basis. In individual matching, for each individual program participant, a non-participant who is the closest match to that participant in relevant characteristics (like age, sex, occupation, income, etc.) is selected to serve as the control. Alternatively, the control group can be constructed by matching the distribution of relevant characteristics of the participants with the non-participants. The non-experimental design can be prospective or retrospective. In other words, the control group can be constructed either before or after the program. The net effects of the program can be measured in the same way as in randomized experiments.

The matched control designs would closely approximate the randomized experimental designs if the matching is done perfectly. In reality, it is impossible to obtain perfect matches. There will always be differences between the participants and the non-participants in critical ways that might be attributed to selection in the program and to outcomes. So a matched control design like the one discussed above cannot really avoid the biases that arise from selection.

Propensity score matching (Rosenbaum and Rubin 1983; Dehejia and Wahba 2002; Luellen et al. 2005) is a very widely used matching technique that tries to eliminate selection bias by matching program participants and non-participants on the basis of their probabilities of being selected in the program. It is also a very useful technique when the numbers of characteristics to match are relatively large. The method requires data on relevant characteristics (that might affect selection in the program) for both the participants and the non-participants. Given the actual data on participation and non-participation as well as the data on individual characteristics, econometric models like *logit* or *probit* are used to estimate the probability of being selected in the program for each individual. This estimated probability is called the propensity score. The treatment groups and the corresponding control groups are constructed by matching the propensity scores of the participants with the non-participants within a pre-specified range. The smaller the range, the better would be the matching.

Propensity score matching effectively controls for selection bias due to observable differences. But it cannot control for bias that arises from unobservable characteristics like motivation, for example. So, the reliability of the evaluation findings can be questioned.

Difference-in-Differences and Fixed Effects Regression

Difference-in-differences (DID) approach estimates the treatment effect by comparing changes in outcome in the treatment group following interventions with the changes in outcome in the control group. So, DID estimation would require data on outcome measures for both treatment and control groups before and after the program. Here, the first difference, i.e., the change in outcome measure for a group before and after the program removes all time-invariant differences between the treatment and the control group because the same group is compared to itself across time. The second difference between the treatment and the control group removes all time-varying external factors that are assumed to affect the treatment and the control group equally during the interval of analysis. If outcome evolves similarly in treatment and control groups in the absence of interventions, the second difference would capture the true causal impact of the program. DID can provide correct estimates of the causal effect if the assumption of parallel trends holds, i.e., in the absence of the treatment, the trends of outcome in the treatment and control groups would be parallel.

Fixed effects regressions are generalized versions of the DID approach when there are multiple time periods and/or multiple treatment groups. Fixed effects models are estimated by regressing outcome on dummies for treatment group(s) and time periods and controlling for variables that can potentially influence the outcome.

Reflexive Control Designs

In reflexive control designs, the treatment group serves as its own control. The pre-program outcome measures of the treatment group are compared with the post-program measures to estimate the effects of the program. Reflexive control designs are very common in full-coverage programs where there is no non-participant to construct a control group. However, the validity of the evaluation crucially depends on the assumption that external factors have no influence on target performance in terms of outcome measures. Since that is a very strong assumption, these types of designs should be avoided for program evaluations.

A relatively better reflexive control design for full-coverage programs is the interrupted time series design. In this design, repeated measures of the outcome variables of the participants are taken both before and after the program. The pre-program sample of the outcome measure is then used to estimate a pre-program trend of the outcome variable and also to forecast the future pattern if the same trend continues. The post-program sample of outcome measure is used to estimate the actual post-program trend. The effect of the program can be estimated by comparing the forecasted trend with the actual post-program trend using statistical procedures.

A major limitation of the interrupted time series design is data requirement. A large number of repeated observations of the program participants are required to accurately estimate a trend and forecast. However, for most public programs such detailed time series data does not exist. Moreover, forecasts become very unreliable over longer forecast horizon. So, for programs that have long gestation periods, interrupted time series evaluations might not be very reliable.

Regression Discontinuity Design

Regression discontinuity design is used to evaluate programs where there are cut-offs or thresholds above or below which the program interventions are delivered. For example, microcredit programs might have an eligibility criterion based on income or land holdings. In such cases, individuals just above the threshold can serve as valid control for those individuals who are just below the threshold and eligible for the treatment. In other words, it is assumed that in close proximity to the threshold, individuals belonging to treatment and control groups are very similar and the selection bias is zero. So long as the rules governing selection of beneficiaries are strictly adhered to, a regression discontinuity design can effectively estimate the causal impact of the program. However, in public sector programs the assignment rules are often not strictly followed, the underlying data based on which selections are made might not be reliable and there might not be enough individuals around the threshold to construct treatment and control groups that are large enough to draw statistically valid inferences. In such cases, a regression discontinuity design will fail to estimate the true causal impact.

Instrumental Variables Approach

An instrumental variable estimation addresses the selection bias by looking for an exogenous variable (to serve as instrument for treatment assignment) that can predict assignment to treatment, albeit imperfectly, but does not influence the potential outcome directly (Imbens and Angrist 1994; Angrist et al. 1996). If such an instrument exists, an instrumental variable estimation can correctly identify causal impact of an intervention. However, it might not always be possible to find a strong instrument which limits the use of this approach in non-experimental evaluations.

Properly implemented randomized trials can capture true causal impacts of programs and have high internal validity. However, the external validity of this approach, i.e., generalizing the results beyond the context of the evaluation, is highly debated. They are also very expensive and not always practical for evaluation of public sector programs. The non-experimental approach can be low on internal validity due to problems associated with handling of selection biases. But they can achieve high external validity due to availability of large nationally representative data sets. While each of these approaches has its own merits and demerits, together they complement each other and enrich the evaluation of public sector programs (Dehejia 2015).

Newer Approaches to Evaluation

The following paragraphs present brief overviews of some of the newer approaches using multi-criteria evaluation such as the Iron Triangle, Alternate Service Delivery Framework (ASDF), and Results-Oriented Management and Evaluation (ROME) followed by Theory-Based Evaluations.

The Iron Triangle of Project Management and Evaluation

The Iron Triangle of Project Management, also called the Triple Constraints in Project Administration, is a widely used concept in project management. Project constraints highlighted by the Iron Triangle include the time or the schedule for the delivery of outputs, cost or the resources required to produce the outputs and the quality of processes and products delivered by the project. The success is therefore evaluated on whether the project was completed on time, within the budget initially allocated for this purpose, and at the defined level of quality that was promised (see Pollack et al. 2018). The Iron Triangle is a useful concept but represents an incomplete construct for project evaluation as it is solely focused on outputs and does not consider the outcome (long-term impact) and the reach (winners and losers as a result of the project). Two recent examples pointed out by Husser (2019) demonstrate the serious flaws of this concept as an evaluation tool. The Boeing 737 Max 8 would be deemed as a great success by the Iron Triangle criteria. The project was completed on schedule, within the budget, and met the specified standards of quality. However, subsequently the project turned out to be a disaster, resulting in the loss of lives and billions of dollars due to serious design flaws. A second is that of the Sydney Opera House that was termed as a spectacular failure by the Iron Triangle criteria. The project was delivered 10 years behind schedule with a cost over-run of AU $95 million. The career of the project architect was destroyed. Yet the project turned out to be a great success as it was later hailed as a great masterpiece of modern architecture, it attracted 8 million visitors a year and recovered cost over-runs within the first two years.

Alternative Service Delivery Framework for Evaluation

The alternative service delivery framework (ASDF) represents a dynamic consultative and participatory process of public sector evaluations that inform public sector reform and restructuring to improve the delivery of public services to citizens by sharing governance functions with individuals, community groups, private for profit and non-profit sectors, other government and beyond-government entities. As part of this evaluation, government role and responsibility are reconsidered for each individual function as possible options for (a) direct delivery, (b) managing, (c) funding, and (d) regulating. As a deliverer, a governmental entity would self-regulate, fund the service, and also deliver. As a manager, the activity of delivery would be performed by someone else but governmental entity would retain the responsibility of managing, funding, and regulating. As the role changes, the activities performed by a governmental entity change but the responsibility of ensuring that services delivered meet the quality and cost-efficiency standards remains with the governmental entity.

As part of the ASDF evaluation, governmental entities/units examine their programs, projects, and activities using the following criteria (see Shah 2005, p. 222):

1. *Public Interest Test*: Does the program area or activity continue to serve public interest? If yes, continue to next step, if not, abandon.
2. *Role of Government Test*: Is there a legitimate and necessary role for the government in this program area? If yes, continue to next step, if not, abandon, and examine service shedding, privatization, divestiture, regulation, and employee takeover options.
3. *Jurisdictional Alignment Test*: Is the assignment of the option to your order of government or to your agency appropriate? If yes, continue to the next step. If not, seek reassignment/realignment.
4. *External Partnership Test*: What activities or programs should or could be transferred in whole or in part to the beyond-government sector? If yes, examine options such as contracting out/franchising/licensing, government owned/contractor operated, public-private partnerships, private, not-for-profit agency/self-help/volunteers, etc. If not, continue to next step.
5. *Business Principles Test*: If the program or activity is to continue, does it meet business principles in terms of efficiency of its operations? If not, consider restructuring as an autonomous agency or improve its organization and management culture. If yes, go to the next step.
6. *Affordability Test*: Is the resultant package of programs and activities affordable within the budgetary/fiscal constraints? If not, see what program or activities could be abandoned.

Result-Oriented Management and Evaluation (ROME)

ROME represents a holistic results-focused approach to evaluation as viewed both by the public managers as well as the citizens at large. Under ROME, a results-based chain provides a framework for evaluating public

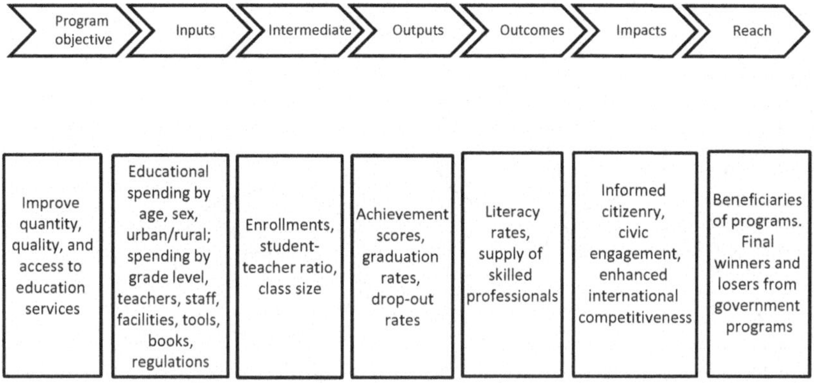

Fig. 2.1 Results chain in ROME. (Source: Shah 2005)

sector performance (see Andrews and Shah 2001). Figure 2.1 illustrates this results-based chain, which suggests that to enforce a culture of accountability for results, one needs to monitor ***program activities*** and ***inputs*** (resources used to produce outputs), including ***intermediate inputs***, ***outputs*** (quantity and quality of goods and services produced), ***outcome*** (progress in achieving program objectives), ***impact*** (program goals), and ***reach*** (people who benefit or are hurt by a program).

ROME provides an integrated approach to managing for results and citizens-based evaluation of those results (see Fig. 2.2). Under ROME, public managers are held to account, through output-based contracts, for achieving defined outputs within the allocated budget but have full flexibility and control over the choice of inputs and organizational structures. On the other hand, citizens, through their political representatives (legislatures), would have outcome contracts with the Cabinet, and the Cabinet, in turn would have outcome contracts with top executives of government agencies. Internal management evaluations examine compliance with management contracts. External, citizens' or civil society or think tanks' evaluations review the entire results-based chain to determine the effectiveness of government programs.

In ROME, citizens exercise their voice, choice, and exit options (where available) through these evaluations. Because of this, citizens must be informed, possibly organized and engaged (see Fig. 2.3). This is facilitated if there is fiscal transparency and government practices managing for

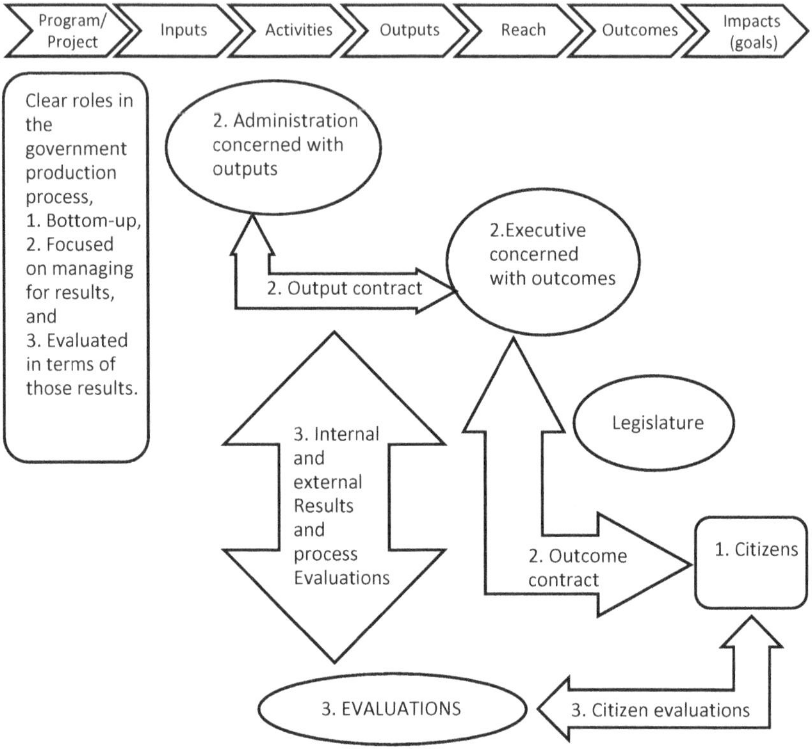

Fig. 2.2 Road map for ROME. (Source: Andrews and Shah 2005)

results so that citizens can see at the 'store-front' what government promises to deliver at what cost as is practiced in New Zealand.

Results-oriented evaluations are considered an integral part of the governing/managing for results framework. In New Zealand, public managers are required to develop processes to ensure that their performance against contracts is monitored and then results are evaluated. Key performance indicators are used to measure efficiency (unit cost of output), efficacy (a measure of degree of achievement of output results) and progress towards achieving specified outcomes. Internal management processes, therefore, enforce an internal learning loop for future program improvements. External, citizens-based evaluations create an external learning loop for program review and restructuring (see Fig. 2.4).

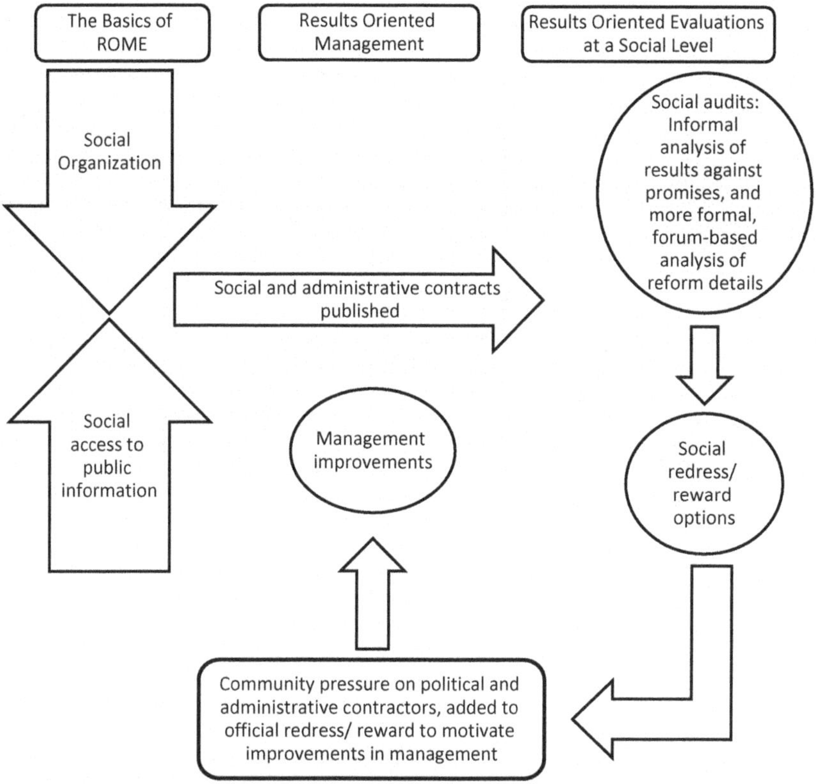

Fig. 2.3 Involving citizens in results-oriented evaluations. (Source: Andrews and Shah 2001)

Theory-Based Evaluation

The outcome-based evaluation research has been mostly focused on evaluating the success or failure of programs in achieving the program objectives and not on why or how the programs succeeded or failed. While economic appraisals of programs tried to achieve efficient allocation of scarce resources, a growing number of failures of public sector programs have rendered such appraisals ineffective for all practical purposes. Even if a program is economically viable and cost-efficient to start with, the resources invested are necessarily a waste from the society's perspective if the program fails in its goals. This is more so if the program makes no

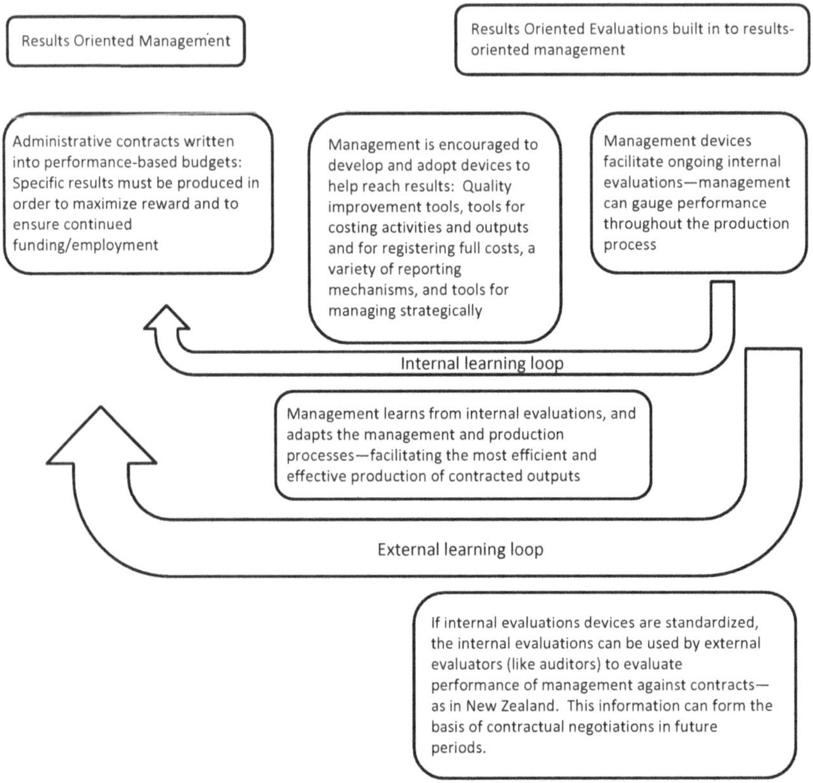

Fig. 2.4 Result-oriented evaluations as an integral part of result-oriented management. (Source: Andrews and Shah 2001)

significant and systematic addition to society's knowledge base in terms of better planning, design, and implementation of such programs that would be crucial for successes of similar programs in the future. *Failures are stepping stones to success*—only if we learn from our failures.

So, evaluation needs to do more than studying the effectiveness of programs. It needs to look inside the 'black box' where inputs are transformed into outputs without any knowledge of how or why. It needs to establish a chain of causality between inputs, activities, outputs, and outcomes which it can test, accept, or reject. This is the essence of theory-based evaluation.

All programs have some implicit theories. These are the expectations or beliefs of the program sponsor, program designers, program managers, and practitioners about how interventions will bring about the desired effects. A theory-based evaluation formalizes these beliefs and assumptions "in terms of a phased sequence of causes and effects" (Weiss 1997a, p. 501). Be it theory-driven evaluation (Chen and Rossi 1980, 1989), theories of change evaluation (Weiss 1987, 1995, 1997a, b), realistic evaluation (Pawson and Tilley 1997), or the logic models (Corbeil 1986; Rush and Ogborne 1991), the fundamental idea of theory-based evaluation is to develop a series of intervening steps leading from input to outcome specifying at each step the causes and their effects. The evaluator then collects data at each step to see whether the postulated relationship holds up. However, if the causal link breaks down, it implies that the next step in the link cannot be achieved and the program is at risk of failure. Accordingly, the design and/or the implementation of the program can be modified.

A program fails either because of failure in implementation of program activities or because of failure of the activities to produce the desired results (Suchman 1967). So, a program contains in it two types of theories—a theory of implementation and a theory of the program (Weiss 1997b). Implementation theory is concerned with the operation of program activities assuming that an appropriate implementation would bring about the intended effect. Program theory, in contrast, addresses the mechanisms that mediate between activities and outcome. An understanding of the distinction between the two helps to distinguish between the implementation issues and the conceptual issues involved in a program. This in turn facilitates improved program design and operation. For example, consider a job-training program whose objective is to help participants get jobs by providing them training in necessary job skills. A typical outcome evaluation of the program would estimate the net effect by comparing the employment rates between the treatment group and the control group. If the net effect is not positive (i.e., the employment rate in the treatment group is not higher than that of the control group), the program is considered a failure, and the only suggestion or insight such evaluation would have is not to promote similar programs in the future. A theory-based evaluation, however, would look into the underlying theory of the program. A plausible theory might be that people are unemployed because they do not have skills. The training program would help participants to develop skills and with skills they will get jobs. In this case, the program mechanism is skill development. A theory-based evaluation would examine the causalities among job training, skill, and employment. No relationship between job training and skill development would imply a failure in implementation the training program is inadequate and should be redesigned to make it more effective. However, if no causality is found between skill development and employment, that would indicate a failure of the program theory. If skills are not enough to get jobs, a modification or alteration of the theory is warranted. An alternative theory might be that to get jobs, the trainees need skills, self-confidence, ability to market skills, and information on job opportunities. Accordingly, career fares, resume-writing workshops, and mock interviews can be included as additional program activities. The participants will gain skills and self-confidence from the training program. The resume-writing workshops and mock interviews will give them the ability to market their skills and also contribute to their self-confidence. While career fares will provide them with information on job opportunities. With skills, self-confidence, ability to market skills, and information on job opportunities, the participants will get hired. In theory-based evaluation, each of these assumptions can be tested. For example, some of the trainees might be asked not to participate in the career fare. If the employment rate of the group that participated in the career fare is not very different from the group that didn't, it would imply that career fares are unnecessary components of the program and can be eliminated in future programs.

So, theory-based evaluation is a continuous process where the evaluators are involved with the program from its planning and design stage through implementation to its very end. In consultation with program designers, the evaluators disaggregate the assumptions of the program into small logical steps, question flawed assumptions and logical leaps, test existing theories, show what works and what doesn't, and propose alternative theories. The evaluation also provides continuous feedback to the program managers about the performance of different program components and helps them to understand what types of modifications are needed. So, evaluation becomes participatory.

Theory-based evaluation provides information on the underlying mechanism of a program. If a program fails, the evaluation can identify which chain of assumption in the program theory broke down and why the program failed. Very often public programs are based on the criterion of desirability rather than what is achievable (Chen and Rossi 1980). Theoretical underpinnings of such programs are shaky with flawed reasoning or no reasoning at all. These programs are more likely to meet with failure because "if the program theory is wrong, there is a good chance that the program is wrong too..." (Weiss 1997a, p. 507). The feedback mechanism and the participatory nature of theory-based evaluation can help the stakeholders understand why the program goals are unrealistic and therefore need to be modified or abandoned. A considerable amount of resources can be saved in the process.

Negative findings in outcome evaluations can meet with resistance from program stakeholders. The program designers or administrators can be fixated with ideas that do not work. A theory-based evaluation doesn't just pass judgment on the worth of a program. It shows which things work and which do not. So, this type of participatory evaluation can be a very useful instrument for "organizational unlearning" (Davidson 2006) and can lead to the development of better strategies. Moreover, theory-based evaluation provides program managers feedback on operations and effectiveness of program activities. It helps them to identify and correct any implementation problems that these activities might have. So, the evaluation can also assist in better program deliveries.

Theory-based evaluation studies the mechanisms through which program activities bring about the desired outcomes. Such evaluative assessment can reveal whether the program is ready for a full-scale summative evaluation or if it requires further development or modification (Wholey 1994; Donaldson and Gooler 2003). For programs with long-term goals, theory-based evaluation can use the causal mechanism to identify intermediate markers of progress and examine if the program is heading in the right direction. It can also distinguish between the essential components that are crucial for the success of the program and the unnecessary components that can be eliminated without any adverse consequences. All these would result in substantial cost savings.

The study of successful mechanisms from repeated evaluations can develop a knowledge base that can be used for improved planning, design, and implementation of programs in future. Mechanisms that have been proved to be successful can be replicated in future programs, whereas less successful mechanisms can be avoided. So, the utility of a theory-based evaluation goes beyond the program. Even if a program fails, the knowledge from its evaluation can be instrumental in successes of similar programs in the future.

A theory-based evaluation is much more expensive than any standard evaluation practices. Since it collects data at each step of the causal link, the requirements of time, effort, and money are also substantially larger. Consequently, for large-scale programs (e.g., a national poverty alleviation program), such evaluations can be very time consuming and prohibitively expensive. In such cases, Lipsey and Pollard (1989) suggested a two-step mechanism—instead of just one final outcome evaluation, an additional intermediate evaluation between input and outcome should be considered.

In public programs, the program activities interact with the social environment (the social and cultural characteristics of the community) to produce the outcomes. Most of these factors that can potentially influence outcomes are not measurable and cannot be included in the evaluation process. The standard evaluation techniques can account for these factors by comparing the effects of the program between the participants and a control group. However, a theory-based evaluation doesn't use a control group. It relies entirely on the causal link and an established causality can itself be affected by the presence of these factors. So, there is no guarantee that these causal mechanisms can be replicated in a new environment. But they still do represent a good staring point.

Conclusion

In this chapter, we presented a synoptic view of program evaluation. The methods discussed serve different purposes. Methods like cost-benefit analysis, cost-effectiveness analysis, or data envelopment analysis address the question of efficiency in the allocation and utilization of funds. In multiple-objectives evaluation, the emphasis is more on accountability in public sector programs, effectiveness of programs, and sustainability of program benefits. The evaluation is concerned with issues like identification of program beneficiaries, assessing their requirements, tailoring of interventions to meet those requirements, monitoring of interventions to ensure that the appropriate interventions are being delivered to the participants, and finally the overall effectiveness of the interventions in achieving the program objectives. So, a multiple-objectives evaluation plays a big role in program planning, design, and implementation. A theory-based evaluation assigns an even bigger role to evaluation in public programs. It goes deeper into the mechanism through which the interventions bring about the desired effects. It analyzes the causal links between interventions and outcomes. So, instead of passing a summative judgment on whether a program succeeded or failed in achieving its objectives, theory-based evaluation shows why it succeeded and why it failed. Thus it contributes to the development of more effective programs in the future.

Evaluation is different from other social research in that it derives its questions from policymakers, program sponsors, program managers, and stakeholders (Weiss 1997a). So the applicability of any specific evaluation method depends on the questions that the evaluator has been asked to address. When the evaluation question is deciding upon alternative interventions aimed at producing similar effects, cost-effectiveness analysis might be more suitable. But it is not useful at all when the problem is prioritizing among different programs addressing different problems. A cost-benefit analysis will be more appropriate in that case. Similarly, data envelopment analysis might not have the valuation problems associated with the cost-benefit or cost effectiveness analysis. But its applicability is limited to comparing efficiencies of similar programs only. For programs whose efficacies have already been established, a multiple-objectives evaluation might be enough for performance evaluations. However, for pilot studies or for programs which have not been tested before, a theory-based evaluation is much more desirable. But it is also more time consuming and more expensive than any other evaluation methods. So, the choice of the evaluation method would also depend upon the availability of time and resources.

Annex: An Example of a Multi-Criteria Evaluation Approach—The Practice by the World Bank Operations Evaluation Department/the Independent Evaluation Group

The World Bank has been a premier institution using MCE in evaluating its programs and projects. The approach used by the World Bank Evaluation Department (earlier the so-called Operations Evaluation Department, OED, and now the Independent Evaluation Group, IEG) has evolved over time. The OED/IEG approach used the following criteria.

Relevance of Objectives

Definition: The extent to which the project's objectives are consistent with the country's current development priorities and with current Bank country and sectoral assistance strategies and corporate goals as expressed in Poverty Reduction Strategy Papers, Country Assistance Strategies, Sectoral Strategy Papers and Operations Policy papers.

The IEG considers the following factors in overall relevance: government ownership and commitment; explicit Bank strategy; results framework; analytical underpinning; flexibility; strategic focus; appropriateness of instrument mix, Bank capacity; Bank and IFC coordination; and Bank and other development partners' collaboration.

Rating of relevance by OED/IEG:

High/Mostly Relevant: Most of the major objectives were highly relevant.
Substantial/Partially Relevant: Most of the major objectives are at least substantially relevant.
Modest/Partially Relevant: Most of the major objectives were not highly or substantially relevant.
Negligible/Not Relevant: Most of the major objectives were irrelevant or negligibly relevant.

Efficacy

Definition: The extent to which the project's objectives were achieved, or expected to be achieved, taking into account their relative importance.

Rating of Efficacy by OED/IEG:

High/Achieved: Major objectives were fully met, or expected to be fully met, with no shortcomings.
Substantial/Mostly Achieved: Major objectives were met, or expected to be met, with only minor shortcomings.
Modest/Partially Achieved: Major objectives were met, or expected to be met, but with significant shortcomings.
Negligible/Not Achieved: Most objectives were not met, or expected not to be met, due to major shortcomings.

Efficiency (by OED; the IEG Dropped This Criterion)

Definition: The extent to which the project achieved, or is expected to achieve, a return higher than the opportunity cost of capital and benefits at least cost compared to alternatives.

Ratings by OED (Note: IEG discontinued this criterion)

High: Project represents sector/industry best practice in terms of cost-effectiveness, and economic returns (if estimates are available) greatly exceed the opportunity cost of capital.

Substantial: Project meets sector/industry standards in terms of cost-effectiveness, and economic returns (if estimates are available) exceed the opportunity cost of capital.

Modest: Project fails to meet sector/industry standards in terms of cost-effectiveness, and economic returns (if estimates are available) are near the opportunity cost of capital.

Negligible: Project is well below sector/industry standards in terms of cost-effectiveness, and economic returns (if estimates are available) are significantly below the opportunity cost of capital.

Sustainability (by OED; the IEG Dropped This Criterion)

Definition: The resilience to risk of net benefits flows over time.

Assessments of sustainability take into account nine factors:

Technical resilience

Financial resilience (including policies on cost recovery)

Economic resilience

Social support (including conditions subject to Safeguard Policies)

Environmental resilience

Government ownership (including by central governments and agencies, and availability of O&M funds)

Other stakeholder ownership (including local participation, beneficiary incentives, civil society/NGOs, private sector)

Institutional support (including supportive legal/regulatory framework, and organizational and management effectiveness)

Resilience to exogenous influences (including terms of trade, economic shocks, regional political, and security situations)

OED Ratings:

Highly Likely: Project net benefits flow meets most of the relevant factors determining overall resilience at the "high level," with all others rated at the "substantial" level

Likely: Project net benefits flow meets all relevant factors determining overall resilience at the "substantial" level
Unlikely: Project net benefits flow meets some but not all relevant factors determining overall resilience at the "substantial" level
Highly Unlikely: Project net benefits flow meets few of the relevant factors determining overall resilience at the "substantial" level
Not Evaluable: Insufficient information available to make a judgment

Result (New Criterion by the IEG)

Definition: To what extent specified output targets were met.

Ratings by IEG:

Met: Specified output targets were fully met.
Mostly met: Major output targets were met.
Partially met: Some output targets were met.
Not Met: Most output target were not met.

Outcome/Effectiveness

Definition: The extent to which the project's major relevant objectives were achieved, or are expected to be achieved, efficiently.

Ratings by OED/IEG (Note that the IEG has consolidated the ratings into four as follows).

Highly Satisfactory/Achieved: Project achieved or exceeded, or is expected to achieve or exceed, all its major relevant objectives efficiently without major shortcomings.
Satisfactory/Achieved: Project achieved, or is expected to achieve, most of its major relevant objectives efficiently with only minor shortcomings.
Moderately Satisfactory/Mostly Achieved: Project achieved, or is expected to achieve, most of its major relevant objectives efficiently but with either significant shortcomings or modest overall relevance.
Moderately Unsatisfactory/Partially Achieved: Project is expected to achieve its major relevant objectives with major shortcomings or is expected to achieve only some of its major relevant objectives, yet achieve positive efficiency.

Unsatisfactory/Not Achieved: Project has failed to achieve, and is not expected to achieve, most of its major relevant objectives with only minor development benefits.

Highly Unsatisfactory/Not Achieved: Project has failed to achieve, and is not expected to achieve, any of its major relevant objectives with no worthwhile development benefits.

An important limitation of the OED approach to the assessment of outcome is that the outcome is considered independent of sustainability. A project may be judged "Highly Satisfactory" while it may not have been sustained.

Institutional Development Impact (IDI; by the OED Only)

Definition: The extent to which a project improves the ability of a country or region to make more efficient, equitable, and sustainable use of its human, financial, and natural resources through: (a) better definition, stability, transparency, enforceability, and predictability of institutional arrangements, and/or (b) better alignment of the mission and capacity of an organization with its mandate, which derives from these institutional arrangements. IDI considers that the project is expected to make a critical contribution to the country's/region's ability to effectively use human, financial, and natural resources, either through the achievement of the project's stated ID objectives or through unintended effects.

OED Ratings:

Substantial: Project as a whole made, or is expected to make, a significant contribution to the country's/region's ability to effectively use human, financial, and natural resources, either through the achievement of the project's stated ID objectives or through unintended effects.

Modest: Project as a whole increased, or is expected to increase, to a limited extent the country's/region's ability to effectively use human, financial, and natural resources, either through the achievement of the project's stated ID objectives or through unintended effects.

Negligible: Project as a whole made, or is expected to make, little or no contribution to the country's/region's ability to effectively use human, financial, and natural resources, either through the achievement of the project's stated ID objectives or through unintended effects.

The IEG no longer uses this criterion.

The Bank Performance

The OED in addition also rated the Bank performance based upon "Quality at Entry" and "Supervision" as follows.

The Quality of Entry ratings took into consideration: project consistency with Bank strategy for the country; grounding in economic and sector work; development objective statement; approach and design appropriateness; government ownership; involvement of stakeholders/beneficiaries; adequacy of technical analysis; economic and financial impact analysis; environmental assessment; impact on poverty reduction and social issues; institutional analysis; adequacy of financial management arrangements; readiness for implementation; and assessment of risk and sustainability.

The Supervision ratings took into account two major factors: focus on development impact and adequacy of supervision inputs and processes. The focus on development impact includes: timely identification/assessment of implementation and development impact; appropriateness of proposed solutions and follow-up; effectiveness of Bank actions. The Supervision ratings took into account: adequacy of Bank supervision resources; supervision reporting quality; attention to fiduciary aspects, and attention to monitoring and evaluation.

OED Ratings on Bank Performance

Highly Satisfactory: Bank performance was rated as Highly Satisfactory on both quality at entry and supervision, or Highly Satisfactory on the one dimension with significantly higher impact on project performance and at least Satisfactory on the other.

Satisfactory: Bank performance was rated at least Satisfactory on both quality at entry and supervision, or Satisfactory on the one dimension with significantly higher impact on project performance and no less than Unsatisfactory on the other.

Unsatisfactory: Bank performance was not rated at least Satisfactory on both quality at entry and supervision, or Unsatisfactory on the one dimension with significantly higher impact on project performance and no higher than Satisfactory on the other.

Highly Unsatisfactory: Bank performance was rated as Highly Unsatisfactory on both quality at entry and supervision, or Highly Unsatisfactory on the one dimension with significantly higher impact on project performance and no higher than Unsatisfactory on the other.

The IEG instead rates Bank performance based upon (a) strategic relevance at country level and (b) effectiveness of Bank interventions. The effectiveness is assessed by relevance, result, efficacy, and overall effectiveness criteria.

The Borrower Performance (by the OED Only)

Definition: The extent to which the borrower assumed ownership and responsibility to ensure quality of preparation and implementation, and complied with covenants and agreements, towards the achievement of development objectives and sustainability.

OED rated borrower performance on there counts: (a) preparation; (b) implementation; and (c) compliance. The preparation took into consideration institutional and financial constraints. The implementation considered macro and sectoral policies/conditions; government commitment; appointment of key staff; counterpart funding; and administrative procedures. The implementing agency performance was also considered. The compliance considered all major covenants and commitments undertaken by the borrower.

Ratings

Highly Satisfactory: Borrower performance was rated Highly Satisfactory on at least two of the three performance factors.
Satisfactory: Borrower performance was rated at least Satisfactory on two of the three factors.
Unsatisfactory: Borrower performance was not rated at least Satisfactory on two of the three factors.
Highly Unsatisfactory: Borrower performance was rated Highly Unsatisfactory on at least two of the three factors.

The IEG no longer rates the borrower performance as indicated by the above criterion.

Source: World Bank (2002, 2020).

References

Andrews, Matthew, and Anwar Shah. 2001. *From Washington to ROME: A Road Less Traveled by Public Sector Reformers.* Washington, DC: Operations Evaluation Department, World Bank.

Andrews, Matthew and Anwar Shah, 2005. Citizen-Centered Governance: A New Approach to Public Sector Reform. In *Public Expenditure Analysis*, ed. Anwar Shah, Chapter 6, 153–182. Washington, DC: World Bank.

Angrist, Joshua, Guido Imbens, and Donald Rubin. 1996. Identification of Causal Effects Using Instrumental Variables. *Journal of the American Statistical Association* 91 (434): 444–455.

Banker, R.D., and R.C. Morey. 1986a. Efficiency Analysis for Exogenously Fixed Inputs and Outputs. *Operations Research* 34 (4): 513–521.

———. 1986b. The Use of Categorical Variables in Data Envelopment Analysis. *Management Science* 32 (12): 1613–1627.

Barnow, B., G. Cain, and A. Goldberger. 1980. Issues in the Analysis of Selectivity Bias. In *Evaluation Studies Review Annual*, ed. E. Stromsdorfer and G. Farkas, vol. 5. San Francisco: Sage.

Boruch, Robert F. 1997. *Randomized Experiments for Planning and Evaluation: A Practical Guide.* Thousand Oaks: Sage.

Briggs, A., and P. Fenn. 1998. Confidence Intervals or Surfaces? Uncertainty on the Cost-Effectiveness Plane. *Health Economics* 7: 723–740.

Charnes, A., W.W. Cooper, and Edwardo L. Rhodes. 1978. Measuring the Efficiency of Decision Making Units. *European Journal of Operational Research* 2 (6): 429–444.

———. 1979. Short Communication: Measuring the Efficiency of Decision Making Units. *European Journal of Operational Research* 3 (4): 339.

———. 1981. Evaluating Program and Managerial Efficiency: An Application of Data Envelopment Analysis to Program Follow Through. *Management Science* 27 (6): 668–697.

Charnes, A., W.W. Cooper, A.Y. Lewin, and L.M. Seiford. 1994. *Data Envelopment Analysis: Theory, Methodology, and Application.* Boston: Kluwer.

Chen, H., and P.H. Rossi. 1980. The Multi-Goal, Theory-Driven Approach to Evaluation: A Model Linking Basic and Applied Social Science. *Social Forces* 59 (1): 106–122.

———. 1989. Issues in the Theory-Driven Perspective. *Evaluation and Program Planning* 12 (4): 299–306.

Corbeil, R. 1986. Logic on Logic Models. In *Evaluation Newsletter*. Ottawa: Office of the Comptroller General of Canada.

Davidson, E. Jane. 2006. The "Baggaging" of Theory-Based Evaluation. *Journal of Multidisciplinary Evaluation* 4: iii–xiii.

Dehejia, Rajeev. 2015. Experimental and Non-experimental Methods in Development Economics: A Porous Dialectic. *Journal of Globalization and Development* 6 (1): 47–69.

Dehejia, R., and S. Wahba. 2002. Propensity Score Matching Methods for Non-experimental Causal Studies. *Review of Economics and Statistics* 84 (1): 441–462.

Department of Finance. 1987. *The Choice of Discount Rate for Evaluating Public Sector Investment Projects: A Discussion Paper*. Department of Finance, Australia.

Donaldson, Stewart, and Laura Gooler. 2003. Theory-Driven Evaluation in Action: Lessons from a $20 Million Statewide Work and Health Initiative. *Evaluation and Program Planning* 26: 355–366.

Duflo, Esther, Rachel Glennerster, and Michael Kremer. 2007. Chapter 61 Using Randomization in Development Economics Research: A Toolkit. In *Handbook of Development Economics*, vol. 4, 3895–3962. https://doi.org/10.1016/S1573-4471(07)04061-2.

Flay, B.R., T.Q. Miller, D. Hedeker, O. Siddiqui, C.F. Britton, B.R. Brannon, A. Johnson, W.B. Hansen, S. Sussman, and C. Dent. 1995. The Television, School and Family Smoking Prevention and Cessation Project: VIII. Student Outcomes and Mediating Variables. *Preventive Medicine* 24 (1): 29–40.

Heckman, J., N. Hohmann, J. Smith, and M. Khoo. 2000. Substitution and Dropout Bias in Social Experiments: A Study of an Influential Social Experiment. *Quarterly Journal of Economics* 115 (2): 651–694.

Husser, Phillpe. 2019. Do Not Stick to the Iron Triangle in Project Management. https://www.philippehusser.com/do-not-stick-to-the-iron-triangle-in-project-management-2/

Imbens, Guido W., and Joshua D. Angrist. 1994. Identification and Estimation of Local Average Treatment Effects. *Econometrica* 62 (2): 467–475.

Kittelsen, S.A.C., and F.R. Førsund. 1992. Efficiency Analysis of Norwegian District Courts. *Journal of Productivity Analysis* 3 (3): 277–306.

Kusek, Jody Zall, and Ray C. Rist. 2004. *Ten Steps to a Results-Based Monitoring and Evaluation System*. Washington, DC: The World Bank.

Levin, Henry M. 1983. *Cost Effectiveness: A Primer*. Beverly Hills: Sage.

Lipsey, M.W., and A.J. Pollard. 1989. Driving Toward Theory in Program Evaluation: More Models to Choose From. *Evaluation and Program Planning* 12 (4): 317–328.

Luellen, Jason K., William R. Shadish, and M.H. Clark. 2005. Propensity Scores: An Introduction and Experimental Test. *Evaluation Review* 29 (6): 530–558.

McClendon, McKee J. 1994. *Multiple Regression and Causal Analysis*. Itsaca: F. E. Peacock.

O'Brien, B., and A. Briggs. 2002. Analysis of Uncertainty in Health Care Cost-Effectiveness Studies: An Introduction to Statistical Issues and Methods. *Statistical Methods in Medical Research* 11: 455–468.

Owens, D.K. 1998. Interpretation of Cost-Effectiveness Analysis. *Journal of General Internal Medicine* 13: 716–717.

Pawson, R., and N. Tilley. 1997. *Realistic Evaluation*. London: Sage.

Pearce, D., G. Atkinson, and S. Mourato. 2006. *Cost-Benefit Analysis and the Environment: Recent Developments*. Paris: OECD.

Pollack, Julien, Jane Helm, and Daniel Adler. 2018. What Is the Iron Triangle, and How It Has Changed? *International Journal of Managing Projects in Business* 11 (2): 527–547.

Quade, Edward S. 1967. Introduction and Overview. In *Cost-Effectiveness Analysis*, ed. Thomas A. Goldman. New York: Frederick A. Praeger.

Rosenbaum, Paul R., and Donald B. Rubin. 1983. The Central Role of the Propensity Score in Observational Studies for Causal Effects. *Biometrika* 70: 41–55.

Rossi, Peter Henry, and Howard E. Freeman. 1993. *Evaluation: A Systematic Approach*. Newbury Park: Sage.

Rush, B., and A. Ogborne. 1991. Program Logic Models: Expanding Their Role and Structure for Program Planning and Evaluation. *Canadian Journal of Program Evaluation* 6 (2): 95–106.

Scriven, Michael. 1967. The Methodology of Evaluation. In *Perspectives of Curriculum Evaluation*, AERA Monograph Series on Curriculum Evaluation, ed. Ralph W. Tyler, Robert M. Gagne, and Michael Scriven, vol. 1. Chicago: Rand McNally.

———. 1991. *Evaluation Thesaurus*. Newbury Park: Sage.

Shadish, William R., Thomas D. Cook, and Donald T. Campbell. 2001. *Experimental and Quasi-Experimental Designs for Generalized Causal Inference*. Boston: Houghton Mifflin.

Shah, Anwar. 2005. On Getting the Giant to Kneel: Approaches to a Change in the Bureaucratic Culture. Chapter 9. In *Fiscal Management*, ed. Anwar Shah, 211–228. Washington, DC: World Bank.

Squire, Lyn, and Herman G. van der Tak. 1975. *Economic Analysis of Projects*. Baltimore: Johns Hopkins University Press.

Suchman, E.A. 1967. *Evaluative Research: Principles and Practice in Public Service and Social Action Programs*. New York: Russell Sage Foundation.

Todd, Petra. 2007. Chapter 60 Evaluating Social Programs with Endogenous Program Placement and Selection of the Treated. In *Handbook of Development Economics*, vol. 4, 3847–3894. https://doi.org/10.1016/S1573-4471(07)04060-0.

Tulkens, H. 1993. On FDH Efficiency Analysis: Some Methodological Issues and Application to Retail Banking, Courts and Urban Transit. *Journal of Productivity Analysis* 4 (1–2): 183–210.

Van Hout, B.A., M.J. Al, G.S. Gordon, and F.F. Rutten. 1994. Costs, Effects and C/E-Ratios Alongside a Clinical Trial. *Health Economics* 3: 309–319.

Weiss, Carol H. 1987. Where Politics and Evaluation Research Meet. In *The Politics of Program Evaluation*, ed. D. Palumbo. Newbury Park: Sage.
———. 1995. Nothing as Practical as Good Theory: Exploring Theory-Based Evaluation for Comprehensive Community Initiatives for Children and Families. In *New Approaches to Evaluating Community Initiatives: Volume 1, Concepts, Methods and Contexts*, ed. J.P. Connell, A.C. Kubisch, L.B. Schorr, and C.H. Weiss. Washington, DC: The Aspen Institute.
———. 1997a. How Can Theory-Based Evaluation Make Greater Headway? *Evaluation Review* 21 (4): 501–524.
———. 1997b. Theory-Based Evaluation: Past, Present, and Future. In *Progress and Future Directions in Evaluation, New Directions for Evaluation*, ed. D.J. Rog, vol. 76. San Francisco: Jossey-Bass.
———. 1998. *Evaluation.* Upper Saddle River: Prentice Hall.
Wholey, J.S. 1994. Assessing the Feasibility and Likely Usefulness of Evaluation. In *Handbook of Practical Program Evaluation*, ed. J.S. Wholey, H.P. Hatry, and K.E. Newcomer. San Francisco: Jossey-Bass.
World Bank. 2002. Guidelines and Criteria for OED Project Evaluations. Operations Evaluation Department, Unpublished Note, July 1, 2000, The World Bank Group.
———. 2020. Guidance. The Independent Evaluation Group, Unpublished Note, January.

CHAPTER 3

Economic Evaluation of Projects

Robin Boadway

Principles of Valuation

This chapter summarizes the principles that are used to evaluate projects from an economic point of view. The term 'project' should be thought of in the broadest of senses. It can refer to individual investment projects, like the building of a bridge or a dam. More broadly, it can include general expenditure programs, like education, health care, or nutrition spending. Or, it can refer to government policies like reforms of the tax-transfer system, or the regulation of economic activities. Our use of the term 'project' in what follows should be taken as including all of these. Economic evaluation of a project implies a measure of its net benefits in monetary terms, as opposed to, say, an evaluation as to its political feasibility.

Attaching a monetary measure to the benefits and costs of a project raises the fundamental question of whose benefits and costs are relevant. We follow the convention used in much of the economics literature referred to as the principle of *welfarism*, which holds that what ultimately

R. Boadway (✉)
Economics, Queen's University, Kingston, ON, Canada
e-mail: boadwayr@econ.queensu.ca

© The Author(s) 2020

A. Shah (ed.), *Policy, Program and Project Evaluation*,
https://doi.org/10.1007/978-3-030-48567-2_3

counts is the welfare of the individuals in the society.[1] Thus, the objective of project evaluation is to measure the benefits and costs accruing to those individuals who are affected.

Measuring the benefits or costs of a project to any given individual involves asking how much the individual would be willing to pay to have the benefit or to avoid the cost. What they would be willing to pay will typically differ from what they actually have to pay. They may not have to pay anything if the project involves public goods or services provided free of charge. But, even if they do pay something, it will likely be less than the amount they would be willing to pay, their *willingness-to-pay*. In other words, they will obtain some *surplus* from it, which implies that market prices will not suffice.

Technically, the willingness-to-pay for a project's benefits (or the minimum amount those affected would be willing to accept to bear the project's costs) is measured by some generalized notion of the *compensating variation* (CV, for short). The standard definition of the CV is obtained implicitly from the following equation:

$$V\left(p_0, m_0\right) = V\left(p_1, m_1 - \mathrm{CV}\right)$$

where $V(p,m)$, the so-called *indirect utility function*, is the individual's utility as a function of the vector of prices of commodities p and income m, with the subscripts 0 and 1 referring to the pre-project and after-tax project prices and income. Alternatively, the CV can be measured directly by making use of the *expenditure function*, $E(p, U)$, which indicates the amount of income required to achieve utility level U when prices are p. The compensating variation can then be written:

$$\mathrm{CV} = E\left(p_1, U_1\right) - E\left(p_1, U_0\right)$$

[1] The term 'welfarism' is due to Sen (1970), who used it to describe the property of a social welfare function which orders alternative resource allocations according to the levels of utility achieved by members of the society. Sen has been critical of the principle of welfarism, arguing that other characteristics of social well-being, such as freedom, justice, non-discrimination, equality of opportunity, and so on, should also count. Project evaluators sidestep this issue by arguing either that the projects under consideration have no particular effect on these virtues or that if they do it is impossible to measure them so they ought to be weighted according to the values of those ultimately responsible for decision-making.

A number of features of the CV are worth noting:

- In the special case in which only one price changes, the CV is equivalent to the conventional consumer surplus, the area beneath the demand curve and the horizontal price line.[2]
- More generally, the CV as defined measures the change in utility at a set of reference prices p_1, those of the final situation. In the two-good case, this is the distance between the initial and final indifference curves measured with lines whose slope reflects the relative prices of the final situation.
- The measure of welfare change is not unique: any set of reference prices could have been used. For example, use of the initial prices yields the so-called *equivalent variation*, EV. More generally, different reference prices give rise to different *money metric* measures of utility change. The actual monetary measure of welfare change will differ depending on the money metric used, but they will all be roughly the same.[3] Given the errors of measurement and uncertainties usually involved in actual project evaluation, it will make little practical difference which measure is used. We shall follow the convention of referring to our welfare changes measures as CVs, but it should be recalled that we could be using any of the money metric measures discussed here.
- The prices in the expression for welfare change can refer to either goods purchased by the individual or factors supplied.
- The CV measure refers especially to the case in which all inputs and outputs have prices associated with them, and consumers can vary quantities at will. If neither of these properties holds, the CV formulation must be suitably amended. But the same principles are involved: CV measures the consumer's willingness-to-pay.

[2] Technically speaking, it is the area beneath the compensated demand curve associated with the pre-change utility level. This area will differ from the area beneath the uncompensated demand curve because of income effects. For typical project evaluations, the difference will not be important, given the limitations of data.

[3] For example, in the case of a single price change, each welfare change measure will correspond to a consumer surplus area beneath a demand curve, but the actual demand curve that is appropriate will vary according to the measure used. For the CV, the compensated demand curve corresponding to the utility level of the final situation will be appropriate, while for the EV, that corresponding to the initial utility level is used. The two will differ only because of income effects. See Boadway and Bruce (1984) for a more complete discussion.

- If the benefits and costs occur over different periods of time, they must be converted using a discount rate to a monetary equivalent at a given point in time. Typically, this will involve discounting to the present at the individual's discount rate to give a present value (PV).

These CVs are the building blocks of project evaluation. But, any given project will give rise to a spectrum of CVs, one for each individual affected by the project. How do we go about aggregating individual CVs together? The problem is that, while the CV indicates in monetary terms an individual's change in welfare, there is no objective way of comparing CVs across persons. Two alternative procedures may be followed.

The first is to follow the precept advocated by Harberger (1971a) and to treat a rupee as worth a rupee no matter whose hands it is in. In this case, individual CVs can be summed to an aggregate CV intended to measure the net benefits to all members of the society. Though this procedure is most frequently used in practice, the theoretical case for it is highly disputed in the literature.[4] Proponents will usually cite one or more of the following arguments, each one intended to support the view that the aggregate CV measures in some sense the efficiency benefits of the project: (i) the government has tax-transfer policy instruments available for redistribution, and should be presumed to be using them to undo any differences in the value of a rupee to various households; (ii) there are many projects being undertaken, and their redistributive effects should be roughly offsetting; and (iii) if the aggregate CV is positive, that is *prime facie* evidence that those who gain could hypothetically compensate those who lose and still be better off. These arguments have failed to convince the critics of the procedure, and the debate stands unresolved. Perhaps the strongest argument for aggregating CVs is a purely practical one: given that aggregate data are all the evaluator has available, it is impossible to do anything but measure aggregate CVs, perhaps supplementing that where possible with evidence about the gainers and losers so that the policymaker can make an informed judgment.

The second procedure is to incorporate *distributive weights* directly into the project evaluation according to some preconceived notion of deservedness. This is not a straightforward exercise. For one thing, the distributive weights ought, in principle, to be applied to individual CVs. But, that

[4] A comprehensive summary of the arguments against using this procedure may be found in Blackorby and Donaldson (1990).

will not be possible for the reason cited above that individual CVs cannot be measured. The best that can be done is to apply distributive weights to different types of benefits and costs according to some evidence about how important they are to individuals of various circumstances (income, needs, etc.). The other main problem with this is choosing the weights. This inevitably involves a value judgment, presumably one that will not command consensus. A common procedure is to parameterize the social welfare function that aggregates household utilities using a single parameter, a common one being the degree of aversion to inequality. For example, suppose individual *i*'s level of utility measured in some money metric is Y_i. Then, let the social welfare function used to aggregate the monetary measures of various households be:

$$W(Y) = \Sigma(Y_i)^{1-\rho} / (1-\rho)$$

The parameter ρ is the coefficient of aversion to inequality, or more formally the elasticity of the marginal social utility of Y_i, or $\rho = -W''(Y_i)Y_i/[W'(Y_i)]$. It captures the extent to which one wants to put higher values on monetary gains accruing to households with lower Y_i's. Given that there is likely no agreement over its exact value, the evaluator can provide estimates of the net benefits of the project based on different values for ρ, leaving it to the policy-maker to decide among them.

What we are left with then are two ways of addressing the distributive effects of a project. The first simply uses aggregate CV measures to estimate costs and benefits of alternative projects, and reports on whatever patterns of distribution of benefits among individuals of different incomes can be estimated. The other is to incorporate distributional weights into the CV measures themselves, using a range of such weights. In either case, the policy-maker is left to choose among options.

The above procedure relies on individual CVs to capture the full benefits and costs of the project. Two caveats are in order before turning to the details of project evaluation. The first is that sole reliance on CVs reflects fully a welfaristic social objective function, and that may not be universally accepted. Policy-makers may be interested in some non-welfaristic objectives as well. These will often not be measurable in monetary terms, in which case the evaluator may simply report the consequences of the project for these other objectives. For example, the effect of the project on society's minorities, or on anti-discrimination objectives, can be reported alongside the monetary net benefits. The second caveat is that there may be external benefits or costs from the project that should form part of the project evaluation. In principle, these should be measured in willingness-to-pay terms, though that will often be challenging given that external effects are typically difficult to quantify.

The Decision Rule

The purpose of project evaluation is to calculate the net benefits of a project in such a way as to form a basis for informing policy-makers as to whether the project should be undertaken. The private sector is engaged in these sorts of calculations on a continuing basis, and it is natural to begin by asking why economic project evaluation should be any different from calculations of financial profitability that are used to guide the investment decisions of firms. In fact, there are several factors which make economic evaluation distinct from private profitability:

- Market prices generally deviate from marginal social values if there are distortions in the economy. The source of the distortions might be government policies (e.g., taxes, tariffs, regulations) or they might be inherent in the market economy (e.g., monopoly).
- There may be externalities, either beneficial or detrimental, which will not be reflected in market prices. Environmental pollution is an obvious example of a negative externality, while the generation of useful information that cannot be appropriated is a positive externality. Because these effects are difficult to quantify, let alone value, the task of economic valuation is typically more difficult than private profitability calculations.
- Some inputs or outputs may have no explicit market price attached to them, such as the value of time saved on a public transportation facility, or the value of improvements in health and longevity. Though these can be quantified, they are nonetheless difficult to put a money value on.
- Economic values must include indirect benefits resulting from induced changed elsewhere in the economy. This will be relevant when outputs change on markets in which there is a distortion, since a distortion results in the benefit to users of changes in the quantity purchased differing from the cost to suppliers of making the changed quantities available.

- Projects may not be self-sufficient, but may require financing from the public purse. Since it is costly for the government to raise revenues, the excess burden of public financing must be taken into account in valuing projects. Private projects will use private sources of financing whose cost is taken into account directly in the rate-of-return calculation.
- The discount rate used for public projects, the *social discount rate*, will differ from the private discount rate because of capital market distortions.
- And, as mentioned, public projects may take into account equity or other social considerations.

All of these points imply that we must take into account a number of considerations not found in financial profitability studies. How this is done will occupy the remaining sections of this paper. In the rest of this section, we address the rule to be used as a basis for deciding on the economic desirability of a project.

The Present Value Criterion

A project will be worth doing if the sum of its benefits is at least as great as the sum of its costs, measured in monetary terms. Given that benefits and costs will occur across several time periods, and that rupees today are worth more than the promise of rupees next year, both streams must be converted to a common time period, conventionally taken to be the present period. Thus, the net benefit of the project will be its net present value (NPV), defined as the present value of the benefits (PVB) less the present value of the costs (PVC), or:

$$\text{NPV} = \text{PVB} - \text{PVC} = \Sigma\left(B_t - C_t\right) / \left(1+i\right)^t$$

where B_t and C_t are the benefits and costs and i is the one-period social discount rate in period t, assumed to be constant, and t goes from 1 until the termination date of the project. If this PV is positive, the project should be undertaken. Or, if the policy-maker is restricted to considering mutually exclusive alternatives, the one with the largest PV should be undertaken. Such alternatives might include identical projects with alternative starting times, projects differing only in scale, projects of differing durabilities, or alternative groups of projects.

There are a number of issues in implementing the PV criterion that ought to be mentioned. They are as follows.

Alternative PV Formulations I: The Benefit-Cost Ratio

Policy-makers often like to have a simple summary statistic indicating how beneficial a project is. The benefit-cost ratio, defined as the ratio of the present value of benefits to the present value of costs or PVB/PVC, provides an intuitively appealing measure of the extent to which benefits outweigh costs. As long as it exceeds one, it can be relied on to indicate whether a project has a positive NPV. But, it can be misleading in the case of ranking projects which are mutually exclusive alternatives, so it cannot be used to choose the project which maximizes net social benefits. The reason is that it does not account for the scale of the project.[5]

The fact is that the benefit-cost ratio uses precisely the same information as the NPV, but presents it in a slightly different form. If policy-makers find it to be useful, it is not difficult to supplement it with the NPV to ensure that the NPV criterion is being satisfied.

Alternative PV Formulations II: The Internal Rate of Return

The internal rate or return (IRR) consists of a net present value calculation of a different sort. The IRR is defined as the discount rate which makes the present value of the stream of benefits less the present value of the stream of costs identically zero. Algebraically, the IRR is defined as the value of λ that satisfies the following equation:

$$\Sigma\left(B_t - C_t\right)/\left(1+\lambda\right)^t = 0,\ t = 1,\ldots,T$$

As can be seen, this is a fairly complex equation to be solved for λ. In fact, it is a polynomial of a degree T, the length of the time horizon. This can be seen by multiplying the equation by $(1 + \lambda)^T$, which leads to an equation of the form $a\lambda + b\lambda^2 + c\lambda^3 + \cdots + k\lambda^T = 0$. In general, this equation can have as many as T solutions for λ. The number of solutions will correspond to the number of times $B_t - C_t$ changes sign. Fortunately, this will not typically be a problem since, for most projects, $B_t - C_t$ will change sign

[5] A simple example will illustrate. Consider two projects, A and B. Project A has a present value of benefits and costs of PVB = 2,000,000 rupees and PVC = 1,000,000 rupees, giving a benefit-cost ratio of 2 and an NPV of 1,000,000 rupees. Project B has PVB = 1,200,000 rupees and PVC = 400,000 rupees, for a benefit-cost ratio of 3 and a NPV of 800,000 rupees. While project B has a higher net present value, it yields a lower NPV.

only once, being negative initially while capital costs are being incurred, and then positive for the rest of the project life. In these circumstances, the IRR will not only be uniquely defined, but it will also indicate to the policy-maker whether the project is socially profitable—if λ exceeds the social discount rate i, the NPV of the project will be positive.

But, like the benefit-cost ratio, the IRR can be unreliable since it may not rank mutually exclusive alternatives according to their NPVs. Moreover, this problem is not simply one of scale. The problem arises because projects with different time profiles can have different NPVs at different discount rates—projects whose benefits accrue later in life will be particularly penalized at high discount rates. This is something that the IRR cannot possibly take account of. For example, suppose two different projects each cost 1 million rupees, so they have a net benefit of −1 million in year zero. Project A generates no net benefits in period 1 and 1.21 million rupees in period 2, while project B generates all its net benefits of 1.15 million rupees in period 1. The IRR of project A is 0.10, while that of project B is 0.15, so the latter would be chosen on the IRR criterion. Suppose the discount rate is $i = 0.02$: the NPV of project A is 0.163 million rupees, while that of project B is 0.127 million rupees. Project A would be chosen. Suppose now the discount rate is 0.07: the NPV of project A is 0.057 million rupees, while that of project B is 0.075 million rupees, making the latter the preferred project. Clearly, when the time profile of projects differs considerably, the ranking can depend upon the discount rate, something which the IRR cannot accommodate.

This implies that if the time profiles of projects differ, the IRR cannot be used to determine which one maximizes NPV, even among those that are of similar scales. If the choice is between a long-lasting project and one with a short time horizon, the IRR is prone to be unreliable.

Capital Budgeting

Suppose that, for whatever reason, the policy-maker has an upper limit on the capital budget that can be used for the projects under consideration. The budget can be used for financing various combinations of projects. In principle, the choice of projects is straightforward: choose the combination of projects within the budget limit which maximizes the total NPV of the projects combined, where the NPV calculation is precisely the same as before. This might, of course, entail not undertaking the one which has the highest individual NPV in order that the aggregate NPV is the highest possible. As before, use of the benefit-cost ratio and the IRR criterion will generally be unreliable.

The discount rate might be thought to be an issue here, since the capital budget is fixed, so there is no opportunity to borrow and lend. But, as we discuss below, given our assumption of welfarism, the discount rate for project evaluation, the so called social discount rate, is the rate at which the benefits and costs of the project are discounted by those individuals in the economy who actually obtain them. In the absence of externalities, and assuming that households are free to borrow and lend on capital markets, the social discount rate is the after-tax interest rate faced by households on capital markets.

Although the principles of project evaluation when there are capital budgeting constraints are clear (and not really any different from project evaluation in the unconstrained case), there are nonetheless a number of conceptual issues that must be dealt with in practice, including the following.

Unused Capital Funds If the collection of projects do not exhaust the capital budget allotted, the issue of what becomes of the unused funds is relevant. If they revert to general revenues and serve to relax the government's overall budget constraint, this must be taken into account. In effect, the excess burden of whatever public financing is available must be incorporated into the project evaluation in a manner discussed below. Projects which use less funds will naturally incur less excess burden on this account. In other words, the procedure for taking account of the actual amount of funding for various options is the same as for project evaluation in the absence of the capital budget constraint. The latter simply puts an upper bound on the capital available.

Multi-Period Capital Costs The evaluation will need to take account of the extent to which different projects incur capital costs over a period of years, and how the capital budget constraint deals with that. Again, nothing new in principle is involved here. As long as all costs and benefits are appropriately accounted for, including the cost of public funds, the only constraint imposed by the capital budget is a restriction on the amount of funds available over time. The capital requirements for different projects may have different time profiles. As long as they are properly costed in the periods in which they are incurred, there should be no problems. The evaluator must still choose the combination of projects which maximizes the aggregate NPV and does not violate the capital budget allotted.

Future Project Capital Requirements Similar considerations apply with capital funding that may be required for expansion of replacement investment some periods down the road. To the extent that capital constraints apply to these, they will obviously have to be satisfied.

The Treatment of Inflation

If the general level of prices is rising over time, market interest rates will reflect that. For example, if the inflation rate is π and it is fully anticipated, the nominal discount rate i will differ from the real one r in a given period according to:

$$(1+i)=(1+r)(1+\pi)$$

(This, of course, neglects any taxes that might be payable on capital income.) In principle, project evaluation should include only real benefits and costs—purely inflationary changes in values should not be included.

There are two equivalent ways to ensure this. The first is to conduct the project evaluation entirely in nominal terms. All benefits and costs would be evaluated in current rupees, using nominal prices projected for each future period. And the nominal social discount rate should be used. The alternative is to use constant-rupee prices, obtained by deflating current-valued ones by the price index relative to some base period, but to discount the flow of net benefits and costs using the real discount rate r. It is straightforward to show that these two procedures will yield the same NPV.[6]

The prescription is perhaps easier than its application. Future inflation rates are difficult to estimate, especially expected ones. What is important is that consistent procedures be used. The use of nominal discount rates must not be mixed with benefit and cost evaluations that do not include an allowance for inflation. Perhaps the safest procedure is to use constant rupee prices so as to avoid the need to estimate future inflation rates.

[6] To see this, note that the relation between real and nominal prices is given by $p_t = (1+\pi)^t p_0$, where p_t is the nominal price level in period t, while p_0 is the real price using a base year of zero. The NPV using nominal prices can be written:

$$NPV = \Sigma p_t X_t / \left[(1+r)(1+\pi)\right]^t = \Sigma p_0 X_t / (1+r)^t$$

where X_t is the vector of net benefits in year t. Note that $(1+\pi)^t$ is the price index for period t.

Terminal Value
A vexing issue in project evaluation is identifying the end of a project's useful life, that is, the terminal period. The terminal period determines the number of periods *T* over which the project may be evaluated. Presumably, the project should cease once its future discounted present value falls to zero. The problem is that this may be far into the future, where projections become less reliable.

Setting aside estimation problems, whatever terminal date is chosen, there will undoubtedly be some fixed capital left over. To the extent that the capital has some value, its so-called *scrap value*, that value should be included as a benefit of the project. This will also be difficult to measure. If the capital can be put to another use (e.g., office equipment, vehicles), its value in that use should be included as a benefit. If the capital has no alternative use, the scrap value would consist of the value of the materials that could be salvaged.

It is even conceivable that scrap value could be negative. For example, the site of the project may leave an environmental or health hazard if it is not cleaned up. This clean-up should be treated as part of the cost of shutting down the operation.

Choice of a Numeraire

An issue that distinguishes various approaches to project evaluation concerns the unit of measurement, or *numeraire*. The numeraire serves as the standard against which all other benefits or costs are evaluated, given the distortions that exist in the economy. It is important to recognize that the choice of numeraire is basically arbitrary in the sense that it does not affect the outcome of the evaluation: project evaluation done under any numeraire can be converted into that for any other by using the appropriate conversion factors.

In the literature, two approaches have been predominant. The first, more traditional, approach is to value all benefits and costs in terms of current consumption expenditures by households. Although we shall outline how to value particular sorts of items, it is worth mentioning some key types of benefits and costs that require special attention.

Present Versus Future Consumption
Naturally, items that occur in later periods must be converted to the current period by a discount factor. In particular, having converted all

within-period inputs and outputs into their values in terms of consumption, the discounting must use a consumption discount rate (i.e., the rate at which household can transform present into future consumption on capital markets).

Foreign Exchange

When foreign exchange markets are distorted by tariffs and other trade measures, the market exchange rate no longer reflects the economic cost of converting foreign products into domestic consumption. A shadow price of foreign exchange must be determined which incorporates the effects of the distortions on the true opportunity cost to the economy of acquiring foreign exchange to purchase imported goods, or conversely to sell foreign exchange acquired from the sale of domestic goods abroad. The foreign price of all traded commodities involved in a project must be converted to domestic consumer prices using the shadow price of foreign exchange.

Public Financing

Public funds cannot be treated as having the same value as funds in the hands of consumers because it is costly to reallocate funds from the households to government. Given that there will be a deadweight loss of using the tax system to do so, a rupee in the hands of the government will be more valuable than in the hands of households. The appropriate conversion factor for converting public funds to private fund is the marginal cost of public funds (MCPF)—the opportunity cost of transferring a marginal rupee from the private sector to the public sector. To the extent that the project entails changes in public sector revenues, these must be valued at the MCPF.

Investment Relative to Consumption

By the same token, because of capital market distortions, a rupee's worth of investment is worth more than a rupee's worth of consumption: the former would yield a stream of consumption whose present value exceeds one rupee. That suggests that to the extent that the project crowds out investment or enhances it, the effect on investment must be valued at the opportunity cost of investment.

Distributive Equity Considerations
It might be judged that a rupee of consumption is worth more to persons of low income than to persons of high income. If it is desired to incorporate such judgments into the project evaluation, the numeraire should specify consumption in the hands of a particular income level of household. Consumption accruing to other households must therefore be discounted by the appropriate distributive weight.

The use of current-period household consumption (perhaps in the hands of a particular income group) as the numeraire therefore entails using conversion factors for future consumption, for changes in foreign currency use, for net public sector funding, for changes in investment, and possibly for consumption accruing to different income groups. What results is a measure of the NPV of the project measured in present consumption to the benchmark income group.

The second approach is that first advocated by Little and Mirrlees (1974) for the OECD, but since widely used by the World Bank (e.g., Ray 1984). Their numeraire is foreign exchange in the hands of the government. The use of this numeraire entails the use of analogous conversion factors as above, but the conversion is typically done in the reverse direction. Thus, any changes in output or use of non-traded commodities must be converted into foreign exchange using effectively the reciprocal of the shadow price of foreign exchange. Also, domestic consumption changes are considered to be less valuable than rupees in the hands of the government for a couple of reasons. First, as above, there is a deadweight loss involved in diverting funds from the private sector to the public sector. But, second, it is reckoned by Little and Mirrlees that funds in the hands of government will be available for investment, which as before is more valuable than consumption because of capital market distortions. So a consumption conversion factor is required to evaluate domestic consumption benefits in terms of government revenues. And, such distributive weights as are deemed necessary are also used to convert consumption of different income groups into that of the benchmark group (taken to be the lowest income group).

The upshot to repeat is that the two procedures should give the same result, as should a procedure which uses any other numeraire. In what follows, we shall implicitly follow the traditional approach and use present-period consumption as the numeraire.

Cost-Effectiveness Versus Benefit-Cost Analysis

The most complete and informative type of project evaluation estimates the NPV of the benefits and costs of all alternatives being considered. This can be a mammoth task. In some circumstances, it is either sufficient or only possible to measure project costs. For example, if one is comparing alternative methods of delivering the same services, it may be necessary only to measure the costs of the various methods, that is, to conduct a *cost-effectiveness analysis.* Thus, one might be interested in comparing the costs of administering a tax or tariff collection system. Or, one may be comparing the costs of different ways of patrolling one's borders. Assuming that the same services are accomplished by various alternatives, a comparison of PVCs should suffice to pick out the socially desirable one. Of course, as long as PVBs are not estimated, it is not possible to say whether any of the alternatives has a positive NPV.

If benefits are conceptually impossible to measure, one has no choice but to measure only the costs. This might be true even if the benefits differ among projects. This does not necessarily render cost-effectiveness analysis of no use. The policy-maker can be presented with the present value of the costs of different alternatives, and the policy-maker can then assume responsibility for deciding which alternative, if any, should be undertaken.

In principle, the analog of cost-effectiveness analysis might need to be done from the benefit point of view. If costs cannot be measured, it might still be informative to compare the benefits from various options. More generally, if some, but not all, of the costs or benefits cannot be measured, it may still help the policy-maker to know the magnitudes of those that can. Some information is typically better than none.

Sensitivity Analysis

Rarely will all parameters be known with full confidence, especially those which are not reflected in market values, which require value judgments, or which will occur in the future. In these cases, presenting calculations using different parameter values will indicate how sensitive the results are to the reported values. The policy-maker will at least know for which parameter values judgment becomes important. There are no general principles for conducting sensitivity analyses. Apart from experimenting to see which parameters are critical for the results of the evaluation, it is also useful to set out the evaluator's judgment of the most likely set of parameter values, as well as lower-bound and upper-bound calculations.

Valuing Inputs and Outputs

The core problem of project evaluation involves putting monetary values on the various benefits and costs of the project. These should reflect the willingness-to-pay. Benefits and costs can come in a variety of different forms, including the purchase or sale of products and factors of production on markets, the provision of non-marketed benefits or costs such as externalities and intangibles, and the net benefits arising from indirectly affecting resources allocated on other markets, which themselves are distorted. We consider each type of benefit or cost separately.

Market Inputs and Outputs

Projects that involve expenditures on goods and services (as opposed to, say, transfers or regulations) will typically involve purchasing some primary or intermediary inputs on markets, and perhaps selling some outputs on markets (e.g., electricity, water, transportation services). At the same time, markets may well be distorted. They may have taxes, tariffs, or subsidies imposed on them; they may be monopolized; or, they may simply be functioning imperfectly. The measurement of benefits and costs of marketed items involves taking account of these distortions. This results in a social, or *shadow*, value or cost for a marketed item which is typically different from the market value or its consumer surplus.

To understand the meaning of a shadow value, consider the case of a project which uses an input X purchased on a market in which the demand price exceeds the supply price. Let p be the supply price (marginal cost) and $q = p + t$ be the demand price, where t is the distortion. For concreteness, think of the distortion as a tax imposed on the input. Figure 3.1 depicts the market for X. The demand curve $D(q)$ shows the quantity demanded at various demand prices, while the curve $S(p)$ shows the quantity supplied at various supply prices. By adding the distortion t vertically to the supply curve, we obtain the curve $S(p + t)$ showing the amount that would be supplied at various demand prices. Market equilibrium occurs at the output X_1 where the supply price is p_1 and the demand price q_1. Suppose now the project purchases an amount ΔG from the market. The demand curve will shift rightward by ΔG, causing the supply and demand prices to rise to p_2 and q_2. As can be seen from the diagram, the project demand ΔG is satisfied partly from an increase in supply, ΔX_S, and partly from a reduction in demand, $-\Delta X_D$. This carries with it an opportunity cost consisting of the cost to suppliers of supplying the additional amount

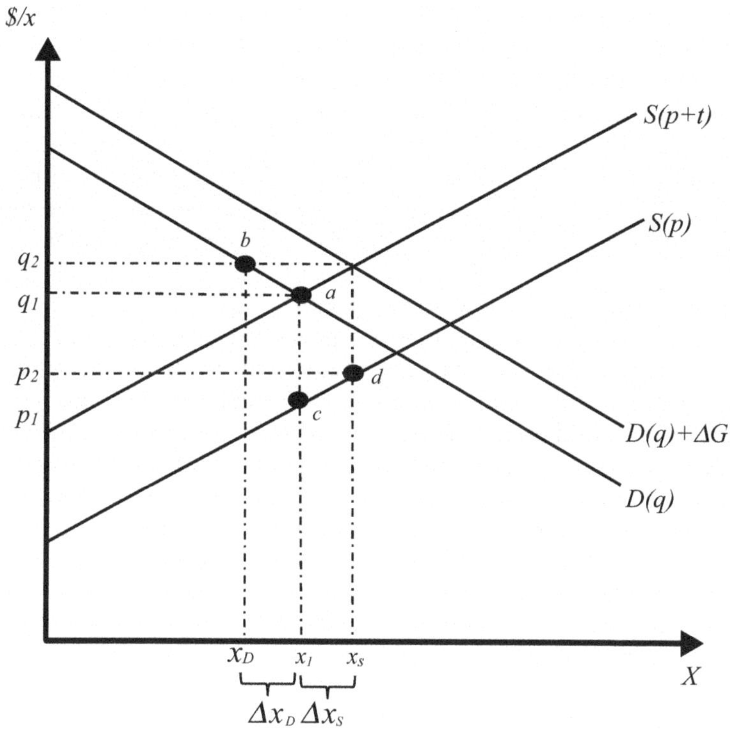

Fig. 3.1 Shadow price of a project input. (Source: Author)

ΔX_S, or $X_1 cdX_S$, and the reduction in benefit to demanders from forgoing purchase of the amount ΔX_D, or $X_1 baX_D$. The sum of these two items gives the shadow value of the input used in the project.

If the project is relatively small, so will be the price changes. Then the shadow value can be written as:

$$X_1 baX_D + X_1 cdX_S = q\Delta X_D + p\Delta X_S$$

The shadow price per unit of input purchased by the project is then given by:

$$s = \frac{p\Delta X_S}{\Delta G} + \frac{q\Delta X_D}{\Delta G}$$

This states that the shadow price s is a weighted average of the supply and demand prices, with the weights being the shares of the project requirements that are obtained from an increase in supply and a reduction in demand. It is sometimes referred to as Harberger's weighted-average shadow price rule. It can be applied both to the purchase of inputs and the sale of outputs, where in the latter case the project output displaces market supply and induces market demand. In the special case where the supply price (marginal cost) is constant (the elasticity of supply is infinite), the shadow price is simply p; while if the demand price is constant (demand is infinitely elastic), the shadow price is $q = p + t$.[7]

An important class of cases in which prices might be constant is that of a small open economy which faces fixed-world prices. In this case, the shadow price of either a tradable input or a tradable output simply reflects the prevailing world price measured in foreign currency terms. The sale of a traded commodity (even on the domestic market) ultimately gives rise to a supply of foreign exchange according to the world price of the good sold, while a purchase gives rise to a demand for foreign exchange. There are no indirect effects on markets for non-traded products. But, if foreign exchange markets are distorted, the conversion of increments of foreign exchange into domestic consumption equivalent values requires a shadow price of foreign exchange.

The Shadow Price of Foreign Exchange

Construction of a shadow price of foreign exchange is analogous to the above procedure. Assuming that trade must balance and the exchange rate is determined as a market clearing price (i.e., is flexible), the demand for foreign exchange reflects the domestic purchase of imports, while its supply comes from the sale of exports. If there were a common tariff at the ad valorem rate τ, and if e is the rupee price of a unit of foreign currency (the market exchange rate), the supply of foreign exchange will depend upon e, while the demand will depend on $e(1 + \tau)$. A project which uses one rupee worth of a tradable product will shift the demand for foreign exchange to the right. A similar argument as above then leads to the shadow price of foreign exchange being given by:

[7]These weighted-average shadow prices might be augmented by distributive weights if desired. We discuss the use of distributive weights later.

$$s = \frac{e\Delta X_s}{\Delta G} + \frac{e(1+\tau)\Delta X_D}{\Delta G}$$

where ΔG is the demand for foreign exchange generated by a project. If there were several different tariff rates τ_i for different products, the shadow price of foreign exchange would become:

$$s = \frac{e\Delta X_{Si}}{\Delta G} + \frac{\sum_i e(1+\tau_i)\Delta X_{Di}}{\Delta G}$$

For project evaluation purposes, this shadow price must be applied to the world price in domestic currency of all traded goods. No domestic taxes need to be taken into account.[8] Of course, if the exchange rate is not purely flexible, or if the domestic economy has market power in international markets, those things must be reflected in the shadow price.

The Shadow Wage Rate

One final application of the shadow pricing of marketed items concerns the price of labor. Labor markets not only have significant taxes imposed on them, but they are also prone to imperfections, especially unemployment. This implies that there will be a difference between the demand price for labor paid by employers and the opportunity cost of workers supplying the labor. In principle, a weighted-average shadow price can be devised and used. But, there are some complicating factors. The supply price of labor may be difficult to measure. For example, in the presence of involuntary unemployment, it will be less than the after-tax wage rate. It should, however, exceed zero given that leisure time has a value, but no market price will correspond to it so its measure will be imprecise. Also, wage differentials may exist for the same labor in different locations. To the extent that this reflects costs of moving, no particular problems arise. The supply price of labor is the wage paid in the new location, since that includes compensation for the costs of moving.

[8] Moreover, if equity is a concern, distributional weights need not be attached to traded inputs and outputs of items of importance to, say, low-income groups since they do not directly affect the domestic consumption of those goods. In the Little-Mirrlees approach, which uses foreign exchange as the numeraire, this makes the valuing of traded commodities particularly easy: world prices in rupees.

Wage differentials may be taken to reflect a segmented labor market where, for institutional reasons, wages are higher in one location (say, urban areas) than in another (say, rural areas), $w_U > w_R$. A worker from the rural area who is hired in the urban area at a wage w_U has only an opportunity cost of w_R, his output in the rural area. In this case, it is argued that the shadow wage should be a weighted average of w_U and w_R, where the weights correspond to the proportions in which hired workers are drawn from elsewhere in the urban area and from the rural area. Indeed, w_R might even be taken to be zero if there is excess labor in the rural sector, as in the Little-Mirrlees approach and the UNIDO *Guidelines* (Dasgupta et al. 1972).

Others find this argument unconvincing. Harberger (1971b), for example, using a variant of the well-known Harris and Todaro (1970) model, argues that the wage differential between the urban and the rural sector represents an equilibrium phenomenon, just like the wage differential between two locations on account of the cost of moving. To see the argument in its simplest form, suppose w_U is artificially above the market-clearing level for institutional reasons, but that w_R is free to adjust as workers move. In the absence of moving costs and assuming risk neutrality, workers will migrate until their expected urban wage equals their urban wage, $w_R = pw_U$, where p is the rate of unemployment and urban jobs are assumed to be filled randomly. Suppose a project creates jobs in the urban area, and that they are filled from the pool of the unemployed. Each job created will induce a migration from the rural area of $1/p$ workers, enough to ensure that the equilibrium condition $w_R = pw_U$ is satisfied. The opportunity cost of attracting these workers is w_R each, or w_R/p in total. By the equilibrium condition, this is just w_U, the wage paid to a worker who has been hired. Thus, market wages become the shadow wage rate. Thus, it is important to be sure of how the labor market functions before settling on a shadow wage rate.

If equity is a concern, it will be particularly important to incorporate distributive weights into the shadow wage rate, given that most of the income of lower income workers will be consumed by them. This will be the case whichever shadow wage formulation is used. Again, we shall return to the issue of distributive weights below.

Special Problems with Capital Inputs

The costing of inputs of a capital nature gives rise to some additional problems over and above the need for shadow pricing discussed above. These arise because of the durable nature of capital assets: outlays must be made for them before they generate a stream of benefits. This gives rise to two sorts of problems. First, capital acquisitions must be financed up front, either by government funding or by making use of capital markets. Either source of finance involves distortions, which implies that the opportunity cost of financing exceeds the amount of funds required. Though this problem is endemic to capital acquisition, it is more general than that. Projects may generate insufficient revenues even for ongoing costs. We defer until later the general problem of the opportunity cost, or shadow price, of project financing.

We deal here with the second problem, which is how to measure the costs of capital inputs given that their use is stretched over a number of periods into the future. As in the case of private-sector project evaluation, two methods of capital cost accounting could potentially be used—cash flow or accrual. Cash flow accounting involves simply including all outlays and inflows as they occur. Capital expenditures are costed in full ('expensed') when they are made, with appropriate shadow pricing used if they are purchased from distorted markets as discussed above. Capital expenditures must include all gross investment expenditures—additions to a project's capital stock, replacement investment, and any scrap value salvaged at the end of the project's useful life. Costs of financing and ongoing depreciation do not enter directly into the calculation of costs over and above the initial cash flow expenditures: that would be double counting. They may enter indirectly to the extent that financing gives rise to excess burdens, or to the extent that capital that has depreciated has been replaced.

Accrual accounting attempts to attach costs to the use of capital in the future rather than at the time of initial outlay. These costs are of two sorts—depreciation and financing costs. Depreciation is meant to reflect how much capital is 'used up' in each period of use, either due to obsolescence, wear and tear, or due to changes in the relative price of the asset. In other words, it measures the extent to which the value of the asset falls over the period. The financing costs represent the forgone interest associated with holding real capital rather than putting the same funds into the financial capital market. Again, one must not mix elements of cash and accrual accounting. If the latter is used, no capital expenditures of any kind should be treated as costs when they are incurred; rather they are costed as they are used up.

Cash and accrual accounting for capital costs are alternative ways of presenting the same information. In principle, the present value of the accrual costs of a capital investment should equal its cash flow (or the present value of its cash flow for a sequence of investment expenditures). But, accrual accounting is inherently more difficult to use since it involves attributing a depreciation sequence to the use of capital, something which cannot readily be observed from market prices. Moreover, the principles of shadow pricing are much less transparent when using accrual accounting. For that reason, cash accounting is typically used for project evaluation in the public sector. The private sector prefers to use accrual accounting because of the information it provides to shareholders. It indicates the period-by-period profitability of a firm which is engaged in a multitude of ongoing projects. Presumably if financial accounts were on a project-by-project basis, cash flow accounting would serve at least equally as well.

Intangibles and Non-marketed Inputs and Outputs

Public projects by their very nature often produce benefits or generate costs for which market prices are not readily available, or which are intangible and cannot readily be priced on markets. Examples include health and safety improvements, environmental improvements or degradation, time saved traveling, and the acquisition of new knowledge or skills. In some projects, these intangible or non-priced benefits are among the most important outputs. Their valuation should be guided by the same principles as above—willingness-to-pay for benefits, and the analog for costs, willingness-to-accept. The difficulty is of course that no guidance is available from market prices, so the monetary values must be inferred by other means.

Two common means can be used for evaluating intangibles. The first is to use the method of *hedonic pricing*, which is to use households' observed behavior elsewhere in the economy to reveal the value they implicitly place on intangibles. The second is to use survey techniques to ask a sample of households directly what value they place on the intangible under consideration. Consider some examples of each in turn.

Value of Time Saved

Public transportation projects such as roads, airports, bridges, and public transit facilities often have as their main objective the saving of time by users of the project as well as by users of alternative means of transportation. The value of time saved traveling depends upon the alternative uses to which the time will be put—whether to productive work or to leisure or non-market activities. In the case of the former, the value of time saved traveling might be the marginal productivity of time spent working, which in a competitive setting can be valued at the tax-inclusive wage rate. This presumes: (i) that labor markets are competitive, (ii) that workers are indifferent between time spent commuting and time spent working, and (iii) that there are no indivisibilities so that time saved can be put to productive use rather than leading to more free time for the worker. If one or more of these is violated, the calculation of time saved must be amended accordingly.

If time saved traveling accrues to households in the form of increased leisure, valuation is more problematic: the household is effectively substituting leisure time for commuting time, neither of which is readily measurable. The wage rate is of relatively little use here, as the following analysis shows. An individual will have different marginal benefits associated with time spent working (MB_W), leisure time (MB_L), and commuting time (MB_C). At the margin, if the individual can freely choose between leisure and working time (for a given commuting time), the equilibrium choice will satisfy $MB_L = w + MB_W$, where w is the wage rate. Since MB_W is presumably negative, the value of leisure is less than the wage rate. If the transportation project substitutes leisure time for commuting time, the value of time saved will be $V_C = MB_L - MB_C$, which is even less than the wage rate.

The value of V_C cannot be observed directly, but must somehow be estimated from other sources. One method commonly used is to infer V_C using transportation mode choices elsewhere in the economy. If consumers have a choice between two ways of getting from point A to point B which differ in the time cost as well as in resource costs, one can statistically estimate the amount of money consumers are just willing to pay at the margin to take the faster mode of transport. That is an application of the hedonic pricing method.

Once a value of time is obtained, it can be used to generate a monetary measure of the benefits of any project which involves time saved. A transportation project will typically both divert traffic and generate an increase in travel. The benefit of the former will include the monetary value of time saved for all diverted trips plus any changes in real resource costs for diverted trips (fuel, capital equipment, etc.). The benefit of generated traffic requires an estimate of the new demand created by the transportation facility, which will also depend upon the value of time saved. Another example of a project for which the value of time is relevant concerns recreational facilities in remote areas, such as national parks. Users will include both those diverted from other sites and newly generated demand. The willingness-to-pay for the use of the new site will depend upon the value of time.

Value of Reduced Risk of Death

Another example of the hedonic pricing technique involves valuing the saving of lives due to a project. (Similar principles apply to reducing the risk of disease or injury.) Health care programs, safety regulations and transportation projects are all examples where this can be used. Again, the monetary value to be attached to a reduction in the risk of death or injury should in principle be the willingness-to-pay for such a reduction by the households potentially involved. In other words, how much would consumers be willing to pay to achieve the given reduction in risk?[9]

In some cases, that valuation is implicit in the measurement of the benefits from using the project. For example, if travelers voluntarily choose to use a transport facility that carries with it a risk of accidental death, and if a demand curve for the facility has been estimated, the latter will include the value that travelers place on using the facility over and above any costs associated with risk. But for some projects, the costs or benefits of changes in the risk of loss of life must be attributed separately. An implicit 'value of life' can be obtained by observing other situations in which households implicitly put a value on the risk. For example, different types of jobs have systematically different risks of death, injury, etc., and those risks ought to be reflected in market wage differentials. Statistical techniques may then be used to estimate an implicit or hedonic value associated with different degrees of risk on the job.

Of course, statistical techniques must be used and interpreted with care. There are likely to be very many factors which go to explain wage differentials, and it is important to control for the most important of

[9] Evaluating reductions in the risk of death by *ex ante* willingness-to-pay, that is, without knowing precisely who will be saved, is not without controversy. Some would argue that as a society, loss of life should be evaluated from an *ex post* point of view since some persons will be saved for certain. This would give much larger values to each life saved. There will also typically be other benefits and costs associated with project that reduce the risk of death or injury, such as loss of output, and psychic costs to friends and relatives. They are valued in the usual way.

these. Moreover, it is possible that different households have different degrees of risk aversion: the least risk averse will be willing to accept a lower wage differential to work in riskier jobs. In these circumstances, wage differentials may not measure the cost of risk to the average person.

Costs of Environmental Pollution

Transportation projects or industrial projects may cause various sorts of pollution to neighboring residents. For example, a new airport will increase noise levels in the vicinity. Estimates of the cost of noise might be obtained indirectly from property values. Ceteris paribus, property values should be lower in noisier locations. Once again, hedonic pricing techniques can in principle be used to obtain monetary measures of environmental costs. In principle, property values should reflect the monetary value of attributes associated with various locations. The trick is to control for all the various attributes so that the cost associated with the environmental cost at stake can be obtained. To be useful for the project, these estimates must be for circumstances similar to those of the project. In the case of noise pollution, estimates from other airport locations might be suitable.

Survey Techniques: Contingent Valuation

Data limitations may preclude the use of statistical techniques to obtain hedonic values for intangibles. In this case, other methods must be found to place a value on them. One way to do so is to conduct a survey. Rather than relying on households to reveal their valuations directly or indirectly through their market behavior, they could be asked directly through a survey. Those surveyed are typically asked how much they would be willing to pay for the good or service in question—their willingness-to-pay—or, if appropriate, how much they would be willing to accept to give something up. Thus, households might be surveyed to determine their willingness to pay to create a national park or to protect an endangered species. Or, if a new airport is being contemplated near a residential area, residents might be asked for their willingness to accept increased noise levels at various times of day.

Naturally, surveys must be constructed with some care to ensure that respondents fully understand the nature of the project being evaluated. But even so, there are several potential pitfalls with survey techniques. Two important ones are as follows. First, those who complete a survey may not be a representative sample of those who might be affected by the project. If the sample is relatively small, there may be a biased group in the sample. But a more likely problem is that of self-selection—those who choose to respond may be those who feel most strongly about it. A second general problem is that responses may not be truthful. Since there is no penalty for being dishonest, those who feel strongly about an issue will have an incentive to exaggerate their willingness-to-pay. Thus, contingent valuation methods must be used and interpreted with some care.

Subsidies

Some projects may provide benefits in the form of subsidies to users. Economists would generally oppose the use of subsidies because they interfere with market efficiency. Nonetheless, there are some circumstances in which policy-makers may be justified in using subsidies:

- There may be externalities associated with an activity, such as innovations or human capital improvements, whose benefits partly accrue to others.
- Subsidies might be justified to divert resources away from other distorted sectors, such as subsidized public transit to reduce road congestion.
- Users might face cash flow problems in the purchase of needed inputs because of inadequate access to capital markets, an example being the use of fertilizer or irrigation in agriculture.
- Governments, especially those in developing countries, might have limited instruments at their disposal to achieve redistributive and other social objectives, and must resort to subsidies as second-best policy instruments.

As defensible as these arguments might be if applied with care, there is always a danger that arguments for subsidization can be contrived on market failure grounds, but without quantitative estimates to support them. That is always a danger with second-best analysis in which market prices no longer reflect social values, and potentially anything goes. In any case, project evaluators might simply have to take as given a project as proposed by the policy-maker, and evaluate it as such.

The monetary value of subsidies is obtained from the standard use of CVs, or consumers and producers surpluses. Consider the example of, say, an input like fertilizer or irrigation provided at preferential rates to the agricultural sector. Figure 3.2 depicts the market for the input being

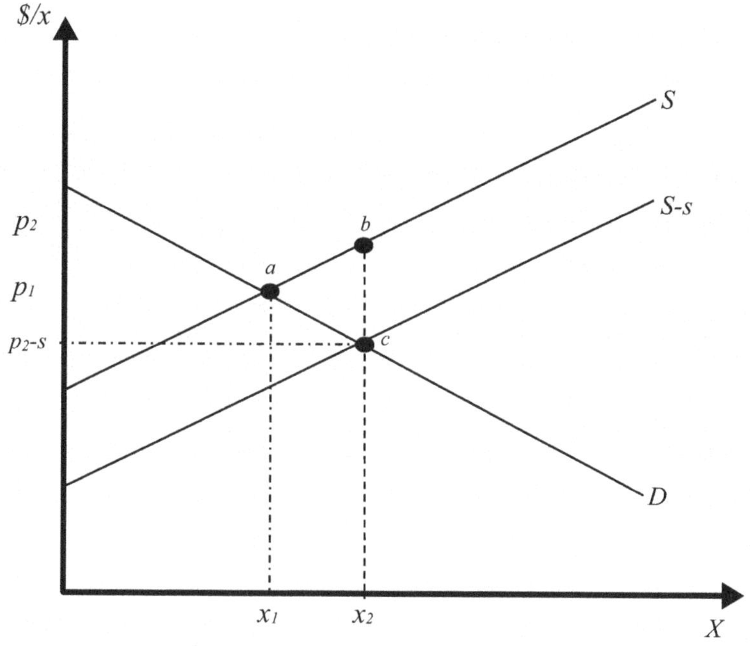

Fig. 3.2 Effect of an input subsidy. (Source: Author)

subsidized. In the absence of the subsidy, the price of the input is p_1, and the demand by the agricultural sector is X_1. When the price is subsidized at the per unit rate *s*, demand rises to X_2 and the price to suppliers rises to p_2. The total benefit to the agricultural sector, or its aggregate willingness-to-pay, is the area beneath the demand curve, X_1acX_2. In the project evaluation, this would enter as a benefit to be set against the costs of the subsidy.

The standard case against subsidization can be readily seen from Fig. 3.2. If the input comes from a competitive industry, the supply curve represents the schedule of marginal production costs. Then the cost of supplying the increment in demand is given by the area beneath the supply curve, X_1abX_2. This exceeds the benefit by the area *abc*, the standard excess burden of the subsidy. Thus, the project would be judged not to be socially beneficial unless there were other compensating benefits arising from shadow pricing, distributive weights, etc. For example, if the agricultural product were tradable, but the input being subsidized were non-tradable, it is possible that the premium put on X by using a shadow price of foreign exchange would be enough to make the project profitable in social terms.

An equivalent way to see the same point is to focus on changes in net benefits to the parties involved—consumers, producers, and the government. The consumers surplus from the fall in price is the area $p_1ac(p_2 - s)$. The producers surplus from the rise in price that suppliers receive is p_1abp_2. The cost to the government is the amount of the subsidy $p_2bc(p_2 - s)$. Aggregating all these changes leaves a net loss to society of abc as before. The usefulness of this approach is that it identifies benefits and costs by parties involved, and so enables the evaluator to attach distributive weights if desired.

It should be emphasized that pure transfers of purchasing power from one household or firm to another per se should be typically attributed no value. But, they may affect the NPV of a project indirectly. For one thing, as with the subsidy, they may affect the allocation of resources in a distorted market, as in the above example, and as in the more general cases to be considered below. Thus, it is not the amount of the subsidy that is relevant and counts as a social cost, but how it affects resource allocation. Second, if distributive weighting is used, the social value of the transfer may be more to one or other of the donors and recipients.

Indirect Benefits and Costs

In measuring the shadow price of an input purchased on a distorted market, we concentrated on the implications of that distortion alone. But, if there are distortions in other markets elsewhere in the economy, induced changes in outputs on those markets also give rise to net benefit changes which must be accounted for in project evaluation. These are referred to as indirect benefits and costs. The general principle, due to Harberger (1971a), is an application of the theory of second best and is as follows. Consider an economy in which there are d sectors ($j = 1,\ldots,d$) which have a distortion between demand price, q_j, and supply price, or marginal cost, p_j. Let t_j be the distortion per unit of output ($t_j = q_j - p_j$) and let it be fixed for simplicity. Then, if a project causes changes in the output on any of these distorted markets on which it is not directly involved because of general equilibrium interactions, net benefits of the following sort must be included in the evaluation of the project:[10] $\Sigma_j\ t_j\Delta X_j$, where ΔX_j is the change in output on market j.

A simple example will illustrate. Consider an urban transit project that partly diverts traffic from congested expressways. Because of the congestion, the marginal social cost of a trip on the road exceeds the cost to the traveler: each traveler increases the cost spent traveling to other road users. As a consequence, there is too much traffic. By diverting traffic, the urban transit system relieves congestion and generates an indirect benefit. Figure 3.3 illustrates the indirect benefit. In the absence of the urban transit project, the demand curve for road trips is D_X in the right panel. Given a cost per trip to travelers of p_X, which includes the time cost, fuel, vehicle operating costs, and so on, the demand for road trips is X_1. But, because of congestion, the marginal social cost per trip is MSC_X. For simplicity, we assume that these costs per trip are constant. Next, an urban transit project is introduced. As in the left panel, the demand curve for urban transit trips is D_Y. At a price of p_Y, Y_2 trips will be taken. The price includes all costs incurred by the traveler. Since the two types of trips are substitutes, the urban transit system will divert some travelers from the roads, causing the demand curve D_X to shift to the left. The number of road trips falls to X_2. The benefits of the urban transit system now include both the direct benefits—those calculated from the surplus generated in the left panel—and the indirect benefits. The latter are given by the area *abcd* in the right panel, which is the distortion times the changes in trips.

The same principles apply whatever the source of the distortion. Moreover, the fact the distortion exists suggests that explicit attempts could be made to increase the amount of traffic diverted. For example, the price of urban transit trips, p_Y, could be reduced below marginal cost even though that causes a deadweight loss in the urban transit market. The

[10] Formally, let the representative consumers' utility be given by $U(X_1,\ldots,X_n)$. The change in utility from a change in demands is given by $dU = \Sigma(\partial U/\partial X_i)dX_i$. Consumers will set relative prices equal to their marginal rates of substitution so $q_i = (\partial U/\partial X_i)/(\partial U/\partial X_n)$, assuming good n is the numeraire. Then, we can write $dW = \Sigma q_i dX_i$, where dW is the change in utility measured in terms of the numeraire $(dW = dU/(\partial U/\partial X_n))$. Now, suppose public project demands are G_i and market supplies are Y_i; then $dW = \Sigma q_i(dY_i + dG_i)$. Since $\Sigma p_i(dY_i) = 0$ by the economy's production possibilities frontier, we have $dW = \Sigma t_i dX_i + \Sigma p_i dG_i$, where $t_i\ (= q_i - p_i)$ is the tax, or other, distortion. Finally, consider the change in a commodity used by or produced by a project, say, dG_k. The welfare change measure becomes $dW = \Sigma_{i\neq k} t_i dX_i + t_k dX_k + p_k dG_k$. The latter two terms can be shown to correspond with the value or cost of the public commodity dG_k evaluated at the weighted average shadow price as above. The first term is what we are calling the indirect effect, following Harberger (1971a). Further details on this are provided in Boadway and Bruce (1984). See also Drèze and Stern (1987).

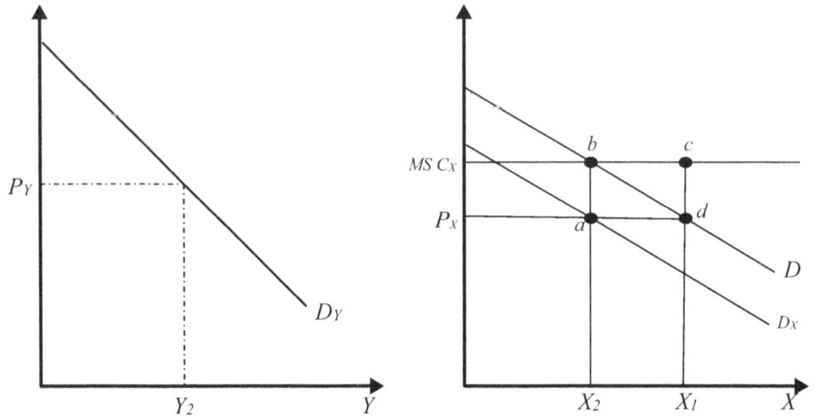

Fig. 3.3 Indirect effect on a distorted market. (Source: Author)

optimal second-best urban transit pricing policy would be that for which the incremental deadweight loss in urban transit just offsets the incremental indirect benefit created by a price reduction.

The Social Discount Rate

Once benefits and costs in each period are evaluated, they must be discounted to a common value. What discount rate should be used? The principle is clear enough: just like the principle of welfarism dictates that current values should be those reflecting individual households' willingness-to-pay, so it dictates that the discount rate should reflect the rate at which households value future relative to present benefits and costs. If capital markets were perfect, so that all households were able to borrow and lend at the going interest rate, they would organize their personal affairs so that the after-tax market interest rate they face is their intertemporal rate of substitution. Thus, the after-tax market interest rate would be the discount rate for project evaluation, the so-called *social discount rate*. (Of course, either a real or a nominal version could be used depending upon whether benefits and costs were measured in current or constant rupee values, as discussed above.)

In practice, there are a number of complications which must be considered in selecting the actual discount rate. Some of them are as follows.

Heterogeneous Household Interest Rates

Households may face differing discount rates. For example, if capital income is taxed at the personal level, different households will be in different tax brackets, or may have access to different types of assets on their marginal borrowing or lending. As well, some households will be creditors and others debtors. If the borrowing rate differs from the lending rate, the social discount rate will be ambiguous. And, different households may face different interest rates because of differences in risk. For example, they may have differing wealth holdings, and therefore different abilities to provide collateral. The social discount rate will have therefore to be a compromise, given that the stream of project benefits and costs cannot typically be disaggregated by type of household.

Capital Market Imperfections

Various kinds of imperfections may exist in capital markets. Households may not be able to borrow freely because of liquidity constraints. If they are quantity-constrained, the true discount rate faced by households will not be reflected in any market interest rate: it will typically be higher. Capital markets themselves may not be perfectly competitive, but may contain features of monopoly or of information asymmetries. Again, this makes it difficult to know the true rate at which households who are affected by projects discount future net benefits.

Externalities in Capital Markets

There may be external benefits associated with household saving. To the extent that households save for bequests, that saving may benefit others in the society who attach a value to the well-being of future generations. If so, there will be a free-rider problem associated with household savings, resulting in too little savings. Compounding this, there may also be externalities associated with the investment that is financed by household saving. The 'new growth theory' has emphasized that new knowledge comes with investment, knowledge whose benefits cannot be entirely appropriated by those doing the investing. In these circumstances, there will also be too little investment and hence too little saving.

Even if one acknowledges that these sources of externality exist and that as a consequence there is too little saving set aside for investment or for future generations, it is not obvious what implications, if any, this should have for the social discount rate. It has often been argued that the social rate of discount should be lower than the market interest rate on this account, and that would certainly be true from the point of view of supporting measures which increase saving above its market-determined level. But, the application of that argument to project evaluation is more tenuous. If the project involves benefits accruing to future generations, it might be argued that they should be discounted at a favorable rate on externality grounds. But standard projects which are not primarily intended to provide benefits to future generations have no particular claim to a low discount rate on these grounds. The rate at which existing households discount present versus future benefits accruing to themselves is the after-tax market interest rate they face, and that should be the discount rate for project benefits.

The project may well induce changes in the level of savings or investment in the economy. If so, it will create an indirect benefit or cost as a result of capital markets being socially inefficient. It would be appropriate to treat that as a benefit of the project in its own right, but not necessarily as one which calls for a lower social discount rate.

Other Arguments: Risk and Distributive Weights

Two further arguments might arise in discounting present versus future benefits of a project. The future will undoubtedly be uncertain, so that one does not know for sure precisely what benefits and what costs are likely to accrue as a result of the project. There are techniques for dealing with project risk, which may or may not involve the discount rate. We deal with those separately below.

By the same token, the treatment of present versus future benefits may be colored by the fact that those who obtain future net benefits are deemed to be more or less deserving than those who obtain current net benefits. If so, there may be a call for attaching distributive weights to future versus present beneficiaries. Again, we postpone discussion of this until the issue of distributive weights is addressed below.

The Numeraire

We have argued that the after-tax interest rate might be an appropriate project discount rate since it reflects the rate at which households in the economy discount present versus future consumption. In so doing, we have implicitly been assuming that the numeraire for project benefits and costs is current household consumption. As we have mentioned, different numeraires could be used, and the choice of numeraire should have no effect on the outcome of an evaluation. But, the choice of numeraire could affect the discount rate. For example, in the Little-Mirrlees approach, the numeraire is foreign exchange in the hand of the government. The discount rate then reflects the relative value of future versus present foreign exchange in the hands of the government. The determination of this can be quite complicated if it is assumed, as do Little and Mirrlees (1974), that governments can use these funds for investment and there are significant capital and foreign exchange market distortions. For a good discussion, see Ray (1984), and also Squire and van der Tak (1975).

Oppurtunity Cost of Finanacing

We have mentioned that pure transfers of funds among households, firms, and governments should themselves have no effect on project benefits and costs. But if such transfers occur through distortionary means, or if they induce changes in outputs on distorted markets, they will have efficiency consequences. One important example of these induced welfare effects concerns the use of public funds to finance projects. Two issues are involved here. First, the transferring of funds from the private to the public sector through taxes is costly if distortionary taxes must be used to facilitate the transfer. That being so, account must be taken of the additional costs incurred in the financing of projects out of public funds. Second, projects which involve significant capital costs may be (justifiably) financed by borrowing from capital markets. Given that capital markets are distorted, this sets in train welfare costs which must be included as a cost of undertaking the project. We discuss these two in turn. It should be borne in mind that the costs being identified here are over and above the benefits and costs associated with project outputs and inputs already discussed.

The Marginal Cost of Public Funds

Many projects in the public sector do not cover their costs; they require public funds. The problem is that obtaining a rupee's worth of funds through taxation costs more than a rupee. That is because there is a deadweight loss or excess burden associated with raising revenues through distortionary taxation.[11] In evaluating projects, what will be important is the deadweight loss at the margin. Given that the deadweight loss is typically convex in the tax rate—it is approximately proportional to the square of the tax rate—the marginal deadweight loss can be significantly higher than the average deadweight loss per rupee of the tax system as a whole. The marginal cost of public funds (MCPF) is simply defined as one plus the marginal deadweight loss of raising additional tax revenues. If the MCPF is high, the hurdle rate of return that a project which relies on public funding would have to achieve can be substantially higher than for private projects.

To understand the MCPF, consider Fig. 3.4, which depicts the market for, say composite consumption, denoted *X*. In the absence of the project

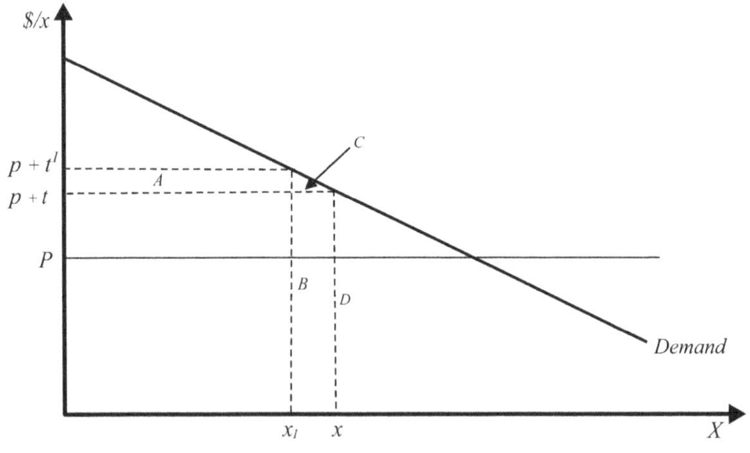

Fig. 3.4 Market for composite consumption good. (Source: Author)

[11] Even if the funds are not obtained from current taxes, there will be a deadweight loss involved. Funds raised through borrowing will induce a deadweight loss. Since borrowing is simply postponed taxes, the deadweight loss will be incurred later on when the loan is eventually repaid. As well, borrowing through printing money will create a deadweight loss as a result of inflation. Of course, if there are unemployed resources, this deadweight loss may be mitigated.

being evaluated, there is a per unit tax of t on consumption. It could be interpreted as a general sales tax, or as a general payroll tax. For simplicity, we assume that the supply price of composite consumption is fixed at p, so consumers face a price of $p + t$. If the project were introduced, the tax rate would have to rise to t' to finance it. We can identify the various costs and benefits of the additional financing required. The change in tax revenue, ΔR, is simply area A minus area B. The deadweight loss from the tax before the tax increase is area D. The change in deadweight loss from the tax increase is then given by $C + B$. The MCPF of transferring an increment of resources from the private to the public sector by increasing the tax rate is given by one plus the incremental deadweight loss per rupee of revenue, or:

$$\begin{aligned} \text{MCPF} &= 1 + \frac{\Delta D}{\Delta R} \\ &= 1 + \frac{(B+C)}{(A-B)} \end{aligned}$$

For small changes, we can neglect the small triangular area C. Then the MCPF may be written as:

$$\begin{aligned} \text{MCPF} &= 1 + \frac{B}{(A-B)} \\ &= 1 - \frac{t\Delta X}{(X\Delta t + t\Delta X)} \\ &= \left[1 + t\Delta X / X\Delta t\right]^{-1} \\ &= \left[1 - \tau\eta\right]^{-1} \end{aligned}$$

where τ is the tax rate expressed in *ad valorem* terms— $t/(t + p)$—and η is the uncompensated price elasticity of demand for consumption.

The MCPF will typically exceed unity. In fact it can be considerably above unity. For example, suppose that the elasticity of demand η is 2, and the tax rate τ is 0.25. Then, the MCPF is 2! The methodology can be extended to take account of more than one tax base, and even to take equity considerations into account (Ahmad and Stern 1991).

The MCPF is relevant for attaching a shadow price to funds used to finance public projects. For each rupee of financing, a charge of (MCPF – 1) should be attributed as a project cost: it is the excess burden induced by the requirement to use distortionary taxes. If lump-sum revenue sources were available, project financing would represent a pure transfer, and would therefore have no efficiency implications.

The Opportunity Cost of Borrowed Funds

Additional problems arise in a dynamic setting when capital markets are distorted. Consider the case of a project whose initial capital costs are financed by borrowing.[12] Let ΔB be the amount borrowed and invested. Suppose the capital market distortions arise from a tax on capital income. Then the gross (pre-tax) rate of return on investment, ρ, exceeds the net (after-tax) return on savings, r. Figure 3.5 illustrates the effect of borrowing. The project borrowing of ΔB will represent a demand for funds on the capital market, and can in general come partly at the expense of reduced investment, ΔI, and partly from induced savings, ΔS. As in our discussion of the weighted-average shadow pricing problem above, the

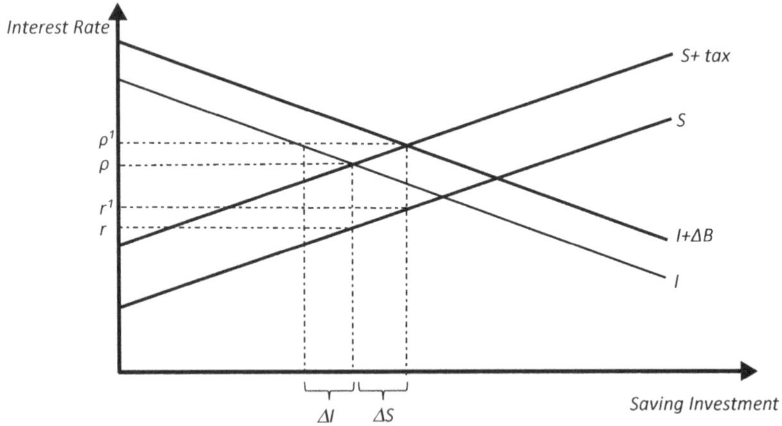

Fig. 3.5 Effect of borrowing. (Source: Author)

[12] This example draws on Feldstein (1972a), which in turn draws on a seminal paper by Marglin (1963).

opportunity cost of the additional financing depends on the opportunity costs of the forgone investment and induced saving.

The opportunity cost of an additional rupee of saving, measured in terms of current consumption which we take to be our numeraire, is simply one rupee. This is the amount of current consumption forgone. To obtain the opportunity cost of a rupee's worth of forgone investment, we need to identify the stream of consumption it would have yielded. The simplest case to consider is that in which the returns to the forgone investment would have been entirely consumed. One rupee's worth of investment with a rate of return ρ will then yield a stream of consumption benefits of ρ in perpetuity. The present value of this perpetual stream is then ρ/r, which is then the opportunity cost of one rupee's worth of forgone investment. Note that because of the capital market distortion—$\rho/r > 1$—the opportunity cost of a rupee's worth of forgone investment exceeds one dollar.

Taking these two opportunity costs together—unity for savings and ρ/r for investment—we can construct the social opportunity cost per rupee of borrowing (SOC):

$$\text{SOC} = \frac{\Delta S}{\Delta B} + \frac{\rho}{r}\frac{\Delta I}{\Delta B}$$

The SOC is used in a manner similar to that of the MCPF just discussed. In this simple case, the amount that would have to be added as a cost to the project at the time of borrowing would be simply (SOC − 1) ΔB. If the debt was paid down later rather than being held in perpetuity, there would be a net welfare gain determined by the difference between SOC and unity.

This simple case illustrates the principles involved in determining the excess burden associated with providing debt financing to a project. (Naturally, if tax finance induces changes in investment and/or savings, a similar calculation could be carried out for that.) More complicated situations can readily be imagined. One simple extension is to suppose that a fraction σ of the returns to investment is re-invested, the remainder being consumed. Then a rupee of investment will accumulate at the rate $\sigma\rho$ per period, so by time t, the amount accumulated will be $e^{\sigma\rho t}$, leading to an amount of consumption at time t of $(1 - \sigma)\rho e^{\sigma\rho t}$. Discounting this stream of consumption to the present yields a present value of forgone consumption of $(1-\sigma)\rho/(r-\sigma\rho)$. Now, the SOC becomes

$$\mathrm{SOC} = \frac{\Delta S}{\Delta B} + \frac{(1-\sigma)\rho}{(r-\sigma\rho)}\frac{\Delta I}{\Delta B}$$

Other assumptions could be made about the stream of consumption that would be obtained in the future from one rupee's worth of current consumption.

The SOC obviously depends upon the extent to which the borrowed funds crowd out private investment as opposed to inducing increased investment. That depends on the responsiveness of savings and investment to the interest rate, on which evidence is rather mixed. But, generally, the more elastic is the supply of savings relative to the demand for investment, the greater will be the proportion of the debt coming from induced savings, and vice versa.

There is a special consideration that merits some attention, and that is that savings might be invested in foreign assets rather than in domestic investment in an open economy setting (which is typically the relevant one). Thus, project borrowing might come from three potential sources now—domestic savings, domestic investment, net foreign capital flows. The relevant SOC then depends upon the type of tax distortions in place. If a tax applies to domestic investment, the opportunity cost of a rupee of forgone investment will exceed one rupee for the reasons discussed above. If there is a tax on capital income earned by savers, that will be a distortion between the rate of return on savings and both the return on domestic investment and that on foreign assets. If project financing displaces the accumulation of foreign assets, the opportunity cost will again exceed unity using analogous arguments to the above. But, if no tax on capital income is applicable at the personal level, which may be approximately so in developing countries, there will be no distortion on the accumulation of foreign assets: the opportunity cost of displacing a rupee's worth of foreign assets will simply be one rupee, the same as for increased savings. Therefore, in a small open economy setting, where all marginal finance involves changes in foreign asset holdings, the SOC of one rupee's worth of project financing will just be one rupee. There will be no need to make an adjustment for the cost of financing.

The procedure described above is based on the net present value criterion, which seeks to identify all sources of benefits and costs measured in terms of a common numeraire and then discounts it at the social discount rate. If domestic consumption is the numeraire, an appropriate discount rate would be the after-tax rate of return on savings, at least assuming that capital markets worked reasonably well. Capital market distortions would be taken account of as a form of cost entering into the numerator of the project's present value calculation. An alternative procedure for taking account of the cost of financing when capital markets are distorted has been championed by Harberger (1969). He advocates using a weighted-average discount rate for discounting project benefits and costs: the pre-tax and after-tax rates of return to capital are weighted by the shares of project financing coming from forgone investment and increased savings, respectively. Though this method has simplicity as its virtue, its results will typically not correspond with the procedure outlined above, so it will not accurately reflect the true NPV of the project. More details of the circumstances under which the two methods differ may be found in Feldstein (1972a) and Boadway and Bruce (1984).

Risk and Uncertainty

One of the most vexing problems in project evaluation concerns the treatment of uncertainty. The problem is that the stream of future benefits and costs is not known with certainty. At best, the evaluator may know the probability distribution of benefits and costs. Perhaps more to the point, the households who are affected by the project will not know with certainty the stream of costs and benefits. Given our assumption of welfarism, it is from their perspective that the benefits and costs must be evaluated. Project evaluation practice typically proceeds on the assumption that the distribution of future benefits and costs is, in fact, known to the affected households. This is undoubtedly an heroic assumption, but one whose consequences we first consider, since it is the standard approach.

Consider the simple case of a household whose real income next period is y_i with probability p_i, where $\Sigma p_i = 1$. The various outcomes represent different exhaustive and mutually exclusive 'states of the world' that are possible. Under certain reasonable assumptions, the household can be supposed to rank alternative combinations of y_i according to expected utility, defined as $Eu(y) = \Sigma p_i\, u(y_i)$. The fact that the values of y_i differ implies that the household faces some risk. Assuming the household to be risk-averse ($u'' < 0$), the household would be willing to pay something to avoid this risk. This willingness-to-pay, referred to as the cost of risk and denoted k, is defined implicitly as follows:

$$u(\hat{y}-k)=\sum_i p_i u(y_i)$$

where $\hat{y}=\sum_i p_i y_i$ is the expected real income. The value of k, for a given distribution of y_i values, evidently depends on how risk-averse the household is. To see this, note that to a first-order approximation, the cost of risk can be shown to simplify to[13]:

$$k \cong -\frac{1}{2}\left(\frac{u''(\hat{y})}{u'(\hat{y})}\right)\text{var}(y_i)$$

This indicates that the cost of risk depends both on the dispersion of incomes, as indicated by the variance, and the degree of risk aversion, measured here as the co-called coefficient of absolute risk aversion, $-u''(\hat{y})/u'(\hat{y})$.

As with other project benefits and costs, there may also be indirect costs of risk associated with a project. For example, recall the social opportunity cost of project financing, which included the opportunity cost associated with crowded-out investment. Suppose that the investment crowded out had a risky return, so that its pre-tax rate of return ρ included a risk premium of, say, β. If the investment is forgone, this risk is no longer borne. Thus, the above SOC formula would have to be amended to reflect that. For example, in the simple case in which all project proceeds are consumed, the SOC would now be given by:

[13]To see this, we can use a Taylor series approximation to obtain $u(y_i) = u(\hat{y}) + u'(\hat{y})(y_i - \hat{y}) + \frac{1}{2}u''(\hat{y})(y_i - \hat{y})^2 + R$, where R is the sum of the higher-order terms. Similarly, given that k is relatively small, a first-order approximation of $u(\hat{y} - k)$ can be obtained as $u(\hat{y} - k) \cong u(\hat{y}) - ku(\hat{y} - k)$. Combining these in the above definition of k yields:

$$u(\hat{y})-ku(\hat{y}-k)\doteq\Sigma p_i\left[u(\hat{y})+u'(\hat{y})(y_i-\hat{y})+\frac{1}{2}u''(\hat{y})(y_i-\hat{y})^2\right]$$

which can be rearranged to obtain the expression for k in the text.

$$\text{SOC} = \frac{\Delta S}{\Delta B} + \frac{(\rho - \beta)}{r} \frac{\Delta I}{\Delta B}$$

The cost of risk identifies the willingness-to-pay of a household faced with a known distribution of outcomes. It is what, in principle, would have to be included as a cost in a project evaluation which otherwise uses discounted expected benefits and costs to calculate the NPV.[14] The difficulty, even assuming that the distribution of future costs and benefits is known, is that the cost of risk is not readily observable since it does not correspond with any market price. One is left with making arbitrary adjustments to account for the riskiness of benefits and costs.

There may be a way out in certain circumstances. Even though a project's benefits and costs may be risky, those risks may be diluted by risk pooling or risk spreading. Risk pooling occurs if the project's benefits and costs are diversified in the 'portfolios' of households. If the project returns in question are independently distributed compared with other sources of income accruing to the household, the variance of the entire portfolio will be less than the sum of the variances of individual elements. The more independent income streams there are, the smaller will be the portfolio variance, with the latter approaching zero as the number of assets increases. The extent to which this may be applicable in the case of a project's returns depends on the case in question. But to the extent that the riskiness facing the household is made negligible by risk pooling, the cost of risk on a given project can be ignored.

Alternatively, public projects may be subject not to risk pooling by the representative household, but risk spreading within the public sector itself. Instead of pooling risks among a number of independent projects, a project's risk might be diminished by sharing the risk among a large number of households, something which may well occur for the typical public project. Returning to our analysis of the cost of risk-taking above, consider an asset with a random return of y, which is shared equally among n households. The variance of the return faced by each household, var. (y/n), can

[14] As in the case of capital market distortions, some persons advocate taking account of risk by incorporating it into the discount rate. There may be special cases in which the use of a risk-adjusted discount rate to discount expected benefits and costs is equivalent to treating the cost of risk as a cost and discounting at a risk-free discount rate that represents how consumers actually discount future versus present consumption. But, in general, the two procedures will not be equivalent.

be shown simply to be equal to var. $(y)/n^2$. Therefore, the cost of risk k can then be written as:

$$k \cong -\frac{1}{2}\left(\frac{u''(\hat{y})}{u'(\hat{y})}\right)\frac{\mathrm{var}(y)}{n^2}$$

As n increases, the risk per person obviously decreases rapidly. Moreover, the total risk from the project, nk, also diminishes, approaching zero as n rises. This result, due to Arrow and Lind (1970), suggests that when the risk is spread among a large number of taxpayers, the cost of risk can be ignored. Again, whether the conditions are right for this to be the case depends upon the circumstances. The project must be small relative to total national output, and independent of it. And, as the number of persons increases, the return per person must fall, a condition that would not be satisfied for public goods, for example.

As the discussion in this section indicates, costing risk in project evaluation is a difficult proposition. The risks are not readily observable and their costs cannot be inferred from market information. Moreover, the analysis is premised on the notion that households have a good idea of the probability distribution of outcomes, something which may well not apply in practice. Given this, the analyst is often left with taking account of risk in an ad hoc manner. One common practice is to report optimistic (upper-bound) estimates, pessimistic (lower-bound) estimates, and best-guess estimates, and let the policy-maker weigh the alternatives according to some notion of how likely each scenario might be.

Distributive Weights

The principles of project evaluation have been presented with reference to measuring benefits and costs according to some numeraire (e.g., rupees worth of consumption), where values are imputed according to those that apply to the actual households in the economy. Little explicit account has been taken of the fact that a unit of numeraire might be 'worth more' to one household than to the next. If so, summing up rupees values of consumption would be akin to summing up numbers of apples and oranges. We have discussed the rationale for this procedure of treating a rupee as rupee no matter whose hands it is in. But the procedure remains controversial, if only because this procedure itself implicitly assigns welfare weights to households. There are suggested ways of getting around that, such as by invoking hypothetical compensation arguments, but they are not entirely compelling to all persons (see, especially, the summary statement by Blackorby and Donaldson 1990).

Concern with the normative implications of simply aggregating rupee values of benefits and costs has led some observers to advocate incorporating distributive weights into the calculus to take account of the fact that one rupee is worth more to one household than another (e.g., Drèze and Stern 1987; Ahmad and Stern 1991). At the outset a vexing question arises: what distributive weights should be used? There is obviously no single correct answer to this question, since a value judgment is involved. Thus, the practice has been to report results for a range of judgments, and let the policy-maker decide. For example, a common procedure is to adopt a very simple form of social weighting procedure by parametrizing the social welfare function into one involving a single parameter—the coefficient of aversion to inequality. We saw earlier that a social welfare function of the form

$$W(Y) = \Sigma \frac{(Y_i)^{1-\rho}}{(1-\rho)}$$

has only a single parameter ρ. Varying ρ from zero to infinity spans the range of coefficients of aversion of inequality for all inequality-averse social welfare functions. In principle, benefits and costs accruing to various households could be weighted by their marginal social utility β_i, which is given by

$$\beta_i = \frac{\partial W}{\partial Y_i} = Y_i^{-\rho}$$

(with $\rho = 0$ corresponding to the case where no welfare weights are used). The problem with this procedure is that it is very difficult to attribute benefits and costs to households according to their real income levels. For some categories, it might be possible. Thus, wage payments for workers might be so weighted, as has been the practice in various applications of the Little-Mirrlees methodology. But generally that will not be possible.

An alternative, less demanding procedure is to attribute welfare weights to commodities according to what might be known about the mix of persons that consume them. To see how this works, consider the change in social welfare from a given project:

$$dW = \sum \beta_i \cdot dY_i$$

where dY_i is the change in real income accruing to household i as a result of the project. Suppose the project involves changes in prices facing households. Then, using the principles of consumer theory, the change in real income for household i can be written $dY_i = -\sum_j x_j^{\,i} dp_j$. Substituting this into the expression for dW, one obtains:

$$dW = \sum_j R_j X_j dP_j$$

where X_j is the aggregate consumption of good j, and $R_j = \sum_i \beta_i x_j^{\,i}/X_j$ is referred to by Feldstein (1972b) as the distribution characteristic of good j. As can be seen, it is a weighted average of the β_i terms, where the weights are the proportions of good i consumed by household j. Costs and benefits can be weighted by their distributive characteristics, and the distributive characteristics can themselves be constructed using various assumptions about the marginal social incomes, β_i, or equivalently the coefficient of aversion to inequality, ρ. Obviously this is much less demanding than disaggregating each benefit and cost to individual households, though still not a trivial exercise.

An example of the use of distributive characteristics of this sort was presented by Harberger (1978). It is simply an illustrative case involving the measurement of the welfare cost of an excise tax. Figure 3.6 depicts the market for commodity X, with demand curve labeled D and supply curve labeled S. An excise tax drives a wedge between supply and demand prices and results in an equilibrium price and output of q_1 and X_1, compared with q_0 and X_0 in the absence of the tax. Producer prices in the two equilibria are p_0 and p_1. Consumers lose q_1abq_0 from the tax, while producers lose q_0bcp_1. The government obtains tax revenues of q_1acp_1. If distributive weights are attached to these gains and losses according to how various income groups share them, the change in welfare will be:

$$\Delta W = -R_D\left(q_1abq_0\right) - R_S\left(q_0bcp_1\right) + R_G\left(q_1acp_1\right)$$

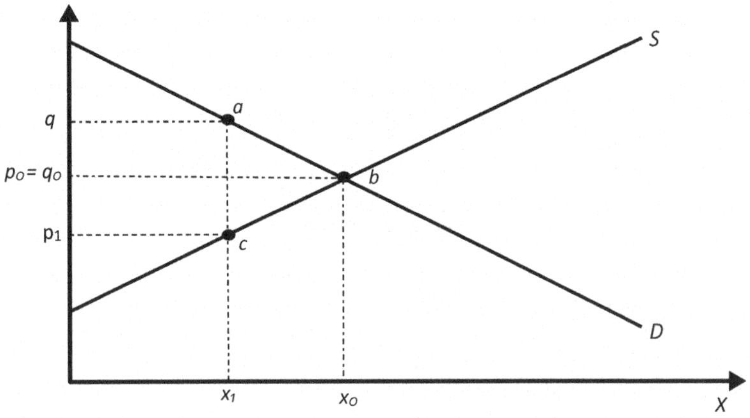

Fig. 3.6 Market for a commodity. (Source: Author)

where R_D, R_S, and R_G are the distributive characteristics associated with consumers surplus, producers surplus, and government revenue, respectively. Of course, if there were no aversion to inequality, these distributive characteristics would all equal unity, so the welfare change would be simply the standard loss in surplus, $-abc$.

Concluding Remarks

In this chapter, we summarized the main issues in the evaluation of projects. It is obvious from our discussion that project evaluation is very much an art, though one with scientific underpinnings. Our purpose has been to indicate what those scientific underpinnings are, so that readers can have an economic perspective on what is involved. The technical literature on project evaluation is a well-established one, but one which must evolve with times. Recent advances in economic theory have probably not yet been incorporated into project evaluation principles to the extent that they could be. For example, the importance of asymmetric information and its implications for market behavior and market failure have been very much in the forefront of economic analysis. Yet, little has been done to incorporate imperfect information into project evaluation rules. This is particularly true insofar as the existence of imperfect information has implications for unemployment. Similarly, there has been considerable research activity into studying the determinants of growth, and whether or not unfettered markets are conducive to high growth rates. Little of this has found its way into applied welfare economics. Finally, the importance of illegal or underground activity has been increasingly recognized. This too might have implications for project evaluation. As with everything else in economics, project evaluation will presumably evolve.

References

Ahmad, Ehtisham, and Nicolas Stern. 1991. *The Theory and Practice of Tax Reform in Developing Countries*. Cambridge: Cambridge University Press.

Arrow, Kenneth J., and R.C. Lind. 1970. Uncertainty and the Evaluation of Public Investment Decisions. *American Economic Review* 60: 364–378.

Blackorby, Charles, and David Donaldson. 1990. A Review Article: The Case Against the Use of the Sum of Compensating Variations in Cost-Benefit Analysis. *Canadian Journal of Economics* 23: 471–494.

Boadway, Robin W., and Neil Bruce. 1984. *Welfare Economics*. Oxford: Basil Blackwell.

Dasgupta, Partha, Stephen Marglin, and Amartya Sen. 1972. *Guidelines for Project Evaluation*. New York: UNIDO.

Drèze, Jean, and Nicholas Stern. 1987. Theory of Cost-Benefit Analysis. In *Handbook of Public Economics*, ed. Alan J. Auerbach and Martin S. Feldstein, vol. 2, 909–989. Amsterdam: North-Holland.

Feldstein, Martin S. 1972a. The Inadequacy of Weighted Discount Rates. In *Cost-Benefit Analysis*, ed. Richard Layard, 311–332. Harmondsworth: Penguin.

———. 1972b. Distributional Equity and the Optimal Structure of Public Sector Prices. *American Economic Review* 62: 32–36.

Harberger, Arnold C. 1969. Professor Arrow on the Social Discount Rate. In *Cost-Benefit Analysis of Manpower Policies: Proceedings of a North American Conference*, ed. G.C. Somers and W.D. Wood. Kingston: Queen's University Industrial Relations Centre.

———. 1971a. Three Basic Postulates for Applied Welfare Economics: An Interpretive Essay. *Journal of Economic Literature* IX: 785–797.

———. 1971b. On Measuring the Social Opportunity Cost of Labour. *International Labour Review* 103: 559–579.

———. 1978. On the Use of Distributive Weights in Social Cost-Benefit Analysis. *Journal of Political Economy* 86: S87–S120.

Harris, J.R., and M.P. Todaro. 1970. Migration, Unemployment and Development: A Two-Sector Analysis. *American Economic Review* 60: 136–142.

Little, Ian M.D., and James A. Mirrlees. 1974. *Project Appraisal and Planning for Developing Countries*. New York: Basic Books.

Marglin, Stephen A. 1963. The Opportunity Costs of Public Investment. *Quarterly Journal of Economics* 77: 274–289.

Ray, Anandarup. 1984. *Cost-Benefit Analysis: Issues and Methodologies.* Baltimore: Johns Hopkins Press for the World Bank.

Sen, Amartya K. 1970. *Collective Choice and Social Welfare.* San Francisco: Holden Day.

Squire, Lyn, and Herman G. van der Tak. 1975. *Economic Analysis of Projects.* Baltimore: Johns Hopkins Press for the World Bank.

CHAPTER 4

The Marginal Cost of Public Funds: Concept, Measurement, and Applications

Bev Dahlby

Introduction

Taxes impose a cost on the economy if they alter taxpayers' consumption, production, and asset allocation decisions, leading to a less efficient allocation of resources. Raising an additional dollar of tax revenue costs the private sector more than a dollar if the allocation of resources in the economy becomes more distorted. The marginal cost of public funds, MCF, is a measure of the cost imposed on the private sector in raising an additional dollar of tax revenue.

As Boadway notes in Chap. 3, the marginal cost of public funds should be used in evaluating the opportunity cost of financing public sector expenditures. It also provides a guide for tax reform by revealing which taxes impose the greatest welfare losses in generating additional revenues. The MCF can also be used to measure the gains from tax reforms that shift the burden from the high-cost tax bases to ones with lower costs.

In this chapter, we provide an introduction to the concept of the marginal cost of public funds (MCF), examples of how the MCFs can be

B. Dahlby (✉)
School of Public Policy, University of Calgary, Calgary, AB, Canada
e-mail: bgdahlby@ucalgary.ca

© The Author(s) 2020

A. Shah (ed.), *Policy, Program and Project Evaluation*,
https://doi.org/10.1007/978-3-030-48567-2_4

measured, and examples of how they can be applied to guide tax reform and public expenditure policies. In keeping with the theme of this volume, the emphasis is on using the MCF as a tool for public policy analysis. No attempt is made to provide a review of the literature, the theoretical foundations in welfare economics, or the full range of applications. Readers who want to probe more deeply into these topics are referred to Dahlby (2008).

The second section contains a brief introduction to the conceptual foundations of the MCF with numerical examples of how it can be calculated from parameters that measure the responsiveness of taxes and how non-tax distortions and concerns about the distributional effects of a tax increase can be incorporated in the MCF. The third section discusses three approaches to measuring the MCF—basic formulas using basic economic models and parameter values, simulations of the effects of tax changes using computable general equilibrium (CGE) models, and econometric estimates of the responsiveness of tax bases or tax revenues. The fourth section provides two examples of the use of the MCF in public policy analysis. The first is an assessment of the gains from a tax reform that shifts some of the tax burden from the corporate to the personal income tax base in Alberta. The second example illustrates how the MCF can be used to derive optimal matching rates for intergovernmental infrastructure grants in a federation with horizontal and vertical fiscal externalities and differences in fiscal capacities among the subnational governments. The final section contains some brief concluding remarks.

Conceptual Foundations

The intuition behind the MCF can be explained using the familiar demand and supply model. Figure 4.1 shows the market demand curve, D, and the market supply curve, S, for a commodity x. In the absence of taxation, x^0 units of the good would be produced and consumed, and the price of the good would be q^0. If a tax of t^1 dollars per unit of x is imposed on the producers of this commodity, the consumer price would increase to q^1, the price that producers receive would decline to $p^1 = q^1 - t^1$. The quantity of x produced would decline to x^1. The total tax revenue collected by the government would be $R^1 = t^1 \cdot x^1$ or area q^1agp^1. The increase in the price paid by consumers would cause a reduction in consumer surplus equal to the area q^1abq^0, and the decline in the producer price would cause a loss of producer surplus equal to area q^0bgp^1. The loss of consumer and

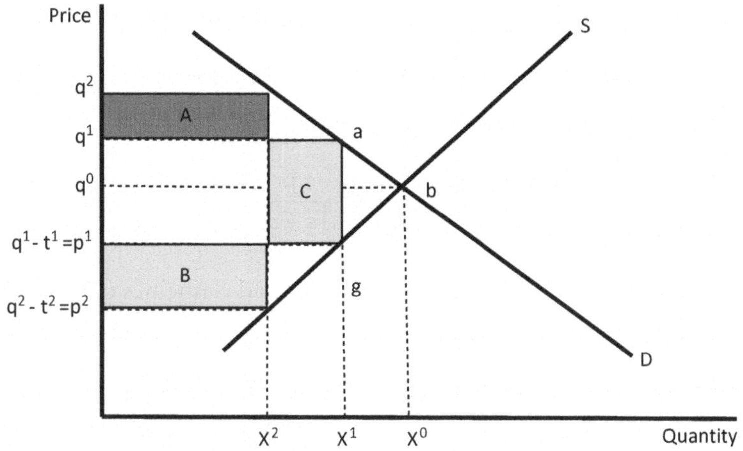

Fig. 4.1 The marginal cost of funds for an excise tax. (Source: Author)

producer surplus exceeds the revenue raised by the tax by the area of the triangle *abg*, which is a measure of the excess burden of the tax.

Now consider the cost of raising additional tax revenue by increasing the tax rate to t^2. The consumer price increases to q^2, the producer price declines to p^2, and output declines to x^2. The change in total tax revenue, $\Delta R = t^2x^2 - t^1x^1$, would be equal to shaded areas $A + B - C$. The reduction in the net output of the economy (the value of the lost output to consumers less the opportunity cost of the resources to producers) is given by the area between the demand and supply curves over the output range $x^1 - x^2$. This net output loss can be approximated by the area C.

The MCF is equal to one plus the reduction in the value of the net output of the economy per dollar of additional tax revenue, or:

$$\text{MCF} = 1 + \frac{C}{A+B-C} = \frac{A+B}{A+B-C} \tag{4.1}$$

Since $A + B$ is the loss of consumer and producer surplus for a very small tax rate increase, the MCF can also be interpreted as loss of consumer and producer surplus per dollar of additional tax revenue. This formula indicates that the MCF is greater than one if the output of x declines. As Fig. 4.1 indicates, area C will be larger (and therefore the MCF will tend to be larger) when the reduction in output is larger or when the size of the initial tax distortion is larger.

From the definition of the MCF in (4.1), the following formula for the MCF can be derived:

$$\text{MCF} = \frac{\eta - (1-\tau)\varepsilon}{\eta - (1-\tau)\varepsilon + \tau\varepsilon\eta} \tag{4.2}$$

where η and ε are the ordinary or uncompensated elasticities of supply and demand and τ is the ad valorem tax rate, $\frac{t}{q}$. When the supply curve has a positive slope, η is greater than zero, and when the demand curve is downward-sloping, ε is a negative number. Equation (4.2) indicates that the MCF will be larger when demand and supply of the taxed commodity are more elastic and when the existing tax rate is higher. For example, if the elasticity of supply is 4, the elasticity of demand is −2, and the ad valorem tax rate 0.333, then the MCF is 2. Therefore, in this situation, raising a $1 tax revenue costs the private sector $2. The MCF is the sum of the taxpayers' direct loss of $1 from the increase in taxes, and the indirect loss of $1 from the reduction in the value of output.

Equation (4.2) can also be used to show the relationship between the MCF and the responsiveness of tax revenues to changes in the tax rate. For a small change in the tax rate, Δt, the change in tax revenues, $A + B - C$, is equal to $\left(\frac{dR}{dt}\right)\Delta t$ where $\frac{dR}{dt}$ is the derivative of total tax revenues with respect to the tax rate. Area $A + B$ is equal to $x\Delta t$, the change in total tax revenue that would occur if the tax base x does not change when the tax rate is increased. Therefore, cancelling out the Δts in the numerator and denominator, an alternative expression for the MCF is:

$$\text{MCF} = \frac{x}{\frac{dR}{dt}} = \frac{\frac{R}{t}}{\frac{dR}{dt}} = \frac{1}{\rho} \tag{4.3}$$

where ρ is the elasticity of tax revenue with respect to the tax rate. This implies that the MCF will be higher the less responsive tax revenue is to an increase in the tax rate. For example, if the tax rate increases by 10 percent, but the tax revenue only increases by 5 percent because of the decline in output, then the elasticity of tax revenue with respect to the tax rate is 0.5 and the MCF is 2.

This illustrates the key relationship between the MCF and the responsiveness to tax revenues to the tax rate. This relationship is popularly known as the Laffer curve, named after Arthur Laffer, who drew a curve illustrating this relationship on a napkin for Ford Administration officials in 1974. Figure 4.2 shows the Laffer curve when the output of the taxed commodity declines when the tax rate is increased. $\frac{dR}{dt}$ is the slope of a tangent line to the Laffer curve, and $\frac{R}{t}$ is the slope of a line from the origin to a point on the Laffer curve. Therefore, the MCF at t^1 is the ratio of the slopes of $0a$ to bb'. If, as shown in Fig. 4.2, the Laffer curve is an inverted U shape, the slope of bb' will be less than the slope of the ray $0a$, and the MCF will be greater than one.

In Fig. 4.2, tax revenues are a maximum when the tax rate is t^*. If the government is maximizing tax revenues, the MCF is infinitely large because at that tax rate a small increase in the tax rate harms producers and consumers but does not generate any additional revenues for the government. If the government is operating on the negatively sloped section of

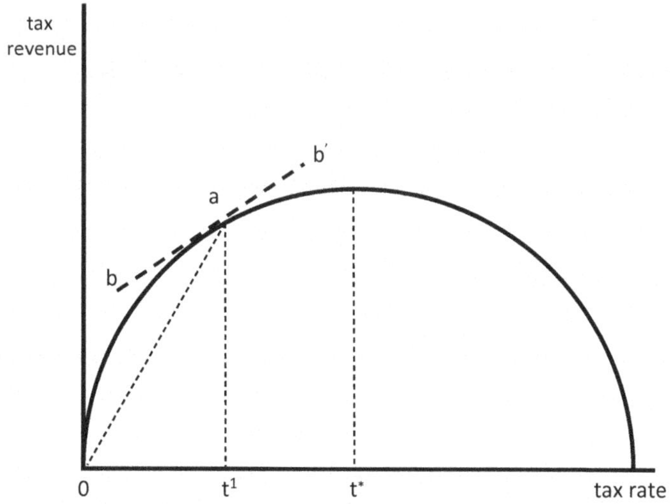

Fig. 4.2 The marginal cost of public funds and the Laffer curve. (Source: Author)

the Laffer curve, the MCF is not defined because the government can increase revenues by lowering the tax rate. In that situation, raising revenues does not involve a "cost" on the private sector, but provides a net benefit. Neither a Leviathan nor a benevolent government should operate on the downward-sloping section of the Laffer curve because a tax rate decrease would make taxpayers better off and the government would collect more tax revenues.

The formulas for calculating the MCF can be generalized to the common situations where governments obtain revenue from more than one tax base and these tax bases are interdependent. Suppose that a government imposes taxes on n different tax bases. The size of the *i*th tax base will, in general, be affected, τ_i, as well as the tax rates that are imposed on other tax bases because of substitution or complementarity relationships among the tax bases. The revenue obtained from tax base i is equal to $R_i = \tau_i B_i(\tau)$ where τ is a vector of tax rates $(\tau_1, \tau_2, \ldots, \tau_n)$ and B_i is size of the tax base i. Total tax revenue, R, is the sum of the tax revenues obtained from the n tax sources, or

$$R(\tau) = \sum_{i=1}^{n} R_i = \sum_{i=1}^{n} \tau_i B_i \tag{4.4}$$

Since the harm from a small tax increase is $B_i \Delta\tau_i$, while the change in total revenue is $\left(\frac{\partial R}{\partial \tau_i}\right)\Delta\tau_i$, a general expression for the $\text{MCF}_{\tau i}$ is:

$$\text{MCF}_{\tau_i} = \frac{B_i}{\frac{\partial R}{\partial \tau_i}} = \frac{\alpha_i}{\rho_i} \tag{4.5}$$

where $\alpha_i = \frac{R_i}{R}$ is the proportion of total tax revenue obtained from tax base i and $\rho_i = \left(\frac{\partial R}{\partial \tau_i}\right)\left(\frac{\tau_i}{R}\right)$ is the elasticity of total tax revenue with respect to tax rate i. Note that ρ_i is equal to $\sum_{j=1}^{n} \alpha_j \rho_{ji}$, where ρ_{ji} is the elasticity of revenue from tax base j with respect to τ_i. Therefore, if ρ_{ji} is positive and an increase in the tax rate on tax base i increases tax revenue from tax base

j, perhaps because they are substitutes for consumers, then the MCF will be lower than in the single taxed good case. On the other hand, if an increase in the tax rate on tax base i reduces revenue from tax base j because they are complementary goods, then the MCF will be higher than in the case where only tax base i is taxed.

To this point, it has been assumed that only taxes drive a wedge between the consumer price (which indicates the social marginal benefit of a commodity) and the producer price (which measures the social marginal cost of producing the commodity). Thus, in the absence of non-lump-sum taxes, the private market would produce an efficient allocation of resources. However, private market may fail to allocate resources efficiently if some firms can exercise monopoly power in setting the prices of their products or if there are externalities, such as pollution, in consumption or production activities. Box 4.1 and 4.2 provide numerical examples of how monopoly power and harmful externalities can be incorporated in the MCF.

Box 4.1 A Numerical Example Comparing the MCF in a Competitive Market and Under Monopoly

Suppose the market demand function is $x = a - bq$, the marginal cost of producing the product is a constant c, and t is the per unit tax imposed. In a competitive market, the equilibrium price would be $q = c + t$. For simplicity, assume that no other taxes are levied in other markets. The formula for the marginal cost of public funds would be a special case of (4.2) where the elasticity of supply, η, is infinite:

$$\text{MCF} = \frac{1}{1+\tau \cdot \varepsilon} \tag{4.6}$$

For concreteness, suppose $c = 1$, $a = 20$, $b = 8$, and $t = 0.25$. The market price is $q = 1.25$ and the ad valorem tax rate is $\tau = \frac{0.25}{1.25} = 0.20$. Output would be $x = 10$. It can be shown that at this point on the demand function, the elasticity of demand is $\varepsilon = -1$. Plugging the values for τ and ε into the above equation, the MCF is 1.25. In other words, raising an addition dollar of tax revenue would impose a burden of $1.25 on the private sector.

(*continued*)

Box 4.1 (continued)

Now consider the marginal cost of raising tax revenue if a monopolist can set the price of the product. With a linear demand function and a constant marginal cost of production, the monopolist will maximize after-tax profits by setting the price half way between the maximum price that consumers are willing to pay for the product, which is $\frac{a}{b} = \frac{20}{8} = 2.5$, and the marginal cost plus tax, $c + t = 1.25$. Therefore, under a profit-maximizing monopoly the price will be 1.875 and output will be $x = 5$. At this point on the demand curve, the elasticity of demand is $\varepsilon = -3$. The distortion created by the monopolist is $d = q - (c + t) = 0.625$. Measured as a proportion of the monopolist's price, this distortion is $\delta = \frac{d}{q} = 0.333$.

As shown in Dahlby (2008, pp. 67–70) the MCF for an excise tax on a monopolist's product is:

$$\text{MCF} = \frac{1 - \delta \cdot \varepsilon \cdot \frac{dq}{dt}}{1 + \delta \cdot \varepsilon \cdot \frac{dq}{dt}} \tag{4.7}$$

Note that this expression for the MCF differs from the MCF in a competitive market in that the numerator has an additional positive term $-\delta\varepsilon\frac{dq}{dt}$, where $\frac{dq}{dt}$ is the rate at which the monopolist increases the price of the product in response to a tax increase. With a linear demand curve and constant marginal cost, $\frac{dq}{dt} = 0.5$. The term reflects the additional distortion because the monopolist has set the price above the marginal cost plus the tax and responds to the tax increase by further increasing the price of the product. Plugging the values of $\delta = 0.333$, $\frac{dq}{dt} = 0.5$, and $\varepsilon = -3$ in (A2), the MCF is equal to 2.73, which is considerably higher than in the equivalent MCF for an excise tax increase in a competitive market. In essence, the MCF is higher when taxing a monopolist's product because a tax increase exacerbates the distortion in the allocation of resources since the monopolist will raise the price of the product, further restricting its production.

Box 4.2 A Numerical Example of the MCF for a Tax on a Pollutant
Consider a case where the consumption of a commodity generates a harmful externality. Let the damage caused by the pollutant per unit of output be $d < 0$. Using the symbols and assumptions about demand and supply as in Box 4.1, the MCF from taxing the commodity is given by the same expression:

$$\text{MCF} = \frac{1-\delta \cdot \varepsilon \cdot \dfrac{dq}{dt}}{1+\tau \cdot \varepsilon \cdot \dfrac{dq}{dt}} \tag{4.8}$$

where $\delta = \frac{d}{q}$ is the marginal external damage expressed as a percentage of the price of the product. Note that since $-\delta\varepsilon\frac{dq}{dt}$ is negative, incorporating the externality in the expression will lower the MCF from taxing the commodity. This reduction in the MCF from taxing a polluting commodity is the rationale behind the Pigouvian taxes, such as those levied on carbon emissions.

Note that if the government can levy lump-sum taxes to finance its expenditures, then its MCF is one, the optimal tax rate on the commodity is $\tau = -\delta$, which is a basic expression for a Pigouvian tax.

To illustrate the consequences of incorporating the externality in the calculation of the MCF, we use the same parameter values as in Box 4.1, with $c = 1$, $a = 20$, $b = 8$, $t = 0.25$, $q = 1.25$, $\tau = 0.20$, $x = 10$, and $\varepsilon = -1$. Suppose the marginal damage is $d = -0.5$, then $\delta = -\frac{0.5}{1.25} = -0.4$. Under the assumption of a competitive market and a perfectly elastic supply, $\frac{dq}{dt} = 1$. Plugging these values into (4.8), the MCF is equal to 0.75. The fact that the MCF is less than one in this case implies that raising an extra dollar of tax revenue by raising the tax rate on this polluting commodity imposes a burden of less than a dollar because of the decline in harmful emissions. If the government can raise revenues by levying lump-sum taxes, the optimal Pigouvian tax rate in this case is $t = 0.5$ or $\tau = \frac{0.5}{1.5} = 0.333$.

The MCF has been defined as a measure of the cost, or efficiency loss, imposed on the private sector from raising additional revenue through a tax increase. However, all societies are concerned about the distributional impact of their tax system. Below we show how the distributional impact of a tax increase can be incorporated in the MCF.

Suppose there are H households in the economy. Let β_h represent the value that the society places on an extra dollar of lump-sum income received by household h. It will be assumed that the society has "pro-poor" social preferences such that β_h is higher for households with a lower standard of living as measured by their income or total consumption. The distributional weights are value judgments, reflecting a society's willingness to trade-off gains and losses by different segments of society. Economists often try to help policy-makers apply a consistent set of distributional weights by using an explicit functional form for the relative distributional weights, such as:

$$\beta_h = \left(\frac{y_h}{y_{ave}} \right)^{-\xi} \tag{4.9}$$

where y_h is the disposable income of household h, y_{ave} is average income, and ξ is a parameter that measures the society's aversion to inequality. If $\xi = 0$, all the βs are equal to one and no consideration is given to distribution of the tax burden. On the other hand, if $\xi = 2$, then the β for a household with half the average income is 4 and the β is a household with twice the average income is 0.25.

We will use a simple model to illustrate how social preferences can be incorporated in the MCF. Suppose the entire burden from taxing a commodity is borne by consumers through an increase in the price of the commodity. The social valuation of the households' welfare losses from an increase in the price of commodity i is:

$$\sum_{h=1}^{H} \left(\beta_h \cdot s_h \right) = \omega \cdot X \tag{4.10}$$

where s_h is household h's share of the consumption of the commodity, $s_h = \frac{X_h}{X}$. The ω parameter is known as the distributional characteristic of commodity, and it measures the social harm caused by increasing the total household expenditure on the commodity by a dollar. The ω will be larger when the β_h and s_h are positively correlated. This means that ω will be high for commodities that are consumed mainly by the poor.

We will define the social marginal cost of public funds, SMCF, as the distributionally weighted cost of raising an additional dollar of tax revenue from a particular tax source. In the simple case that we are dealing with, this is simply SMCF = $\omega \cdot$ MCF. See Box 4.3 for a numerical example of incorporating concerns about the distribution of the tax burden in the social marginal cost of public funds.

Box 4.3 Incorporating Distributional Concerns in the Calculation of the MCF

To illustrate how concerns about the distribution of the tax burden across income groups can be incorporated in the SMCF, we use the same example as in Box 4.1 where an excise tax is imposed in a competitive market with a perfectly elastic supply of the commodity. Based on the same parameter values as in Box 4.1, with $c = 1$, $a = 20$, $b = 8$, $t = 0.25$, $q = 1.25$, $\tau = 0.20$, $x = 10$, and $\varepsilon = -1$, the MCF is 1.25. Now consider a society that consists of 10 households with total income of 1000 and average income of 100. In the first column in Table 4.1 shows the shares of total income for each household. Suppose the value that the society places on an additional dollar of income for household h is given by Eq. (4.9) with the income inequality aversion parameter equal to $\xi = 1$. The second column show the βs that correspond to this degree of aversion to inequality.

Consider two cases. First, suppose that commodity is a normal good with the income elasticity of demand of 0.5. Households consume more of the commodity as their incomes increase, but the share of their incomes spent on the commodity declines with income. In the third column in Table 4.1 shows each household's share of the consumption of the commodity. Note that the share of total consumption exceeds the household's share of total income at low income levels and is less than the share of income at high income levels. Multiplying the β_h by the shares of total consumption in column 3 and summing, we obtain a value of 1.28 for the distributional characteristic of the commodity, ω, and the social marginal cost of funds is SMCF = 1.60. Recall that in the absence of distributional weight, the MCF is 1.25.

The fourth column shows the shares of total consumption if the commodity is a luxury and the income elasticity of demand is 1.25. Now the households' shares of total consumption are less than their shares of total income for low-income households and higher than their shares of income for high-income households. In this case the distributional characteristic is 0.878 and the social marginal cost of public funds is 1.10.

Table 4.1 Distributional weights, distributional characteristics, and the SMCF

		Share of total consumption	
Shares of total income	*Distributional weight* β	*Income elasticity of demand equal to 0.50*	*Income elasticity of demand equal to 1.25*
0.038	2.654	0.066	0.027
0.040	2.529	0.067	0.029
0.043	2.347	0.07	0.032
0.048	2.098	0.074	0.037
0.056	1.786	0.08	0.045
0.070	1.434	0.089	0.059
0.092	1.082	0.103	0.084
0.130	0.77	0.122	0.128
0.191	0.522	0.148	0.208
0.293	0.341	0.183	0.353
Distributional characteristic, ω		1.28	0.878
Social marginal cost of public funds, SMCF		1.60	1.10

Source: Author

Measuring the MCF

There are three basic ways of calculating the MCF. One approach is to derive formulas for the MCF that incorporate the tax rates, behavioural responses to the tax rate changes, shares of tax revenues, and (possibly) the distributional characteristics of the tax bases. The MCF is then calculated using known or estimated values of these key parameters. A second approach is to use a computable general equilibrium (CGE) model to simulate the impact of a small increase in a tax rate on the well-being of households and the government's revenues and use of these results to calculate the MCF. A third approach is to use econometric models to estimate the tax sensitivity of the tax bases or tax revenues and then use general formulas such as (4.5) to calculate the MCF. In this section, we will review some examples of each of these approaches and then discuss their advantages and limitations.

Formula-Based Calculation

In the second section, we showed how formulas for the MCFs can be derived for a few simple situations. These formulas can incorporate multiple tax rates and bases, households, and non-tax distortions. Estimates of the key responses of tax bases to tax rate changes, effective tax rates and tax shares, and non-tax distortions drawn from the previous economic studies, or supplied by the researcher, can be plugged into the formulas to calculate the MCFs. An example of this approach is Chandoevwit and Dahlby (2007), who calculate the MCFs for alcohol, tobacco, and fuel excise taxes in Thailand. They used estimates of own and cross price elasticities of demand for 10 categories of expenditure on goods and services in Thailand to measure the demand responses of these commodities to changes in the tax rates on alcohol, tobacco, and fuel. Estimates of the effective tax rates on the 10 expenditure categories were obtained from input-output tables. Budget shares of consumers were obtained from an household expenditure survey. The non-tax distortions created by environmental and public externalities, market power, addition, and smuggling were also incorporated in model, with parameter values drawn from a wide variety of sources.

Chandoevwit and Dahlby (2007) found that the non-market distortion created by smuggling, market power, and addiction significantly affected the magnitudes of the MCFs. Based on the benchmark parameter values, the MCFs are 0.532 for fuel excise taxes, 2.187 for tobacco excise taxes, and 2.312 for alcohol excise taxes. Pro-poor distributional weights and expenditure shares for 90 household groups were used to calculate the distributional characteristics of the expenditure categories. The distributional characteristics were used to calculate the SMCFs, but SMCFs had the same ranking as the MCFs. Finally, the authors found that a revenue-neutral marginal tax reform—reducing the excise tax rates on alcohol and tobacco by one percentage point and increasing the fuel excise tax—would result in a net efficiency gain equal to 1.72 Baht for every additional Baht of fuel tax revenue. The authors' concluded that a revenue neutral shift from alcohol and tobacco taxes to fuel taxes would improve economic efficiency and have a positive distributional impact.

CGE Computations of the MCFs

CGE models can be used to estimate the MCFs for various taxes by shocking the model with a small tax rate increase and calculating the ratio of the burden on households to the additional revenue collected. Barrios et al. (2013) used the CGE model GEM-E3 model (General Equilibrium Model for Energy-Economy-Environment interactions) to compute the MCFs for taxes on labour and household consumption of energy for 24 EU countries based on 2005 data. The model used effective rates, defined as the ratio between the tax revenues to the corresponding tax base, rather than statutory rates. Seven types of taxes were included in the model—indirect taxes, environmental taxes, direct taxes, value-added taxes, production subsidies, social security contributions, and import duties.

An essential feature of the model was the inclusion of labour market distortions that result in involuntary unemployment. Unemployment benefits were included in the model as a transfer from the government to the household sector to offset income losses from unemployment. Higher social security payment in response to higher unemployment was also built into the model. Another feature of the model was that, in calculating the MCFs for small tax rate increase, the additional revenues were allocated to the rest of the world (such as through foreign aid payments) so that the MCFs reflected the income losses from the tax increase and did not include the income effects from spending the additional revenues on public goods or domestic transfers. This is important because this makes the MCFs consistent with the analytical framework for defining the MCFs in Section "Conceptual Foundations" where expenditure effects are ignored.

Table 4.2 shows the estimated MCFs for labour taxes and green taxes for the EU countries. The GDP weighted average was 1.90 for labour taxes with a wide range from 1.30 in Estonia to 2.41 in France. For the green taxes, the GDP weighted average MCF was 1.08, ranging from 0.62 in Bulgaria to 1.42 in France. For every country, the MCF for labour tax was higher than for the green tax. Barrios et al. (2013, p. 21) conclude that "relying on green taxation to raise revenues, rather than labour taxation, would be expected to be more efficient for the economy as a whole."

Econometric Models

The key behavioural parameters in the calculation of the MCFs are the responses of tax bases to tax rate increases, or equivalently, the response of total revenues to tax rate changes, i.e. the slope of the Laffer curve. Dahlby and Ferede (2012) used panel data and Dahlby and Ferede (2018) use time series data on the corporate income tax, personal income tax, and sales tax bases for the Canadian provinces to estimate their tax sensitivities and to compute the MCFs for these taxes. Their basic approach is to estimate equations of the form:

$$lnB_{jt} = \eta_{jo} + \eta_{jc} \cdot \tau_{ct} + \eta_{jp} \cdot \tau_{pt} + \eta_{jc} \cdot \tau_{st} + X_{jt} + u_{jt} \quad (4.11)$$

Table 4.2 The MCFs for labor taxes and green taxes in the EU

	Labor taxes	*Green taxes*
EU average (GDP weighted)	1.90	1.08
Simple average	1.73	0.90
Austria	1.82	0.87
Belgium	1.98	0.63
Bulgaria	1.56	0.62
Czech Rep.	1.49	0.81
Germany	1.96	1.14
Denmark	2.31	0.86
Estonia	1.30	0.79
Greece	1.59	0.85
Spain	1.79	0.89
Finland	1.61	0.63
France	2.41	1.42
Hungary	1.53	0.86
Ireland	1.33	0.62
Italy	1.68	1.10
Lithuania	1.45	0.84
Latvia	1.42	0.82
Netherlands	1.57	0.83
Poland	1.63	1.26
Portugal	1.82	0.93
Romania	1.43	0.89
Sweden	2.06	0.87
Slovenia	1.66	0.95
Slovakia	2.19	1.06
United kingdom	1.81	1.13
Coefficient of variation	17.38%	22.21%

Source: Barrios et al. (2013, Table 2, p. 27)

where j is an index for the corporate, personal, and sales tax rates, τ_{jt}, in year t, $j = c, p, s$; $ln\ B_{jt}$ is the log of tax base j; X_{jt} denotes a vector of other control variables in tax base j regression which includes federal statutory tax rates, other provinces' tax rates, and various variables to capture relevant province-specific shocks; and u_{jt} is the error term. The η_{kj} coefficients, are the semi-elasticities of tax base k with respect to tax rate j and shows the percentage change in tax base k from a one percentage point change in the corporate, personal, and sales tax rates respectively. The own semi-elasticity estimates, η_{jj}, are expected to be negative, while the cross semi-elasticities, η_{kj}, could be positive or negative.

Table 4.3 The marginal cost of public funds for major provincial income taxes in 2018

	Corporate income tax	*Provincial income tax*	*Provincial sales tax*
Newfoundland and Labrador	***	3.81	1.82
Prince Edward Island	***	2.80	2.44
Nova Scotia	***	---	1.62
New Brunswick	***	2.51	1.59
Quebec	3.46	3.06	1.92
Ontario	2.62	6.76	---
Manitoba	***	2.42	1.41
Saskatchewan	***	2.27	1.53
Alberta	3.39	1.77	###
British Columbia	2.19	3.88	---

Source: Author

Notes: Calculations based on 2018 tax rates, average revenue shares 1972–2013, and estimates of the semi-elasticities of the tax bases based on data from 1972 to 2013 in Dahlby and Ferede (2018)

*** Indicates that a tax rate increase would reduce total tax revenues in the long run

--- Indicates that the MCF could not be computed because the tax rates were stationary and the semi-elasticities could not be estimated

The MCF for Alberta was not calculated because the province does not levy a sales tax

Table 4.3 shows the MCFs for the provincial governments for 2018 based on the Dahlby and Ferede (2018) estimates of the semi-elasticities of the three tax bases. The MCFs for corporate income taxes are not reported for six provinces because at the 2018 tax rates these provinces were on the downward sloping sections of their long-run total revenue Laffer curves, i.e. a reduction in their corporate income tax (CIT) rates would increase their long-run total tax revenues. Note that these are the provinces with the smallest populations, and the econometric results indicate that the (absolute value) of the semi-elasticity of the corporate tax base is inversely related to the province's population. For the other provinces, the MCFs for the CIT range from about 2.19 in British Columbia to 3.46 in Quebec. The MCFs for the personal income tax (PIT) range from 1.77 for Alberta to 6.76 for Ontario. In Alberta and Quebec, the MCF for the CIT exceeds the MCF for the PIT whereas this ranking is reversed in Ontario and British Columbia. Note also that in all of the provinces where both the MCFs for both the PIT and the provincial sales tax (PST) could be calculated, the MCF for the provincial sales tax was lower. This is consistent with many other studies which indicate that general sales taxes are less distortionary than personal income taxes.

The three approaches to calculating the MCFs have advantages and disadvantages. It is relatively easy to derive formulas for the MCF for a particular set of taxes. They also provide analysts with a platform for an intuitive explanation of the results, which is important for convincing policy-makers of their usefulness. However, applications depend on the availability of reliable estimates of the key behavioural parameters. This approach is also limited in its ability to incorporate all relevant tax base interactions, especially when calculating the MCFs for major sources of tax revenues such as the corporate income tax. CGE models are able to capture the interdependence of tax bases, but the framework can be very rigid, especially if the analyst has to use an "off the shelf" CGE model. CGE models are also black boxes, with a lot of uncertainty about key parameters in most cases, and it may be difficult to convey to policy-makers the intuition behind the results. Econometric-based estimates of the MCF are grounded in observed responses to tax rate changes, but they are only as reliable as the underlying econometric models and data, and they cannot cover the range of tax base interactions that is possible with a CGE model. The choice of the approach then depends on the particular taxes to be modelled, the availability of data and estimates of behavioural parameters, and relevant CGE models.

Using the MCF to Evaluate Tax Reforms and Public Expenditure Programs

Evaluating opportunities for tax reform and public expenditure programs are two most obvious applications of the MCF concept. In this section we provide examples of how the MCF can be used to measure the potential gains from tax reform and to derive the matching rate for intergovernmental grant to induce optimal expenditures on infrastructure by subnational governments.

Evaluating Tax Reforms

The MCFs for excise taxes in Thailand in Section "Formula-Based Calculation" illustrated how differences in the MCFs among the taxes can be used to indicate the direction of welfare improving tax rate changes. In this section, we show how the MCFs can be used to calculate the gain from the recent corporate income tax cuts in Alberta. In May 2019, the newly elected Government of Alberta announced that it would reduce the province's general statutory CIT rate from 12 percent to 11 percent on July 1, 2019, and then to 10 percent in 2020, 9 percent in 2021, and to 8 percent in 2022.[1]

As Table 4.3 indicates, the MCF for the CIT in Alberta in 2018 was 3.39, while the MCF for PIT was 1.77. We will assume that the reduction in corporate income tax revenue will be offset by an increase in the top marginal personal income tax rate. The first step is to calculate the increase in the personal income tax rate needed to generate, in the long run, the additional PIT revenues needed to offset the reduction in CIT revenues following the four percentage point cut in the CIT rate. In fiscal year 2018–19, Alberta received $4.871 billion in corporate tax revenues and $11.874 billion in personal income tax revenues. Using the Dahlby and Ferede (2018) estimates of the own and cross semi-elasticities of the tax bases with respect to a CIT rate change, the four percentage point reduction in the CIT rate will reduce the province's annual total revenues by $586 million in the long run. Similarly, using the own and cross semi-elasticities of the tax bases with respect to a PIT rate change, the PIT rate will have to increase from 15 percent to 16.3 percent to offset this decline in CIT revenues. These post-2022 tax rates imply that the MCF for the CIT will decline from 3.385 to 1.886, while the MCF for the PIT will increase from 1.765 to 1.891.

As shown in Dahlby (2008, Chapter 2), the gain from this tax reform, G, can be approximated using the following equation:

$$G = 0.5\left[\left(\mathrm{MCF}_{c0} - \mathrm{MCF}_{p0}\right) + P\left(\mathrm{MCF}_{c1} - \mathrm{MCF}_{p1}\right)\right]\cdot(-\Delta R_c) \quad (4.12)$$

where the MCF_{c0} and MCF_{p0} are the pre-reform and the MCF_{c1} and MCF_{p1} are the post-reform MCFs, P is a price index (discussed below), and ΔR_c is the tax revenue that is shifted from the CIT base to PIT base. The difference in post-reform MCFs is multiplied by the price index P in order to convert it from a money measure of a welfare change at the post-reform prices into a money measure of a welfare change at the pre-reform prices. (See Dahlby 2004, p. 37 for a more detailed explanation of why

[1] See Dahlby and Ferede (2019) and, Ferede and Dahlby (2019) for estimates of the impact of the CIT rate cuts on the Alberta's growth rate.

this adjustment is necessary.) In the current context, this price index can be approximated as:

$$P = 1 + \frac{w \cdot L}{I}(\theta + \rho) - \Delta\tau_P \tag{4.13}$$

where $\frac{wL}{I}$ is the ratio of labour income to total income, θ is the income elasticity of labour supply, and ρ is the elasticity of the marginal utility of income. Assuming that labour income is 70 percent of total income, that $\theta = -0.20$, and $\rho = -2.00$, P is equal to 0.98. Based on this value for the price index, the pre- and post-MCFs for the two taxes, and the shift in tax revenues between the two bases, the annual gain from the tax reform is $473 million or $110 per capita.

Two further points should be made about these calculations. First, the model indicates that at the post-reform tax rates, the MCFs for the two taxes will be almost equal. This implies that there will be no further gains from lowering the corporate income tax rate and increasing the personal income tax rate. Second, the model is based on estimates of the responses to the CIT and PIT bases to change in the tax rates in the long run. During the transition to the new long-run equilibrium, the loss of revenue from the reduction in the CIT rate may exceed the increase in revenue from the higher PIT rate because Dahlby and Ferede (2012) found that the CIT base responds less quickly to a tax rate change than the PIT base. Because of these differences in adjustment rates, which is not reflected in this model, the tax reform may not be revenue neutral in present value terms and a larger increase in the PIT rate might therefore be required.

Designing Intergovernmental Infrastructure Grants[2]

Public infrastructure—the transportation, environmental, educational, and recreational facilities that are provided by governments—contributes to the quality of life and the productive capacity of a country's citizens. In federal countries, infrastructure is provided by all levels of government, and there may be coordination problems because of benefit spillovers and differences in the abilities of governments to finance infrastructure

[2]This section is based on the analysis of federal infrastructure grant programs in Canada in Dahlby and Jackson (2015).

spending. In Canada, the federal government has developed a series of grant programs to help the provincial and municipal governments finance infrastructure projects. Many of these programs are matching grants whereby the federal government provides a proportion of the total cost of the project. In this section, we use the MCF framework to derive a central government's optimal contribution rates to the subnational governments' spending on infrastructure projects.

The rationale for a central government's involvement in the financing subnational governments' spending on infrastructure is based on the presence of horizontal and vertical fiscal externalities and fiscal imbalances between the levels of government. Fiscal externalities arise when the fiscal policies of one jurisdiction affect the well-being of individuals in the rest of the federation. A local government's infrastructure projects can directly benefit residents in other jurisdiction through benefit spillovers, such as the use of local parks, or increases in regional productivity through investments in transportation facilities that improve the movement of people and products. Such productivity improvements can increase the incomes of the residents in other jurisdictions and increase tax revenues of the central government. Horizontal fiscal externalities occur across the same level of government, such as municipalities, whereas vertical fiscal externalities occur between different levels of government, such as a regional government and the central government. Differences in fiscal capacity arise because of differences in per capita tax bases, as well as differences in the tax sensitivity of tax bases, across and between levels of government.

Fiscal externalities and differences in fiscal capacity can lead to a sub-optimal provision of public infrastructure in a federation. An optimal matching grant from a central government induces the subnational government to invest in the infrastructure project up to the point where the total marginal benefit from an additional dollar spent on an infrastructure project equals the total marginal cost of spending an additional dollar on that project. Below we develop a simple model of the optimal matching rate.

We will use the following notation:

MB_i is the present value of the marginal quality-of-life benefit to the residents in subnational government i from an additional dollar spent on a given infrastructure project by subnational government i.

MB_o is the present value of marginal quality-of-life benefit to the residents of all other subnational governments from an additional dollar spent on a given infrastructure project by government i.

MCF_i is the marginal cost of public funds of subnational government i.

MCF_f is the marginal cost of public funds of the federal government.
ρ_i is the marginal product of spending on the infrastructure project, i.e. $\frac{dY}{dg_i} = \rho_i$ where Y is the present value of total income and g_i is spending on infrastructure by government i.
τ_i is the tax rate on income generated in subnational government i.
τ_f is the total federal tax rate on income.
m is the federal cost-sharing or matching rate under the infrastructure transfer program.

From the perspective of subnational government i, the optimal expenditure on an infrastructure project occurs when the marginal benefit to its residents from an additional dollar spent on the project is equal to its marginal cost of public funds, MCF_i, times the net amount of revenue that has to be raised to finance a dollar spent on infrastructure, which is $((1 - m) - \tau_i\rho_i)$. The matching grant, m, and the additional revenue generated by the project, $\tau_i\rho_i$ lower the net amount of revenue that has to be raised to finance an additional dollar spent on the project. Consequently, the subnational government's expenditure on the project will be determined by the following equation:

$$MB_i + \left(1 - \tau_i - \tau_f\right)\rho_i = \mathrm{MCF}_i\left[\left(1 - m\right) - \tau_i\rho_i\right] \tag{4.14}$$

Equation (4.14) is a version of the Atkinson and Stern (1974) condition for the optimal expenditure on a public good or service financed by distortionary taxation. The first term on the left-hand side of the equation is the marginal quality-of-life benefit generated by the project and the second term is the increase in the after-tax incomes of the residents of subnational government i from the additional incomes generated by the infrastructure project.

The optimal expenditure on the project occurs when the total direct benefit, $MB_i + MB_o + (1 - \tau_i - \tau_f)\rho_i$, is equal to the cost of financing the project at the lowest possible cost of raising tax revenues. In most federations, the central government has a greater fiscal capacity and therefore a lower marginal cost of public funds than the local governments. Therefore, the optimal expenditure on the project occurs when the following condition is satisfied[3]:

[3] For simplicity, we ignore the effect of the subnational government i's infrastructure spending on the after-tax incomes of the residents in, and the tax revenues of, other subnational jurisdictions.

$$MB_i + MB_o + \left(1 - \tau_i - \tau_f\right)\rho_i = \mathrm{MCF}_f\left[1 - \tau_i \rho_i - \tau_f \rho_i\right] \quad (4.15)$$

The condition for the optimal expenditure in (4.15) differs from (4.14) in that (a) it takes into account the marginal quality-of-life benefits for the residents in other jurisdictions, MB_o; (b) it takes into account the additional revenue that will accrue to the federal government, $\tau_f\rho_i$, which allows the federal government to lower taxes or increase spending on federally provided public services; and (c) it is based on the lowest-cost method of raising the additional revenues that could be used to finance the project, MCF_f.

The optimal matching rate for a transfer to fund the infrastructure project creates the incentive for subnational government i to spend on the project an amount that satisfies the condition in (4.2). Substituting $MB_i + (1 - \tau_i - \tau_f)\rho_i$ from (4.14) into (4.15) and solving for m yields the following expression for the optimal matching rate:

$$m = \frac{MB_o}{\mathrm{MCF}_i} + \frac{\mathrm{MCF}_f}{\mathrm{MCF}_i}\tau_f \rho_i + \left(1 - \frac{\mathrm{MCF}_f}{\mathrm{MCF}_i}\right)\left[1 - \tau_i \rho_i\right] \quad (4.16)$$

The optimal matching rate has three distinct components. The first term on the right-hand side of (4.16) reflects the quality-of-life benefit spillovers to residents in other jurisdictions. The matching rate increases with the extent of these benefit spillovers to the residents of other jurisdictions, MB_o, and is decreasing in the marginal cost of public funds of the jurisdiction that provides the infrastructure, MCF_i. This means that when the subnational government that provides the infrastructure has a higher marginal cost of funds, the matching rate should be lower, for any given direct benefit spillover, because it is more costly to provide this spillover.

The second term on the right-hand side of (4.16) reflects the vertical fiscal externality from an additional dollar spent on the project. This component is increasing in the additional revenue that accrues to the federal government from the project and is increasing in the ratio of the federal MCF_f to the subnational government's MCF_i. In other words, the higher the subnational government's MCF relative to the federal MCF, the lower the matching rate should be because it is more costly to induce the subnational government to spend more on the project.

The third term only arises when there is a difference in the marginal cost of raising revenues between the federal government and the subnational government. Note that this component will be larger when the ratio of the federal and subnational governments' MCFs is lower and when the project generates less revenue for the subnational governments.

To illustrate how the optimal matching rates can be computed, consider a project that only yields quality-of-life benefits, i.e. $\rho_i = 0$. Suppose the benefit spillover to the residents of other jurisdictions is equal to \$0.10 per dollar of expenditure on the project, i.e. $MB_o = 0.10$. Furthermore, suppose that the $MCF_o = 1.77$ and $MCF_f = 1.25$, which corresponds to the MCF for the PIT in Alberta and an estimate of the MCF for the Canadian federal government. The matching rate for this quality-of-life is 35 percent, with 6 percentage points due to the benefit spillover and 29 percentage points due to the difference between the MCFs of the two levels of governments.

Now consider a productivity-enhancing project, where the present value of the increase in output from an additional dollar spent on the project is \$1.10 or $\rho_i = 1.1$, and there are no quality-of-life benefit spillovers, $MB_o = 0$. If the subnational government's tax rate is 10 percent and the central government's tax rate is 25 percent, the optimal matching rate would be 46 percent based on the same MCFs used in previous calculations for a quality-of-life project. The vertical tax externality accounts for 19.4 percentage points of the matching rate, while the difference in the fiscal capacities of the two levels of governments accounts for the other 26.1 percentage points of the optimal matching rate. It is interesting to note that the matching rates that we have computed in these two examples fall within the range of matching rates in federal infrastructure grants in Canada. As well, Dahlby and Jackson (2015) found that federal government's matching rates for productivity-enhancing projects have generally been higher than those for quality-of-life projects as these examples suggest.

Concluding Remark

The first chapter of Dahlby (2008) starts with the following quote from Martin Feldstein (1997, pp. 211–212)—"There are many fascinating theoretical and empirical issues to be addressed in public finance. But none is more important than measuring the effects of tax rate changes and the costs of incremental tax revenues." Feldstein's assessment of the importance of the subject addressed in this chapter still holds true, nearly 25 years later. In this chapter, we have tried to convey through a series of applications why the MCF is of central importance and remains relevant for the evaluation of public expenditures and tax reforms by public finance economists today.

References

Atkinson, A., and N. Stern. 1974. Pigou, Taxation and Public Goods. *Review of Economic Studies* 41: 119–128.

Barrios, S., J. Pycroft, and B. Saveyn. 2013. The Marginal Cost of Public Funds in the EU: The Case of Labour Versus Green Taxes. *Taxation Papers*, Working Paper N.35–2013, European Commission. https://ec.europa.eu/taxation_customs/sites/taxation/files/docs/body/taxation_paper_35_en.pdf

Chandoevwit, W., and B. Dahlby. 2007. The Marginal Cost of Public Funds for Excise Taxes in Thailand. *eJournal of Tax Research* 5 (1): 135–167.

Dahlby, B. 2008. *The Marginal Cost of Public Funds: Theory and Applications.* Cambridge, MA: MIT Press.

Dahlby, B., and E. Ferede. 2012. The Effects of Tax Rate Changes on Tax Bases and the Marginal Cost of Public Funds for Canadian Provincial Governments. *International Tax and Public Finance* 19: 844–883.

———. 2018. The Marginal Cost of Public Funds and the Laffer Curve: Evidence from the Canadian Provinces. *FinanzArchiv* 74: 173–199.

———. 2019. Simulating the Growth Effects of the Corporate Income Tax Rate Cuts in Alberta. *SPP Research Papers* 12 (30) (with Ergete Ferede). https://www.policyschool.ca/wp-content/uploads/2019/09/Alberta-CIT-Dahlby-Ferede.pdf

Dahlby, B., and E. Jackson. 2015. Striking the Right Balance: Federal Infrastructure Transfer Programs, 2002–2015. *SPP Research Papers* 8 (36). https://www.policyschool.ca/wp-content/uploads/2016/03/federal-infrastructure-transfer-dahlby-jackson.pdf

Feldstein, M. 1997. How Big Should Government Be? *National Tax Journal* 50: 197–213.

Ferede, E., and B. Dahlby. 2019. The Effect of Corporate Income Tax on the Economic Growth Rates of the Canadian Provinces. *SPP Research Papers* 12 (29). https://www.policyschool.ca/wp-content/uploads/2019/09/Canada-CIT-Dahlby-Ferede.pdf

CHAPTER 5

Theory-Based Evaluations: Guidelines for Case Studies in Program and Project Evaluation

Ewa Tomaszewska

Introduction

Theory-based evaluation is an approach to evaluating intervention programs that are based on an explicit theory of change, or logic, that underlies the intervention being evaluated.

The development of the theory involves specification of causal links and assumptions by which the intervention or program is expected to lead to various changes in the socioeconomic environment and ultimately to a certain desired outcome. The theory of change is often presented in the form of a flowchart, or logic model, that illustrate how the causal links are expected to lead to that outcome. The evaluation attempts then to assess each of the links to see whether they have materialized and what has changed. With evidence, the evaluator can follow through the causal assumptions to explain how the intervention program has contributed to

E. Tomaszewska (✉)
HDR, Ottawa, ON, Canada
e-mail: Ewa.Tomaszewska@hdrinc.com

© The Author(s) 2020

A. Shah (ed.), *Policy, Program and Project Evaluation*,
https://doi.org/10.1007/978-3-030-48567-2_5

the desired outcome, and if the intended outcome has not been achieved, where the break in causal assumptions had occurred.

This chapter presents an application of theory-based evaluation to a few examples of public sector reforms frequently promoted by the World Bank from the point of view of their impact on reduction in corruption among public sector officials. The specific examples of reforms include the following:

- Case A: Privatization Programs
- Case B: Judicial and Legal Reforms
- Case C: Civil Service Reforms
- Case D: Trade Liberalization
- Case E: Tax Administration Reforms
- Case F: Direct Anticorruption Activities (Anticorruption Agencies, The Office of The Ombudsman, Transparency Rules, and Decentralization).

For each case, a theory and or logic model of causal assumptions and systemic changes are presented that explain how the original reforms lead to a reduction in corruption in the public sector. This is followed by a discussion of those causal assumptions, the type of data that would be needed to analyze and evaluate the changes that took place, and possible sources of such data.

The key lines of impacts leading to a reduction in corruption that are modeled in each case are outlined below.

Case A: Privatization Programs

Privatization programs have the main purpose of improving the economic efficiency. State-owned enterprises slated for privatization undergo economic restructuring to make them profitable. Privatization changes profoundly the way the economy works. Among various changes, corporate subsidies and preferential credits from the government are phased out as the government is not directly involved in the operations of private companies. This reduction in the supply of public finance and emergence of a new class of business owners reduce the opportunities for corrupt behavior by public officials.

Case B: Judicial and Legal Reforms

The primary aim of these reforms is to increase the efficiency and effectiveness of the legal and regulatory framework. This in turn is expected to make the legal system more market-friendly, better capable to deal with recent changes in the economy, and ultimately to promote economic development. Many of these reforms are likely to have an indirect effect of decreasing opportunities for corruption to judges, court support staff, and other public officials leading to an overall decrease in public sector corruption.

Case C: Civil Service Reforms

The primary purpose of civil service reforms is to create a skilled and efficient government workforce that can effectively and efficiently deliver public services. At the same time, professional, well-motivated, well-managed, adequately paid, and accountable civil service workers are less likely to engage in corruption or even have less opportunities to do so.

Case D: Trade Liberalization

Trade liberalization entails a greater degree of deregulation of foreign trade, removal of certain licensing requirements, simplification of tariff codes and lowering of tariffs. This reduces the opportunities and the need to engage in various forms of corrupt behavior by public officials and business community.

Case E: Tax Administration Reforms

The primary purpose of tax reforms is to enhance compliance among taxpayers to raise collection and tax revenue as well as to rationalize tax administration efforts and minimize administrative costs per dollar of tax revenue. Promoting greater efficiency in tax collection and encouraging greater compliance among taxpayers will indirectly impact on the opportunities for corruption to tax officials and the need for citizens to pay bribes.

Case F: Direct Anticorruption Activities

Direct institutional measures such as an anticorruption agency, or the office of the ombudsman, are thought to be a key element of fighting with corruption. The key feature of these institutions is their mandate to investigate cases of alleged or suspected corruption, education and promotion of transparency, rule of law, and anticorruption. This is then expected to lead to a change in behavior of public officials and lower the incidence of corruption.

In the following sections, the above-mentioned cases are detailed.

Case A: Privatization Programs

Privatization has been one of the major areas of reforms promoted in World Bank–financed projects. The main purpose of privatization is to improve economic efficiency.[1] Private companies tend to be more efficient, perhaps because the market discipline they face is very strong, whereas state-owned firms are seen as enterprises that cannot go bankrupt. But privatization changes profoundly the way the economy works. For example, in a privatized economy, preferential subsidies and credits are phased out as the government is not directly involved in the operations of private companies. This decrease in the supply of public finance implies a decrease in opportunities for corruption to public officials. This may lead to lower corruption rates, even if no new direct measures to curb corruption have been implemented. Projects with a strong privatization program component may thus be a good candidate for a theory-based evaluation of the World Bank projects in terms of their contribution to anticorruption. Below we outline a framework for an evaluation study.

Program Theory

The first step in the theory-based evaluation involves specifying a chain of causal assumptions by which the program is expected to cause corruption rates to fall. Below we discuss two possible chains of developments associated with privatization that can be expected to bring about lower corruption rates: decrease in the supply of public finance and emergence of a new private sector constituency.

Decrease in the Supply of Public Finance

As mentioned in the introduction, the primary purpose of privatization is to improve economic efficiency. There is a notion that a state-owned company cannot go bankrupt and thus the discipline of costs and effects

[1] Privatization may also have other goals such generating revenues for the government or attracting foreign investment.

facing it is relatively weak. The government often ends up subsidizing these enterprises or granting preferential loans. This supply of public finance offers numerous opportunities for corruption to public officials. For example, enterprise directors may try to influence the politicians and bureaucrats to grant them inflationary subsidies and credits (see Kaufmann and Siegelbaum 1997). Privatization breaks this link between businesses and government, as the essence of a private economy is that businesses have to survive on their own merit. Because subsidies are no longer available, business owners concentrate their efforts on the bottom line and strive to improve their economic efficiency. They do not contact public officials regarding their business matters, and as a result, opportunities for corruption to public officials decrease.

Development of a New Private Sector Constituency

It may also be the case that privatization helps foster the development of a new private sector constituency. This may be in particular the case if privatization is accompanied by the creation of many new enterprises. Business owners may be able to organize themselves and exert pressure on the government to adopt more business-friendly attitude and regulations (e.g., remove some licensing requirements). They may even be able to expose cases of suspected corruption or deficiencies in the regulations. If this is the case, local and federal governments may feel an increasing pressure to implement reforms that would eliminate most obvious deficiencies in the system and decrease opportunities for corruption to public officials.

Figure 5.1 illustrates these chains of causal assumptions.

The Analysis

Information regarding all causal assumptions in the chain of developments from implementation of the privatization program to measures of corruption rates will then be collected. The assumptions will be tested to determine whether they are satisfied. If any of the links breaks down, the privatization program in question is not likely to contribute to the decrease in corruption. Below we discuss several vulnerable assumptions which should be carefully addressed in the actual evaluation.

Decrease in the Supply of Public Finance

Let us suppose that a number of state-owned enterprises have been privatized and that subsidies or preferential credits are no longer allowed in the

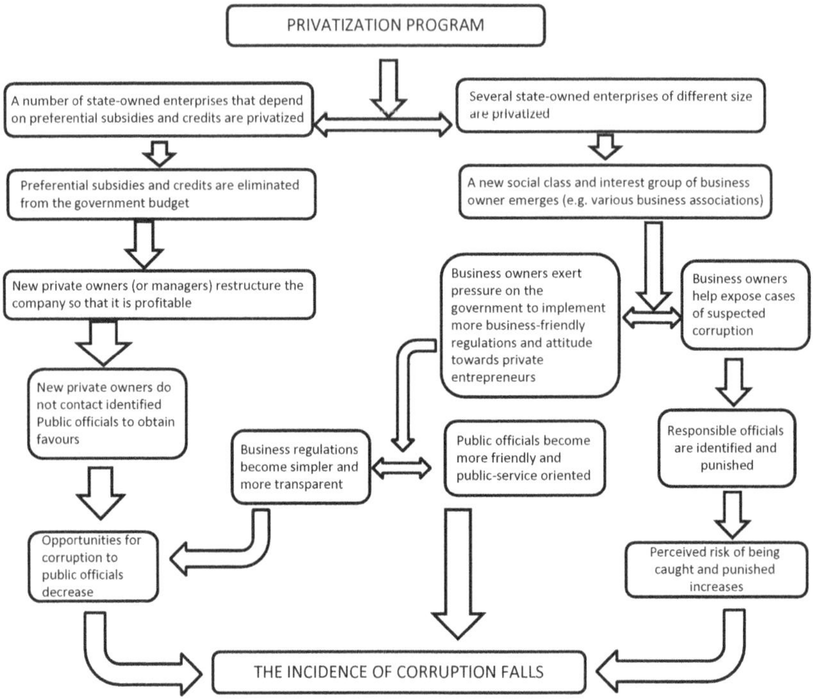

Fig. 5.1 Causal assumptions in impact of privatization programs on corruption. (Source: Author)

government budget. This forms a basis for an economy where firms compete on the basis of merits and not connections. But the end result will depend on the implementation of the privatization process itself. For example, state monopolies may be taken over by a small number of private individuals at undervalued prices and conditions that do not fully take into account the value of the enterprise. In this case, it may happen that only the owners, or the operators of the enterprises, change. The new owners may be able to preserve their monopoly positions and will not feel the pressure to restructure the company. They may even be able to influence politicians and bureaucrats to introduce new legislation providing market protection (e.g., difficult entry into the industry) or preferential tax treatment. This scenario is particularly likely if the new owners had some previous connections with the government before privatization, such as when the new owners are members of the former ***nomenklatura***. As a result, old corrupt relationships between business and government may be re-established. The causal assumption "New owners restructure their company so that it is profitable" and all other assumptions down that chain break down. The incidence of corruption may actually increase.

The effects of privatization will thus depend to a large extent on the design of the privatization process, or the method of privatization. Spontaneous privatization and management buyouts are most likely to produce such negative results.[2] These methods of privatization are often ad hoc and not very transparent as to the conditions and timing of sale or who can put in a bid and thus offer numerous opportunities for corruption. Also, privatization through tenders and trade sales may be risky in this regard if the agency administering the sale is unable to maintain independent status and has problems with internal monitoring. Kaufmann and Siegelbaum (1997, page 443) indicate that: "On the theory that corruption begets corruption, as old-guard economic actors are reinforced in their beliefs that the old techniques still work, those methods of privatization prone to be corrupt in their implementation should be associated with higher levels of corruption in the post-privatization environment." In other words, public officials may be able to re-establish old opportunities for corruption, or find new ones. The assumption "Opportunities for corruption to public officials decrease" breaks down.

Suppose now that the new private owners of a state-owned company did restructure the enterprise so that it can compete effectively in the market place. The new owners do not have to contact public officials to obtain favors such as subsidies, tax reductions, or other forms which affect costs of operations. But the new owner may feel harassed by public officials in some other way or face obstacles of some other nature. For example, they may have difficulties obtaining various licenses (such as an import license) or certificates allowing them to continue operations (e.g., fire safety certificates). These problems may arise in particular in situations in which privatization is not accompanied by a comprehensive program of economic liberalization. As a result, opportunities for corruption to public officials do not necessarily decrease.

[2] For taxonomy and an overview of privatization methods, see Kaufmann and Siegelbaum (1997) and Berg and Berg (1997). Kaufmann and Siegelbaum (1997) also provide an extensive discussion about the corruption potential of various methods during the process of privatization and in the post-privatization economy.

Development of a New Class of Private Business Owners

This chain of causal assumptions may break at the very beginning if initially (i.e., before privatization) the economy is highly concentrated, and then a small number of individuals succeed in taking over the state-owned companies. This case is similar to that described in the previous section: the new private owners become private monopolists who want to maintain this position. They start lobbying politicians and bureaucrats to introduce measures protecting them from competition. As a result, the incidence of corruption does not necessarily decrease. Again, spontaneous privatization, management buyouts, and tender sales are most likely to produce this negative effect.

Suppose now, however, that state-owned companies have been taken over by several new owners so that concentration in the post-privatization economy is not very high. The new business owners may fail to organize themselves, voice their concerns, and exert pressure on the government to implement more business-friendly regulations. This may be the case in particular in situations where the business constituency is very fragmented and dispersed. But even if they succeed to organize themselves, their actions may not be effective if there is no political will on the part of politicians. For example, if the local government derives its revenues from local taxes (i.e., in a decentralized government structure), it may be interested in fostering the development of the local businesses. On the other hand, if the government obtains its revenues from the central government in the form of transfers, the support for business reforms will be much smaller. As a result, the causal assumptions that "Business regulations become simpler and more transparent" and that "Public officials become more public-service oriented" break down.

The chain of causal assumptions from "Business owners help expose cases of suspected corruption" to "The incidence of corruption decreases" is vulnerable in a way similar to the chains of causal assumptions underlying the programs of anticorruption agencies. Responsible officials may remain unpunished, if there is no real commitment on the part of politicians and the government to fight corruption.

The Data

To carry out the analysis, the following information will be required.

Decrease in the Supply of Public Finance

A lot of basic information about the privatization program should be available from country sources. In particular, it should be possible to obtain information about privatization methods employed, enterprises selected for privatization (their main lines of business, market share, etc.), sale price (and how their market value has been determined), bidders, and the winners. The structure of the post-privatization economy (concentration ratios in various industries, prices, employment, etc.) can be analyzed to determine the extent of changes both in quantitative and qualitative terms. This exercise will help identify potential or real abuses in the privatization process as well as determine potential market power of the newly privatized enterprises and thus the probability that they will become cost-efficient and will not seek special protection from the government. Country experts could also be interviewed and asked to assess the likelihood that old corrupt relationships between the government and business will be re-established.

It seems that there are no readily available data to determine the number and the nature of contacts between private businesses and public officials. To obtain this type of information, a survey of newly privatized enterprises may be necessary. The owners, or the managers, can be asked about their recent experience with public administration, the nature of the problems encountered, and how these problems were resolved. A survey of perhaps country experts or former public officials could provide insider information about the common practices in the bureaucracy, its quality, and the morale of civil servants. This information will help assess the nature of relationships between businesses and public officials as well as the probability that public officials will substitute some new forms of corruption for the lost opportunities for corruption.

Development of a New Private Sector Constituency

As in the case of decrease in the supply of public finance, it should be possible to obtain some basic information from country sources. The structure of the post-privatization economy can be analyzed to determine the number and the size distribution of private businesses. Business directories can be examined to determine the number and the nature of business associations. Country experts can be interviewed and asked to provide some insights about the activities of these business associations and their relationships with the government.

It should also be possible to obtain information about existing business regulations and recently introduced changes. These regulations may be examined and evaluated in terms of their simplicity and transparency. However, interviews with businesses may also be necessary to help identify problems.

Regarding the attitude of public officials, it seems that there are no readily available data to evaluate the attitude of public servants. A survey of businesses will be necessary to obtain this type of information. Business owners, or managers, can be asked about their recent experience with public administration, for example, whether public officials were helpful and treated them with respect.

Country sources may also provide information about cases of corruption exposed by business associations and whether responsible officials were identified and punished. In addition, country experts can be asked to express their opinion whether the existing problems have been really resolved or whether what happened amounted to "looking for scapegoats." This will help determine whether the perceived risk of being caught on corruption and then punished is likely to increase.

Case B: Judicial and Legal Reforms

In recent years, judicial and legal reforms have become an important area of public sector reforms funded by the World Bank in developing and transition economies. Some examples of these reforms include the following:

- Upgrading the training of judges, support staff, and legal practitioners
- Modernization of court operations (including provision of equipment, development of information systems, and strengthening of general management)
- Public education campaigns and improvements in the dissemination of legal information
- Assistance in drafting laws and updating of the legal and regulatory framework
- Improving accessibility to judicial services and developing alternative dispute resolution mechanisms
- Institutional development (such as promoting judicial independence, strengthening enforcement of judicial rulings)

The primary aim of these reforms is to increase the efficiency and effectiveness of the legal and regulatory framework. This in turn is expected to make the legal system more market-friendly and better capable to deal with recent changes in the economy, and ultimately to promote economic development. But many of these reforms are likely to have an indirect effect of decreasing opportunities for corruption to judges, court support staff, and other public officials. For example, reforms strengthening judicial independence weaken outside interference in court proceedings and appointments of judges. This eliminates some opportunities to public officials, government agencies, or "well-connected" individuals to exert influence on judges and "buy" favorable rulings and in this way evade responsibility for corruption. Projects with a strong judicial reforms component may thus be good candidates for theory-based evaluation of the World Bank projects in terms of their contribution to anticorruption. Below we discuss a few characteristics of judicial reforms which may contribute to anticorruption and outline the framework for an evaluation study.

Program Theory

The first step in the theory-based evaluation involves specifying a chain of causal assumptions by which the program is expected to cause corruption rates to fall. As mentioned in the introduction, judicial reforms involve a number of complex programs designed to achieve various objectives such as increasing professionalism of the judiciary and court personnel, speeding up processing of cases, improving access to legal services, making the legal system more transparent, strengthening enforcement of judicial rulings, and strengthening judicial independence. Below we discuss the mechanism by which strengthening the enforcement of judicial rulings, independence of the judiciary, and transparency of the legal system may bring about lower corruption rates in courts and even in the public service sector in general.

Strengthening Enforcement of Judicial Decisions

One problem plaguing the legal system in many developing countries is poor enforcement of judicial decisions. Court judgments are often simply ignored by the parties whom they bind. Enforcement officials lack support from the courts and the police and often cannot work effectively. Weak enforcement combined with relatively high litigation costs and slow processing of cases discourages recourse to the legal system by ordinary citizens as well as undermines the respect for law. Cases of corruption may go on unreported, and even if they are reported, the involved officials may remain unpunished. Reforms which introduce and/or strengthen the mechanism of enforcement of judicial decisions should thus increase the probability that cases of suspected corruption will be reported and that convicted officials will actually be punished. This in turn may have the effect of curbing corruption.

Transparency of the Legal System

In some countries serious shortcomings exist in the application and interpretation of the laws and legal procedures. Cases are often ill-managed, partly due to outdated technology but partly due to outdated procedures and poor professionalism of the judiciary. The existing procedures may be difficult to apply to the new developments in the economy and do not work well in situations of increased business activity and complexity. As a result, judicial decisions are unpredictable and of low quality, and the legal system has substantial backlogs and bottlenecks. In this situation, businesses and private citizens may realize that they have to pay a bribe to speed up the processing of their cases or to obtain a favorable decision. Thus reforms which establish standards of legal procedures, improve court infrastructure, or develop information systems will make the system more transparent and more predictable. This in turn will have an indirect effect of decreasing opportunities for corruption.

Independence of the Judiciary

In the past, in many transition and developing economies the principle of independence of the judiciary branch of government was often ignored. In communist countries, appointments of judges were based on political correctness (such as party membership and party activities) rather than qualifications and ethical standards. Judges could have been dismissed overnight for delivering a ruling inconsistent with the official ideology or with instructions provided by the executive branch of government. But even in many (non-communist) developing countries political patronage in appointments was quite strong. These deficiencies, combined with low salaries and an underfunded court administration in general, have created a system where outside interference in court proceedings is strong and not unusual, and corruption is pervasive. Public officials, government agencies, or "well-connected" individuals may try to exert pressure on judges, blackmail them, and/or bribe them, make them deliver favorable rulings and in this way evade responsibility for corruption. When judiciary becomes more independent, some cases of alleged corruption will go to trial and involved public officials may be convicted. This in turn may discourage some public officials from engaging in corrupt activities in the first place and results in lower corruption rates.

Figures 5.2 and 5.3 illustrate these chains of causal assumptions.

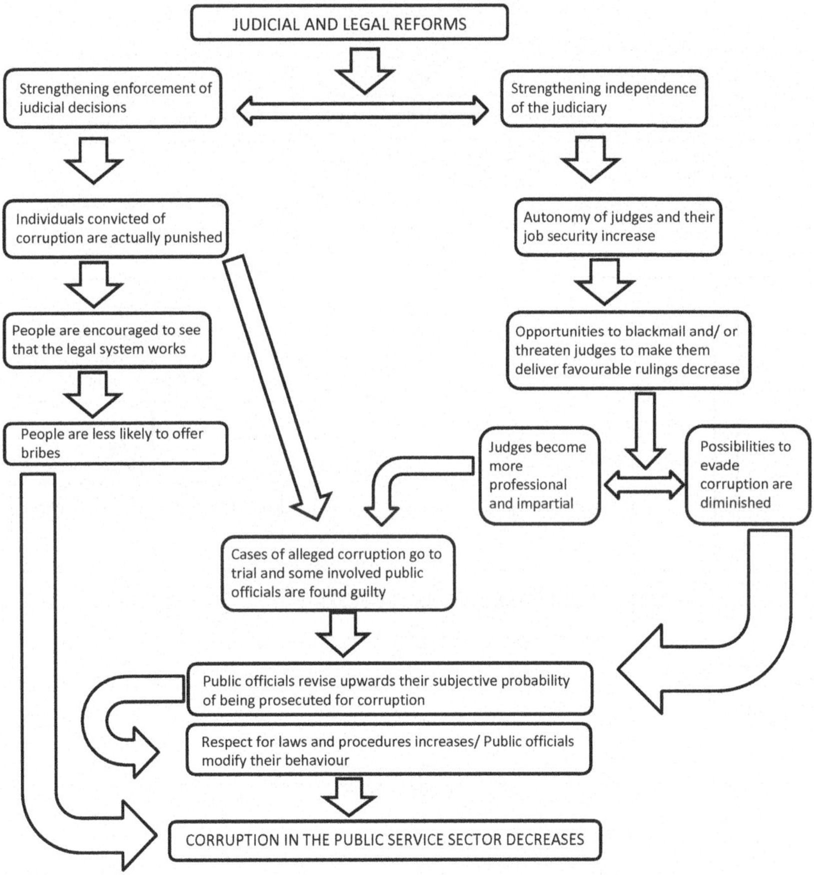

Fig. 5.2 Causal assumptions in impact of judicial and legal reforms on corruption (part 1). (Source: Author)

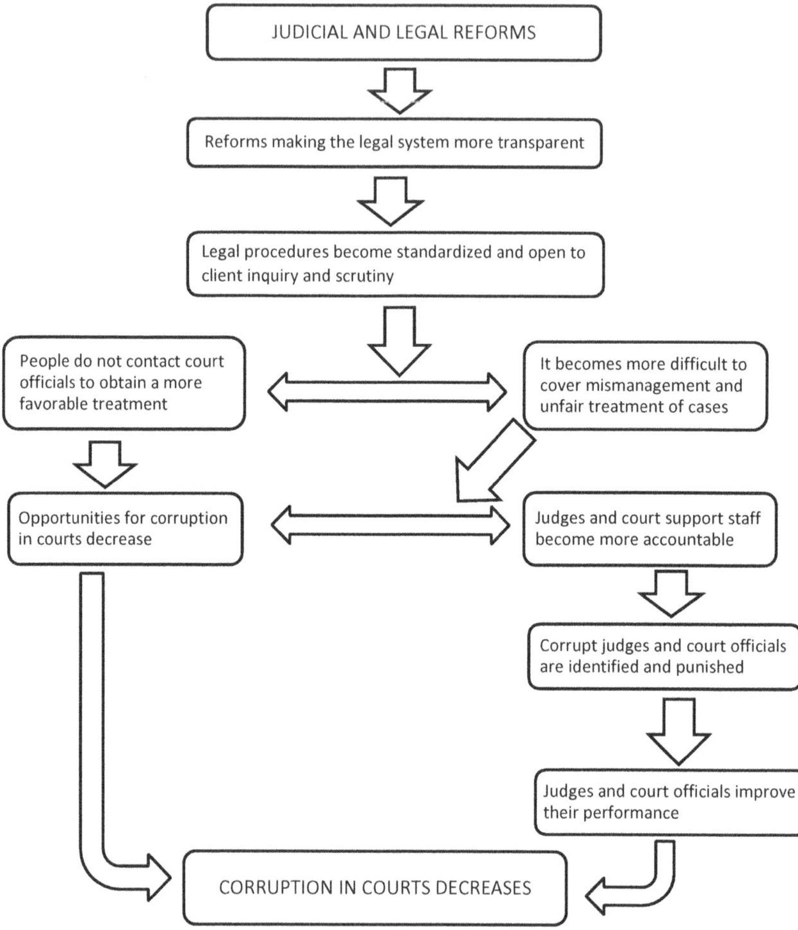

Fig. 5.3 Causal assumptions in impact of judicial and legal reforms on corruption (part 2). (Source: Author)

The Analysis

Information regarding all causal assumptions in the chain of developments from implementation of legal reforms to measures of corruption rates will then be collected. The assumptions will be tested to determine whether they are satisfied. If any of the links breaks down, judicial reforms in question are not likely to contribute to the decrease in corruption. Below we discuss several vulnerable assumptions which should be carefully addressed in the actual evaluation.

Strengthening of Enforcement

Strengthening of enforcement of judicial rulings should in fact diminish the chances of escaping the punishment by corrupt public officials. However, for various reasons, the punishment may be rather light and without a ban on future employment in the civil service. In addition, it may be impossible to recover funds defrauded by the official because (for example) the money has already left the country. If this is the case, the ultimate goal of corruption, personal enrichment, has been achieved. The punishment itself is just the cost, or the risk, of engaging in corrupt activities, and most likely it will be associated with an increase in the level of bribes. As a result, the assumption that public officials revise their subjective probability of being prosecuted and punished for corruption, as well as the assumption that people change their perception of how the legal system works and become less likely to offer bribes, may all break down.

It may also be the case that the office of the prosecutor is not truly autonomous and independent from the executive branch. Anticorruption investigations may be politically motivated (e.g., as an election agenda) and lack consistency and long-term commitment. If this is the case, trials on corruption charges and meting out the punishment may improve things for a while but will not change the morale of public officials. Again, the assumption that respect for laws and procedures increases breaks down.

Strengthening Independence of the Judiciary

Strengthening independence of the judiciary should in fact eliminate some possibilities to exert pressure on judges and lead to judges becoming more impartial. However, the organizations investigating a case of corruption, collecting the evidence, and preparing the case may be in general underfunded and inefficient. They may lack properly trained and experienced staff and/or equipment and be unable to do their job effectively. On the other hand, officials under investigation may be able to destroy or distort evidence. As a result, there may be insufficient evidence presented in court to convict a public official suspected of corruption. The law may also be full of loopholes, and the government system of decision making may be non-transparent, making it difficult to determine the key players in a decision process. The assumption that possibilities to evade responsibility for corruption are diminished breaks down.

Another potential problem is that that judges may be poorly educated (or their education has become obsolete) and/or have insufficient access to legal information and professional training. As a result, some judges may make errors in their judgments, and the assumption that judges become more professional and impartial breaks down.

Transparency of the Legal System

An important condition of the effectiveness of the discussed reforms is that they cover all aspects, or all stages, of a case as well as all aspects of business activities. Otherwise, corrupt officials may be able to substitute one area or form of corruption for another. People may still feel that they have to bribe court officials to obtain proper treatment. In other words, the assumption that people do not contact court personnel may not be satisfied.

The discussed reforms will not work well if there are no mechanisms through which dissatisfied clients could voice their concerns and file a formal complaint (and expect that their complaint will be looked into seriously). Another problem may be underdeveloped civil society institutions and a low probability that civil society will vigorously scrutinize individual judges and courts. If this is the case, the assumption of increased accountability of judges and court staff will not be satisfied.

The Data

Below we discuss the data required to carry out the analysis and discuss possible sources.

Strengthening Enforcement

A lot of basic information about the legal system should be available from country sources. Court data on convictions could be analyzed together with records on punishment. Operations of enforcement agencies could be analyzed from the point of view of their power (i.e., what they can and cannot do), their effectiveness, and efficiency (e.g., the number of interventions, the results of the intervention, time it takes to conclude a case). This exercise will help test the assumption that individuals convicted of corruption are actually punished.

It seems that there are no readily available data to determine whether people are less likely to offer bribes or whether public officials revise upwards their subjective probability of being prosecuted for corruption. This information could be obtained perhaps from interviews with country experts. Users of selected government services (where corruption was a serious problem) could also be surveyed to determine the change in quality of service after introduction of legal reforms.

Strengthening Independence of the Judiciary
Actual independence of the judiciary may be difficult to measure. The constitution may well acknowledge the independence of the judiciary branch but in practice the court system may be an element of a complex political structure. Thus, interviews with country experts may be necessary to determine the degree of actual autonomy and job security of judges. Country experts could also be asked to express their opinion about the degree of professionalism and impartiality of judges as well as the quality of legal information and legal training available in that country.

Court records could be examined to determine the number of corruption cases as well as the number of convictions. This information could then be analyzed together with publicly available corruption ratings. If a country where corruption is pervasive does not see many cases of corruption in courts, the judicial reforms are not really having a significant impact on corruption. The local laws could be examined by legal practitioners to determine whether there are any loopholes in the law. Law enforcement agencies could be examined to determine their effectiveness in criminal investigations. Civil servants could be surveyed about how the decision making in their agencies looks like. All these exercises will help test the assumption that it is more difficult to escape responsibility for corruption after judicial reforms have been introduced.

Transparency of the Legal System
It should be possible to obtain from country sources information about legal procedures for a few selected typical transactions. This information could be examined by legal practitioners to determine the existence (and degree) of discretionary power and potential for abuse in the court system. This exercise will help test the assumption that legal procedures become standardized and open to client scrutiny.

The court system could also be examined to determine whether there are any "watchdog" institutions (or commissions) which review cases of judicial incompetence. Country experts could also be interviewed in this regard and asked for opinion. This will give an idea about the true accountability of judges and court personnel.

It seems that there are no readily available data sources to test the other assumptions. A survey of service users may be necessary to determine whether people still contact court officials and whether it is possible to cover mismanagement. Service users could also be asked about their most recent experience with courts, the quality of service, delays, problems, and how these problems were resolved. A survey of perhaps former court personnel may provide some information about the possible existence of other opportunities for corruption in courts after the introduction of transparency rules.

Case C: Civil Service Reforms

Civil service reforms have been one of the major areas of public sector reforms promoted in the World Bank financed projects. Some examples of these reforms include the following:

- Rationalization of staffing involving elimination of redundant workers, elimination of "ghost" and vacant positions, reduction in civil service size (through retrenchment, early retirement, or hiring freeze), elimination of non-essential services, elimination of overlaps and duplication of responsibilities, computerization of personal files
- Improvement of human resources management involving introduction of clear and consistent rules that govern hiring, promotion, salary, delineation of duties, responsibility for results, evaluation of performance
- Improvement of compensation
- Improved management of service delivery through development of new roles and missions, improved budgeting and financial management.

The primary purpose of these reforms is to create a skilled and efficient government workforce that can effectively and efficiently deliver public services. However, well-motivated, well-managed, public-service-oriented, and accountable civil service workers are less likely to engage in corruption or even have less opportunities to do so. Projects with a strong civil service reforms component may thus be good candidates for theory-based evaluation of the World Bank projects in terms of their contribution to anticorruption. Below we discuss a few examples of civil service reforms that may contribute to anticorruption and outline the framework for an evaluation study.

Program Theory

The first step in the theory-based evaluation involves specifying a chain of causal assumptions by which the program is expected to cause corruption rates to fall. As mentioned in the introduction, civil service reforms involve a number of changes in how government agencies are run and how government workforce is designed and managed with the purpose to increase efficiency. Below we discuss the mechanisms by which an increase in compensation and improved management of service delivery may lead to lower corruption rates.

Improved Compensation of Civil Service Workers

One problem typical for public sector employment in many developing countries are very low real salaries. In some countries the salaries are even below subsistence level and several times lower than in the private sector (in positions requiring similar skills). In this situation corruption is seen as a source of supplementary income, and civil service workers explain their corrupt behavior by the need to support their families.

When compensation in the public sector is increased, public officials become better able to support their families. There is a widely shared feeling that corruption is morally repugnant. Thus, some public officials may stop asking for or accepting bribes out of personal pride. Better compensation in civil service also attracts more and better able job applicants increasing competition for government jobs and increasing the status of a position in civil service. The morale in civil service increases, making some public officials less likely to request and accept bribes.

Another reason why better compensation in civil service may decrease the incidence of corruption is that a higher salary increases the cost of losing a job when caught on corruption. Public officials will stop asking for bribes because they are afraid they may lose their jobs. This argument is similar to wage-preventing-shirking models according to which employers offer a wage above the level which clears the market in order to prevent shirking on the job.

Figure 5.4 illustrates these chains of causal assumptions.

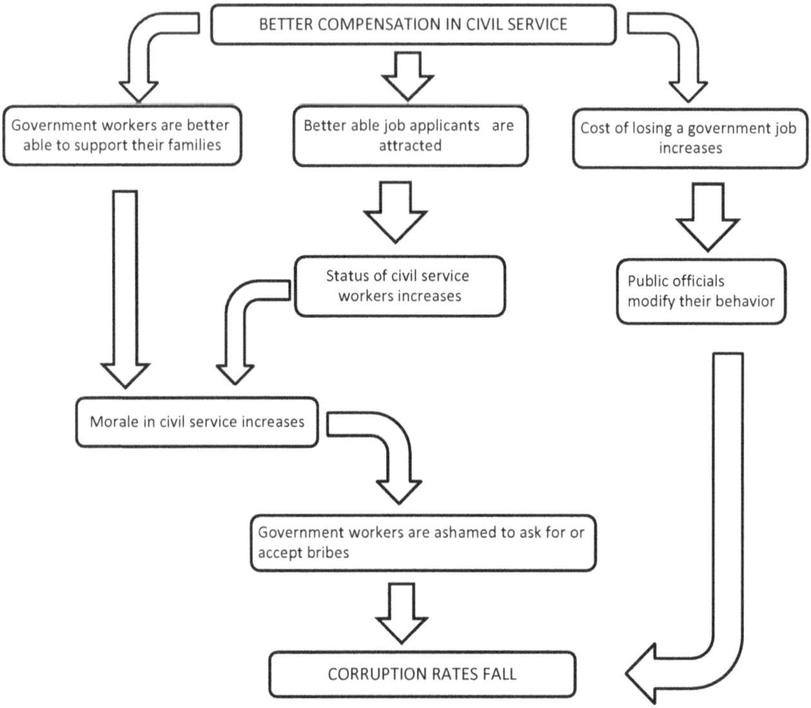

Fig. 5.4 Causal assumptions in impact of civil service reforms on corruption: improved compensation example. (Source: Author)

Improved Management of Service Delivery

In some developing countries bureaucratic processes are not well described. For example, clients may be asked to bring new documents repeatedly and then sent to another office with little explanation. Complaints about mistreatment or allegation of corruption may be difficult to investigate because it is unclear who is responsible for the matter.

When responsibilities between government agencies become more clearly defined, overlaps and duplications eliminated, bureaucratic processes become simpler, more transparent and consistent, leaving less ambiguity as to the proper procedure. It becomes more difficult to send away a client without a decision and without an explanation, and it becomes easier for citizens to question how their matters are being dealt with. It may also be the case that it becomes more difficult to cover mismanagement and fraud.

When it becomes more difficult to send away a client without a decision or explanation, some delays are eliminated and people have less incentive to offer a bribe. When it becomes easier for citizens to question how they are treated, they become more aware of their rights and less willing to pay a bribe to obtain service. Finally, when it becomes more difficult to cover mismanagement and fraud, public officials realize that they have to modify their behavior. As a result, the incidence of corruption falls.

Figure 5.5 illustrates these chains of causal assumptions.

The Analysis

Information regarding all causal assumptions in the chain of developments from implementation of civil service reforms to measures of corruption rates will then be collected. The assumptions will be tested to determine whether they are satisfied. If any of the links breaks down, judicial reforms in question are not likely to contribute to the decrease in corruption. Below we discuss several vulnerable assumptions which should be carefully addressed in the actual evaluation.

Improved Compensation of Civil Service Workers

Very small increases in compensation (insufficient to make them comparable to those in the private sector) may not work. The assumptions that government workers are better able to support their families, that more and better able applicants apply for government jobs, and that the cost of losing a government job increases will all break down.

However, some civil service officials—even if they are well paid—may still be unable to resist the temptation of bribes and will become corrupt if mechanisms of accountability are very weak. In particular, if the probability that corrupt behavior will be caught and punished is very small, the assumption that public officials modify their behavior (and become honest) breaks down.

It may also be the case that improved compensation fails to increase the morale in civil service. Front-line civil service workers may be demoralized by the example of their supervisors who continue old corrupt practices, by inconsistencies and unfairness of promotions, delineation of

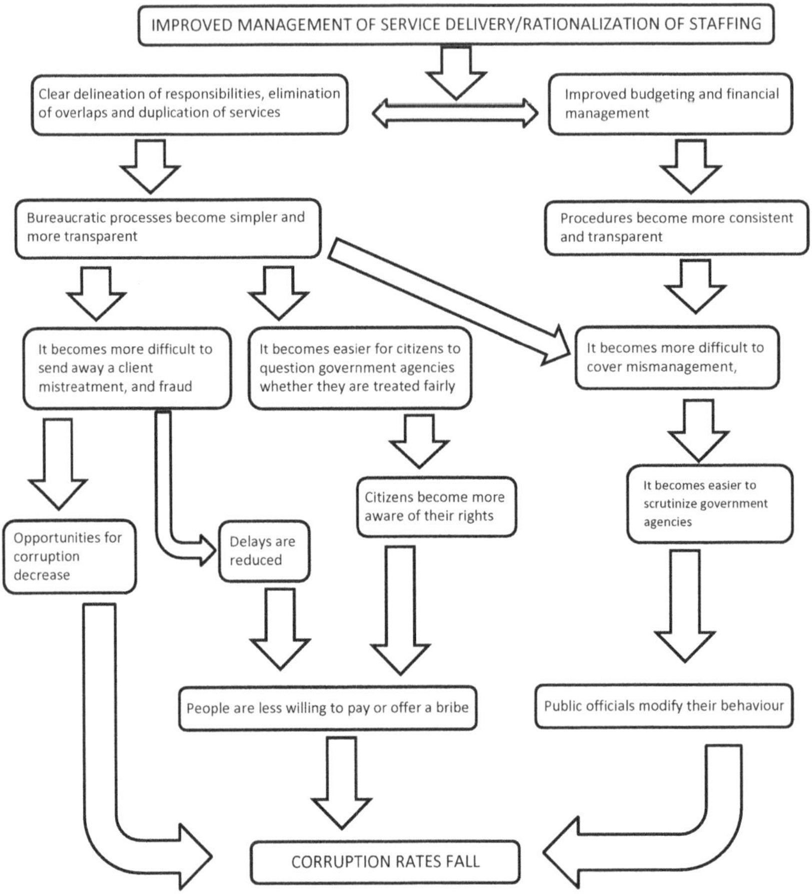

Fig. 5.5 Causal assumptions in impact of civil service reforms on corruption: improved management of service delivery example. (Source: Author)

responsibilities, or evaluation of performance. As a result, the incidence of "petty corruption" may still be high.

Improved Management of Service Delivery
Clear delineation of responsibilities, elimination of overlaps and duplications, improved budgeting and financial management should in fact make rules and procedures more consistent and more transparent. In some cases

it may no longer be possible to request a bribe due to simplification and clarification of procedures. But there may be cases subject to discretionary decision of a public official. Public officials may be able to exploit this power and extract bribes. In other words, corruption in some areas may in fact decrease but it may actually increase in other areas. If this is the case, the assumption that opportunities for corruption to public officials decrease breaks down.

It may also be the case that government agencies are not very likely to be scrutinized. Civil society institutions may be underdeveloped, there may be no laws protecting "whistle blowers," nor laws requiring cooperation of the investigated agencies. In other words, it may be very difficult to scrutinize government agencies and determine if any abuses of power have in fact taken place. As a result, public officials may not necessarily modify their behavior.

The Data

Below we discuss the data required to carry out the analysis and discuss possible sources.

Improved Compensation in Civil Service

It should be possible to obtain from country sources information about compensation in civil service as well as compensation in the private sector in positions requiring similar skills and involving similar responsibilities. Data on costs of living and job applications for government positions should also be available. This information can be analyzed to determine the real wages in civil service (and whether they allow to support a family) and their competitiveness compared to the private sector.

Court records could be examined to determine the number of corruption cases and convictions and compared with publicly available corruption ratings and surveys of public services. This information will help test the assumption that public officials modify their behavior in order to keep their well-paid jobs.

It seems that there are no readily available data to assess the level of morale of civil service workers. A survey of civil service workers may be required to obtain this type of information. The respondents may be asked to assess their job satisfaction, contribution to society, rules governing promotions and performance evaluations, and professionalism of their supervisors and co-workers. Country experts could also be interviewed to collect this type of evidence.

Improved Management of Service Delivery
Some basic information about the management of public services delivery should be available from country sources, for example, the number of ministries and government agencies, their internal organization and mandates, rules concerning budgeting and financial management. This information could then be examined by experts to determine whether there are any inconsistencies and potential for abuse of power. This exercise will help test the assumption that various procedures have become simpler and more transparent after introduction of civil service reforms.

It seems that there are no readily available data to test the other assumptions. A number of surveys may be required to obtain the necessary information. For example, service users may be surveyed about their experience with public service delivery. Such a survey will help determine whether there are delays in processing of applications and whether people have to pay bribes. Country experts may also be asked to rate people's awareness of their rights, the image that various government agencies have, and assess the probability that government agencies will be scrutinized and that corrupt behavior will be detected and punished.

Case D: Trade Liberalization

It is often claimed that trade liberalization leads to a fall in corruption rates. Various forms of trade liberalization have been promoted in many projects funded by the World Bank. Projects with a strong trade liberalization component may thus be a good candidate for a theory-based evaluation of the Bank projects in terms of their contribution to anticorruption.

Program Theory

The first step in the theory-based evaluation involves specifying the chain of causal assumptions by which the program is expected to cause corruption rates to fall. Trade liberalization involves a few types of reforms such as: (1) elimination of import license requirements, (2) simplifying and unifying the import tariff code, and (3) lowering or eliminating import tariffs. Below we discuss some theories of how each of these reforms may contribute to anticorruption.

Elimination of Import License Requirements
Obtaining an import license may be a troublesome procedure for an applicant. Processing time may be unreasonably long and accompanied by additional delays. There may also be restrictions on the number of licenses issued for a particular class of goods. Applicants may find they have to pay a bribe to a public official to speed up the processing of the application or to obtain a permit at all. When licenses are no longer required, importers do not have to contact public officials as often and public officials have one less opportunity to extract a bribe.

Simplifying and Unifying the Tariff Code
It may be the case that import tariffs are highly non-uniform and that there are different rates for similar categories of goods or tariff exemptions within a certain category. Importers may have then an incentive to offer a bribe to a custom official to classify its good in a lower tariff category or as a tariff exemption. When the tariff code is uniform, this gain from forging the custom documents (changing slightly the classification of goods) disappears and so does the opportunity when custom officials may request a bribe.

Lowering or Eliminating Import Tariffs
One argument why lowering or eliminating import duties may have an effect of curbing corruption is an extension of the argument outlined in the previous paragraph: if there are no import tariffs, or they are small, the incentive to forge custom documents disappears and so does the opportunity when custom officials may request a bribe.

As a result of these reforms, incentives to offer a bribe to a public official (such as a custom officer or an officer from business services) become much weaker. Some reasons for which bribes were paid no longer exist, or the extent of discretionary power (and the possibility to give a more favorable decision to those who "pay") that some officials had becomes much weaker. Then the incidence of corruption in customs and business services decreases. The diagram in Fig. 5.6 summarizes this chain of causal assumptions.

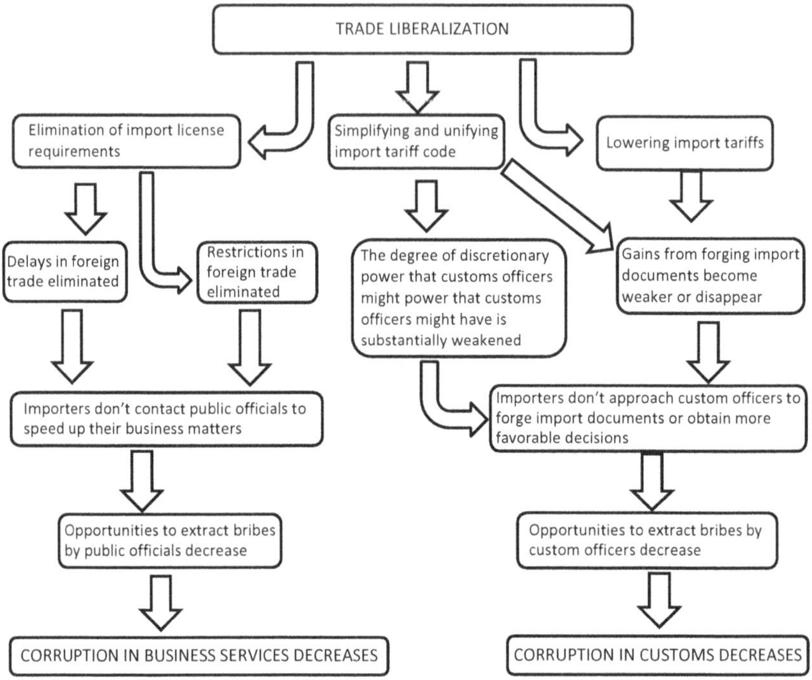

Fig. 5.6 Causal assumptions in impact of trade liberalization on corruption. (Source: Author)

The Analysis

Information regarding all causal assumptions in the chain of events from trade liberalization to decrease in corruption will then be collected. The assumptions will be tested to determine whether trade liberalization has had or likely to have its expected impact on corruption rates. If any of the links breaks down, trade liberalization is not likely to contribute to the decrease in corruption. As an example of this type of analysis, let us consider elimination of import licenses. Below we analyze several vulnerable causal assumptions.

Elimination of Import Licenses

Suppose that import licenses were eliminated but we find out from importers that there are still some delays and restrictions in foreign trade, although now these delays and restrictions are of a different nature. Importers still feel compelled to contact public officials to speed up their business matters. If that is the case, the decrease in corruption that we were hoping to achieve through elimination of licenses is not likely to materialize.

Suppose now that we find that delays and restrictions were in fact eliminated but we also find out that importers still spend a lot of time with public officials, this time on some other matters. If that is the case, the decrease in corruption is not likely to materialize.

Suppose now that delays and restrictions in foreign trade were in fact eliminated and importers don't have to contact public officials to speed up their business matters. This decreases opportunities to extract bribes by public officials from import licensing. But public officials may also have other sources of extortion and now concentrate their attention on those sources. As a result, the overall rate of corruption may not necessarily decrease.

Simplification of the Tariff Code

Suppose that the import tariff code has been simplified: several exemptions have been eliminated, the tariff level has been lowered, and the number of tariff rates has been decreased. It is no longer possible for importers to "negotiate" with the customs officers to classify a shipment into a lower tariff category.

But this does not imply that the degree of discretionary power that customs officials might have is substantially weakened. There may be other regulations which allow customs officers to harass importers in other ways. For example, they may be able to subject the goods to lengthy control procedures, or reject documents presented by importers because of some minor errors. Importers may realize that they still have to approach customs officers and offer bribes to speed up their business matters. If this is the case, the causal assumption that the degree of discretionary power of customs officers is weakened, that importers do not approach customs officers to obtain a more favorable decision, and that opportunities to extract bribes decrease will all break down.

The Data

To carry out the above analysis the following information will be required.

Elimination of Import Permits

A lot of information on trade liberalization may be available from various country and international sources. For example, it should be possible to collect from country sources information on which import licenses were eliminated, what the volume and share of imports affected by licensing requirements was, the number of licenses issued each year, etc.

Delays and Restrictions in Foreign Trade

Some information on delays in trade may probably be obtained from government sources. For example the dates of when an application for a license was submitted and when it was approved will give data on how long it took to obtain a license. Data on trade volumes before and after elimination of licenses should also give an idea of whether delays in foreign trade have decreased after elimination of the licenses. For example, if trade volume has not increased at all, we will have some doubts whether delays have been reduced. However, a survey of service users may be necessary to obtain more insights into the problem, such as those below:

- How long did it take to obtain a license? Were additional documents required to obtain a license? How much money an importer could lose due to delays or restrictions?
- Did public officials have some discretionary power in processing of applications and issuing a license?
- Did elimination of licenses reduce the time necessary to collect all documents and finalize a transaction? Were licenses replaced by other administrative procedures? Did other existing procedures become suddenly more "complicated" and time consuming?

Contacts Between Importers and Public Officials

It seems that there is no readily available data on the nature of contacts between service users and public officials. A survey of service users may thus be necessary to obtain the required information, such as:

- How many visits to the business service office were necessary to obtain a license? How many visits were necessary to deal with other business matters? What were the contacts with officials like? Were officials friendly and helpful?
- What is the nature of contacts with officials now (after elimination of import licenses)? Are they now more friendly or helpful?

Opportunities to Extract Bribes by Public Officials
As with contacts between importers and public officials, it seems that there are no readily available data to assess the opportunities in a country and whether officials are likely to focus on other sources of extortion if old sources dry up. A survey of, perhaps country experts or former public officials, could provide insider information about the common practices in public service offices, quality of bureaucracy, and morale of civil servants.

Corruption in Business Service
A survey of service users may be necessary to obtain also this kind of information.

Degree of Discretionary Power of Customs Officials/Contacts Between Importers and Customs Officers
Some information in this regard may be inferred from the tariff code itself and other foreign trade regulations. They may be analyzed by experts from the point of view of consistency and presence of loopholes. A survey of importers may also be useful to obtain real-life examples of harassment on the part of customs officers. These data will help identify deficiencies in the system.

Case E: Tax Administration Reforms

Tax administration reforms have been one of the major areas of public sector reforms promoted in World Bank–financed projects. Some examples of these reforms include computerization of records and data bases, reducing the complexity of tax laws, switching to self-assessment of taxes by taxpayers, establishment of large taxpayers' units, broadening of tax base (e.g., through the introduction of VAT). The primary purpose of these reforms is to enhance compliance among taxpayers to raise collection and tax revenue as well as to rationalize tax administration efforts and minimize administrative costs per dollar of tax revenue. But encouraging greater compliance among taxpayers and rationalizing certain processes will indirectly impact on the opportunities for corruption to tax officials, even if no new direct measures to curb corruption are introduced. Projects with a strong tax administration reform component may thus be a good candidate for a theory-based evaluation of the World Bank projects in terms of their contribution to anticorruption. Below we discuss a few tax administration reforms which may contribute to anticorruption and outline the framework for an evaluation study.

Program Theory

The first step in the theory-based evaluation involves specifying a chain of causal assumptions by which the program is expected to cause corruption rates to fall. As mentioned in the introduction, tax administration reforms involve a number of reforms. Below we discuss how simplification of the tax system, self-assessment of tax obligation, and incentive bonuses for tax inspectors may contribute to anticorruption.

Simplification of the Tax System

The tax administration literature indicates that complex tax systems are more difficult to administer, which results in low effectiveness and efficiency of the tax system.[3] One problem is that complex tax laws may be a major source of opportunities for corruption to tax officials. For example, sometimes the tax code has a large number of taxes and tax rates with large inter-industry disparities and numerous exemptions. Then a taxpayer has an incentive to offer a bribe to a tax official in exchange for classifying her business into a lower tax rate category (or a category where the total tax payments are smaller). Another example is when tax rules are ambiguous and difficult to interpret. If this is the case, a taxpayer has an incentive to offer a bribe to a tax official in exchange for a favorable decision (i.e., a lower tax assessment). Also, a tax inspector may threaten a taxpayer to interpret the rules in a way which is unfavorable to the taxpayer unless she pays a bribe. Simplification of the tax system (reduction of the number of taxes and rates, removal of tax exemptions, introduction of tax rules that are easy to understand and interpret) eliminates, or at least alleviates, all these problems. As a result, corruption in tax administration falls.

Self-Assessment of Tax Obligation and Self-Payment of Taxes

In this system, the taxpayer calculates her tax obligation herself according to publicized rules and submits the tax payment with the tax declaration directly to a processing center. There is no direct personal contact between a tax official and the taxpayer when the tax obligation is determined and then paid. As a result, it becomes much more difficult to offer or request

[3] For references see Silvani and Baer (1997, p. 10).

a bribe, for example, in exchange for a lower tax assessment or to obtain proper service.

Bonus Incentives for Tax Inspectors
Sometimes the problem of corruption in tax administration is addressed through direct measures such as bonuses for tax inspectors for discovering cases of tax evasion. When bonuses become a part of a tax inspector's income, the relative attractiveness of a bribe falls. If the bonus is large enough compared to the potential bribe, corruption will disappear. But even small bonuses may have some effect. For example, some tax inspectors may feel that the status of their job has increased; they may refuse an offered bribe either because of a higher personal income and a higher morale or because of a higher perceived cost of losing the job should corruption be detected. As a result, corruption rates in tax administration falls.

Figure 5.7 illustrates this chain of causal assumptions.

The Analysis

Information regarding all causal assumptions in the chain of events from implementation of anticorruption measures to decrease in corruption rates will be collected. The assumptions will be tested to determine whether they are satisfied. If any of the links breaks down, the activity in question is not likely to contribute to the decrease in corruption. Below we discuss several vulnerable assumptions which should be carefully addressed in the actual evaluation.

Simplification of the Tax System/Self-Assessment of Tax Obligation
It seems that simplification of the tax system should in fact eliminate much of the discretionary power that tax officials may have when they assess the tax obligation. The system of self-assessment and self-payment of tax should also eliminate some contacts with tax officials and opportunities when tax officials may try to extort a bribe. However, a tax administration may be disorganized in many ways, and field-level officials may be poorly trained and supervised. Tanzi and Pellechio (1995) mentions that in some countries tax laws are not compiled in a code (page 2, footnote 2), or that it is very difficult, if not impossible, for a taxpayer to obtain a copy of the tax regulations (page 4, footnote 2). Even if copies of tax regulations are available, tax officials may be not informed about recent changes in procedures and regulations. If this is the case, the taxpayer may get frustrated

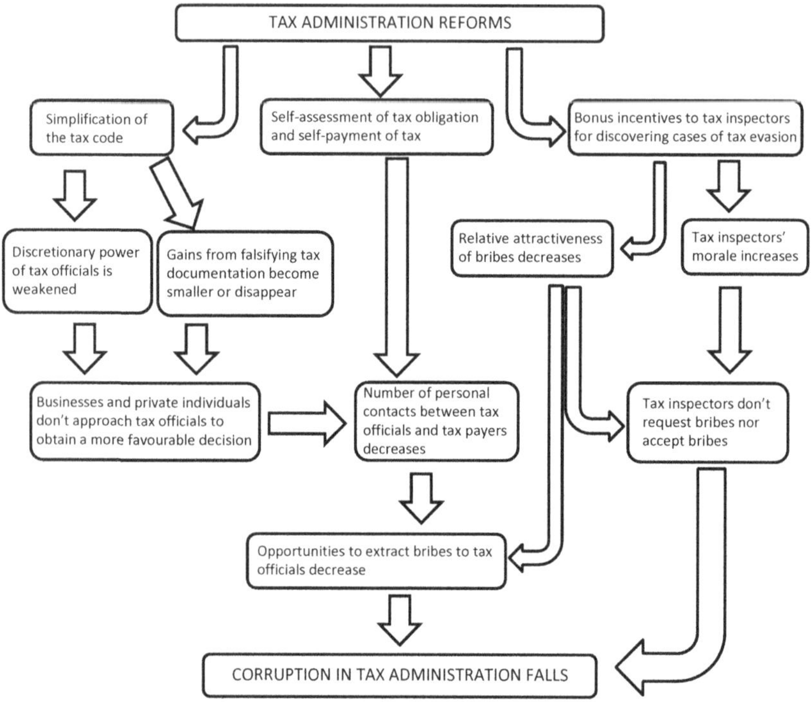

Fig. 5.7 Causal assumptions in impact of tax administration reforms on corruption. (Source: Author)

and realize that she has to pay a bribe when she deals with tax officials, this time to get proper service. In extreme cases, the taxpayer may not even know that she legally falls into a lower rate category, or tax officials may manipulate with taxpayers' files in order to extract a bribe.[4] In other words, the causal assumptions that the number of contacts between taxpayers and tax officials or that opportunities to extract bribes decrease may break down.

[4] For example, focus groups in the Tanzania national integrity survey reported that personal files frequently went missing if people did not pay a bribe. See CIET International (1996, page 23).

Bonus Incentives for Tax Inspectors
Monetary incentives may encourage a number of tax inspectors to be honest and report cases of tax evasion. However, Tanzi and Pellechio (1995) report that sometimes this has produced perverse incentives. Specifically, tax inspectors have purposely not informed taxpayers of their obligations so that violations take place, penalties are collected, and bonuses are paid (see Tanzi and Pellechio (1995), page 4). If this is the case, taxpayers may find it necessary to offer a bribe to a tax official to obtain proper and informative service. One can also think about possibilities when taxpayers and tax inspectors collude so as to raise a tax inspector's income through bonuses and minimize a taxpayer's payment of taxes and penalties. This may take place in particular in systems where there are many rates so that the tax inspector and the taxpayer can "agree" on a rate and where penalties are relatively small or their application can be delayed through the appeal process. If these problems occur, the assumptions that tax inspectors' morale increases or that opportunities to extract bribes shrink break down.

The Data

To carry out the analysis, the following information will be required.

Simplification of the Tax System
A lot of information about the tax administration and the tax system should be available from country sources. It should be possible to obtain information about various taxes that individual and corporate taxpayers have to pay, number of rates, exemptions, documents required from the taxpayer. The amount of tax obligation can be calculated under a number of hypothetical assumptions regarding income, its source, type of business, etc., to see whether there is a potential for substantial tax savings if these hypothetical assumptions change slightly. This requires a good knowledge of the tax system; interviews with country experts may be necessary to identify deficiencies in the system. This exercise will help determine whether there are any potential gains from falsifying tax documentation, or whether tax officials have any degree of discretionary power.

It seems that there are no readily available data to determine the number and the nature of contacts between taxpayers and tax officials and opportunities to extract bribes that tax officials might have. To obtain this type of information, a survey of service users may be required. Businesses and private individuals can be asked about their recent experience with tax administration, the nature of their problems, contacts with tax officials, and how the problems were resolved.

Self-Assessment and Self-Payment of Tax

If should be possible to obtain from country sources information which will help determine how easy it is for a taxpayer to calculate and pay her tax obligation. The relevant information includes availability of copies of tax rules, clarity and simplicity of these rules and tax declaration forms, availability of qualified staff to answer tax questions that a taxpayer may have, forms of tax payment (e.g., direct deposit, personal check mailed to the tax office), and their reliability in reaching the tax office.

Regarding personal contacts with tax officials and opportunities to extract bribes, a survey of service users may be required. This would be a similar survey as that for simplification of the tax system.

Bonus Incentives for Tax Inspectors

Information about tax inspectors' salaries, incentive bonuses, as well as possible penalties for tax evasion, will help to get an idea about relative attractiveness of bribes and bonuses. For example, if penalties are large and bonuses are rather small, a taxpayer may still be able to bribe a tax inspector "to look the other way." The record of detected cases of tax evasion, or system of supervision of tax inspectors, can also be useful indicators.

Other information necessary for this evaluation may be difficult to obtain from country or international sources. A survey of country experts, and perhaps former tax officials, may be necessary to obtain some insights about the morale of tax inspectors before and after the introduction of bonus incentives. A survey of detected tax evaders may help determine whether tax inspectors have any additional opportunities to extract bribes. One problem with such a survey is that the approached tax evaders may refuse to participate and their answers may not be truthful. However, the resentment expressed by respondents may give an indication of deficiencies in the system.

Case F: Direct Anticorruption Activities (Anitcorruption Agencies, the Office of the Ombudsman, Transparency Rules, and Decentralization)

It is often claimed that corruption has to be fought through direct institutional measures such as an anticorruption agency, the office of the ombudsman, transparency rules in the government, or decentralization of the government. Various forms of these reforms have been promoted in many projects funded by the World Bank. Projects with a strong component pertaining to direct anticorruption activities may thus be a good candidate for a theory-based evaluation of the Bank projects in terms of their contribution to anticorruption. Below we outline the framework of such a study.

Program Theory

The first step in the theory-based evaluation involves specifying the chain of causal assumptions by which the program is expected to cause corruption rates to fall. Below we discuss some theories of how anticorruption agencies, the office of the ombudsman, transparency rules, and decentralization may contribute to anticorruption.

Anticorruption Agencies

One of the main mandates of anticorruption agencies is to investigate cases of alleged corruption and abuse of power. As a result of these investigations, several cases of corruption are exposed and the perpetrators are punished. In this way, the agency sends out a message to all public officials that corruption will not be tolerated. Public officials start to realize that the probability of detection and punishment is high, modify their behavior, and become honest. As a result, corruption rates fall.

A second function that anticorruption agencies typically play is prevention. The agency staff identifies major causes of corruption in the country and areas where it is likely to arise. It indicates systemic deficiencies in procedures, regulations, and law which allow corruption to thrive and go on unpunished. The agency then makes recommendations for improvements. These improvements eliminate the opportunities for corruption to public officials and increase the probability of detecting and punishing corrupt behavior. In view of these changes, public officials modify their behavior and become honest.

Another aspect of an anticorruption agency's work involves education of the general public. Through a series of educational campaigns, people are made aware about corruption and its costs to society as well as their rights to public services. They change their attitude toward corruption, becoming more willing to report wrongdoing and more likely to refuse a request for a bribe.

Figure 5.8 summarizes this chain of causal assumptions.

The Office of the Ombudsman

The office of the ombudsman gives a citizen a chance to complain about mistreatment received from public officials when all, or almost all, other means of making an effective complaint have been exploited. As a third-party institution, the office of the ombudsman is able to reevaluate the case objectively and intervene if there was neglect or if the decision in the case was unjust. In this way, the citizen receives proper service and some egregious cases of abuse of power are exposed and the perpetrators punished. As a result of a number of successful interventions, in particular those highly publicized, people become more aware of their rights, and because they know they can turn to the office if they are mistreated, they are less likely to tolerate corruption.

Depending on its mandate, the office of the ombudsman may also play a preventive role. It can identify practices that are contrary to law and recommend improvements. In this way, public officials are made aware of deficiencies in the procedures used by them and given incentives to develop practices consistent with law. As a result, the opportunities for corruption to public officials shrink and corruption rates fall.

The diagram below summarizes the chain of these assumptions. The link between "Several cases of corruption are identified" and "Corruption falls" is not direct, thus a dotted line is used in the diagram. However, the causal links are the same as in the diagram (see Fig. 5.9) for anticorruption agencies between the links "Several cases of corruption are identified" and "Corruption falls."

Transparency Rules

The idea behind transparency rules is that government operations should be open to public scrutiny. The decision-making process must be clear and free of secrecy, and actions taken by public officials that may generate

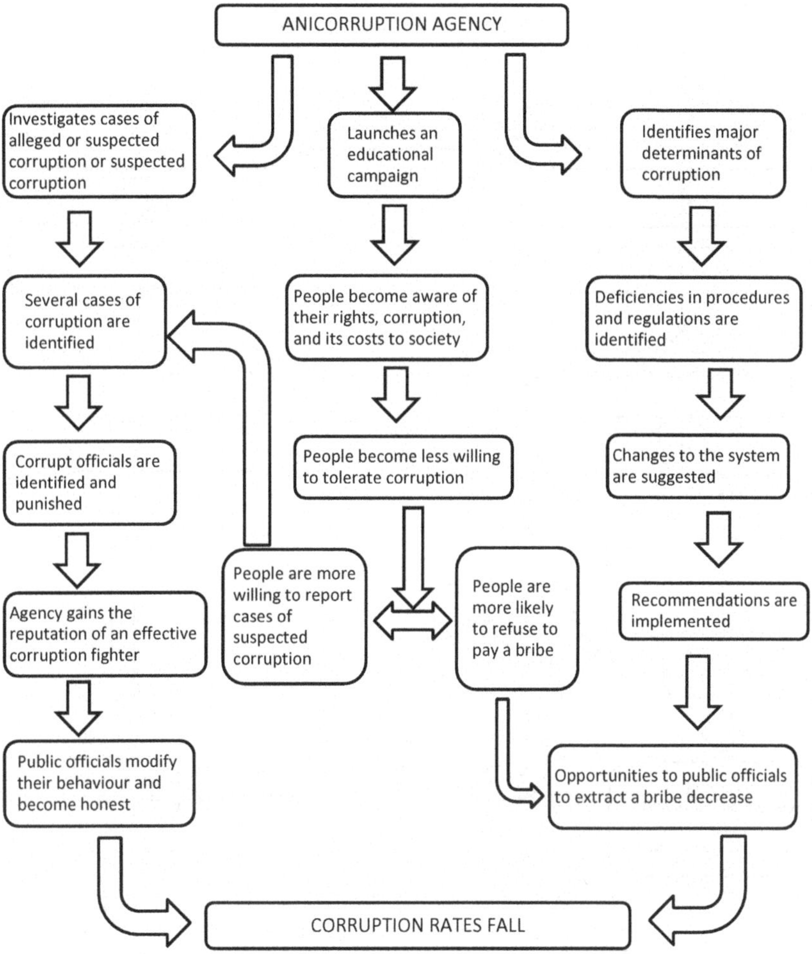

Fig. 5.8 Causal assumptions in impact of direct anticorruption activities on corruption: example of anticorruption agency. (Source: Author)

suspicion must have a sound explanation and proper documentation. In these circumstances, it is much more difficult to hide any wrongdoing such as mismanagement of public funds, theft of public assets and fraud. Public officials become more accountable for their actions, opportunities for corruption decrease, and corruption falls.

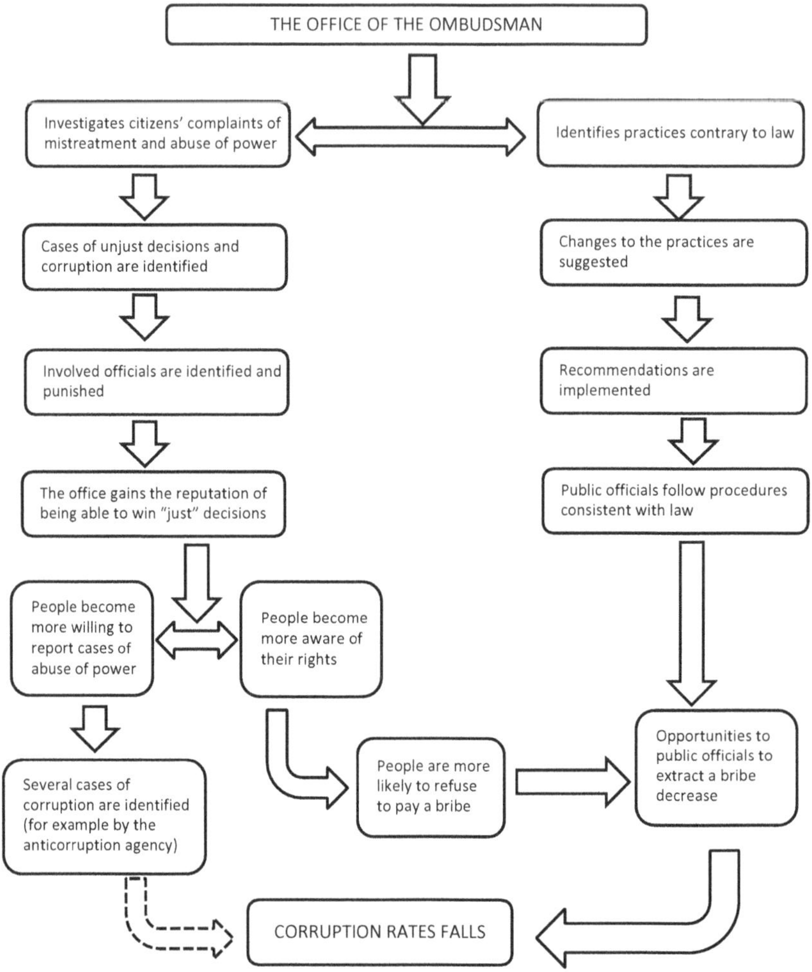

Fig. 5.9 Causal assumptions in impact of direct anticorruption activities on corruption: example of office of the ombudsman. (Source: Author)

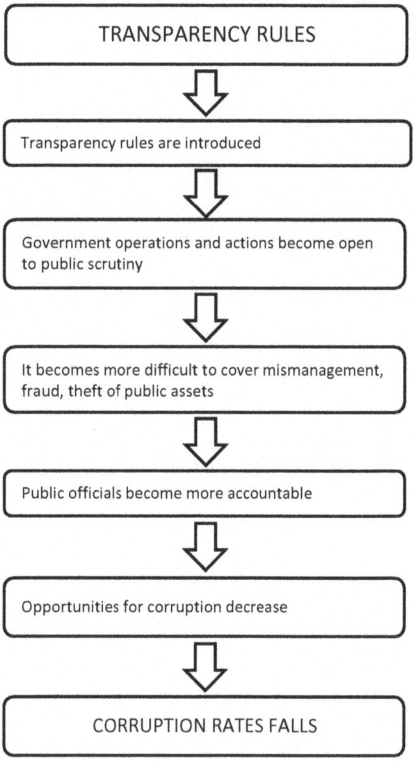

Fig. 5.10 Causal assumptions in impact of direct anticorruption activities on corruption: example of transparency rules. (Source: Author)

The diagram in Fig. 5.10 illustrates this chain of causal assumptions.

Decentralization
The local government is closer to service users and may thus have a better understanding of local needs and capabilities than the central government in the capital far away. In a decentralized system, public programs can thus be modified to better address specific local problems. This may give the local government a greater sense of influence on the performance of the local economy and the local communities a greater sense of influence on their well-being. In this system, it may be easier to encourage community participation in terms of expressing their interests and expectations and being involved in the implementation of programs. In such a decentralized system, people are more able to compare what has been collected

from them in taxes, various charges, and possibly volunteer work, with the quality and quantity of services delivered. Any inconsistencies in this regard are more easily detected and raise the question of how the money is being spent. Also, many people involved in the decision-making and service delivery process are well known in the local community and changes in their lifestyles are relatively easily observable. Inconsistencies in the lifestyles of public officials and their salaries or the state of the local economy and local public services are more easily detected. All these factors make it more difficult to hide mismanagement and fraud. This, in turn, makes public officials more accountable and decreases the incidence of corruption (see Fig. 5.11).

The Analysis

Information regarding all causal assumptions in the chain of events from implementation of anticorruption measures to decrease in corruption rates will then be collected. The assumptions will be tested to determine whether they are satisfied. If any of the links breaks down, the activity in question is not likely to contribute to the decrease in corruption. Below we discuss several vulnerable assumptions which should be carefully addressed in the actual evaluation.

Anticorruption Agency

Suppose that an anticorruption agency has been created and that the agency has three major mandates as specified in the diagram: investigation of suspected cases of corruption, education of the public, and prevention.

If the agency is understaffed and underfinanced, it is likely that it will fail to identify any major cases of corruption and the whole chain of developments in the left-hand side column in Fig. 5.8 will break down. The agency will become a façade without any real power.

Even if the agency exposes several cases of corruption, it may still be the case that the responsible officials are not identified nor punished. The reason may be that the agency is not truly independent from political influence; it may be discouraged from pointing at specific responsible individuals. The existing legal system may also have many loopholes and deficiencies which allow the suspected officials to escape the punishment. For example, they may be able to transfer stolen funds overseas, or obtain only an insignificantly small punishment. If this is the case, the decrease in corruption is not likely to materialize.

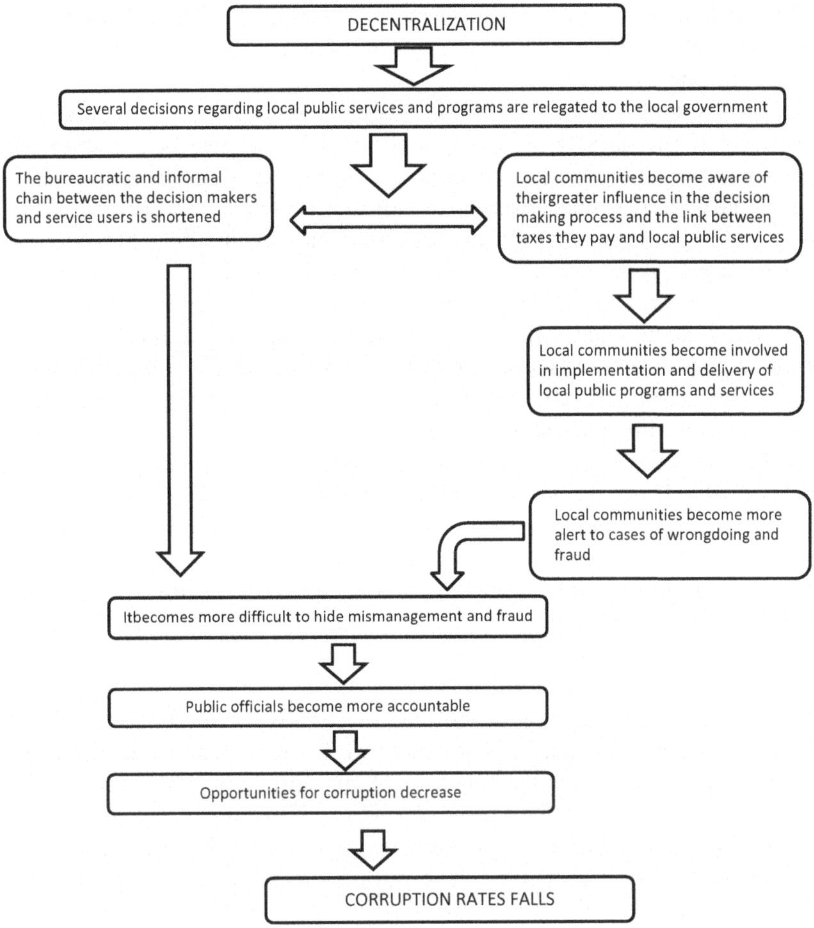

Fig. 5.11 Causal assumptions in impact of direct anticorruption activities on corruption: example of decentralization. (Source: Author)

Suppose now that the agency does discover several cases of corruption and that corrupt officials are punished. This may scare off some officials and the corruption rate may fall, at least temporarily. But this will not be sustainable if the actions of the agency were politically driven and designed to show the public some quick results. The agency will be seen as a "witch hunter" rather than a dedicated corruption fighter and it may fail to establish high reputation. If this is the case, in the long run public officials are not likely to modify their behavior and corruption rates are not likely to fall significantly.

The assumptions in the middle column describing the educational function of the anticorruption agency seem less vulnerable. It is in the agency's control to design an informative and suggestive educational campaign. However, it may still be the case that people are aware of corruption and its costs to society and that they don't like it (i.e., they become less willing to tolerate corruption), but they feel compelled to pay bribes (i.e., they are not more likely to refuse to pay a bribe). For example, they may feel that they have no choice because complaints are ineffective and there are no alternative service providers. This suggests that for the educational function of the anticorruption agency to be effective, its investigative function must have some success.

The assumptions underlying the preventive function may also easily break down. If the agency is understaffed and underfinanced, it will likely fail to identify deficiencies in the system and/or find an effective solution to these deficiencies. But even if some deficiencies are identified and changes suggested, they may simply not be implemented or may be ignored.

The Office of the Ombudsman

The chain of assumptions describing the investigative function of the office of the ombudsman is vulnerable in a way similar to assumptions underlying the investigative function of the anticorruption agency. The office may be understaffed and underfinanced and unable to investigate citizens' complaints properly. There may be loopholes in laws and regulations which make it very difficult to punish the responsible officials. The office itself may be subject to political pressure and fail to establish a reputation of an independent institution. Finally, even if people become more aware of their rights, they may still feel that they have to pay bribes (i.e., they are not less likely to refuse to pay a bribe) for the same reasons as those in the case of anticorruption agency.

The causal links describing the preventive function may easily break down at the implementation stage: the recommendations may simply not be implemented. But even if changes are implemented, public officials may still continue old corrupt practices because of lack of supervision and a small probability of detection and punishment. Finally, even if certain changes are implemented and public officials follow procedures consistent with law, there may be other deficiencies in the system and other potential sources of extortion. Public officials may concentrate their attention on those other sources and the overall rate of corruption may not necessarily decrease.

Transparency Rules
The causal assumptions underlying transparency rules seem to be relatively robust compared with anticorruption agency and the office of the ombudsman. However, transparency rules will have little impact on corruption if civil society, for some reason, is not very likely to vigorously exercise its right to scrutinize the government. This may be the case, for example, in young democracies where civil society institutions (e.g., investigative journalism) and effective opposition are not well developed. In these situations people may have a good reason to fear some form of retaliation on the part of public officials alleged to be involved in wrongdoing. In this way, the link "Public officials become more accountable" breaks down.

There is also a possibility that public officials will become more sophisticated and learn new ways to hide corruption. As a result, opportunities for corruption to public officials do not necessarily decrease after the introduction of some transparency rules.

Decentralization
As in the case of transparency rules, the causal assumptions underlying decentralization seem to be relatively robust. However, the success of decentralization in curbing corruption depends on civil society institutions. If local communities, for some reason, are not very active, or if there is no effective local opposition, there may still be cases of corruption which go on unpunished. In other words, the assumption that public officials become more accountable breaks down.

The Data

To carry out the above analysis, the following information will be required.

Anticorruption Agency

Basic Functions of the Agency
A lot of information about the activities of the anticorruption agency should be available from country sources. It should be possible to obtain

information on funding, staff, number of cases investigated, number of cases brought to court, number of convictions, number and forms of educational campaigns, and the amount of identified deficiencies in procedures and regulations and number of suggested changes. These data can be analyzed using quantitative and qualitative techniques to test most of the causal assumption underlying the preventive function as well as the initial assumptions in the chain of assumptions for the investigative and educational functions. For example, a poor record of identified cases of corruption in a country which consistently scores low in a number of corruption surveys, a large number of inconclusive and unfinished investigations, lack of focus and strategy imply that the assumption "Several cases of corruption are identified" is not in fact met. As a result, the investigative function of the anticorruption agency is not likely to contribute to a decrease in corruption rates.

Intermediate Links in the Chain of Causal Assumptions

It seems that no readily available information exists to determine whether the anticorruption agency in fact has a reputation of a corruption fighter, whether people are aware of their rights and the corruption problem, and whether they are willing to report cases of suspected corruption or likely to refuse to pay a bribe. A survey of businesses, citizens, and perhaps country experts may be necessary to collect this type of information. Private individuals could be asked to express their opinion whether certain behavior by public officials such as requesting "additional payment" constitutes corruption and whether this is justifiable under any circumstances. They could also be asked whether they have ever refused to pay a bribe and why (whatever their decision was). Businesses and country experts could be asked about the anticorruption agency, consistency of its activities and impact on an "average" public official.

Behavior of Public Officials, Opportunities to Extract Bribes

It seems that there are no readily available data to assess the opportunities to extract bribes in a country and whether officials are likely to focus on other sources of extortion when old sources dry up or when it becomes more difficult to exploit those old sources. A survey of, perhaps country experts or former public officials, could provide insider information about the common practices in public service offices, quality of bureaucracy, and morale of civil servants.

The Office of the Ombudsman
Similar type of data are required to evaluate an anticorruption program involving creation of an office of the ombudsman as these required to evaluate an anticorruption agency.

Basic Functions of the Office
A lot of information about the activities of the office of the ombudsman should be available from country sources. It should be possible to obtain information on funding, staff, number of interventions, identified practices contrary to law, and suggested changes. These data can be analyzed using qualitative and quantitative techniques to test the first three assumptions for both the investigative and preventive functions identified in Fig. 5.9. For example, a poor record of identified practices contrary to law in a country where petty corruption is widespread implies that the preventive function of the office is not likely to contribute much to a decrease in corruption.

Intermediate Links in the Chain of Causal Assumptions
It seems that no readily available data exists to determine whether the office enjoys a high reputation in the public or whether its activities make people more aware of their rights. A survey of citizens, and perhaps also of users of the office, could provide the necessary information. Citizens could be asked whether they have heard anything about the office, or whether they have learnt anything about their rights since the time the office was created. Service users could be interviewed about their overall experience with the office and the impact of this experience on their lives and their families. Citizens could also be asked whether they have ever refused to pay a bribe and whether they would report a case of corruption (and why).

Opportunities to Extract Bribes
The same type of information is required as that for anticorruption agencies. The same type of survey could provide this information.

Transparency Rules
Some information necessary to test the causal assumptions could be collected from country sources. Various information on local governments may be helpful in this regard, for example, government size and structure, its governance style, record of consultations with local communities, handling of complaints and suggestions, procedures for obtaining information about government finances, and operational activities.

Country experts could be surveyed on the political situation at the local level, in particular on activities of parties at the local level and presence of political opposition. For example, if the government is very slow in responding to citizens' complaints and if there is no effective local opposition, the assumption that public officials become more accountable will likely break down.

An independent audit of the local government could reveal whether there are any inconsistencies in government finances or possibilities for "creative accounting."

Decentralization

Some information necessary to test the initial causal assumptions could be collected from country sources. Various information on local public services and participation of local communities may be useful, for example: types of public services run by the local governments, record of consultations with the local communities, handling of complaints and suggestions, participation of local communities in the implementation/delivery of services (composition of local school boards and presence of members from the general public, local social programs initiatives and involvement of volunteers, etc.). A survey of local communities may also be necessary to obtain more insights on the types and quality of local public services and involvement of local communities in the delivery of these services.

As in the case of transparency rules, country experts could be interviewed about the political situation at the local level. For example, a time-consuming mechanism of complaints combined with lack of effective opposition may cause the assumption of greater accountability of public officials to break down.

References

Berg, Andrew, and Elliot Berg. 1997. Methods of Privatization. *Journal of International Affairs* 50 (2): 357–390.

CIET International. 1996. *Service Delivery Survey: Corruption in the Police, Judiciary, Revenue, and Land Services.* Dar es Salaam: CIET International and EDI World Bank.

Kaufmann, Daniel, and Paul Siegelbaum. 1997. Privatization and Corruption in Transition Economies. *Journal of International Affairs* 50 (2): 419–458.

Silvani, Carlos, and Katherine Baer. 1997. *Designing a Tax Administration Reform Strategy: Experiences and Guidelines.* IMF Working Paper WP/97/30, March.

Tanzi, Vito, and Anthony Pellechio. 1995. *The Reform of Tax Administration.* IMF Working Paper WP/95/22, February.

CHAPTER 6

A Framework for Evaluating Anti-Corruption Policies and Programs

Jeff Huther and Anwar Shah

The impact of corruption on public service delivery performance and poverty alleviation is widely recognized (see, e.g., Tomaszewska and Shah 2000 for empirical evidence). A wide consensus has also recently emerged that corruption is a symptom of failed governance (see World Bank 2000a), and hence curtailing corruption requires addressing the causes of misgovernance. Nevertheless, the menu of potential actions to curtail corruption is very large so a framework is needed that provides guidance on ordering potential actions. Prioritization of various actions depends on both the conceptual and empirical views of what works and what does not work in the context of particular countries. Such a framework is also needed for evaluating country anti-corruption programs and policies. This chapter proposes a framework for such evaluations.

J. Huther
Board of Governors, Federal Reserve Board, Washington, DC, USA
e-mail: jeffrey.w.huther@frb.gov

A. Shah (✉)
Governance Studies, Brookings Institution, Washington, DC, USA

© The Author(s) 2020

A. Shah (ed.), *Policy, Program and Project Evaluation*,
https://doi.org/10.1007/978-3-030-48567-2_6

A Simple Evaluation Framework

To focus attention on the corruption aspects of development programs, we use a framework based on the incentives for opportunistic behavior by public officials.[1] To distinguish between highly corrupt and largely corruption-free societies, consider the conditions that encourage public officials to seek out or accept corruption:

- The expected gains exceed the expected costs of undertaking a corrupt act.
- Little weight is placed on the cost that corruption imposes on others.

The first point is based on pure self-interest: corruption will only take place when officials expect to derive net positive benefit from the transaction. Successful anti-corruption programs will lower the expected gains and raise the expected penalties of corrupt behavior. That is, anti-corruption programs must change the cost-benefit calculations of public officials who believe that the expected net benefits of corruption are positive. A self-interested individual will seek out or accept corruption if the expected gains outweigh the costs, i.e. when:

$$E[B] = n \times E[G] - \text{prob}[P] \times [P] > 0$$

where

E is the expectations operator
n is number of corrupt transactions
G is the gain from the corrupt transaction
prob[P] is the probability of paying a penalty
P is the penalty for the corrupt activity

[1] We recognize that corruption entails the actions of private agents as well as public officials (the "demand side" for corruption in the case of bribery). We focus only on the supply of corruption by public officials because a government that is unable to improve the incentives of its own employees is unlikely to affect private sector agents (i.e. demand can safely be thought of as constant in highly corrupt societies) since a government has significantly fewer policy actions for discouraging corruption by private agents than for discouraging corruption among public officials.

Based on cost-benefit considerations, anti-corruption programs can influence corruption through four mechanisms—reducing the number of transactions involving public officials, reducing the scope for gains from each transaction, increasing the probability of paying a penalty, or increasing the penalty from corrupt behavior. The factors influencing each element of a public official's cost-benefit analysis are described in the following paragraphs and listed in Table 6.1.

Table 6.1 The influence of anti-corruption programs on officials' cost-benefit analysis

Number of corrupt transactions	*Gross gains from corruption*	*Probability of paying penalty*	*Magnitude of penalty*	*Actions not influencing cost benefit analysis*
Bureaucratic culture—Streamlining services	Economic reform—Improving competitive environment	Anti-corruption agencies	Rationalization of laws	Raising awareness of public through seminars
Creating or raising public service standards	Scaling down individual public projects	Parliamentary oversight		Public opinion surveys
Reducing public employment	Bureaucratic culture	Ombudsman		Raising public sector wages
Reducing public sector size	Referenda on large public projects	Financial accountability		Reducing wage compression
Financial liberalization		Media independence		
Increasing transparency		Judicial independence		
Decentralization of public services		Citizen participation		
Economic reform—Privatization		Rule of law		
		Ethics office		

Source: Authors

Reducing Expected Gross Benefits[2] The expected net benefit derived from corruption is context-dependent on the factors that influence a public official's expectations—a country's historical treatment of corrupt activities, the quality of the judicial framework, the strength and scope of enforcement institutions, and the potential for changes in these characteristics for escaping the procedures of legal recourse with illegal maneuvers. Thus relevant anti-corruption policies geared towards reducing the gross gains will vary with the institutional environment of each country. Transaction value can be reduced by scaling down of individual projects, requiring popular referenda for large projects with votes both on tax and expenditure allocation choices, de-monopolizing public services, promoting competition in the private sector, increasing the share of financing from domestic taxes or user charges,[3] and bringing a culture of new contractualism to the public sector.

Reducing the Number of Transactions Policies which reduce the number of transactions that create opportunities for graft and private capture of public programs can include streamlining bureaucracy, economic or financial liberalization (e.g. deregulation, freer trade, etc.), improving service standards, and decentralizing government services. Privatization can reduce the number of transactions but, as recent experience in Eastern Europe shows, the privatization process itself involves transactions which may strengthen the hold of vested and sometimes corrupt interests so businesses operating in a competitive environment, free of state financing, and with adequate governance safeguards may or may not emerge from privatization.

[2] A large subset of expected benefits is captured in the commonly cited formula, Monopoly + Discretion − Accountability (Klitgaard 1988). By focusing on the actions of individual officials, we hope to highlight the difficulties in improving accountability and the implications of greater accountability on a country's institutional framework. In addition, in a country with adequate governance arrangements, discretion by public officials may be welfare-enhancing—it is discretion, after all, that is likely to provide efficiency gains in the public sector (even for public services that are not highly contestable).

[3] Domestic finance is important because it forces deliberate choices on the trade-off between the pain of taxation and the pleasure of spending by the government and the citizenry.

Increasing the Probability of Paying Penalties[4] Increasing the probability of penalties is a three-step process: detection, prosecution, and exacting the penalty. In cases where corruption is extortion for jobs that should be done as a matter of public service, improved detection is straightforward—increase citizen participation in the electoral process, establish citizens' charters specifying expected service standards, allow media independence, make interactions between the public and private sectors more transparent, and strengthen the rule of law so that both individuals and the media do not fear reprisals.

Increasing the Magnitude of Penalties There are corrupt societies which have stiff penalties for corruption, suggesting the magnitude of penalties may not be a strong deterrent to corruption.[5] In general, people may not respond much differently to, say, an increase in penalties from five to ten years in prison, as Malaysia did in 1997 with no discernible change in perceptions of corruption (as measured by Transparency International). In some countries, however, the legislation setting penalties may be ambiguous or penalties may be set at the discretion of judges. In either case, a country may discourage corruption by clarifying corruption penalties. While the Bank may provide assistance in clarifying legislation, setting criminal penalties is outside the scope of its work.

In cases where corruption is in the form of bribes to alter the normal course of government, increased transparency of government operations reduces the opportunity for undetected corruption (e.g. clearly defined bidding processes, open judicial proceedings, strict rules on gift-giving) and increasing the number of competitors reduces the potential gains while increasing scrutiny of bidding processes. Prosecution requires judicial independence and transparency. For the judicial system to exact

[4] There may also be losses that occur with certainty, for example if an official has to "buy" a position that offers potentially large gains from corrupt activities. While this type of situation should not affect the officials cost-benefit analysis (since the price paid for the position is a sunk cost), it does raise an equity issue. In cases where endemic corruption has led to a tradition of buying public positions, serious anti-corruption efforts could, conceivably, include partial compensation for current office holders (declining in value with tenure). In practice, such a system is likely to be too prone to abuse to be feasible.

[5] For example, countries such as China and Vietnam, which are perceived to have relatively high levels of corruption, have sentenced people to death for graft.

penalties, it must have sufficient resources and independence. To the extent that penalties are reputational, media independence is a crucial element to deterrence.

While a more complete treatment would include the incentives of private sector agents who interact with public officials, policies affecting private sector incentives are largely outside the scope of Bank work. Policies which increase the magnitude of penalties or the expected probability of paying penalties, however, are likely to have similar effects on the private sector as they do on the public sector. The focus on public officials excludes consideration of policies, typically in countries with low levels of corruption, that penalize private sector efforts to participate in corruption in other countries. These policies are potentially relevant to anti-corruption efforts, but are outside the scope of our framework (and most Bank work). In terms of domestic policies, we believe that the focus on public officials is appropriate even if well-designed policies may reduce the incentives of the private sector to engage in corruption. The argument is that a government which cannot influence the incentives of its own officials is unlikely to be able to reduce private sector incentives to engage in corruption (see Table 6.1).

In the formulation above, an official's income does not have an effect on whether or not to engage in corrupt activities. Two concerns have been raised with this approach. One is that officials paid less than subsistence income are forced to undertake corrupt activities to survive, the second is that, at some high level of income, officials should be unwilling to risk that income to gain more through corrupt activities. Both arguments require an assumption that officials are motivated to follow the rule of law regardless of whether they see it as a threat to their income from corrupt activities. The argument put forward in this chapter is that officials are not so motivated in countries in which the rule of law is weak.[6]

The large number of potential incentive targets and anti-corruption actions listed in Table 6.1 raise two questions:

- How to establish the priorities of anti-corruption campaign
- Which actions should be used to meet those targets

[6] A similar argument applies on the penalties side. The alternatives to public sector employment tend to be worse in countries with high levels of corruption. Given poor alternatives, we would expect public officials to be unwilling to risk their careers for small temporary gains. While in some cases an argument can be made for desperation on the part of public officials, more generally it seems likely that officials in highly corrupt societies do not see the rule of law as a risk to their careers.

Economic theory suggests that high-priority programs are those that address large welfare losses caused by corruption. Two practical considerations make prioritization based on welfare losses difficult: quantifying corruption losses is often not possible and large losses are often the result of multiple governance failures. The result is that prioritization of anti-corruption campaigns must rely on the analysis of an individual country's economic, political, and bureaucratic conditions.

Prioritization based on welfare losses highlights one of the problems with using survey data to construct an anti-corruption program. High visibility corruption, which is likely to be identified by surveys, may have significantly lower welfare costs than less visible corruption. It is possible, for example, that the public is highly aware of corruption causing marginal losses in traffic enforcement, utility hook-ups, or business permits but largely ignorant of the economic distortions caused by revenue losses through tax evasion by wealthy individuals and large corporations.

In determining which actions should be used, Table 6.1 suggests actions which vary depending on the weaknesses of a specific government. For a country in which the government that is disproportionally large, actions which reduce the size of government are likely to reduce the scope for corruption. For a country in which a few officials appear to have become very wealthy in public service, actions should aim to reduce the gross gains from corruption. For a country in which few are held accountable for corrupt activities, anti-corruption efforts should focus on judicial independence resources.

Empirical evidence for individual anti-corruption efforts is listed in Table 6.2. Widespread corruption, however, is likely to be the result of multiple governance failures so successful anti-corruption campaigns are likely to be multi-pronged. For example, an official's cost-benefit analysis suggests that raising public sector wages, by itself, is unlikely to lead to lower corruption.[7] A program that ties wage increases to increases in satisfaction with public services, however, may encourage public officials to trade income from corrupt sources for legitimate income. The

[7] This assertion is supported indirectly by observation in countries facing widespread corruption that wealthy officials are at least as susceptible to corrupt activities as poor ones (among examples of wealthy officials convicted of corruption are two former South Korean presidents, a former Pakistani prime minister, and a former mayor of Beijing). In economic terms, we are arguing that, for an average individual, the utility of wealth function is not highly concave. Evidence directly supporting this assertion is difficult to obtain, given the need to make inter-personal comparisons of utility.

Table 6.2 Empirical evidence on selected anti-corruption programs

Program	*Empirical evidence*
Anti-corruption agencies	Anti-corruption agencies have been successful in Chile, Hong Kong, New South Wales, Australia, and Singapore (Klitgaard 1988; Segal 1999 and World Bank 2000a). Developing country officials however do not see these as effective anti-corruption tools in countries with endemic corruption (Shah 2007)
Public opinion surveys	Public opinion surveys have served as a useful tool in articulating more precisely citizens' concerns (e.g. Bangalore scorecard and a "corruptometer" by an Argentine NGO). International surveys, such as those compiled by transparency international, highlight countries in which corruption is perceived to be endemic
Raising public sector wages	Van Rijckeghem and Weder (1997) find no short-run impact (as the income from bribery dominates total income). Gurgur and Shah (1999, 2002) find a negative yet insignificant effect. Treisman (1999a, b, 2000, 2007, 2010) and Swamy et al. (1999) find no relationship. The Swiss Development Corporation experience in the forestry sector in Pakistan also confirms this. In corrupt societies public positions are often purchased by borrowing money from family and friends. Raising public sector wages simply raises the purchase price and subsequent corruption efforts to repay loans. Of course raising public sector wages which do not allow the employee to satisfy the basic needs of his/her family are likely to reduce petty corruption
Reducing public sector size	Tanzi and Davoodi (1998) and La Porta et al. (1997) find that reduction in public sector size leads to less corruption. Gurgur and Shah (2002) find that this result only holds when important variables such as judiciary, democratic institutions, colonial heritage, decentralization, and bureaucratic culture are omitted. Elliott (1997) finds an inverse relationship between the budget size and corruption. Privatization in some countries (e.g. Russia) has led to increased corruption and exploitation. Thus appropriate role of the government is the critical element for discussion on corruption
Financial accountability	Gurgur and Shah (1999, 2002) find a negative yet insignificant association
Media independence	Freedom of press is negatively correlated with the level of corruption (see Brunetti and Weder 1998)
Judicial independence	Judicial independence reduces corruption as confirmed by Ades and Di Tella (1995, 1996, 1997), Goel and Nelson (1998), and Gurgur and Shah (1999, 2002)
Citizen participation	Citizen participation leads to reduced corruption as confirmed in Gurgur and Shah (1999, 2002)

(*continued*)

Table 6.2 (continued)

Program	*Empirical evidence*
Decentralization	Huther and Shah (1998), Gurgur and Shah (2002), Ivanyna and Shah (2011, 2014), and Fisman and Gatti (2002) find a negative relationship between decentralization and corruption. See also Arikan (2004), Carbonara (1999), Crook and Manor (2000), Fan et al. (2009), Bardhan and Mookherjee (2005), Shah et al. (2004), and Shah (2015) for surveys of the literature
Bureaucratic culture	Gurgur and Shah (1999, 2002) find a positive relationship between command and control type civil service orientation and corruption

Source: Authors

effectiveness of such a program may be further enhanced if it is jointly undertaken with efforts to increase the probability of paying penalties, say through efforts to increase judicial independence.

Corruption in the Presence of Altruism

While the presence of wide-spread corruption suggests a lack of altruism among public officials, some may be motivated, in part, by a desire to perform civic duties or a desire to help others. In corrupt societies, however, otherwise altruistically motivated officials may participate in corruption because:

- Officials believe that their careers can be advanced by corrupt practices.
- Corruption acts as an insurance against risk in an unstable and uncertain political environment.
- Officials may believe that their marginal contributions to the burden of corruption are insignificant.
- Corruption may be reinforced by prejudice or tradition.
- Officials may believe that their actions are an appropriate "fend for yourself" response in an inhospitable environment with large income inequalities.

Policies which promote altruistic behavior face significant hurdles. Widespread corruption is likely to be influenced by multiple factors. Consequently, an anti-corruption program which focuses on officials' concerns for others is unlikely to be effective unless it simultaneously addresses these factors—awareness or selective enforcement campaigns may fail if officials do not believe most other officials will not change their ways, creation of ethics offices and ombudsmen may actually lead to greater entrenchment of underlying prejudices or traditions, and public opinion surveys may confirm officials' views of their clients.

While policies that promote altruism seem unlikely to be successful by themselves, programs which influence officials' cost-benefit analysis may also reinforce altruistic motivations. Efforts to improve service delivery or policies which reward performance should be effective from either a cost-benefit or altruistic perspective.

Adapting World Bank Evaluation Methodology to the Evaluation of Anti-Corruption Programs

The above discussion provides us with some background to apply the World Bank methodology in evaluating anti-corruption programs. In the following, the key criteria used in the World Bank methodology are discussed.[8]

Relevance

World Bank defines relevance as "the extent to which the project's objectives are consistent with the country's current development priorities and with current Bank country and sectoral assistance strategies and corporate goals."[9] Thus anti-corruption programs are judged to be relevant if they have the potential to achieve their objectives given a country's existing institutional and policy environment.

Schacter and Shah (2004) argue that judgment about relevance combine two distinct factors: technical relevance and welfare relevance. Technical relevance refers to the impact of specific activities on the incidence of corruption and the welfare relevance relates to the relative importance, for growth and poverty reduction of a particular type of corruption.

[8] This section draws heavily upon Mark Schacter's comments on an earlier version of this note. Several of his comments have been added verbatim.

[9] For details on the definitions in this section and World Bank methodology more generally, see World Bank (2000b).

Highly relevant Bank-supported interventions target (a) the known causes of given types of corruption and (b) the forms of corruption that are believed to have a strong negative effect on growth and poverty reduction. As a first step, Bank-supported intervention is assessed on whether it is likely to have an impact on a given form of corruption by changing the incentives of public officials (technical relevance). This requires identification of the particular causes of corruption in the particular country setting. The intervention then must be assessed on how that particular type of corruption is likely to be affecting growth and poverty reduction. This requires a view on the link between a particular form of corruption and development within a specific country (welfare relevance).

So the evaluation of the relevance of a Bank-supported intervention combines judgments about both the suitability of any particular intervention (targeting) and the importance of one particular form of corruption relative to any other (potential for welfare gains). For example, one could imagine a case where an intervention was well suited to the form of corruption in question, but where the particular form of corruption had relatively little negative impact on growth and poverty reduction. Explicit anti-corruption efforts such as setting up of anti-corruption agency, ethics office, and requiring no bribery pledge, for example, are likely to be less effective in countries lacking a functioning legal system, without accountability of government, or inadequate financial transparency. Given this breadth of issues, we have used a stylized view of countries based on broad categories of "Poor," "Fair," and "Good" governance to classify countries by incidence of corruption and the likely consequences of anti-corruption efforts (see Table 6.3).[10]

Efficacy

The World Bank defines efficacy as "the extent to which the project's objectives were achieved, or expected to be achieved, taking into account their relative importance." This requires measurement of the effect of a given set of anti-corruption activities on levels of corruption or corrupt activities. Of interest is the measurement of changes in levels of corruption as well as the degree to which observed changes can credibly be attributed to the anti-corruption interventions. Both these issues are subject to large

[10] For a discussion of the measurement of quality of governance and country rankings, see Huther and Shah (1998) or Kaufmann et al. (1999).

Table 6.3 Ratings on relevance of a menu of anti-corruption programs

Program	*Country's quality of governance*			*Comments*
	Weak	*Fair*	*Good*	
Raising public awareness of corruption through seminars	Not relevant	Low	Medium	In countries with weak governance, corrupt practices and agents are generally well known
Raising awareness of public officials through seminars	Not relevant	Low	Medium	Public officials may be aware of corruption but unwilling and/or unable to take action due to incentive problems in countries with weak governance
Anti-corruption agencies/ ombudsman	Not relevant	Low	Medium	With endemic corruption, anti-corruption agencies or ombudsman may actually extort rents. Positive influence if pre-conditions for good governance exist
Ethics office	Not relevant	Low	Medium	Positive influence may be limited to societies with good governance
Raising public sector wages	Negligible	Low	Medium	May have positive impact on petty corruption but little impact on grand corruption. Negative impact if part of problem is excessive public employment
Reducing wage compression	Negligible	Negligible	Negligible	More relevant as an incentive mechanism for career development. May increase corruption if the public sector is viewed as lucrative career option by greedy elements of society
Merit-based civil service	Low	Medium	High	May be derailed by bureaucratic processes in highly corrupt societies
Public opinion surveys	Low	Medium	Medium	Public opinion surveys have served as a useful tool in articulating citizens' concerns (e.g. Bangalore scorecard)

(*continued*)

Table 6.3 (continued)

Program	*Country's quality of governance*			*Comments*
	Weak	*Fair*	*Good*	
Financial accountability	Low	Low	Medium	Appropriate when democratic accountability and a substantial accounting/bookkeeping infrastructure with some integrity are in place
Parliamentary oversight	Low	Medium	Medium	Parliamentary oversight can be helpful but parliamentary micro-management not an effective form of governance
Reducing public employment	Medium	Low	Low	May reduce opportunities for corruption
Decentralization	Medium	Low	Low	May improve accountability and may increase sense of social purpose for public officials
Client-based civil service/bureaucratic culture	Medium	Medium	Low	Success depends upon service delivery orientation of public service, reinforced by accountability for results
Economic policy reform	High	Medium	Low	Reduces potential corruption by shifting decision-making to the private sector
Media and judicial independence, citizen participation	High	Medium	Low	Allows for detection, followed by accountability
Reducing public sector size	High	Medium	Low	By reducing the number of government activities, officials can focus on primary objectives of the state
Rule of law	High	Medium	Low	Essential for any progress

Source: Authors

measurement errors. Judgments need to be made about the degree to which Bank-supported interventions have (i) reduced, (ii) had no impact upon, or (iii) led to an increase in the levels of various forms of corruption in the country. For practical purposes, efficacy evaluation will need to focus on the relationship between Bank-supported interventions and changes in key corruption drivers.

Efficiency

The World Bank defines efficiency as "the extent to which the project achieved or is expected to achieve, a return higher than the opportunity cost of capital and benefits at least compared to alternatives" (see World Bank 2000b, p. 3). An anti-corruption program is considered *efficient* if it generates maximum reduction in the incidence of corruption (good targeting) and associated welfare gains at the least cost. The same data constraints noted above apply here. Efficiency would ideally be based on the cost of Bank-supported interventions in relation to outcomes at the level of corruption. In the absence of direct measures of levels of corruption, assumptions about changes in levels of corruption have to be based on changes in proxy measures. Therefore, the evaluation will focus on the relationship between the cost of anti-corruption interventions and changes in incentives.

Sustainability

The World Bank defines sustainability as "the resilience to risk of net benefit flows over time" (see World Bank 2000b, p. 4). The assessment of sustainability would take into account political, economic, financial, social, and external factors. In terms of anti-corruption activities, sustainable actions are likely to be those which change the expectations of the accountability of public officials. Risk reduction in anti-corruption efforts, like risk reduction in financial management, is likely to be aided by diversification. In countries with limited restraints on corruption, anti-corruption activities which rely on a single office, official, or regulation face a high risk that benefits will be lost over time. Conversely, broad-based efforts to improve accountability, reduce the monopoly power of government, or create judicial independence are likely to create sustainable reductions in corruption. Table 6.4 provides a summary of these ratings.

This framework highlights the difficulty of an anti-corruption campaign—successful campaigns reduce the welfare of some public officials. In this environment, Bank staff have to operate opportunistically in pursuing anti-corruption policies. The implication is that anti-corruption campaigns cannot be applied uniformly in terms of either timeframe or policy reach. As a result, some evaluations may show that in some countries, at some times, anti-corruption efforts are not worthwhile either because political opportunities do not exist or because welfare gains are not likely to be significant.

Table 6.4 Summary of proposed rating factors for anti-corruption programs

Relevance	Program objectives consistent with country's development priorities, with Bank strategy Program design underpinned by analytical work that recognizes country-specific public sector mission and values, opportunities and constraints, and an informed view of potential impacts of alternative actions Judgments as to (a) the degree to which the anti-corruption programs were targeted to corruption drivers and (b) the relationship between those drivers, corruption, and welfare outcomes
Efficacy	The extent to which the project's objectives were achieved, or expected to be achieved, taking into account their relative importance in curtailing corruption Judgments to be made about the degree to which Bank-supported interventions have (i) reduced, (ii) had no impact, or (iii) led to an increase in the levels of various forms of corruption in the country. As a proxy focus on the relationship between Bank-supported interventions and changes in key corruption drivers
Efficiency	Generates most reductions in corruption and associated welfare gains for the least cost Targets corruption that has large costs
Sustainability	The resilience to risk of net benefit flows over time based upon an assessment of political, economic, financial, social, and external influences

Source: Authors

Conclusion

As noted earlier, path dependency is critical in determining the relative efficacy of various anti-corruption programs. For example, in a largely corruption-free environment, anti-corruption agencies, ethics offices, and ombudsman serve to enhance the standards of accountability. In countries with endemic corruption, the same institutions serve a function in form only and not in substance. Under a best-case scenario, these institutions might be helpful, but the more likely outcome is that they help to preserve the existing system of social injustice.

Successful anti-corruption programs are those which address the underlying governance failures, resulting in lower opportunities for gain and a greater likelihood of sanctions. Thus, programs have to be targeted to a country's existing quality of governance. Past experiences of the industrialized world confirm these conclusions since, without exception, these countries did not achieve reduction in corruption by introducing technocratic solutions but, rather, by encouraging a sense of public duty among

Table 6.5 Effective anti-corruption programs based on governance quality

Incidence of corruption	*Governance quality*	*Priorities of anti-corruption efforts (based on drivers of corruption)*
High	Poor	Establish rule of law; strengthen institutions of participation and accountability; limit government interventions to focus on core mandate
Medium	Fair	Decentralization and economic policy reforms; results-oriented management and evaluation; introduction of incentives for competitive public service delivery
Low	Good	Explicit anti-corruption programs such as anti-corruption agencies; strengthening financial management; raising public and officials awareness; no bribery pledges; fry big fish; etc.

Source: Authors

officials through accountability for results. Such an accountability culture came about by empowering people and decentralizing decision-making (see Shah 1999). These conclusions suggest the following stylized presentation of anti-corruption measures based on the existing quality of governance (see Table 6.5).

Addressing the governance failures which distort officials' cost-benefit assessment is likely to be the only route to success in countries with high levels of corruption and poor governance since direct dialogue on corruption is likely to be counter-productive (resulting in simply another level of corrupt officials under the name of anti-corruption offices). In countries with poor governance quality, external advice can promote economic liberalization, judicial reform, and greater public participation in public expenditure decisions without explicitly raising contentious issues of corruption and, one hopes, without threatening their existing relationships. In countries with modest levels of corruption and governance quality, where the existing governance structure has the capacity to reform, it is important to focus on improvements in readily identifiable output indicators rather than uncertain measures of corruption as measures of success. In countries with high governance quality, explicit efforts to reduce corruption are likely to be successful—commissions on corruption, ombudsmen, ethics offices, and the like can rely on an infrastructure of public accountability and transparency to ensure that their findings result in lower incentives to commit corrupt acts.

Annex: Framework for Evaluation of the Relevance of Anti-Corruption Policies—Principal-Agent Theory and New Institutional Economics

Moral Hazard Issues

a. One intellectual framework often used for analyzing corruption is principal-agent theory, as developed in the economics literature in recent decades. In this framework, there is a principal (say a supervisor) dealing with an agent (say an employee) in a situation of asymmetric information. Specifically, the agent knows more about the details of his work than does the principal. The objectives of the principal and the agent are normally not identical. The principal can collect various types of information (with specified costs of information collection) and she can specify the criteria according to which the agent will be rewarded or punished. A rich literature has developed spelling out the kinds of reward systems and information collection mechanisms that will enable the principal to maximize the attainment of her objectives, subject to the resource and information constraints. It is generally assumed in this literature that both the principal and the agent are self-interested, rational, and calculative.
b. One way to apply this framework to corruption in public bureaucracies is to suppose that top-level politicians and administrators want public services to be delivered without corruption on the part of the employees. In that case, the top-level decision-makers would set up a meritocratic civil service along the lines described long ago by Max Weber. Recruitment would be by examination, salaries would be generous, employment would be secure as long as the rules were not broken by employees, retirement pensions would be generous but would be contingent on following the rules, and so forth. Of course there would be clear lines of authority, and accounting systems and auditing procedures would be put in place to monitor employee performance and uncover corruption.
c. If we look at the incentives facing the employee, we see that there are benefits and costs of engaging in corruption. The rational, self-interested bureaucrat calculates the expected net benefits to himself of breaking the rules and engaging in illicit exchanges with private

interests, extortion of private actors, and theft of public assets. As discussed above, the benefits can be monetary or non-monetary, and easy or hard for outsiders to detect. The expected costs to the bureaucrat are the probability of paying a penalty times the magnitude of the penalty. The penalties can take the form of fines, imprisonment, loss of job and pension, public humiliation, and so forth.

d. The top-level decision-makers can manipulate the benefits and expected costs in various ways. The bribes that public officials can extract are strongly influenced by the value to private interests of the services the officials have to offer. In an economic regime of price controls, exchange restrictions, directed credit, import quotas, industrial licensing, public officials have a very strong bargaining position vis-à-vis private interests. Thus economic liberalization ("neoclassical" economic policy reform) can be a powerful tool for curbing corruption. The expected costs of corruption depend on the probabilities of detection, prosecution, and exaction of a penalty. The probability of detection can be increased by inspections and audits. The most corrupt countries are most in need of these agencies. Inspections and audits can only be effective when the agencies conducting them are not corrupt themselves. This is less likely to be the case the more corrupt the country is. The penalty of dismissal and loss of pension can be exacted by the public agency itself, while the probability of prosecution and judicial punishment depend on the competence and motivations within the judicial system.

e. A widely used formula for analyzing corruption control is Corruption = Monopoly + Discretion − Accountability (Klitgaard 1988). Corruption can sometimes be reduced by permitting competition among public agencies (in granting licenses or permits, for example). Corruption can also be controlled by limiting the discretion of public employees, for example by allowing an employee only certain types of actions. Accountability can be enhanced by inspections, audits, and follow-up procedures that result in penalties for discovered violations. It should be noted, however, that discretion is not necessarily the enemy of organizational efficiency. Organization theorists and practitioners have found that the most efficient organizations are not those that follow the rules rigidly in a Weberian manner, but those that permit and encourage their members to exert effort, exercise initiative, and take responsibility (as discussed in

Clague 1993 and many other places). Understanding this type of behavior requires us to move away from the strictly rational self-interest assumption of principal/agent theory, and to recognize the possibility of group identity, internalization of group goals, and *esprit de corps*. Organizations that succeed in eliciting effort, initiative, and responsible behavior from their employees are found much more frequently in the private sector of developed countries than in their public sectors, and they are probably extremely rare in the public sectors of less-developed countries. But the possibility of creating such organizations in the public sectors of poor countries should not be ruled out, and this has implications for designing rules to curb corruption in these organizations (see the discussion of reforming the Mexican internal revenue service in Das-Gupta and Mookherjee 1998).

f. Principal/agent theory can also be used when we relax the assumption that top-level decision-makers are interested in the corruption-free delivery of public services. In this analysis, the principal may be the public and the political leaders may be their agents. This is known as the theory of common agency. The degree of control that the public exerts over political leaders is obviously much less strict than the control of a supervisor over her employee. However, some of the same principles apply: the principal should collect information and reward and punish agents according to their performance. A rich body of democratic theory has been devoted to this problem, and the outlines of a properly functioning democratic system are well known. All countries fall short of the ideal of democratic accountability, but the shortfalls are especially severe in most less-developed countries, most of which cannot be considered to be democracies at all. Even most of those that meet the minimal conditions of electoral democracy do not have good systems of accountability of politicians and public officials. Strengthening institutions of accountability is one important strategy of corruption control, but principal/agent theory is not particularly helpful in analyzing this problem. For this, we turn to institutional analysis.

Institutional Analysis of Corruption

g. The New Institutional Economics (NIE), a development of the last few decades, helps to explain how institutions affect economic development and how institutions change over time. In addressing these issues of the determinants and the consequences of different institutional arrangements, the NIE has broadened its assumptions from those of traditional neoclassical theory to include a wider range of causal factors. At the same time, some branches of political science have developed a style of analysis similar to economics and they have also devoted much attention to the role of institutions in political outcomes. Thus there is a new style of institutional analysis that has been developed by both economists and political scientists. While it is often called the New Institutional Economics, that name is perhaps no longer appropriate, and in any case the analysis recognizes that economic development can only be understood by taking politics seriously. In other words, a country's economic progress depends critically on its political as well as its economic institutions.
h. In the NIE, institutions are the humanly devised rules of the game. Institutions form a complex set of rules, some fundamental for the society and others applicable only to particular organizations. Organizations are institutions themselves, and they are players in economic and political games that are conducted under other institutions. An important idea in the NIE is that the games can have multiple equilibria. For example, within an organization or within a political framework, if other people follow the rules, then it is in each individual's interest to do so too. On the other hand, if rule breaking is widespread, individuals find it to their advantage to ignore the formal rules.
i. A situation in which no rules prevail can be called one that is not institutionalized. A prominent analysis of politics in less-developed countries characterizes these countries as lacking in institutionalization (Huntington 2002). While not all institutions are beneficial to society, the near absence of institutions is considered to be a very serious problem for development.
j. Institutional analysis can take place on different levels. One can take as given the more fundamental institutions of society and examine the choices at a lower level. For example, given a functioning mar-

ket economy, one can analyze the organizational forms best suited to a small biotech firm or to a national retail chain. Alternatively, given a society's culture and democratic constitutional framework, one can analyze how different campaign finance rules affect political outcomes. At a deeper level, one can visualize the constitutional political order or the cultural characteristics of societies as institutions that have emerged out of the largely self-interested actions of individuals. As one progresses from smaller-scale to larger-scale institutions, the role of conscious planning of the institution diminishes. The important economic and political institutions of most societies are not the result of conscious planning by small groups of people but are the unplanned outcomes, over long periods of time, of the actions of very many individuals and groups, all seeking their own goals.

k. An important concept in the NIE is that of "coordinating on the rules of the game." Societies tend to function better when there are predictable rules of behavior. There are few situations worse for societies than anarchy. Thus whatever rules prevail at a given time, there are normally many individuals and groups with a strong interest in seeing that the rules are respected. One implication is that the basic institutions of society normally change very slowly over time. However, the idea of coordinating on the rules contains the possibility of rapid changes from one political order to another. Clearly this is more likely to occur in lower-level institutions than in higher-level ones. For example, individual companies in a market environment can often be "turned around" quickly, and individual agencies in the public sector can experience a fundamental change in the rules of behavior and in the accompanying attitudes of employees. Moreover, societies sometimes experience fairly rapid change from one political order to another. One example is the European colonization of Africa, which changed the top-level political order in a couple of decades in many colonies. The collapse of communism is of course another example.

l. In the NIE framework, corruption is a manifestation of institutional failure, and its remedy is sought mainly in strengthening certain institutions (and perhaps in weakening certain others). One part of institutional analysis is to describe a set of institutions that would make an economy or a society function well. The other (and more difficult) part is to determine how institutions have changed through history and how interventions might help to move them in a desirable direction. In this latter endeavor, we do not have precise theorems, but rather generalizations about patterns of development observable in history. This task is made more difficult by the fact that institutions often change slowly and there is an element of path dependence influencing the manner in which institutions change. In other words, where a society has been influences not only the current situation, but where it will be and how it will change in the future.

m. An example of the effect of institutions on an economic system arises in the discussion of transaction costs. Transaction costs are defined as the costs, other than price, which are incurred when trading goods and services and encompass the costs of using the mechanisms of production and exchange. Thus, transaction costs can be viewed as frictions in the economic system, and are affected by the institutions in the environment. In particular, a system characterized by corruption can suffer from inadequate mechanisms of contract enforcement, weak judicial systems, and inadequate provisions for public safety. This in turn will raise the transaction costs in the economy, raising the cost of investment and the cost of public service delivery. Alternately, an economy that reduces the level of corruption can reduce the level of transaction costs.

Source: World Bank (2004).

References

Ades, A., and R. Di Tella. 1995. *Competition and Corruption*. Oxford Applied Economics Discussion Paper, Series. 169 April: 18.

———. 1996. The Causes and Consequences of Competition: A Review of Recent Empirical Contributions. In *Liberalization and the New Corruption*, Institute of Development Studies Bulletin 27(2), ed. B. Harris-White and G. White, 6–11. Brighton: Institute of Development Studies.

———. 1997. The New Economics of Corruption: A Survey and Some New Results. In *Political Corruption*, ed. Paul Heywood. Oxford: Blackwell Publishers.

Arikan, G. 2004. Fiscal Decentralization: A Remedy for Corruption. *International Tax and Public Finance* 11: 175–195.

Bardhan, P., and D. Mookherjee. 2005. Decentralization, Corruption and Government Accountability: An Overview. In *Handbook of Economic Corruption*, ed. S. Rose-Akerman. Northhampton: Edward Elgar Publishing.

Brunetti, A., and B. Weder. 1998. *A Free Press Is Bad News for Corruption.* Wirtschaftswissenschaftliches Zentrum der Universitat Basel Discussion Paper, No. 9809.

Carbonara, E. 1999. *Bureaucracy, Corruption and Decentralization.* University of Bologna Working Paper.

Clague, Christopher. 1993. Rule Obedience, Organizational Loyalty and Economic Development. *Journal of Institutional and Theoretical Economics* 149 (2): 393–414.

Crook, R., and J. Manor. 2000. *Democratic Decentralization.* OED Working Papers Series, World Bank, Washington, DC.

Das-Gupta, A., and D. Mookherjee. 1998. *Incentives and Institutional Reform in Tax Enforcement: An Analysis of Developing Country Experience.* New Delhi: Oxford University Press.

Elliott, Kimbery Ann, ed. 1997. *Corrruption and the Global Economy.* Washington, DC: Institute for International Economics.

Fan, C., C. Lin, and D. Treisman. 2009. Political Decentralization and Corruption: Evidence from Around the World. *Journal of Public Economics* 93: 14–34.

Fisman, R., and R. Gatti. 2002. Decentralization and Corruption: Evidence Across Countries. *Journal of Public Economics* 83: 325–345.

Goel, R.K., and M.A. Nelson. 1998. Corruption and Government Size: A Disaggregated Analysis. *Public Choice* XCVII: 107–120.

Gurgur, Tugrul, and Anwar Shah. 1999. *Major Causes of Corruption.* Operations Evaluation Department Working Paper, World Bank, Washington, DC.

———. 2002. Localization and Corruption: Panacea or Pandora's Box? In *Managing Fiscal Decentralization*, ed. Ehtisham Ahmad and Vio Tanzi, 46–67. London/New York: Routledge Press.

Huntington, Samuel P. 2002. Modernization and Corruption. Chapter 15. In *Political Corruption: Concepts and Contexts*, ed. A. Heidenheimer and M. Johnston, 253–264. New Brunswick: Transaction Publishers.

Huther, J., and A. Shah. 1998. *A Simple Measure of Good Governance and Its Application to the Debate on the Appropriate Level of Fiscal Decentralization.* World Bank Working Paper, Series No. 1894, Washington, DC.

Ivanyna, Maksym, and Anwar Shah. 2011. Decentralization and Corruption: New Cross-Country Evidence. *Environment and Planning C: Government and Policy* 29: 344–362.

———. 2014. How Close Is Your Government to Its People? Worldwide Indicators on Localization and Decentralization. *Economics: The Open-Access, Open-Assessment E-Journal* 8 (2014–3): 1–61. https://doi.org/10.5018/economics-ejournal.ja.2014-3.

Kaufmann, D., A. Kraay, and P. Zoido-Lobaton. 1999. *Governance Matters*. World Bank Working Paper, Series No. 2196, Washington, DC.
Klitgaard, R. 1988. *Controlling Corruption*. Berkeley: University of California Press.
La Porta, R., F. Lopez-De-Silanes, A. Shleifer, and R.W. Vishny. 1997. Trust in Large Organizations. *American Economic Review*, Papers and Proceedings CXXXVII (2): 333–338.
Schacter, Mark, and Anwar Shah. 2004. Combating Corruption: Look Before You Leap. *Finance and Development* 41 (4): 40–43.
Segal, P. 1999. Dealing with Devil: The Hell of Corruption. *Impact*, International Finance Corporation, Spring.
Shah, Anwar. 1999. Governing for Results in Globalized and Localized World. *The Pakistan Development Review* 38 (4): 385–431.
———. 2007. Tailoring the Fight Against Corruption to Country Circumstances. Chapter 7. In *Performance Accountability and Combating Corruption*, ed. Anwar Shah, 233–254. Washington, DC: World Bank.
———. 2015. Decentralized Provision of Infrastructure and Corruption. Chapter 14. In *Decentralization and Infrastructure in the Global Economy: From Gaps to Solutions*, ed. Jonas Frank and Jorge Martinez-Vasquez, 418–454. New York: Routledge Press.
Shah, Anwar, T. Thompson, and H. Zou. 2004. The Impact of Decentralization on Service Delivery, Corruption, Fiscal Management and Growth in Developing and Emerging Market Economies: A Synthesis of Empirical Evidence. CESifo DICE Report. *Journal for Institutional Comparisons* 2 (1): 10–14.
Swamy, A., S. Knack, Y. Lee, and O. Azfar. 1999. *Gender and Corruption*. IRIS Center, University of Maryland, July.
Tanzi, V., and H. Davoodi. 1998. *Roads to Nowhere: How Corruption in Public* Investment Hurts Growth. In New Perspectives on Combating Corruption, Transparency International and the World Bank.
Tomaszewska, Eva, and Anwar Shah. 2000. Phantom Hospitals, Ghost Schools and Roads to Nowhere: The Impact of Corruption on Public Service Delivery Performance in Developing Countries. Processed.
Treisman, D. 1999a. The Causes of Corruption: A Cross National Study. *Journal of Public Economics* 76 (3): 399–457.
———. 1999b. *Decentralization and Corruption: Why Are Federal States Perceived to Be More Corrupt*. Paper Prepared for the Presentation at the Annual Meeting of the American Political Science Association, Atlanta, September 1999, University of California, Los Angeles, August.
———. 2000. The Causes of Corruption: A Cross National Study. *Journal of Public Economics* 76 (3): 399–457.
———. 2007. What Have We Learned About Causes of Corruption from Ten Years of Cross-National Empirical Research? *Annual Review of Political Science* 10: 211–244.

Treisman, Daniel. 2010. *The Causes of Corruption*. San Francisco: Sage Publications.

Van Rijckeghem, C., and B. Weder. 1997. *Corruption and the Role of Temptation: Do Low Wages in Civil Service Cause Corruption?* IMF Working Paper, WP/97/73.

World Bank. 2000a. *Reforming Public Institutions and Strengthening Governance. A World Bank Strategy*, November.

———. 2000b. Evaluation Criteria Review. June 30, Operations Evaluation Department, World Bank, Washington, DC.

———. 2004. *Mainstreaming Anti-Corruption Activities in World Bank Assistance: A Review of Progress Since 1997.* Annex B, pp. 67–70. Operations Evaluation Department, World Bank.

CHAPTER 7

Evaluating External Analytical Advice on Budgetary Institutions and Allocations

Jeff Huther and Anwar Shah

Introduction

The Development Assistance Community routinely carries out a review of a country's expenditure allocations and the budgetary processes used to make those allocations. Such analysis is typically labelled as a Public Expenditure Review (PER) and is used in guiding external assistance needs of a country. The most common format of recent PERs begins with a presentation of an overall picture of the country's fiscal situation. This picture typically focuses on the country's expenditure trends. This presentation provides the background, and frequently the justification, for the specific issues addressed by the review. The picture of the fiscal situation is frequently followed by an analysis of the budget process, which typically provides the foil for recommendations made in the PER. In some cases, providing a picture of the country's fiscal situation and outlining the budget process, may be the only tasks undertaken in the PER. In other

J. Huther
Board of Governors, Federal Reserve Board, Washington, DC, USA
e-mail: jeffrey.w.huther@frb.gov

A. Shah (✉)
Governance Studies, Brookings Institution, Washington, DC, USA

© The Author(s) 2020
A. Shah (ed.), *Policy, Program and Project Evaluation*,
https://doi.org/10.1007/978-3-030-48567-2_7

Table 7.1 Characteristics of a typical formal PER

Topic	*Physical characteristics*
Budget overview	Current state of public finances and expenditure trends
Sectoral reviews	Most include education and health, other sectors depending on circumstances
Intersectoral issues	Common issues include investment prioritization, public sector management, public enterprise efficiency, and civil service reform
Budget process	Typically provides description of bureaucratic constraints on budgetary reforms
Supporting annexes	Usually includes a large number of tables of various budget components and, for traditional PERs, a multicolored map of the country

Source: Authors

cases, PERs selected inter- and intra-sectoral issues (World Bank 1998). Almost all formal reviews, and many informal reviews, also include extensive data on a country's expenditures (see Table 7.1 for general PER characteristics).

The goals of this chapter are to present a framework to evaluate.

1) the quality and timeliness of PER work;
2) the impact of PER instruments on
   - the client's budgetary processes, institutions, and public expenditure allocations; and
   - aid-coordination

PERs can be evaluated based on standard World Bank evaluation criteria of the relevance, efficacy and efficiency of each PER reviewed. Relevance should be evaluated largely based on the consistency of the PERs' objectives with the country's development strategy. Efficacy will measure the success in achieving stated goals in PERs. Efficiency will relate outcomes to the resources used to generate those outcomes. These criteria can be applied to both the PER product and the PER impact. Flexibility, responsiveness, and timeliness are factors that should also be considered when evaluating the effectiveness of PERs. In addition, PERs should also be examined for internalization of the recommendations of previous studies.

This chapter presents a systematic evaluation framework applicable to PERs of all types: what factors should influence when a PER should be undertaken, what tasks a PER should perform, how a PER should be effectively presented, and what actions should be taken to ensure the sustainability and efficacy of a PER's recommendations. The chapter uses World Bank PERs as a reference but the evaluation framework presented here, with minor modifications, would be applicable to all PERs conducted by external development assistance community or by think tanks.

Methodology

The basis of evaluation is the *rating system* of the characteristics of the PER process and documents. These characteristics can be rated based on their influences on the quality, timeliness, and impact of PERs. The rating system will be similar to that used in previous OED work: the characteristics of individual PERs should be evaluated in terms of criteria that can easily be converted to a multi-point scale. The criteria to be considered in the evaluation of quality and timeliness are outlined.

Evaluation of the Quality and Timeliness of Alternate Forms of PERs

PER quality should be evaluated on the basis of (a) clarity of framework and consistency and rigor of analysis, (b) internalization of findings of previous studies, (c) evidence of consultations with relevant levels of government and stakeholders, (d) selection of issues addressed and depth of such analyses, and (e) proper recognition of political, institutional, informational, and economic imperatives of the client. These five characteristics of PER work can be used to determine an overall rating of the quality and timeliness of the PER analysis. The proposed methodology for this evaluation is outlined below.

(a) Rigor, Consistency, and Clarity

The quality of PERs depends significantly on the rigor, consistency, and clarity of analysis and recommendations. If a PER is to be used effectively, the conclusions and the reasoning used to reach those conclusions must be easily accessible to readers from a variety of backgrounds. For the client, this accessibility means that the conclusions of the PER must be presented in persuasive terms with sufficient evidence of the gains from structural adjustment. The evaluation of the clarity, consistency, and rigor of the analysis and conclusions is proposed to follow the matrices in Table 7.2.

Table 7.2 Quality of analysis evaluation (a): Clarity, rigor, and consistency

PER recommendation	Basis for recommendation	Relevance of framework for evaluation[1]	Consistency of recommendation with analysis[2]	Potential for implementation of recommendations[3]	Clarity of presentation[4]	Exposition of presentation[5]

Source: Authors

Notes: [1] Rate on scale of 1–6 where:

1: Framework is appropriate basis for addressing country's expenditure needs
6: Framework is inappropriate basis for addressing country's expenditure needs
[2] Rate on scale of 1–6 where:
1: Recommendation is logical outcome of analysis
6: Recommendation is unrelated to analysis
[3] Rate on scale of 1–6 where:
1: Recommendation is likely, given constraints
6: Recommendation is unlikely, given constraints
[4] Rate on scale of 1–6 where:
1: Analysis is clear, recommendation is clearly stated
6: Analysis and recommendations vague
[5] Rate on a scale of 1–6 where:
1: Analysis and recommendation are concise, systematically presented.
6: Analysis and recommendation are verbose, unstructured

The analysis of budgetary mechanisms and processes may be based on both a conceptual framework and empirical experience. At the conceptual level, the analysis of public expenditures can be based on the appropriate role of the state, the appropriate level of government for given expenditures, and the necessary institutional capacity for efficient expenditures. An analysis based on the appropriate role of the state can provide guidance on the appropriate level of expenditures devoted to public enterprises, the allocations of resources to various sectors, and the appropriate use of market interventions through subsidies. An analysis of the appropriate level of government can provide guidance on the allocation of resources to various levels of government. An analysis of institutional capacity can provide guidance on efficient use of public resources.

The empirical analysis of sectoral expenditures may be based on either generalized experience applied to a specific expenditure (e.g., there are high returns to primary health care) or based on an assessment of a specific expenditure option (e.g., a cost–benefit analysis). The value of either approach is the prioritization of expenditures within a country's economic, political, and institutional capacity constraints. For the external participant, this prioritization provides the basis for an evaluation of the effectiveness of external aid. For the country, this prioritization highlights potential gains from rationalization of its fiscal policies. For both the external participant and the country, the usefulness of the PER depends on the quality of this prioritization.

(b) Internalization of Findings of Previous Studies

Previous studies have led to several "rules of thumb" relating to donor studies that are likely to improve PER quality. It is generally recognized, for example, that the findings of a PER, or any other study, will have the greatest impact if its completion is timed to coincide with overall changes in a country's political and budgetary cycles. It is also generally recognized that clients will be more receptive to the findings of donor studies if the client expresses an openness to review, and participates in the review process. The World Bank has emphasized that any project is more likely to succeed if its agenda and objectives are clearly specified upfront. These general rules of thumb, and recommendations of previous work, can be classified as either suggesting improvements in the process level or at the analysis level. PERs should be evaluated on the degree to which they have incorporated these recommendations (see Table 7.3 for details of the proposed evaluation).

(c) Evidence of Consultations with Relevant Levels of Government and Stakeholders

Formal consultations with the government depend on the government's openness to advice on public expenditures. Informal consultations with government officials, academics, NGOs, the business community, and civil society organizations can usually be made even in the absence of strong government commitment to the review. Additionally, the alternative views of expenditure policy provided by these groups can only improve PER quality. Consequently, one can seek evidence that the views from within the country have been sought and reflected in the PER through interviews in the countries (see Table 7.4).

(d) Selection of Issues Addressed and Depth of Such Analyses

An important component of a PER is the selection of issues to be addressed to achieve a maximum bang for the buck. Analyses of expenditure components that are truly inflexible, for example, will not provide additional guidance to external participants, nor will analyses of widely recognized needs of the highest priority. Examples of the former may include analyses

Table 7.3 Quality of analysis evaluation (b): Internalization of previous work*

Process	*Recommended status*	*Status noted in previous evaluations*	*Current PER**
Mission design	Consensus on a clearly defined agenda is essential	*Ex ante* consensus on the focus of the mission is rarely reached	
Resource costs	Streamline missions, focus on upstream work	Poorly-defined agendas contribute to the cost of expenditure reviews, and can lead to inefficiently large missions	
Timing	PER timed to influence external lending and internal budget	Timing is often not well suited for aid-coordination	
Production delays	White cover report closely follows Main Mission	The time lag between final mission and completed review can be years	
Bank–fund interaction	PER incorporates fund data and policy. Fund uses PER as basis for policy	Interaction is erratic and relies primarily on personal relations	
Internal bank incentives	Greater participation by sectoral experts	Sectoral staff place relatively low priority on public expenditure work	
Analysis	*Recommended status*	*Status noted in previous evaluations*	
Macroeconomic framework	PER recommendations consistent with Fund's macro recommendations	The integration of Fund's macro work is quite limited	
Political economy	PER recommendations consistent with political constraints	Most reports do not worry about the political feasibility of suggested reforms	
Role of state	PER recommendations based on long-term goal of rationalizing responsibilities of all levels of government	Few reports address this topic	
Expenditure policies	Analysis of PER focuses on the quantity and quality of services to be provided through public expenditures	Analyses of sectoral allocation, adequacy of operating expenditures and incidence of public expenditures remain weak	

(*continued*)

Table 7.3 (continued)

Budget process	Budgetary mechanisms clearly described, weaknesses noted	Expenditure work does not examine mechanisms through which government funds are allocated. These mechanisms are critical in translating budget objectives into practice
Institutional capacity and incentives	Recommendations recognize constraints and incentives of institutional structure	These issues are typically not covered

Source: Authors

Notes: *Current status is same as recommended status (1), current status is same as previous evaluation (6)

Table 7.4 Quality of analysis evaluation (c & d): Relevant collaboration and consultations

Source	*Sought advice*[1]	*Incorporated relevant advice*[2]
Government—official		
Government—unofficial		
Legislature		
NGOs		
Local academics		
Local business		
Local civic groups		
Fund—documents		
Fund—meetings		
Other donors		

Source: Authors

Notes: [1] Rate on basis of:

1: sought relevant or mandated advice

6: did not seek relevant or mandated advice

[2] Rate as:

1: sought and incorporated relevant advice

6: sought but did not incorporate advice

of military spending or fixed interest payments. Examples of the latter may include poverty assessments during severe droughts or health assessments in areas without any health care facilities.

Selection of expenditure categories should be evaluated based on efficacy in terms of timeliness, efficiency in terms of potential for changes in expenditure policy, and relevance in terms of the relevance of selected topics to both the external lending strategy and the Borrower's expenditure policies. The overall objective is to determine the potential social gain from changing expenditure policy in the areas selected by the PER for review. The proposed matrix for this evaluation is presented in Tables 7.5 and 7.6.

(e) Recognition of Political, Institutional, Informational, and Economic Imperatives of the Client

Previous studies have found that a lack of awareness of the client's constraints has reduced the efficiency and relevance of PER recommendations. Major constraints on public expenditures include institutional capacity, budgetary, political, and informational constraints. A lack of institutional capacity may lead to inefficient use of expenditures even if the correct sectors have been given high priority. Budgetary constraints, in the form of budgetary inflexibility or limited revenues, can make expenditure recommendations irrelevant as can a lack of acknowledgment of political constraints. PERs that do not recognize informational constraints, in terms of indicators of failure or success of expenditure changes, may make recommendations that either cannot be acted upon, or if acted upon, do not yield measurable results. Consequently, awareness of country constraints should be sought in an examination of PER documents (see Table 7.7).

Overall Quality and Timeliness

The evaluation of each of the characteristics outlined above can be used to obtain an overall rating of the quality and timeliness of the analysis. This overall rating will be based on an equal weighting of each of these five characteristics of quality and timeliness (see Table 7.8).

Table 7.5 Quality of analysis evaluation (e): Summary of inputs and assessments of output potential of PERs

	PER inputs			*Output potential**			
	Primary focus	Secondary focus	Not addressed	Likelihood of expenditure change	Social gain from expenditure change	Timeliness	Relevance given likelihood of change, objective, timeliness
Overall budget							
Institutional/ process weaknesses							
Sectoral allocations							
Total expenditure level							
Revenue collection							
Role of government							
Market failures							
Public enterprises							
Institutional development							
Budgetary process							
Transparency							
Intergovernment expenditures							
Social development							
Education							
Health							
Poverty							
Capital expenditures							

(*continued*)

Table 7.5 (continued)

PER inputs	*Output potential**
Investment projects—Transportation	
Investment projects—energy	
Investment projects—water and sewerage	
Investment projects—social development	
Intrasectoral allocations	
Public sector efficiency	
Reduced employment	
Wage structure	
Rationalization of subsidies/ag. support	
Privatization	

Source: Authors

Notes: Output potential rated on six-point scale and weighted by input importance so issues not addressed and unlikely to improve output potential would not influence rating. Issues not addressed, but that have potential for improving output would reduce rating

Table 7.6 Evaluation of output potential of PERs: Criteria for evaluation of output potential

Potential output	*Evaluation criteria*
Likelihood of expenditure change	Degree of budget flexibility Commitment of client to expenditure change: Local demand for expenditure analysis Likely responsiveness to bank-driven analysis
Social gain from expenditure change	Sectoral potential for social gains
Timeliness	Planned completion date vs. actual Timing of planned completion date and Reassessments of CAS Client's budget cycle

Source: Authors

Table 7.7 Quality of analysis evaluation (f): Evaluation of PERs' treatment of borrower constraints

Constraints[a]	*Degree of relevance for borrower*[a]	*Role discussed in PER or internal documents*[a]	*PER or internal documents' recommendations reflect constraints*[a]	*PER or internal documents suggest ways to ease constraints*[a]
Institutional capacity				
Budgetary constraints				
Political constraints				NA
Informational constraints				

Source: Authors

[a]Rate substantially (1) to negligibly (6)

Evaluation of the Impact of PER Instruments

The impact of PERs is measured by the extent to which the results of the PERs are incorporated into aid-coordination, and into expenditure policies of the countries reviewed.

Table 7.8 Overall rating of PER quality and timeliness

Criteria	*Rating*	*Weighting*	*Weighted rating*
Clarity, consistency, rigor		0.17	
Internalization of previous studies		0.17	
Consistency with fund		0.17	
Selection of issues		0.17	
Government consultations		0.17	
Recognition of constraints		0.17	
Overall quality and timeliness			

Source: Authors

(a) Aid-Coordination Efforts by the Development Assistance Community

Evidence of the impact on the assistance strategy of external participants should be sought in an evaluation of both post-PER documents and the beliefs and attitudes of external participant staff. These impacts can be gauged from evidence on other donors' involvement in PER processes, post-PER program, and policy documents of external participants. Phone calls to donors, which may be followed up by mailed questionnaires, can be used to determine the degree to which donor policies and aid decisions, either implicitly or explicitly, have been influenced by the analysis and recommendations of the PER (see Table 7.9).

(b) Borrower Policies

Evaluation of the impact of the PER on the Borrower can be based on the formal response of government, budgetary changes, institutional changes, indicators on inputs and outputs, and other stakeholders' comments and perceptions about PER contributions (see Table 7.10). Budgetary changes can be evaluated based on changes in expenditure patterns (to the extent data is available), changes in the budgetary process, or reallocations of expenditures to different levels of government. Indicators for inputs will be public sector employment and, for public enterprises, subsidy levels. Where applicable, output indicators will include short-term indicators of shifts in social expenditures (e.g., number of teachers or health workers), privatization of public enterprises, and changes in civil service employment and compensation. Dissemination of PER findings can be evaluated based on interviews with local stakeholders.

Table 7.9 Evaluation of PER impact on donor assistance strategies

	PER analysis	*Analysis cited*[a]	*Analysis invoked*[a]	*PER recommendation*	*Recommendation cited*[a]	*Recommendation invoked*[a]
Bank CAS						
Bank loan/credit conditions						
Bank staff reports						
External participants' documents						
Fund PFPs						
Fund staff reports						
Fund TAs						

Source: Authors

[a]Rate on scale of 1–6 where:

1: Document uses PER analysis or recommendation as basis for own analysis or recommendation

6: Analysis or recommendation of document contradicts analysis or recommendation of PER

Table 7.10 Evaluation of the impact: client expenditure policies

PER recommendation	Impact[a]
Formal response	
Budgetary changes	
Institutional changes	
Changes in social indicators	
Dissemination within country administration	
Awareness of PER analysis by nongovernment agencies	

Source: Authors

[a]Rate substantially (1) to negligibly (6)

Evaluating the impact of PERs on expenditure policies is further complicated by difficulties in separating policy changes due to the findings of a PER from policy changes due to other factors. To address these difficulties, Borrowers' comments to PERs should be sought through telephone interviews or in person, in addition to budgetary and social indicators of PER impacts. Borrowers' commitment to expenditure policy reforms will be measured by Borrowers' comments on the PER, subsequent policy decisions, and by a review of record on internalization and dissemination of PER analyses and recommendations. Field visits can be used to arrive at a deeper understanding of the PER impacts on country policies and institutions through Borrower and stakeholders interviews.

Additionally, each PER should be examined for awareness of distortion of incentives created by aid: were expenditure shifts made to accommodate aid, were expenditure shifts made to encourage more aid, and did the Borrower use budgetary shifts to meet aid requirements while not actually improving expenditure allocations?

(c) Cost-Efficiency

PERs have the potential to be very cost-effective. Advice on public expenditures that leads to changes in expenditure policy can lead to large gains in social welfare for a country. This potential does not, however, guarantee that resources are used efficiently in PER work. This evaluation will include cost efficiency as an indicator of the quality of analysis (although it will be

Table 7.11 Evaluation of the impact: cost-efficiency

Indicator	*Rating*
Potential impact rating	Rate from scale of 1 to 6 where, 1 = impact on average quality of life outstanding, 2 = substantial, 3 = moderate, 4 = modest, 5 = inconsequential, and 6 = negligible
Actual impact rating	Calculate the average of potential and actual impact ratings
Average impact rating	Calculate the average of potential and actual impact ratings
Adjusted average impact rating	Adjusted average impact rating is calculated as follows: Adjusted average impact rating = 7.00 – Average impact rating
PER cost rating	Rate from 1 to 6 where 1 = cost of 0–$50,000, 2 = $50,000–100,000, 3 = $100,000–175,000, 4 = $175,000–250,000, 5 = $250,000–350,000, 6 = $350,000 and above
Cost–benefit ratio	Divide cost rating by adjusted average impact rating
Cost-efficiency	Use the following rating scheme to assign cost-efficiency rate—Cost-efficiency rating (R) for cost–benefit ratio: R1:0.00–0.40; R2:0.40–1.00; R3:1.00–1.10;R4:1.10–1.50;R5:1.50–2.00; R6:2.00 ad above Where, R1 = cost-efficiency highly satisfactory, R6 = cost-efficiency highly unsatisfactory

Source: Authors

given a lower weight in the combined evaluation). The rating of cost efficiency should be based on the relation of the resource cost of the PERs examined, in financial terms and staff weeks consumed, to the PER's potential and actual impact on the client's expenditure policies (see Table 7.11).

Overall Impact

The evaluation of each of the characteristics outlined above can be used to obtain an overall rating of the PER impact, weighted change of country policy by 75 percent, and change in donor-coordination by 25 percent (see Tables 7.12 and 7.13).

Table 7.12 Overall impact rating

PER impact		*Weighting scale*	*Rating*
Impact on Bank/Fund lending strategies		0.30	
Impact on aid-coordination		0.20	
Impact on expenditure policies		0.50	
Overall rating		1.00	

Source: Authors

Table 7.13 Cumulative matrix of PER quality and impacts

Criteria	*Rating*	*Weighting*	*Weighted rating*
PER analysis		0.30	
Clarity, consistency, and rigor		0.05	
Internalization of previous studies		0.05	
Consistency with fund		0.05	
Selection of issues		0.05	
Relevant consultations		0.05	
Recognition of constraints		0.05	
PER impact		0.60	
Impact on Bank/fund lending strategies		0.18	
Impact on aid-coordination		0.12	
Impact on expenditure policies		0.30	
Cost-efficiency		0.10	
Overall rating		1.00	

Source: Authors

Annex: Getting Government Right—The Canadian Approach to PER

Canada in 1994 conducted a whole of government PER review to deal with persistent public sector deficits, a large overhang of debt, and growing citizen dissatisfaction with the public sector. For this review, Canada opted for the so-called alternative service delivery framework for developing public sector reform and restructuring options. As part of the program review process under this framework, departments and agencies were required to review their activities and programs against the following six guidelines and identify programs that are to be strengthened as well as those that are to be discontinued:

1) *Public Interest Test*: Does the program area or activity continue to serve a public interest?
2) *Role of Government Test*: Is there a legitimate and necessary role for the government in this program area or activity?
3) *Federalism Test*: Is the current role of the federal government appropriate, or is the program a candidate for realignment with the provinces?
4) *Partnership Test*: What activities or programs should or could be transferred in whole or in part to the private or voluntary sector?
5) *Efficiency Test*: If the program or activity continues, how could its efficiency be improved?
6) *Affordability Test*: Is the resultant package of programs and activities affordable within the fiscal constraints? If not, what programs or activities should be abandoned?

The Canadian experience with this simple approach to PER using the alternative service delivery framework was highly successful. The federal deficit was cut from 7.5 percent of GDP in 1993 and reached a balanced budget in 1998 and surplus budgets in the late 1990s. The numbers of federal departments were reduced from 38 to 25, and the civil service roll was reduced from 220,000 to 178,000. Allocations to social services, justice, and science and technology were increased, while the remaining services saw a reduction in the budgetary allocations. Citizen-centered service delivery enhancements were achieved by clustering services around the needs of citizens, enacting regulatory reform to encourage competition and innovation, recovering costs from services that benefited special segments, and continuing to reevaluate programs to support alternative service delivery mechanisms. The overall impact of these reforms was an improvement in service delivery and citizen satisfaction (Shah 2005).

References

Shah, Anwar. 2005. On Getting the Giant to Kneel: Approaches to a Change in the Bureaucratic Culture. Chapter 9. In *Fiscal Management*, ed. Anwar Shah, 211–228. Washington, DC: World Bank.

World Bank. 1998. *The Impact of Public Expenditure Reviews: An Evaluation*, Report No. 18573, Operations Evaluation Department. Washington, DC: World Bank.

CHAPTER 8

Inter-Sectoral Allocation Choices

Stuart Landon

Introduction

The size of government has been found to be an important determinant of growth in some empirical studies.[1] In other studies, using data for a broad range of countries, no clear relationship has been found between aggregate public expenditure and growth.[2] For example, government expenditure as a share of GDP in rapidly growing countries, such as Singapore, Korea and Taiwan, is not that different from the average level of spending in developing countries (Rao 1998). The imprecise relationship between aggregate government spending and growth may be the result of aggregate spending data obscuring important differences across spending programs. That is, the impact of a given level of spending on growth may depend as much on the design and efficiency of expenditure programs, and the distribution of expenditure across and within sectors, as on the aggregate level of spending. If spending has not been implemented

[1] See, for example, the regression evidence presented in the World Bank (1997).
[2] See, for example, Rao (1998).

S. Landon (✉)
Victoria, BC, Canada
e-mail: Stuart.Landon@ualberta.ca

© The Author(s) 2020

A. Shah (ed.), *Policy, Program and Project Evaluation*,
https://doi.org/10.1007/978-3-030-48567-2_8

efficiently, or allocated optimally across spending categories, it may be possible to increase growth and welfare by redesigning spending programs, or shifting spending from one sector to another, without increasing the overall level of government spending.

Given that government decisions affecting the inter-sectoral allocation of resources may have important effects on growth and welfare, an examination of the rationales for, and consequences of, inter-sectoral resource allocation decisions is an important component of any development strategy. This examination should provide answers to several questions: Are there sectors that should be given priority in the allocation of resources? Is it sufficient to allocate resources to aggregate sectors or are sub-sector allocations important and, if so, what sub-sectors should receive the highest priority? Does the inter-sectoral allocation of spending depend on the capacity of the state or the stage of development? Are some types of sector-level spending programs more likely to succeed? How does the role played by the private sector affect the inter-sectoral allocation of state resources? The analysis in this chapter attempts to address these questions as they relate to government expenditure programs.[3] In so doing, issues are raised that should be considered by reviews of current public expenditure programs as well as by reviews of proposed spending programs and spending reform initiatives.

The appropriate allocation of public expenditures between sectors involves many factors and is not the same in all circumstances. Although it is not possible to offer universal truths with respect to the inter-sectoral allocation of resources, evidence from a broad selection of countries over many years can be used to identify sector-level spending programs that should generally be given high priority in the allocation of state resources. It is also possible to note problems and constraints, both in general and for specific sectors, which are likely to hinder the success of spending programs. These constraints have implications for the optimal inter-sectoral allocation of resources as well as for the design of expenditure implementation strategies.

[3] The focus of this chapter is public expenditure policy. The analysis does not address the inter-sectoral resource allocation implications of tax policy, the role of labor market policies, savings, trade, exchange rate or macroeconomic stabilization policies. All of these have important implications for development, and all are likely to interact with public expenditure decisions to either assist or hinder growth. The analysis also does not address the large, important and complex issue of which level of government should have responsibility for which types of sectoral expenditures.

The available evidence suggests that priority should be given to spending programs that deal effectively with market failures and improve the operation of governments and markets. In particular, resources should be allocated to improve the capacity, efficiency and quality of government services and administration, to develop an effective legal system to protect and enforce property rights, to design and implement a system of financial regulation, to maintain the existing infrastructure, and to invest in infrastructure that is important to the development of a market economy—transportation, communications and electricity. Spending priority should also be given to improvements in the quality and quantity of primary education and basic health care (public health, disease control, sanitation, water, and basic curative care) as well as to consumption subsidy programs for the very poor, but only if these can be well targeted. In order to improve the quality and efficiency of state spending, it is necessary to allocate resources to evaluations of program effectiveness; that is, to measuring and evaluating the outputs produced given the inputs employed.

Evidence from many developing countries implies that spending programs are not likely to be successful unless they are designed and implemented appropriately. This means that they must be consistent with the administrative capacity available, they must incorporate appropriate incentives, and they must include effective input and output monitoring. In the absence of these factors, increased spending on sector-level programs, even if addressing an important need, is unlikely to be effective.

The experiences of many countries suggest that there are many sectoral spending programs that should generally be allocated few resources. These include subsidies to many state-owned enterprises, industrial subsidies, poorly targeted consumption subsidies, many infrastructure projects, social security programs, tertiary education and hospital care, military spending, and extensive regulatory regimes. Low priority should also be given to spending on programs that displace private sector producers, programs for which the costs of intervention (the direct expenditure costs as well as the administrative costs, the costs of any distortions introduced by the program, and the distortions associated with revenue generation) exceed the costs of the market failure the spending is attempting to address, programs that have a regressive effect on income distribution, and programs that provide opportunities for rent-seeking and corruption.

The following section provides a brief overview of the standard theoretical framework for the analysis of government resource allocation decisions. In the Section "Inter-Sectoral Resource Allocation: Public Sector

Administration", general issues are discussed that relate to the interaction of the administration of the public sector and the inter-sectoral allocation of resources. This is followed with a discussion of sector specific issues in the Section: "Sector-Specific Issues in the Allocation of Government Resources". A concluding section then summarizes the principal findings.

Rationales for Government Intervention in the Allocation of Resources: A Framework for Analysis

It is generally accepted that government intervention in the allocation of resources can improve social welfare only in the presence of market failure. Therefore, before the state intervenes in the allocation of resources between sectors (or within sectors), the source, cause and magnitude of the market failure being addressed should be identified. Only if this is done is it possible to determine the extent to which the proposed intervention in the allocation of resources is likely to successfully deal with the causes and consequences of the market failure and, thus, whether the intervention is likely to be welfare improving. The purpose of this section is to briefly describe several common forms of market failure, and to identify broad issues associated with policies to counteract these types of market failure.

Insufficient Competition

In general, market failure arises from incomplete markets or insufficient competition. The absence of sufficient competition may have three important types of negative effects on an economy. Firms may set prices above marginal cost, firms that are not subject to competitive pressures may be less likely to innovate and pursue least cost methods of production, and, if noncompetitive behavior leads to higher prices, resources will be transferred from consumers to the owners of firms and workers in the noncompetitive sector. This last effect may have detrimental implications for the distribution of income since many of the consumers of the goods produced by noncompetitive firms in developing countries are likely to be poorer than either the workers or the owners of the firms.

Noncompetitive behavior generally occurs when there are few firms in a market or when a small number of firms control a large share of market output.[4] This can result from economies of scale in production, the predatory behavior of established firms, government regulations, or high transportation costs leading to regional monopolies (particularly as a result of a poor transportation infrastructure). Intervention to counteract noncompetitive behavior can involve competition regulation, greater investment in transportation infrastructure, subsidies or state-ownership.

Firms with significant economies of scale and few competitors are often present in industries such as gas, electricity, water, sanitation, airports, ports and telecommunications. Through the development of a regulatory structure, the state could attempt to force firms in these industries to set price equal to average cost, thereby yielding the unsubsidized level of output closest to the efficient level. The use of average cost pricing regulation (or any other form of regulation) would require that resources be allocated to the design and administration of a regulatory framework as well as to the acquisition of firm cost information. Rather than regulate private sector production, the state could directly produce goods that exhibit decreasing costs. However, this would require expenditure on infrastructure, production, distribution and monitoring. Furthermore, unless it was carefully monitored and regulated, there is little reason to believe that a state-owned firm would not exhibit much of the same inefficient behavior as a noncompetitive private firm.

Two important issues arise when considering the inter-sectoral allocation of resources necessary to respond to insufficient competition. First, the factors determining the degree of competition in a market are likely to be continually in flux as changes in technology and the costs of entry alter the form of the industry and the level of potential competition. For example, changes in technology (the introduction of cellular phones) have made the telephone sectors in many developing countries much more competitive. Policies that may be effective at contributing to efficiency at one point in time, such as a state monopoly or state subsidies, may actually reduce competitive pressures at other points in time by restricting the introduction of new technology or the entry of new firms.

Second, parts of some industries (i.e. electricity generation) are potentially competitive since they can be split off from the decreasing cost part of the industry (i.e. electricity transmission). Prior to designing an

[4] It is not always the case that the existence of a small number of firms in a market leads to noncompetitive behavior since the possibility of entry by other firms may induce existing firms to act competitively.

intervention strategy in order to promote competition, it is necessary to determine which parts of an industry are potentially competitive and which parts are truly natural monopolies. Only the truly decreasing-cost noncompetitive segments of an industry need to be regulated.[5] As industries evolve, periodic reviews of expenditure and regulatory policies should be used to determine whether these competition-promoting policies continue to be necessary.

Incomplete Markets

Market failure also occurs when the market for a good does not exist even though the marginal benefit of the good exceeds its marginal cost. This may occur as a result of asymmetric information (complete information is not available to both sides of the market), insufficient market size (the market is not large enough for a firm to cover its fixed costs of production), or because it is not possible to prevent individuals from consuming a good (non-excludability). Several specific types of incomplete markets have implications for the inter-sectoral allocation of state resources.

Public Goods

Public goods are goods that possess two distinct characteristics. They provide benefits to individuals other than the provider at no additional cost to the provider (they are non-rival) and the consumption of the good by individuals other than the provider is difficult (or too costly) to prevent (they are non-excludable).[6] Since the provider of a public good cannot charge other consumers of the good for the benefit these consumers receive from the good, the provider of the good is unlikely to take the benefit to these other consumers into account when determining the quantity of the good to provide. As a result, too little of the good will be provided.[7] In contrast, since private goods are excludable and provide

[5] This is important since regulated monopolies are often given regulatory protection against competition from new technologies (such as telephone monopolies that are protected by regulations that prevent cellular phone use).

[6] Excludability depends on technology in many cases and changes in technology may affect the extent of excludability. For example, air and water pollution may not always have been possible to price, but now monitoring devices are capable of measuring pollutants and, as a result, prices can be charged for these emissions.

[7] If the benefit to others is negative (i.e. the good is a "bad"), too much of the good will be provided.

benefits only to the direct consumers of the good, individual choices will ensure that the optimal quantity of the good is provided.[8] Since a government can force payment for a good through its coercive power, governments can (in theory) ensure that the appropriate level of a public good is provided, where the appropriate level is the quantity of the good at which social marginal cost equals social marginal benefit, and the latter includes the benefit to all consumers of the good.[9] This is usually accomplished by subsidizing private production or through direct public provision.

Many "public goods" are said to be "impure" because they do not possess all the characteristics of a pure public good. This generally occurs because additional consumers impose costs on existing consumers (i.e. they are not non-rival), or because the good combines both public good and private good characteristics that cannot be consumed separately (a characteristic that can also facilitate excludability). For example, health care, education and redistributive policies generally help the beneficiaries directly (and, thus, are a private good), an increased number of beneficiaries raise the costs of these services, and direct beneficiaries of these services are generally excludable. However, the existence of these programs is often believed to bring benefits to individuals other than the direct beneficiaries (a benefit that does not depend on the contribution of these other individuals to the cost of the program) and, thus, they are to some extent public goods.

Asymmetric Information

Asymmetric information implies that the two agents involved in an exchange have different information on, in particular, their individual effort levels and the risks involved in the transaction. This can lead to the absence of markets for some goods and less trade than is optimal. For example, due to inadequate information on risks and effort levels, some individuals may not be able to obtain health insurance from the private sector and some firms may not be able to obtain loans from private

[8] It is important to distinguish public goods from publicly provided private goods. The latter are private goods produced by the public sector.

[9] The concepts of externalities and spillovers are closely related to that of public goods. An externality or spillover is produced when the actions of one economic agent have an impact on the well-being of another agent, and the agent producing the externality is unaffected by the impact of their actions on the second agent's welfare. Thus, the agent providing the externality does not choose to produce at the socially efficient level.

lenders. As a result, even if there exist projects with a positive net rate of return, because borrowers cannot acquire loans (the capital market is incomplete), these private benefits cannot be captured. Under these circumstances, governments have often allocated resources to stimulate the development of markets, particularly those for insurance and credit. However, these government programs are often unsuccessful because they are affected by many of the same information asymmetries that prevented private sector provision.

Redistribution

Redistribution of resources from the better off to the poor can be justified as a response to two types of market failure. First, as a result of asymmetric information (and the resulting moral hazard and adverse selection problems), there rarely exists a private market for income insurance. This is particularly the case in developing countries since they generally have underdeveloped insurance markets. Second, the private provision of redistribution is unlikely to yield the socially optimal level of redistribution because the benefits of redistribution are, to some extent, a public good. Since these benefits are received by everyone, even those who do not contribute resources to the redistribution effort (i.e. free-riders), the actions of private individuals are not likely to provide the socially optimal level of redistribution. These two types of market failure imply that, if the optimal level of redistribution and income insurance is to exist, it must be provided or subsidized by the state.

Section Summary

Market failures generally follow from insufficient competition or missing markets (due to the public good nature of some goods or asymmetric information). Governments have often addressed these problems through regulation, subsidies or direct provision of goods. When evaluating expenditure programs, it is important to identify the source and magnitude of the market failure being addressed in order both to design the appropriate type of intervention and to determine whether the benefits of intervention are likely to outweigh the costs. It is particularly important to determine whether the form of intervention proposed is likely to successfully counteract the market failure, given the capacity of the state, without inducing serious distortions. Even where there exists an identifiable market failure, intervention may not be warranted as the cost of intervention (administrative costs as well as the costs of induced changes in behavior) may exceed the benefits.

In the absence of market failure, government interference in the private provision of goods does not yield positive benefits. On the other hand, this intervention can have negative consequences by using scarce resources (including scarce administrative capacity), and by introducing incentives and distortions that could cause inefficient behavior on the part of private agents. In addition, because the public sector is often characterized by the absence of appropriate incentives, over-manning, inflexible labor markets, ineffective monitoring and control, and poor motivation of management and workers, state provision is often more costly than private sector production (Hemming et al. 1991).

Inter-Sectoral Resource Allocation: Public Sector Administration

This section examines several issues that relate the administration of the public sector to the inter-sectoral allocation of resources. Sector-specific issues are covered in the following Section: "Sector-Specific Issues in the Allocation of Government Resources".

Capacity and Efficiency of the Administration

If a government is to respond effectively to market failures, the state administration must have adequate capacity to both design and successfully implement spending programs. Poor design and implementation can have negative implications for both the quality and quantity of government services. Furthermore, because the state sector provides goods that are used as inputs by the private sector, and administers regulations that restrict private sector behavior, the efficiency and capacity of the state administration has important implications for the performance of private sector firms and, thus, the economy as a whole. Rodrik (1997) suggests that the success of government intervention in East Asia may have had more to do with the effectiveness of policy implementation than with the actual policies chosen.[10]

[10] Rodrik (1997) provides an example of a Kenyan export subsidy scheme that seems to have had little impact on exports, in large part due to the inefficient administration of Kenyan bureaucrats.

Inadequate administrative capacity can lead to crucial flaws in program design. For example, as a result of poor administrative capacity, the civil service may not have the ability to plan, cost or evaluate the impact of competing policy proposals. This may result in inferior programs being chosen and anomalies arising:—hospitals may be built, but not provided with staff or equipment; schools may have teachers, but no books; roads may be constructed, but not maintained. Furthermore, poor program design may mean that civil servants have little incentive to provide a quality service efficiently, while users of the service may be given an incentive to undertake costly overconsumption.

While program design is critical to a project's success, implementation has also often been problematic due to inadequate administrative capacity or the inefficient use of the capacity available. In many cases, often while attempting to respond to perceived market failures, states with weak administrative capacity have tried to implement programs that they did not have the capacity to successfully undertake. The end result (poor quality services and a failure to meet program objectives) may have been more harmful than the inefficiency implied by the original market failure. The failure of interventionist policies in South Asia resulted, in large part, because the scale and form of intervention exceeded the capacity of the civil service.[11] Inadequate administrative capacity has also impeded development in sub-Saharan Africa (World Bank 1997). Due to failures in monitoring and accountability, both key elements in program implementation, there have often been large differences between policy goals and realized outcomes. For example, in Guinea the government designated primary education, basic public health and roads as priorities, but adequate funds were not allocated to these sectors (World Bank 1997). Poor administrative capacity has also meant poor coordination of government departments and agencies and the inability of the state to evaluate spending programs during development and implementation. The end result of all these factors has been higher program costs and poor program performance.

The critical importance of administrative capacity to the success of spending programs has several implications for the inter-sectoral allocation of resources. First, spending programs should be prioritized so that the capacity of the state is not exceeded by the concurrent implementation of

[11] While intervention was ineffective at meeting policy goals, it was effective at creating a large, relatively low-quality and ineffective bureaucracy.

too many (or too ambitious) expenditure programs. Second, since administrative capacity is likely to be a significant constraint in many developing countries, before implementing a spending program, it is necessary to determine the program's administrative requirements and whether these requirements can be met by the resources available. Spending programs that require administrative resources in excess of those available, even if they may yield higher potential welfare benefits, should be passed over in favor of spending programs that have less demanding administrative requirements and, thus, that are more likely to be successfully implemented. Third, programs should be designed taking into account the available administrative capacity. Finally, because the capacity of the state administration affects both the ability of the state to provide necessary public services as well as the performance of the private sector, increasing the capacity of the administration should be an important sectoral spending priority.

While the quantity of administrative capacity is important to the success of expenditure programs, the effectiveness and cost of public spending programs is also dependent on the efficiency with which the available administrative capacity is used. Since the civil service is a monopoly provider of many services, there is often little incentive for government agencies to provide quality services efficiently. This has several implications for the appropriate sectoral allocation of resources. First, spending programs should be designed so that state employees have an incentive to implement programs cost effectively and in a fashion that meets program goals. Designing this type of program is often extremely difficult, a factor that should be taken into account when determining the appropriate sectoral allocation of resources.[12] Second, it is generally inappropriate to implement a spending program that has not been (or cannot be) designed so that the economic agents involved have an incentive to undertake actions that meet the program's goals. Third, spending should generally be directed to programs that have clear and specific goals, rather than vague or general goals. Goals that are clear and specific facilitate monitoring, accountability and the design of incentives.[13] Finally, many of the incentive problems in state administrations follow from the monopoly position of

[12] See Crosby (1996) for a discussion of the complexities of program implementation as well as examples of successes and failures.

[13] Evidence on the success of World Bank structural adjustment loan conditions suggests that the more specific the condition, the more likely it will be met (Huther et al. 1997).

the state and the absence of competitive pressures in the provision of government services. Spending programs are likely to be more successful if they involve a greater degree of competition. This may affect the types of programs chosen, the form of their implementation, and the extent of private sector involvement.[14]

As noted above, increasing the quantity and efficiency of a country's administrative capacity should be an important priority. One way of doing this is to reform the organization, recruitment and compensation of civil servants.[15] In many countries, civil service wages have been compressed so that well-trained and capable managers have been attracted to the private sector (or public enterprises) rather than to the public sector. One method of attracting competent individuals to the state sector is to introduce a pay structure that is competitive with the private sector, and that reflects skill levels, responsibility and ability. In combination with merit (rather than time-served or political connections) as the basis for promotion, and the possibility of dismissal for poor performance, this type of pay structure could provide a strong incentive for workers to perform efficiently as well as to invest in their own managerial and technical skills.[16] To make this compensation scheme effective would require that significant resources be devoted to raising wages and monitoring civil service performance. Successfully implementing a reform of this type would also require a relatively skilled administration, and could take considerable time to be effective in changing attitudes and behavior.[17]

[14] While the problems that arise in the civil service with respect to incentives and control are similar to those that arise in large private sector companies, in a competitive market, the behavior of private sector managers can be controlled, to some extent, through profit-sharing or the threat of bankruptcy. Managerial rent seeking in the public sector is much more difficult to control due to the absence of competition and performance measures (such as profits).

[15] Lienert and Modi (1997) discuss civil service reform issues in detail, while Klitgaard (1997) discusses some of the problems with implementing reforms.

[16] Civil servants are, generally, paid less than their private sector counterparts. For example, in the Philippines, public sector pay is 25 percent of pay in the private sector while, in Singapore, credited with a very efficient civil service, it is 114 percent (World Bank 1997). The civil service in Singapore may be more efficient because the government both pays employees relatively high wages and emphasizes individual accountability (Huff 1995).

[17] The effectiveness of the civil service could also be increased through other reforms (most of which would require some, but perhaps not a large, allocation of resources). For example, recruitment based on merit (such as through a competitive exam) can increase the quality of recruits as well as motivate civil servants by increasing the competitiveness and prestige of a civil service career. The imposition of a common training program for senior civil servants

Size of the Civil Service Wage Bill

In many countries, the size of the civil service wage bill is excessive and too many resources have been allocated to civil service salaries. Central government wages as a share of GDP tend to be much higher in Africa and the Middle East than in East Asia and South Asia because countries in both Africa and the Middle East tend to have relatively high levels of public sector employment (Huther et al. 1997; Rao 1998). In sub-Saharan Africa, employment in the public sector has grown rapidly, more quickly than wages, with particular growth at the lower skill levels (Mackenzie 1991a). As a result, countries in sub-Saharan Africa tend to have high levels of public employment relative to total formal sector employment (often 50 percent or more).[18] Despite the large relative size of the civil services in sub-Saharan African countries, there is no evidence to suggest that these countries have provided a proportionately greater quantity or quality of public services.

Excessive growth in civil service employment has frequently resulted because governments have used the public sector as an employer of last resort to absorb excess labor or as an instrument of political patronage. Furthermore, in many cases, public sector managers have had little incentive to control costs and, as a result, have expanded employment. Finally, extensive intervention by the state in the economy, as pursued by some governments, requires a large civil service and has necessitated the expansion of state sector employment.

A large public sector wage bill can have a negative impact on output growth as well as on the quality and efficiency of the public service. The diversion of significant resources to the public sector may directly

could improve the quality of the state workforce as well as develop a civil service culture. Governments could also avoid undertaking projects that have unclear goals, that have not been allocated adequate resources, or that are too ambitious to succeed, since these types of projects can undermine the morale and effectiveness of the civil service. If program goals are clear it is much easier to introduce mechanisms to measure performance and improve accountability so that merit based pay and promotion can operate successfully. However, clarifying objectives is very difficult for many social services since the output of these services is often hard to measure. Finally, the capacity and efficiency of the civil service can be impeded by political interference. By imposing merit-based recruitment and promotion for all but the top civil service positions, it is possible to improve incentives and reduce the extent and effects of political interference.

[18] For example, the government of Zambia or its agencies employed 75 percent of Zambia's formal sector workers (Mackenzie 1991a).

discourage private sector investment (through higher taxes and lower private consumption). Furthermore, since many of the resources going to the state sector are required to pay wages, there are often too few resources going to non wage inputs.[19] This has reduced the quality and quantity of the services provided and meant that public servants often do not have adequate resources to do their jobs. Large levels of state employment can also increase inefficiency if there do not exist sufficient resources to monitor and coordinate a large civil service. The significant role played by government employment in the formal sectors of many economies may also mean that governments are drawing skilled labor away from the private sector. Excessive public sector employment and public sector wage settlements may also bid up the price of labor in the private sector and so reduce private sector output. Expansion of the public sector can cause government employment to be seen as the best path for advancement in society and, thereby, retard the development of a local entrepreneurial class (Collier and Gunning 1999). Furthermore, if a public sector career is deemed to be more desirable than a private sector career, workers may prefer to queue for public sector jobs, rather than accept employment in the private sector, and individuals may choose to invest in certain forms of university degrees simply to secure public sector jobs.

In many countries, as the civil service wage bill has increased, governments have tried to restrict its expansion by controlling wage growth, particularly for higher skilled workers, rather than by restricting employment growth.[20] This has caused public sector wages to be relatively low in some countries, particularly for more skilled workers.[21] For example, in Uganda, real public sector wages fell so drastically that, by the mid-1980s, workers could not support themselves on a full-time government salary. Similar declines occurred in Ghana, Nigeria and Zambia. In Argentina, between 1982 and 1988, real public sector wages fell by 17 percent while real private sector wages rose by 12 percent (Mackenzie and Schiff 1991). Low wages in the public sector can reduce incentives in the public service and induce well-trained, capable and experienced managers to leave for

[19] For example, the ratio of wage to non-wage expenditures in sub-Saharan Africa is double that in Asia (Collier and Gunning 1999).

[20] Even with falling real wages, growth in the wage bill has often outpaced spending on other inputs (World Bank 1997).

[21] However, in general, public sector wages are a larger multiple of average per capita income in developing countries than in developed countries (Mackenzie and Schiff 1991).

the private sector. In addition, low wages tend to promote corruption, absenteeism, declining morale and poor service.

The excessive size of the wage bill and state employment in many countries suggests that an important policy priority should be to reduce civil service employment.[22] To accomplish this, resources should be allocated to evaluations of individual spending programs and government services. Programs that are not addressing a market failure, or that are dealing with a market failure unsuccessfully, need not be continued. These evaluations could also determine whether private sector provision of publicly provided goods would be more efficient than public provision.

Even if state employees are not fulfilling a useful purpose, in many countries it is very difficult, for political reasons, to reduce public sector employment. Cuts to civil servant numbers have often not been sustained and governments have often preferred to lower wages rather than reduce employment. Since it is generally easier to avoid hiring new employees than to dismiss existing employees, it is critical to carefully analyze the desirability of new spending programs before they are initiated. When evaluating a new spending program, not only should it be determined whether the spending program is necessary and likely to succeed, but it should also be determined whether there are any controls over employment growth in the new program. Furthermore, if a new program is justified as a replacement for an existing program, or if it will be financed by resources that are to be saved by reducing spending on another program, before implementing the new program, it should be realistically determined whether spending and employment in the existing program will actually be reduced.

[22] One way of reducing civil service employment is to eliminate ghost workers and institute controls to prevent their reappearance. Other policies to reduce government employment levels include laying off temporary workers, hiring freezes, voluntary resignation and early retirement packages, dismissal with severance, and privatization (Mackenzie 1991a). Hiring freezes can be very important in countries in which the government has acted as an employer of last resort (particularly for unemployed university graduates as in Sri Lanka). Lienert and Modi (1997) suggest that the costs associated with voluntary retrenchment programs are often high. Early retirement packages (and dismissal with severance) can impose considerable administrative costs, require costly payments, are frequently subject to abuse, often encourage the best workers to leave, and are only effective if rehiring is not allowed. Despite these problems, one study of retrenchment programs found that efficiency gains and salary savings paid for the costs of severance in 1.7 years on average (World Bank 1997).

Monitoring Expenditure Effectiveness

A major problem with developing country expenditure programs is a lack of adequate monitoring. Once a spending program has been put in place, it is important that it be monitored to determine whether the program has been effective at meeting its goals, whether it has been operating cost-effectively, whether there exist flaws in the program's design (i.e. whether it has altered behavior in an unintended fashion), and whether it has had a negative impact on other sectors of the economy.

Monitoring is critical because it is very difficult to design programs that have the intended consequences in all circumstances.[23] For example, while a spending program may include a particular incentive structure, it is important to determine ex post whether this structure has actually induced the desired response from program participants and program administrators (Crosby 1996). Effective monitoring can also ensure that civil servants have fewer opportunities to provide poor service or participate in rent-seeking behavior (corruption), facilitate the search for the best policy design, and allow civil servants to be held accountable for their performance.[24] This accountability is critical to building the capacity and effectiveness of the state administration. Given the importance of monitoring, monitoring program outputs and inputs should be an important spending priority.

Setting up an effective monitoring mechanism is potentially expensive and, generally, difficult. For example, governments may have very limited access to information on program performance because information on performance is difficult or expensive to collect. Monitoring is especially problematic in sectors for which it is difficult to measure output, such as health care and education. Furthermore, in some circumstances, there may be large incentives for program administrators and participants to falsify information, making any information that is available suspect. Even when reliable information is available, it is often difficult to disentangle the consequences of a particular program from the effects of other programs and changes to the economy (van de Walle 1998). These problems may be

[23] Although related to the performance of firms rather than the civil service, Rodrik (1997) suggests that the success of Korea's export incentive programs was due, in part, to good monitoring (as well as observable performance criteria and a professional bureaucracy).

[24] While monitoring of public sector activities may bring poor performances to light, unless government employees are made accountable, little improvement may be seen.

less serious if programs are designed to facilitate monitoring and assessment.[25]

At a minimum, resources should be allocated to an auditing system that can track whether funds budgeted for certain tasks were actually spent on those tasks. This would provide a basic level of accountability and would help ensure that funds are not stolen or diverted to unintended uses. However, monitoring should not be limited to counting inputs, even though these are cheaper and easier to measure, since input use may have little bearing on the quality and quantity of the services provided. In fact, measuring inputs can be damaging because it may give a false sense that resources are being spent appropriately, even though input monitoring provides little incentive to improve quality or efficiency, and may provide an incentive to increase spending unnecessarily in order to meet spending targets.

Private Sector Provision of Goods

In some instances, if the public provision of a good is warranted by market failure, private sector participation in the provision of the good may have several advantages.[26] With respect to the allocation of state resources between sectors, private provision of goods in a sector may reduce the quantity of state resources that must be allocated to that sector. This can be particularly important for countries with weak public institutions, few resources and a meager institutional capacity. Furthermore, if there is

[25] Given the costs and other difficulties associated with monitoring, it may be possible, with relatively limited expenditure, to make civil services more efficient by creating independent monitors (auditors, citizens advisory committees) or by supporting independent business and consumer associations. For example, an independent auditor general could be given the power to randomly examine state activities, come to conclusions about the cost-effectiveness of these activities, and makes recommendations for improvements. An alternative monitoring mechanism is to use consumers of public services as monitors. This could be done by circulating client surveys or by encouraging users to comment on the efficiency and quality of services through other channels. However, these monitoring activities are only likely to be undertaken seriously if they are believed to have some influence on government behavior and policies.

[26] Private sector provision of public goods can involve profit-oriented private firms or nonprofit NGOs. Nonprofit NGOs often provide high-quality low-cost service for religious or ideological reasons, and are common in the education and health sectors. For example, the government of Bolivia has used religious NGOs to manage public secondary schools with some success (World Bank 1997).

sufficient competition between private sector providers, private sector provision may improve efficiency and quality.[27] Contracting out the provision of public services to private firms can also induce the public sector to provide better services since it introduces the threat of contracting out. In addition, private provision of "public" goods, along side public provision, can provide a benchmark against which to measure the performance of public providers.[28] Contracting out, particularly if it involves a foreign firm, may also reduce the opportunities for corruption.[29]

Contracting out the provision of public goods to private entities is not a panacea. Private providers may be just as inefficient as the government sector if there is not sufficient competition between alternative providers. Contracting out also incurs transaction costs in the design, tendering and monitoring of contracts, and these costs are likely to rise as the complexity of a project increases. Problems with the contracting out of government services can also arise if there is political interference in the choice of the winning bid, if performance standards are not clearly specified, if private firms are not given effective performance incentives, and if inadequate resources are devoted to monitoring the behavior of private providers.

User Fees

While user fees do not have a direct effect on the inter-sectoral allocation of resources, they can have an important indirect effect. If user fees are charged for a public service, fewer state resources may be necessary to provide the service, and the resources saved can then be used to provide other services. Furthermore, if the revenues from user fees stay in the sector in which they are collected, they may be used to improve the quality of the service provided or the amount of resources devoted to maintenance

[27] In Latin America, during the 1990s, more than US$35 billion went into roads through private road concessions. In addition to providing resources that the public sector would then not have to provide, these roads have tended to be constructed more efficiently and to higher standards (Burki et al. 1999).

[28] Chile improved access to basic education significantly by providing funds to both the public sector and the private sector based on the number of students enrolled (Huther et al. 1997).

[29] For example, in an attempt to reduce corruption and increase efficiency, Indonesia contracted out its customs inspections to a Swiss firm (World Bank 1997).

(if adequate incentives are in place).[30] On the other hand, user fees may be costly to collect, they may cause the use of a service to fall below the optimal level, and they may be regressive since the demand of the poor for public services tends to be relatively more price elastic. In evaluations of existing and new expenditure programs, the possibility of employing user fees, and the consequences of so doing, should be addressed.

Section Summary

The effectiveness and organization of the government administration has several implications for the sectoral allocation of resources. First, spending programs should be chosen and designed so that they do not exceed the administrative capacity of the state. Second, resources should be allocated to the design and implementation of mechanisms to evaluate and monitor the effectiveness of expenditures. Monitoring of program expenditures, with emphasis on the effectiveness of expenditures at meeting output goals, should be an important spending priority. Third, programs should be designed with clear and specific goals since this improves monitoring and accountability. Fourth, each spending program should be evaluated to ensure that it provides the appropriate incentives to the providers and beneficiaries of the program. Fifth, since the capacity of the administration is a key constraint in many areas, resources should be allocated to expand this capacity in terms of quantity and quality. This may involve the allocation of significant resources to reform the organization and pay structure of the civil service. Sixth, efforts should be made to reduce civil service employment in those cases in which it is excessive as well as to eliminate expenditure programs that are providing goods that are not associated with significant market failures. Seventh, possibilities for contracting out should be investigated since contracting out may reduce the quantity of state resources required by individual spending programs. However, if contracting-out is used, sufficient resources must be allocated to the contract design and monitoring process. Finally, program development should include an analysis of the appropriateness of user fees since these can reduce the level of state resources needed to provide a public service.

[30] Dailami and Klein (1997) suggest that low tariff rates caused Malaysia's power company to neglect O&M.

Sector-Specific Issues in the Allocation of Government Resources

Law and Security

An important deterrent to investment and the expansion of markets in developing countries is the inadequate and inefficient enforcement of property rights and contracts.[31] The poor enforcement of property rights has an impact on the economy through three principal channels. First, the greater the risks associated with the poor enforcement of property rights, the higher is the expected return investors will require to invest in a project. This leads to lower investment, impedes the growth of the capital stock and hinders the development of markets.[32] Second, even if the return to capital is high, poor property rights enforcement may bias investment away from projects that require significant fixed capital, since fixed capital is more difficult to recover when property rights are threatened. Third, the cost of business may be higher and business expansion less vigorous, as private sector agents rely more heavily on nonjudicial forms of contract enforcement. For example, individuals may restrict their dealings to individuals they know well, a practice that can retard development by preventing trade between parties who are not familiar with one another.

Given the importance of property rights to the development of markets and investment, a key spending priority should be the establishment of a legal structure to enforce property rights and contracts. This requires that resources be allocated to the establishment of a police force capable of combating crime, improvements in the legal education of both lawyers and judges, and the enforcement of the decisions of the courts. Resources should also be committed to reducing legal delays since long delays raise the costs of dispute resolution and make it more difficult to enforce

[31] Property rights can be threatened by government expropriation, the poor enforcement of contracts, or by criminal activity. The problem of crime is particularly serious in sub-Saharan Africa, Latin America and the transition economies and has been an impediment to development in these regions. While security could be provided by the private sector, the level of private spending on security may be too low if there are economies of scale in the provision of security or if the external benefits of security spending result in spending that is lower than socially optimal. Barro (1997) finds that improved maintenance of the rule of law increases the growth rate of real per capita GDP.

[32] Fischer et al. (1998) suggest that the risk associated with poorly enforced property rights and a poorly functioning legal system has had a negative effect on private investment in Africa.

contracts. Finally, it is important to implement a program to monitor judges, such as a judicial council, in order to reduce the number of arbitrary rulings and increase the efficiency of the courts.[33]

The enforcement of property rights also requires that property rights be adequately recorded. The allocation of resources to the registration of land titles, for example, can secure the property rights of the owners and facilitate borrowing in credit markets. Evidence from the Thailand titling project indicates that secure land titles allowed more borrowing by farmers and encouraged investment and other land improvements that led to significant increases in productivity (World Bank 1997).[34]

Military Spending

In many developing countries, significant resources have been allocated to military spending.[35] Through its contribution to the maintenance of law and order, military spending can assist in the protection of property rights. However, in many countries, a large and poorly paid military is a vehicle for extortion and corruption that actually makes the investment environment more costly and less secure. Furthermore, while it has been suggested that a large military may be necessary to maintain political stability, there seems to be little evidence of a link between military spending and political stability (Hemming and Hewitt 1991).

It has also been argued that there may be some benefits from technological diffusion associated with military related R&D. However, in most developing countries, the military is a relatively low-tech, low-skill operation that is likely to have few technological externalities. Among developing countries (other than the transition economies of Eastern Europe), only India and Brazil are large military equipment producers (Hemming and Hewitt 1991). Even in these two countries, while military spending

[33] The failure to establish judicial systems that are efficient, fair and not arbitrary has hampered development in many countries. Weak and slow judicial systems have hampered economic activity in the CIS, while courts in much of Latin America are inefficient, corrupt and suffer from political interference (World Bank 1997).

[34] For borrowing to increase when land titles are made more secure, a rural credit market is also necessary. If this market had not existed in Thailand, as is the case in much of Africa, there might not have been as large an effect.

[35] In Africa, these expenditures average 2.9 percent of GNP (compared to public spending on education of 4.9 percent) while in Latin America they average 1.9 percent (World Bank 2000).

may have had some spin-off effects, it is not clear that spending on military R&D was the most productive or efficient way of producing these spin-offs. Furthermore, significant military-related R&D can divert scientists and engineers from the private sector.[36]

In summary, there seems to be little reason to believe that military spending has a significant positive effect on growth. In fact, most evidence suggests that the effect of military spending on growth is negative and that less military spending would raise growth and improve welfare.[37] Obviously, some military spending is necessary, but it should not be seen as an instrument of growth and efforts should be taken to reduce the quantity of state resources absorbed by the military. In countries with large military budgets, resources should be allocated to an examination of the objectives of military spending and the efficiency with which the military has met these objectives. Such an assessment should also determine whether the level of military manpower is appropriate, whether the level of compensation is adequate, and whether the types of equipment purchased by the military meet identifiable needs.

Infrastructure Investment

Investment in infrastructure, particularly, transportation, communication, power and water infrastructure, has often been considered to be a critical development input and a key responsibility of the public sector. There is little doubt that poor infrastructure can greatly hinder development. On the other hand, greater spending on infrastructure does not necessarily improve a country's development prospects if the infrastructure is poorly constructed, poorly managed, or does not fulfill a useful purpose. Poorly planned, inefficient and unnecessary infrastructure spending is consistent with the results in many studies that find government spending on infrastructure to be unrelated to growth (Barro 1991; Baffes and Shah 1998; Gerson 1998).[38] While Easterly and Levine (1997) find a significant

[36] Military spending may possibly have some human capital development attributes if it builds social cohesion or provides education to those who would otherwise be uneducated. However, given the low-skill nature of the armed forces in most developing countries, these factors are likely to be relatively minor.

[37] See Hemming and Hewitt (1991), Arora and Rayoumi (1994), Devarajan et al. (1996), and Baffes and Shah (1998), for example.

[38] In contrast, Cashin (1995) finds that the ratio of public investment to GDP has a positive impact on growth in per worker output. Also, the World Bank (2000) reports that the

positive relationship between infrastructure and growth, they also find that the quality of infrastructure matters more than the quantity of infrastructure (i.e. the percentage of paved roads is more important than the kilometers of roads).

In many countries, infrastructure investment has been undertaken primarily by the public rather than the private sector. As a result, large quantities of public resources have been devoted to infrastructure and considerable strain has been placed on government financial and administrative capacity. Several reasons have been given for the large level of public participation in infrastructure investment. First, in countries with underdeveloped capital markets, the private sector may not be able to raise sufficient capital to finance large infrastructure projects. Similarly, the large sunk costs associated with infrastructure projects imply that they are often too risky in unstable political environments for the private sector to undertake.[39] Both these factors imply that, if infrastructure were to be built, the public sector would have to build it (or subsidize its construction).[40] The problem for governments is distinguishing between projects that have not been built because sufficient domestic private capital is not available and projects that are simply not economic.

The second major reason for public participation in infrastructure development is that the public sector may be able to internalize the externalities associated with these projects better than individual private investors. For example, consider an infrastructure project (such as a road network) that has many beneficiaries. Suppose no one individual benefits sufficiently from the project to build it on their own, but the aggregate benefit of all users of the project exceeds its cost. If it is costly or difficult to exclude users and charge a user fee, or if individual beneficiaries do not perceive the magnitude of the aggregate benefit, the project is unlikely to be built by a private investor. In this case, the infrastructure will only be built if the public sector intervenes and coordinates the building and

availability of advanced infrastructure was the most important location consideration for international firms located in Hong Kong, Singapore and Taiwan.

[39] In addition, considerable financing for private-sector projects often comes from abroad. This exposes private investors to exchange rate risk and the risk of controls on capital movements (Dailami and Klein 1997).

[40] The importance of foreign aid in infrastructure financing may also induce more public sector involvement.

financing of the project.[41] The critical problem with this rationale for government provision of infrastructure is the identification of economically viable infrastructure projects that have not been built due to coordination problems in the private sector.

The third reason for public provision of infrastructure is that, because some types of infrastructure projects are characterized by decreasing costs, the operators of these projects are often monopolies. Public sector involvement in the provision of this type of infrastructure is justified as a method of countering the inefficiencies and high prices of private monopolies. However, because public monopolies generally have little incentive to produce efficiently or treat consumers any differently than private monopolies, it may also be necessary to regulate and monitor public monopolies.

In the case of publicly provided infrastructure, there is often excess demand for the services provided by the existing infrastructure. This gives the perception that there is a shortage of infrastructure and that the public sector should increase infrastructure spending. However, the observed excess demand may be the result of low user fees and this excess demand may disappear or fall if prices are set to cover a greater proportion of costs. In many sectors, particularly gas, electricity and water, user fees have fallen short of costs, sometimes by considerable margins. Rather than meeting a perceived excess demand for infrastructure by using scarce public resources to expand the stock of infrastructure, it may be more efficient to raise user fees. This would reduce the wasteful use of infrastructure induced by low prices, lower the quantity of government resources allocated to infrastructure development, and could induce the entry of private suppliers (Dailami and Klein 1997).

Although it may be necessary for the public sector to coordinate and instigate the development of some infrastructure projects, this does not preclude private sector participation in the construction and management of these projects. In many countries, innovative methods have been used to encourage private participation in infrastructure through a variety of different forms of contracts.[42] Furthermore, state-owned companies that

[41] In Singapore, the government invested to improve the communications infrastructure. Following this investment, a profitable market in financial services developed. Before the government intervened, the firms operating in this market did not undertake to build the infrastructure themselves.

[42] Private companies have participated in the construction and operation of railroads, ports, power and water companies. For example, private operators now operate the water systems in Buenos Aires, Jakarta and Manila (World Bank 2000).

have been successful in their own jurisdictions could be contracted to run infrastructure in other jurisdictions. For example, the Port of Singapore Authority was contracted to operate the Port of Aden in Yemen.

The participation of private operators in infrastructure projects has two important benefits with relevance to the sectoral allocation of resources. First, a private firm may have a greater incentive to control costs and meet production targets than a public sector firm. Second, private participation may reduce the quantity of scarce public administrative and financial resources required to realize an infrastructure project. On the other hand, private sector involvement is likely to necessitate greater government investment in regulation and monitoring in order to ensure that contract obligations are satisfied and to prevent private firms from acting as inefficient monopolists.[43]

Before the public sector invests in infrastructure, or attempts to coordinate the development of an infrastructure project, it is necessary to determine whether the benefits from the project will outweigh its cost. This generally involves some form of detailed project evaluation. While these appraisals are subject to many types of distortions, and can be made to make extremely uneconomic projects look economic, they provide at least a minimal framework with which to evaluate and rank projects. Measures of access to infrastructure services, particularly relative to those of similarly developed countries, can also be used to identify priority sectors for infrastructure investment. These might include the percentage of the population with access to safe water and sanitation, the percentage of the population with access to electricity and the proportion of time electricity is available, as well as the length of the road (paved and unpaved) and rail systems.[44] If the state has already devoted significant resources to infrastructure in a particular sector, the marginal benefit of increased spending is likely to be small. Low measures of access to services may simply imply that the existing infrastructure is being poorly used.

In addition to individual project appraisals, several general criteria can be used to identify the most useful infrastructure projects. Infrastructure that supports the development of market activities (particularly export activities), such as transportation and communication networks, should be

[43] This may be no more significant than the monitoring that would have to be undertaken of state-owned infrastructure.

[44] Output measures of this type can also be used to evaluate the effectiveness of existing infrastructure, something that should be done before new infrastructure is constructed.

given high priority since these are likely to have a large impact on competition and growth. Resources should not be allocated to projects that are likely to be undertaken by the private sector. The level of infrastructure investment undertaken should also depend on the administrative capacity of the public sector and the resources required for the efficient administration and monitoring of the infrastructure. For example, since administrative capacity is generally a constraint, projects that are complex to implement, monitor and evaluate should receive lower priority than more straightforward projects. Furthermore, there is little point in undertaking investment in infrastructure if the resources to operate and maintain the new infrastructure are unlikely to be available or if the new infrastructure would cause funds to be diverted from the operation and maintenance of existing infrastructure.

In summary, infrastructure is an important input in development and large increases in infrastructure are likely to be necessary to support rising incomes and output. However, large quantities of infrastructure investment have strained the financial and administrative capacity of many states, and much of the infrastructure constructed is of poor quality, badly maintained, and inefficiently operated. As a result, in many cases, infrastructure projects have not successfully met their objectives. The resource demands of infrastructure development could be reduced, and the quality potentially improved, through greater private sector involvement in the construction and management of infrastructure. However, if this were done, a greater quantity of resources would have to be allocated to government regulatory and monitoring activities. There is little justification in committing resources to infrastructure if it is not likely to be properly constructed or operated. As found by Easterly and Levine (1997), the quality of infrastructure is often more important than the quantity. Thus, it may be more efficient to allocate resources to improve the quality and operation of existing infrastructure than to construct new infrastructure.

Transportation Infrastructure

Due to its important role in growth and development, particularly in the development of markets, investment in communication and transportation infrastructure should generally be given high priority.[45] Poor

[45] In reviewing the empirical literature on government spending and growth, Kneller et al. (1999) find that only transportation and communication infrastructure spending have a con-

transportation infrastructure makes markets difficult to reach, economies of scale, particularly in manufacturing, difficult to exploit, and production more costly and risky, since input supplies are uncertain.[46] An efficient transportation infrastructure is particularly necessary for export-oriented growth since producers will not invest to produce for more distant markets if they cannot move their product to these markets. Inefficiencies in the transportation networks, including ports and airports, of sub-Saharan Africa have imposed significant costs on exporters relative to their competitors in other countries.

Poor transportation infrastructure may also reduce competition and allow firms to act as inefficient regional monopolists. For example, in countries with poor transportation networks, the regional distribution of goods may be controlled by a single firm. In this case, investment in the expansion and efficiency of agricultural production and the local retail sector may be hindered by the noncompetitive behavior of the local distributor. Improvements in the transportation network can make both the product market and the product distribution system more competitive by facilitating the participation of consumers, producers and retailers in both the local and more distant markets.[47] Improved road links have allowed trucks to provide significant competition for railroads. Furthermore, while ports and airports may have a local monopoly, improvements in transportation links can increase competition by making it feasible for firms to ship to and from other locations. More competition in the transport sector should lower transport costs and encourage expansion of the productive sector.[48]

In most countries, the highest transportation priority should involve improvements to the extent and quality of the road system since this is likely to be the most flexible way of linking markets. Road density and

sistent positive effect on growth. In contrast, Devarajan et al. (1996) find that the larger the transportation and communication spending as a share of total spending, the lower is the growth rate. This could be because the efficiency of this spending has been low or that the infrastructure has not been adequately maintained.

[46] This raises firm costs since firms must keep larger inventories of spare parts and inputs.

[47] The Hong Kong market garden sector expanded considerably after bike paths were improved so that producers could more easily take their produce to market. Evidence from India (World Bank 1997) suggests that lower transportation costs increase agricultural output by making it easier for farmers to get their goods to market.

[48] Fischer et al. (1998) suggest that noncompetitive ports, airlines and rail carriers have led to high transportation costs in Africa.

quality tends to be low in developing countries relative to developed countries, although roads carry 60–80 percent of freight (Burki et al. 1999).[49] Considerable emphasis should be placed on improving the quality of roads since poor quality roads can significantly add to the costs of producers (in terms of time and wear on vehicles).[50]

Operations and Maintenance

In many developing countries, inadequate resources have been allocated to the operation and maintenance (O&M) of infrastructure.[51] As a result, the benefits of the infrastructure have not been realized, the quality of the service provided is poor, the cost of the service is high, and some infrastructure has deteriorated to such an extent that it is not useable. For example, poor maintenance of domestic and agricultural water systems has resulted in large water losses through leakage, and poor maintenance and operation of power systems has resulted in losses that are more than twice as large in low-income countries as in other countries (World Bank 1997). As a result of poor O&M, almost half of all medical equipment in developing countries is unusable, and much of this equipment never reached its normal life span (World Bank 1993). In addition to inadequate maintenance spending, underfunding of operations expenditures has meant that, in some cases, health and education infrastructure has been left unused because of staff and input shortages.

Poorly maintained infrastructure in the transport and electricity sectors, by raising the costs of producers and increasing the risks associated with production, has been a major impediment to private sector development.[52]

[49] In sub-Saharan Africa, roads carry 80–90 percent of passenger and freight traffic and are the only way of reaching many communities (Pennant-Rea and Heggie 1995).

[50] The 88 percent of Tanzania's roads that are in poor condition imposed additional transportation costs equal to a third of export earnings in 1990 (World Bank 2000). Poor quality roads raised transport costs by 17 percent in Zambia in 1992 while in 1993, in Kenya, the failure to spend $40 million on road maintenance resulted in $120 million in increased vehicle operating costs (Pennant-Rea and Heggie 1995). Minten and Kyle (1999) provide evidence that road quality is negatively related to food costs in the former Zaire.

[51] For example, in sub-Saharan Africa, the funds allocated to road maintenance are generally less than half those needed and, in some countries, are less than a third (Pennant-Rea and Heggie 1995).

[52] The interruption of electricity supplies due to poor maintenance can seriously disrupt production and may cause firms to maintain their own costly power generation capacity.

Given the importance of infrastructure to the operation of a market economy, the rate of return to O&M spending is likely to be higher than that on new investment.[53] In addition, spending on infrastructure maintenance on a continuous basis is likely to be less expensive than more irregular spending.[54] These two factors imply that O&M spending should be a priority in most sectors. Simply by ensuring that existing capital is used more efficiently, O&M spending may increase a country's growth rate as well as raise the quality and quantity of services provided.

Shortages in O&M spending are likely the result of this type of spending being one of the easier types of spending to cut. It is generally less impressive than new capital projects, it is rarely supported by foreign donors, it may serve little political purpose relative to other types of spending, and the negative effects of too little maintenance spending generally appear in the future and so are not immediately obvious. There may also be little data on the extent of O&M problems and the adequate level of O&M spending.

One additional cause of inadequate O&M spending is the failure of governments to include sufficient O&M funds in the budgets of new and existing projects. While incorporating reasonable levels of funds for O&M in the budgets of capital projects is a start, this does not guarantee that the budgeted resources will be spent efficiently or on O&M. Thus, resources must also be allocated to the design and implementation of incentive and monitoring mechanisms to ensure that O&M budget allocations are spent effectively. While introducing the appropriate incentives is often difficult, and generally requires considerable administrative capacity, it is critical to ensure that O&M spending is of high quality and does not lead simply to greater spending on wages and employment with little effective impact on the level of actual O&M undertaken. Since the technical and management capacity to effectively undertake O&M expenditures is often lacking (Heller 1991), resources should be allocated to develop this capacity.

[53] For example, the return to road maintenance is quite high, often over 35 percent (Pennant-Rea and Heggie 1995).

[54] Burki et al. (1999) quote a study that found US$43 billion of roads had eroded—a process that could have been prevented with expenditure of US$12 billion. According to Pennant-Rea and Heggie (1995), infrequent road maintenance raises the cost of maintenance by about one-third.

Education

Government subsidies to education may be justified if the social return to education exceeds the private return, so that private spending on education is less than optimal. Universal primary education, for example, may yield a larger social than private return by promoting social cohesion and basic literacy, both of which may improve the functioning of the economy. Higher levels of education may also facilitate the absorption of technology, which can have large network externalities.[55] For instance, by adopting new technologies faster than uneducated farmers, educated farmers are an example for uneducated farmers (World Bank 1998). Education spending, particularly spending on the education of females, also appears to improve family health, childcare and the educational attainment of children, while reducing both child mortality and the birth rate.[56]

Imperfect information and the absence of credit markets have also been used to rationalize government expenditure on education. An individual's investment in education yields an uncertain future payoff that depends on many factors, including individual effort. For this reason, and because those individuals investing in education often have little collateral, it is difficult for education investments to be financed in credit markets. As a result, if left to the private sector, investment in education may be lower than socially optimal. Furthermore, because individuals often have imperfect information about the benefits of education, they may undervalue education and, thus, invest less than is optimal.

Education spending has also been justified as a means of redistributing income and opportunities to the poor. In the absence of complete capital markets and perfect information, the educational opportunities of the poor are severely limited. Spending on primary education is often the largest redistributive expenditure undertaken by the public sector (Burki et al. 1999).

If the social return to education exceeds the private return, the allocation of state resources to education could conceivably have a positive impact on growth. However, in a review of the growth literature, Gerson (1998) finds that, while educational attainment generally has been found to have a positive effect on growth, there does not exist a clear relationship between education spending and growth. Schultz (1999) also finds that

[55] Fischer et al. (1998) suggest that inadequate human capital has reduced the productivity of private capital in Africa.

[56] See Nehru et al. (1995), World Bank (1998) and Schultz (1999).

the empirical evidence on the link between higher levels of education spending and growth is mixed (and is beset by data and measurement problems).[57]

One reason why education spending and growth may not be closely linked is that the efficiency, quality and coverage of education spending differ significantly across countries.[58] Despite the allocation of significant state resources to education, in many cases, education systems are characterized by serious problems. For example, although there is a high social return to educating females, in many countries education spending and programs continue to be biased against females.[59] Furthermore, half the children in Africa, many of whom are female, poor and ethnic minorities, do not go to school (World Bank 1997), while, in developing countries as a whole, approximately 20 percent of children receive less than five years of education (World Bank 2000). Even when children do attend school, the schools in many developing countries are poorly run, inadequately funded, and their teachers are often not well trained or motivated. As a result, the education provided is of poor quality, and many primary schools are characterized by high repetition rates, low graduation rates, and low achievement scores. Mingat (1998) notes that considerable empirical evidence shows the importance of the quality as well as the quantity of education. The high-performing Asian economies have been successful at providing high-quality education as well as ensuring high rates of

[57] For example, Cashin (1995) and Devarajan et al. (1996) do not find a statistically significant link between growth and education spending, while Barro (1991), Easterly and Levine (1997), Baffes and Shah (1998), Mingat (1998) and Temple (1999) find a link between variables related to education spending and growth. Krueger and Lindahl (1998) conclude that the finding of an insignificant effect of education spending on growth is due to measurement errors and that, after correcting for these errors, education spending has a positive effect on growth.

[58] Mingat (1998) notes how developing countries that spent similar proportions of GDP on education had very different outcomes in terms of average number of grades completed, while developing countries that had similar numbers of grades completed spent very different proportions of GDP on education. Gupta et al. (1997) find that efficiency falls at higher levels of per capita spending on education. Thus, higher levels of spending do not necessarily improve outputs. Higher education levels may also not increase the growth rate if the economy is hindered by other distortions. The World Bank (2000) notes, countries with high levels of education but low levels of foreign direct investment do no better than countries with low education levels and low levels of foreign direct investment.

[59] In Côte d'Ivoire and Pakistan, respectively, public spending on boys is two times and one-and-a-half times greater than spending on girls (World Bank 1997).

enrollment.[60] These factors suggest that the principal priority of education spending should be to increase access and improve quality, rather than simply to increase spending.

Improvements in school quality are likely to follow from improvements in teacher training, behavior and motivation. Mingat (1998) notes that the rapidly growing Asian economies tended to pay teachers higher salaries than other countries. In this way, they attracted more qualified individuals to the profession. However, to be effective, higher teacher salaries must be combined with incentive and monitoring mechanisms that induce the provision of high-quality education.[61] At a minimum, this would require that sufficient resources be allocated to measure the output and quality of the education provided (rather than simply the level of spending).[62] Useful educational outcome measures might include enrollment rates by level and gender, standard achievement test scores, the percentage of the population with reasonable access to a school, the proportion of students that attend secondary schools, graduation and dropout rates, literacy rates and the supply of skilled professionals.

Educational outcomes may also improve with the increased availability of school supplies. Considerable evidence suggests that educational supplies (such as books and blackboards) in primary schools have been underprovided, perhaps because it is politically easier to cut spending on supplies than on salaries (Mackenzie 1991c). However, supplies may be an important ingredient for education success since, for example, empirical

[60] In some schools in Ghana and Kenya, after several years of primary school, test results indicated that nothing had been learned (World Bank 1998). For Ghana, Glewwe (1996) found that the social rate of return to improvements in school quality was greater than the return to an additional year of schooling without improvements in quality. One reason for the high unemployment rate of secondary school graduates in Sri Lanka is that the curriculum was poor.

[61] Monitoring can absorb considerable resources that could have been used in the classroom, but may be less costly if local school committees are used as monitors (although they may require training). In Brazil, local school councils have been given some responsibility and have had some positive effects on achievement results (World Bank 1997).

[62] Since input measures do not reflect the quality or efficiency of spending, they are not particularly useful. However, they can be used to compare spending levels across jurisdictions, in particular, relative to the education output produced. Input measures might include the number of teachers in classrooms, teacher–pupil ratios, spending on inputs other than wages, and the qualifications of teachers.

evidence suggests that student achievement depends on the adequate provision of textbooks (Lockheed et al. 1991).[63]

Achievement levels and enrollment rates in primary schools are, according to some empirical evidence, determined to a large extent by the availability of schools.[64] This would suggest that spending priority be given to improving access to schools. On the other hand, Schultz (1999) cites evidence for African countries that shows little relationship between school distance and primary school enrollment.[65] Thus, prior to expanding the number of schools, evidence should be obtained to ascertain whether enrollment has been hindered by the absence of school facilities or some other factor.

In order to improve school quality, it may not be necessary to reduce the pupil–teacher ratio. Low pupil–teacher ratios require more resources and may have little impact on learning. By maintaining relatively high pupil–teacher ratios (for their stage of development), the rapidly growing Asian economies were able to provide universal primary education for the same resources that would have financed only partial coverage at a lower pupil–teacher ratio (Mingat 1998).

In summary, the principal emphasis of state education spending should be on extending access to primary education and on improving the quality of education. This can be done by improving access to schools in areas that do not have them, ensuring that school supplies are available, devoting resources to improved teacher training, and increasing teacher motivation. Higher salaries may attract better-trained and motivated teachers. Some evidence also suggests that providing incentives to teachers and school administrators, while giving more decision-making power to schools, can improve educational outcomes without large increases in funding (Burki et al. 1999). Higher teacher salaries, more schools, greater autonomy and greater spending on supplies are unlikely to be successful without adequate accountability and sufficient monitoring of outcomes. As a result, resources should be devoted to assessing teacher and school performance.

[63] In Ghana, spending on blackboards and classroom repairs has improved educational outcomes. In Vietnam, three times as many commune leaders believed that better school facilities and better teacher training would improve educational outcomes more than a greater number of teachers or better-paid teachers (World Bank 1998).

[64] See the evidence cited in Huther et al. (1997).

[65] Schultz (1999) also notes that spending on more schools tends to improve the educational attainment of poor rural residents, while spending to improve education quality tends to favor rich urban residents.

Primary Versus Tertiary Education

Education spending is biased in many countries in favor of the tertiary sector. For example, as a percent of spending on university education, the per pupil current expenditure on primary education was only 3 percent in sub-Saharan Africa, 8 percent in East Asia/Oceania and 13 percent in South Asia, Latin America and the Caribbean (Huther et al. 1997). In Africa as a whole, spending per student is approximately 44 times greater at the tertiary level than at the primary level, although in Tanzania it was 238 times greater (World Bank 1997). While primary education enrollment rates are lower in Africa than in developing countries in other regions, African enrollment rates at the secondary and tertiary levels are higher. Despite this imbalance, primary enrollment rates in Africa actually fell from 1980 to 1990 (Schultz 1999). The emphasis on tertiary education in Africa contrasts with the considerable emphasis placed by the rapidly growing South East Asian nations on primary education (a policy that yielded enrollment rates of close to 100 percent).

The spending bias against primary education exhibited by many countries is likely to have consequences for the distribution of income, economic efficiency and growth. Considerable empirical evidence indicates that the private and social returns to primary education in developing countries are higher than the returns to investment in tertiary education (Mackenzie 1991c; Psacharopoulos 1994). In addition, the relative rate of return to primary education tends to be higher for the least developed countries (Mingat 1998). Mingat (1998) finds that primary enrollment rates positively affect growth, while secondary and tertiary enrollment rates have an insignificant or negative effect on growth. In addition to having a lower social rate of return, spending on tertiary education benefits far fewer students than spending on primary (or secondary) education, and those who benefit from spending at the tertiary level tend to be from the wealthier segment of society.[66] Thus, for both distributional and

[66] Although governments cover the bulk of the costs of tertiary education in many developing countries, the cost of attendance is usually high enough to exclude the poor (Mackenzie 1991c). As a result, increased spending on university education is likely to increase inequality. Huther et al. (1997) note that, in Costa Rica, the poorest 40 percent of households receive 57 percent of the benefits from primary education, while the richest 20 percent receive 43 percent of the benefits from tertiary spending. Similarly, in Ghana, the richest 20 percent of households receive 45 percent of the subsidies to tertiary education while the poorest 20 percent receive only 6 percent (World Bank 1998).

efficiency reasons, in many countries education spending should be reallocated from the tertiary to the primary education sector.[67]

While efficiency and distributional factors suggest that greater emphasis be placed on primary education, the efficient allocation of resources requires some spending on all levels of education. As countries become more developed, the demand for more educated workers tends to rise, and relatively more resources should be shifted to the tertiary education sector. During the 1970s, higher education enrollment expanded in Singapore at an annual rate of 3.7 percent. During the 1980s, as Singapore became more technologically advanced and the demand for university educated workers rose, tertiary enrollment grew at twice this rate (Huff 1995). Nevertheless, for countries at a relatively early stage of development, tertiary education should remain a low priority.

In addition to responding to differences in the rates of return across education levels, the allocation of state education resources should also respond to differences in the social rate of return across programs within the tertiary education sector. Many lower-income developing countries have postsecondary education systems that prepare students for civil service administrative jobs while providing very little technical training (World Bank 1998). It may be more useful for state resources to promote postsecondary education in the sciences and engineering since this is likely to facilitate the adoption of technology from more advanced economies. Empirical evidence implies that the proportion of students enrolled in science, engineering and mathematics has a positive effect on growth (World Bank 1998).[68]

In general, governments have directly provided education services. The rationale for public, rather than private, provision of education is that direct provision is a more efficient method of regulation and monitoring (Mackenzie 1991c). However, even if education is directly provided by government agencies, these agencies must be monitored in order to assess their effectiveness, while government monopoly provision of education services prevents comparisons with, and competitive pressures from,

[67] In a cross-country study, Gupta et al. (1999) find that shifting spending toward primary and secondary education has a positive impact on enrollment rates as well as on the number of students enrolled through grade 4.

[68] For example, Singapore's rapid expansion of tertiary education did not significantly involve the humanities.

alternative education service providers.[69] In several of the rapidly growing Asian economies, because so much of the return to spending at the tertiary level is private, emphasis has been given to private provision of tertiary education.[70] Furthermore, since a larger part of the benefit of tertiary education is likely to be purely private (in the sense of being reflected in higher wages), a significant part of the cost of tertiary education should be borne by students.[71] Greater cost-recovery at the tertiary level of education and greater provision of university-level education by the private sector (with standards set and monitored by the government) would free up public funds for spending on primary education. Higher fees may also act as an incentive for students to choose worthwhile career paths as well as for schools to offer programs in demand.

With greater emphasis on cost-recovery at the secondary and tertiary levels, the state may be pressured to introduce grant or loan programs in order to ensure access to the relatively less well-off. Student loan programs can be expensive, as loan default rates tend to be high, and are costly and cumbersome to administer, particularly if the loans are contingent on future income. In addition, these programs tend to be regressive since, even when loans are available, the poor generally find tertiary education to be too costly.

In conclusion, least developed countries should emphasize the expansion and improvement of primary rather than tertiary education. Secondary-level and university-level education should only be given greater emphasis as the level of development advances, with much of any

[69] It is common in some countries to have competing education systems (public and private) both financed by the public sector (as in Canada, the Netherlands and Chile). In these systems, as with a purely public system, the state must continue to monitor quality and maintain general curriculum standards in order to protect uninformed parents and students. While operating two parallel education systems may be more expensive from an administrative perspective, the competition engendered by the two systems could potentially have a significantly positive impact on education quality.

[70] In Korea, Japan and Taiwan, the majority of students at the tertiary level are enrolled in private schools (Mingat 1998). In 1995, enrollment in private colleges and universities in Korea was more than four times that of public institutions (World Bank 1998).

[71] Note that market efficiency requires that **social** marginal cost and **social** marginal benefit be equalized. In some studies, the private return to education has been shown to be high. Estimated private rates of return for education in developing countries are 30 percent for primary education and 20 percent for secondary and tertiary education (World Bank 1998). Since the private return to an investment, by its very nature, is captured by the individual undertaking the investment, the individual should bear the cost of earning this return.

increase in spending directed to technical areas such as the sciences and engineering. Increased user fees and private participation at the tertiary level can increase the quantity of state resources available for primary education.

The Health Sector

Many types of primary health services have spillover benefits that accrue to individuals other than the individual directly acquiring the service. As a result, state intervention is necessary to ensure that the efficient quantity of these services is provided. Examples of health-related expenditures that may have important spillover effects include disease control (such as malaria and TB), immunization against infectious diseases, provision of clean water and sanitation, pre- and postnatal care, family planning, public health education (with respect to nutrition, hygiene, smoking and communicable diseases such as AIDS), regulation of the health sector, and environmental regulation.[72] In addition to internalizing the spillovers associated with spending on these services, these types of public expenditures can lower total health costs by reducing the level of curative care required, improve the quality of life, and increase worker productivity.[73] Provision of these primary health-related services, most of which involve preventive actions, has a higher return than curative care and also tends to be less regressive than other types of health expenditures.[74]

The magnitude of the benefit from spending on primary health-related services could potentially be large. For example, the unsafe disposal of waste and the consumption of unsafe water are important contributing factors to both the spread of disease and infant mortality.[75] However, nearly 1.5 billion people in developing countries, most living in rural areas, do not have access to clean water, while 2.6 billion people do not have

[72] It may also be optimal for the government to subsidize the provision of these services if imperfect information causes individuals to undervalue their benefits (World Bank 1997).

[73] See Schultz and Tansel (1997) on the significant negative relationship between disabling health status and wages.

[74] The emphasis placed by the Indonesian government on primary health care in the 1970s and 1980s caused the share of health subsidies captured by the lowest 40 percent of households to rise from 19 percent to 31 percent (Huther et al. 1997).

[75] Gupta et al. (1999) find that shifting spending toward primary care reduces infant and child mortality rates.

access to basic sanitation (World Bank 2000).[76] In addition to improving health status, a large proportion of spending on clean water and sanitation is likely to benefit the poor and, thus, may also reduce inequality.

While some types of health-related spending are associated with benefit spillovers, many types of health spending, particularly spending on curative care, yield primarily private benefits. Nevertheless, governments have often directly provided or subsidized these types of health services for several reasons. First, in many countries, the market for health insurance is underdeveloped or nonexistent. Government direct provision of basic curative services, or provision of insurance against catastrophic health-related events, is intended to counteract the effects of this missing market. Second, since private sector provision of health care is often skewed in favor of urban areas and the rich, public provision can counteract this bias if it emphasizes the provision of services to the poor and rural areas. Third, some regulation of the health care sector may be necessary to compensate for imperfect consumer knowledge. To make this regulation less cumbersome to administer, it may be more efficient for the government to directly provide basic health care.

While there may be a role for government in the provision of health services that are essentially private goods, a subsidized system of comprehensive health services is beyond the means of most governments. This means that governments must be extremely careful in choosing the types of health services to provide and subsidize. For example, the absence of private health insurance has been used to justify the provision of subsidized hospital care by governments. However, hospital care is very expensive and tends to benefit the rich more than the poor (Filmer et al. 1997). Furthermore, empirical evidence indicates that the return to basic health care is higher than the return to tertiary care (Huther et al. 1997).

[76] In sub-Saharan Africa, only one-third of rural residents have access to safe water, as opposed to three-quarters of urban residents. In East Asia, the proportion of the population with access to safe water is 60 percent in rural areas, but almost 100 percent in urban areas. Only 4 percent of rural residents in East Asia have access to sanitation services compared to over 60 percent of urban residents. In sub-Saharan Africa, the proportion of the rural population with access to sanitation is under 30 percent, approximately half the proportion in urban areas. In South Asia, urban population access to sanitation is just over 60 percent, while rural access is under 20 percent. In Latin America and the Caribbean, while access to sanitation is just under 80 percent in urban areas, it is barely over 30 percent in rural areas (Huther et al. 1997).

While basic health clinics are less expensive to provide than hospitals, state spending on basic curative care may not be necessary if there already exists substantial private provision of health services. Under these circumstances, state-provided curative services will either be underutilized or crowd out private sector providers. In either case, state spending is unlikely to substantially alter health outcomes. As a consequence, state spending on curative services should be directed at individuals and areas that do not have access to private health services (generally poorer and rural areas) so that they will not encourage substitution from the private to the state sector. The provision of only extremely basic care in poor areas, for example, is likely to ensure that the rich self-select away from the state system.[77]

Schultz (1999) maintains that it is low levels of health status, and the impact of poor health on human capital development, that has been one of the major impediments to growth in Africa. Fogel (1994) provides historical evidence for developed countries, which indicates that poor childhood nutrition leads to an increase in chronic diseases in later life that has a negative impact on labor force productivity.[78] However, Devarajan et al. (1996) do not find a statistically significant link between growth and the share of government spending on health. Similarly, in a review of the empirical growth literature, Gerson (1998) found that the level of health status has generally had a positive effect on growth, but the level of health spending is not closely related to growth. This finding is consistent with the considerable empirical evidence reviewed in Filmer et al. (1997), as well as the evidence in Gupta et al. (1999), that finds little impact of health spending on health outcomes.

While the impact of health-related spending on productivity and growth may take considerable time to occur (as recognized by Fogel (1994)), the impact on health outcomes should become apparent more quickly. The absence of a positive empirical relationship between health spending and health outcomes may follow from the inefficiency and poor quality of publicly provided health services in many developing countries (World Bank

[77] In the rapidly growing countries of Asia (Korea, Taiwan, Singapore), state spending on health care is relatively small as health care is left to the private sector. There is some state health insurance, but this only expanded as the level of development rose (Rao 1998). In low-income countries as a whole, over 63 percent of total spending on health care is private, relative to 53.6 percent for all countries. The share was almost 75 percent in South Asia and was close to 60 percent in sub-Saharan Africa and Latin America (Filmer et al. 1997).

[78] Fogel attributes about 30 percent of Britain's growth over the last 200 years to improvements in nutrition.

1997). Clinics have often lacked trained staff as well as basic medical supplies, drugs and equipment. In many cases, because of inadequate O&M, equipment has worn out prematurely, while doctors and nurses in public clinics often have little incentive to provide quality care (Filmer et al. 1997). As a result of these factors, clinics have not been able to provide the services for which they were intended, and patients have often chosen private providers even when public services were free or very cheap.[79] Low utilization and poor operation of public health facilities can greatly reduce the effectiveness of public expenditures, while variations in expenditure effectiveness can lead to large differences in health outcomes that are not reflected in spending differences.

The failures of the public health systems in many countries are often due to poor monitoring, accountability, cost control and administration. Incentives for health workers are ineffective or nonexistent, and spending programs often exceed the capacity of the public service. Before increasing the resources going to the health sector, resources should be allocated to improving the quality and efficiency of health spending. This could be accomplished by increased monitoring of health facilities, the measurement of inputs and outputs, and a pay system that provides service provision incentives. Reliance by the state on private providers of health services could lead to competition between private providers and may also improve efficiency and quality.

Since user fees can directly increase the resources available to the health system and restrict demand for health services, the use of user fees may reduce the quantity of state resources required by the health sector. While there is probably scope for increased cost recovery in the health sectors of many developing countries, individuals may be less willing to pay for preventive care than curative care because the benefits of preventive care are less easy to perceive. As a result, it may not be beneficial to charge user fees for many types of preventive care. In Benin, for example, user charges were imposed for curative visits and drugs, while preventive health care services were provided free of charge. Although user fees may reduce the resource requirements of the health sector, they may be difficult to

[79] Berman (1998) suggests that a key reason for the ineffectiveness of India's primary care system was that the number of clinics was expanded without an adequate increase in funding. This meant that staff and input shortages were common, and the quality of service low, with the result that the sick preferred to rely on private sector providers. See also Filmer et al. (1997).

administer and may also have adverse consequences for health consumption and the distribution of income. It may be possible to minimize these adverse consequences by discriminating on the basis of observable characteristics such as age (old and young), the presence of a disability, new mothers, or type of disease.[80]

In summary, most developing countries do not have sufficient resources to finance and operate a comprehensive health care system. Attempts to operate a system of this type are likely to result in inefficient and inequitable health care provision as well as neglect of the basic health services that should be government priorities. The highest returns to government spending in the health sector are likely to come from the provision of basic health services, particularly to the poor and in rural areas (since this would make the distribution of health services more equitable). These basic services would include simple curative care in primary facilities, such as clinics, health education programs designed to improve sanitation and nutrition, public health campaigns, spending on improved access to sanitation and clean water, disease control, and other forms of preventive care. Resources should be allocated to improving the quality and efficiency of existing government health facilities, before expanding the quantity of facilities. Efficiency may be improved and the resources required by the health system reduced through greater private sector participation in the delivery of health services and the greater use of user fees. Resources should not be allocated to the provision of services that are already adequately provided by the private sector or that will be underutilized because they are of poor quality.

Redistribution

Given the high level of poverty and income inequality in developing countries, income redistribution policies have taken on considerable importance. This has occurred for altruistic reasons as well as to maintain political and social stability. As countries develop, two factors are likely to increase the importance of government sponsored redistribution: income growth will make more resources available for redistribution and the traditional extended family support network is likely to weaken. While redistributive policies are likely to grow in importance, the experience of many countries with redistributive programs has not always been positive. Programs have

[80] For a discussion of cost recovery in the health sector see Kochhar (1991).

been poorly designed and poorly administered and, as a result, they have been costly and ineffective (sometimes actually regressive). They have also frequently provided individuals with perverse incentives.

In developing countries, since direct income transfers are rare, redistribution generally takes one of three forms: public works programs, social insurance programs or consumption subsidies (i.e. for health, housing, education, fuel and food). As a result of the frequently high levels of seasonal unemployment in rural areas, public employment programs (road building, irrigation system maintenance, conservation projects) have been used extensively as a method of reducing unemployment and redistributing income to the rural poor. This form of redistribution is particularly common in Africa and South Asia (World Bank 1997). The advantages of these programs are that they may have better incentive effects than cash transfers, and they may expand the infrastructure base (Ahmad and Hemming 1991).

While some public works programs have been successful, they have often suffered from several shortcomings. First, if the wage is set too high, workers other than the very poor will be attracted to the program, the redistributive nature of the program will be weakened, and the cost of a given level of redistribution will be high. On the other hand, if the wage is set too low, workers often have little incentive to work efficiently or effectively and, hence, the quantity and quality of the work accomplished is low. Second, management of these programs is often inadequate and monitoring weak so that the quality of the work is poor. Third, the administration of these programs is often quite involved (since they are spread across rural areas and tend to start and stop during the year), which makes the programs difficult and costly to administer. Fourth, these programs can divert workers from the private sector if they are not put in place only when unemployment is high, either cyclically or seasonally. Fifth, only projects that require large temporary quantities of unskilled labor are likely to be effective. Finally, if these programs do not create infrastructure that serves the poor, they will have a smaller redistributive effect.[81] The quantity of state resources allocated to these types of programs should depend on the extent to which these difficulties can be addressed.

[81] Ravallion (1999) provides a relatively simple way of evaluating these programs. Using this methodology, he finds them to be quite expensive for each dollar of increased income going to the poor.

The second major method of redistribution employed in developing countries is social insurance. This includes programs such as family benefits and, most importantly, pensions. Most of these programs are very poor instruments of income redistribution and poverty alleviation since they benefit only a small part of the population, generally workers in the formal sector and, in particular, civil servants. They are, therefore, heavily biased against the rural poor.[82] Furthermore, because the administration of social insurance systems is extremely complex, they are costly to run, they are often inefficiently administered, and they place large demands on the state's administrative capacity (Jütting 1999). An additional problem with social insurance programs in many developing countries, particularly pension programs, is that they are fiscally unsustainable.[83] This is principally due to poor design and targeting, demographic pressures and political pressures to raise benefits. Given the high costs and other shortcomings of social insurance programs, the quantity of government resources allocated to these programs should be severely limited. They are likely to be appropriate only for countries at a relatively advanced level of development with a large formal sector. For example, countries such as Korea and Taiwan only introduced social insurance gradually, beginning with the most needy and easily covered, after having reached a certain level of development (Rao 1998). If financial markets are well developed, the allocation of state resources to these programs can be reduced by placing more emphasis on private sector involvement.[84]

[82] Social insurance programs cover only 6 percent of the labor force in sub-Saharan Africa, 23 percent in Asia and 38 percent in Latin America (World Bank 1997). It is difficult to use these programs to cover the informal sector, such as rural farmers, because it is difficult to collect taxes or contributions from this sector.

[83] For example, implicit pension debt, as a percentage of GDP, is 296 for Uruguay, 187 for Brazil, 72 for Turkey, 63 for China and 44 for Cameroon (World Bank 1997). These large implicit liabilities could have a negative impact on the future growth of these countries. Using data for OECD countries, Kneller et al. (1999) find a negative relationship between social security expenditures and per capita growth.

[84] For example, a pension program could operate as a fully funded private system (perhaps with mandatory payments) that is regulated by the government. Similarly, the private provision of unemployment insurance could be instituted through a forced savings program involving individual unemployment insurance accounts. The private provision of mandatory social insurance programs has been introduced in, for example, Singapore (Huff 1995), Chile and Australia. However, private programs cannot benefit individuals who have not been able to save adequately due to poverty or unemployment. Schemes of this sort are also only likely to be relevant to workers in the formal sector.

In addition to public works programs and social insurance programs, consumption subsidies have frequently been used as instruments of redistribution in developing countries. These programs come in various forms, but it is common for governments to simply subsidize the prices of basic foodstuffs and fuel, particularly in Africa, the transition economies and the Middle East, and to provide education and health services at little or no cost. Subsidies of this type are frequently available to all consumers and, as a result, are extremely costly and not particularly redistributive. It is also common to sell subsidized goods through state retail outlets that tend to be costly and bureaucratic to administer and which have little incentive to provide good service. Furthermore, since subsidized goods are often rationed, and subsidies drive a wedge between consumer and producer prices, these programs often encourage black market trading, corruption and fraud.[85] By encouraging excessive consumption, subsidies can be wasteful and some subsidies, such as energy subsidies, can be environmentally damaging.

Although they are generally rationalized as instruments of redistribution, consumption subsidies are generally ineffective at income redistribution. In fact, since the rich may actually consume more of the subsidized good, a subsidy may actually be regressive.[86] Gasoline subsidies, for example, which cost developing countries US$270–330 billion annually, largely benefit the nonpoor because they consume more gasoline than the poor (Huther et al. 1997). Housing subsidies also tend to be very poorly targeted in developing countries. Only 20 percent of total housing subsidies reached individuals with incomes below the median in South Asia, Latin America and sub-Saharan Africa (World Bank 1997). While they may not be redistributive, it has been argued that food subsidies improve the nutrition levels of the poor and, thereby, their health status and productivity. However, there is little evidence to this effect (Mackenzie 1991b). In fact, since consumption subsidies are costly and not very effective

[85] For example, it may be possible for consumers to purchase a good at its subsidized price, and then sell it to a producer of the good for a slightly higher price, who then sells it back to the government marketing agency.

[86] See the references in Krueger (1990). This does not apply only to foodstuffs. Subsidies for tertiary education are often justified as a method of assisting the poor when, in fact, most of the beneficiaries tend to be the better-off.

redistributive tools, they may actually absorb resources that could have been more effectively directed toward the poor.[87]

As a result of the problems noted above, state resources should only be allocated to the provision of consumption subsidies if these subsidies can be effectively targeted at the poor and if the associated administrative costs are not excessive. In order to minimize administrative costs, a subsidy should be easy to implement and not involve rationing or a state distribution program. One potentially effective food subsidy of this type is a general subsidy for food that is consumed by the poor, but not the rich. Tunisia has implemented a program of this type by eliminating food subsidies for foods that are only consumed by the nonpoor and by distributing subsidized food in differentiated packaging, using generic ingredients, in order to induce the nonpoor to self-select away from the subsidized food. As a result of these changes, Tunisia's food subsidy expenditures have fallen from 4 percent to 2 percent of GDP (World Bank 1997). Another method of targeting general consumption subsidies is to subsidize food only in regions that have a large proportion of poor residents.[88]

As an alternative to general food subsidies, some countries have introduced food stamp programs directed at the poor. Since these programs must be targeted, they tend to be costly to administer and, in many cases, the accuracy of the targeting is poor. They are also often subject to fraud. These problems can be reduced somewhat by targeting on easily observable characteristics, such as age or whether a woman is pregnant or has a newborn.[89] Food-for-work programs, as with public works programs,

[87]Other methods of subsidizing consumption can be very damaging to the economy even if they do not require large allocations of state resources. For example, restrictions on the prices farmers receive for foodstuffs may lower the price of food, but will also lower the quantity of agricultural output and investment. Similarly, food imports can be subsidized if the exchange rate is overvalued, but this will penalize exports and reduce growth and investment in export industries. Since consumption subsidies directly affect the government's budget, their costs are more clearly evident.

[88]This could have the undesirable consequence of inhibiting mobility out of depressed regions. Another potentially important problem with well-targeted programs is that, while they may reach only the poor, they may reduce the incentive for the poor to leave poverty and, thus, may magnify the extent of poverty. In Sri Lanka, van de Walle (1998) reports, food-stamp programs induced a fall in labor supply (and income) equal to 30 percent of the gross transfer under the scheme.

[89]The World Bank (2000) reports the results of a study that found that food-stamps distributed through health clinics in Jamaica reached 94 percent of malnourished children.

could also be used to direct food subsidies to the poor, but are likely to be expensive to administer.

In summary, public works programs are often costly and inefficient methods of redistribution. In most developing countries, social insurance programs should receive few state resources because they are costly to administer and are poor instruments of poverty alleviation. Unless they are designed to minimize administration costs, ensure appropriate targeting and reduce the incentive for fraud, state resources should not be allocated to food subsidy programs. If a food subsidy program is employed, it should aim to provide only basic food stuffs so that the rich will self-select out of the program.

Regulation

In a number of developing countries, significant government resources have been committed to the administration of extensive regulatory regimes. While some of the regulations involved may have potentially positive benefits, such as financial regulation, environmental regulation, health and safety regulation, and competition regulation, in many cases these benefits are dissipated, and sometimes reversed, by poorly designed and executed regulatory regimes. In other cases, there appears to be little or no economic rationale for the regulations employed. This is particularly the case for regulations aimed at controlling prices or entry into markets, such as the allocation of import and production licenses (Guasch and Hahn 1997).

Extensive regulatory regimes can be extremely costly to an economy. They make use of scarce administrative resources and can be extremely expensive to administer. Regulations can also impose unnecessary costs and restrictions on the private sector and, in this way, hinder investment and growth.[90] Furthermore, if the institutional capacity is not available to efficiently administer regulations, enforcement becomes haphazard and arbitrary, causing the regulations to be ineffective and the investment environment to be uncertain. Overregulation, combined with arbitrary enforcement, also provides government employees with substantial rent-seeking opportunities. Efforts by these employees to exploit the regulatory environment can raise firm costs and undermine the operation and

[90] For example, in 1981 acquiring an export license in Brazil required dealing with 13 ministries and 50 agencies and taking 1470 separate legal actions (World Bank 1997).

legitimacy of the state. Furthermore, in some cases, rather than promoting competition, regulations have been designed to substantially reduce competition. Even when this has not been the case, by imposing large regulatory costs on firms, particularly new firms, regulations have often stifled investment and growth, thereby reducing competition.

Given the considerable costs that are associated with many regulations, poorly designed and executed regulations can be worse than no regulation at all (or very imperfect and limited regulations). Excessive and complex regulations are a particular problem in the CIS, North Africa, the Middle East and South Asia (World Bank 1997). In these regions, regulations have created extensive opportunities for corruption, imposed large costs on firms, and utilized large quantities of state resources.

Since the administration of a regulatory regime can impose large costs on an economy as well as require significant state resources, a regulation should only be put in place if an assessment clearly indicates that it is likely to yield net social benefits in both theory and practice. This assessment should also determine whether the state has the capacity to administer the regulation since, if this capacity is not available, imposition of the regulation is likely to be costly, ineffective and, potentially, counterproductive. If a regulatory system is put in place, sufficient resources must be allocated to its administration or it is unlikely to be effective. In many countries, existing regulatory regimes are costly and use significant state resources (particularly administrative capacity). Given these high costs, state resources should be allocated to an assessment of existing regulations in order to determine which regulations are too costly or ineffective, and whether there exist alternatives to regulation (i.e. methods of fostering competition in noncompetitive markets).

Financial Markets

While many of the regulations used in developing countries are costly and counterproductive, it may be important to allocate sufficient state resources to financial market (particularly bank) regulation. Properly functioning financial markets are critical to ensuring that savings are mobilized and allocated to the most productive investments.[91] Without adequate regulation, financial markets tend to function poorly—financial institutions may

[91] King and Levine (1993) and Wurgler (1999) find that countries with developed financial markets are likely to see more efficient capital allocation.

be more inclined to undertake speculative lending, savers may save less because of the higher level of uncertainty, some firms may issue too much debt, while others may have only limited access to external capital. As with the protection of property rights, the effective regulation of financial markets facilitates the operation of markets and can have a significant payoff in terms of increased output and growth.[92]

As a result of the large potential impact of financial market regulation on growth, developing and implementing a financial regulatory system should be a high priority for state resources, particularly for economies that are at an intermediate stage of development.[93] The goals of this regulation should be to discourage fraud, ensure the soundness of the financial system, clarify the risks being taken by investors and depositors, protect consumers and minority shareholders, and ensure that financial institutions have appropriate incentives to allocate capital to productive investments (as opposed to speculative investments).[94]

Although there may be significant returns to financial market regulation, it is important to avoid excessive regulation that might stymie innovation and competition, or divert resources to particular sectors (World Bank 2000). Financial sector regulation also tends to take considerable time to yield results and is information and skill intensive, both of which are scarce and costly inputs for governments and firms in developing economies. If these regulations are not properly designed and implemented, they may impose unnecessary costs on the economy and hinder growth and investment. In countries with less capable administrations, emphasis should be placed on the development of less resource-intensive forms of regulation.

[92] King and Levine (1993) and Easterly and Levine (1997) find that growth is adversely affected by poorly developed financial systems. Levine (1997) provides an overview of the importance of financial development for growth.

[93] These regulations generally entail the development and imposition of clear and informative auditing standards; the imposition of capital adequacy rules, insider trading and lending rules; the effective monitoring of financial institutions; the enforcement of criteria to maintain the health of financial institutions; and the imposition of strong minority shareholder rights.

[94] See Stiglitz (1998). In Malaysia's banking crisis of the mid-1980s, the more highly regulated banks had losses equal to only 2.4 percent of deposits while the less regulated non-bank sector had losses of 40 percent of deposits (World Bank 1997).

State-Owned Enterprises

In developing countries, significant state resources have been allocated to state-owned enterprises (SOEs). One rationale for the allocation of resources to SOEs is that, when domestic entrepreneurial capital is scarce and domestic capital markets are underdeveloped, it may be necessary for the state to provide goods, such as power, that are required by other sectors as inputs. Governments have also used shortages of domestic financial and entrepreneurial capital to justify investments in the production of essentially private goods, such as steel and cotton, which they believe to be necessary for industrial development. The problem with this rationale is that it assumes that government planners know the correct types of investments to make and when these investments are necessary.

In industries characterized by decreasing average costs, such as telecommunications and power transmission, efficient production requires only one producer. To avoid the emergence of private monopolies in these industries, governments have created state-owned monopolies. However, the operations of these state monopolies have often been characterized by many of the shortcomings of private sector monopolies:—poor service, poor quality and, sometimes, high prices.

Irrespective of the rationale for their existence, the cost of SOE production tends to be high. These firms are likely to have little incentive to operate efficiently since they often do not face private sector competition and their losses are generally covered by the state treasury. Political interference in the investment, pricing, and employment decisions of SOEs is common and frequently reduces efficiency and raises costs. In particular, SOEs are often characterized by over-manning, frequently politically induced, and state-run banks and lending agencies often allocate loans and enforce interest payments in accordance with political directives.[95] Furthermore, due to the political importance, size and monopoly status of SOEs, unions are common and have often been able to obtain large wage settlements and maintain excessive levels of employment. In addition, SOEs are often poorly monitored and, thus, managers have little incentive to act efficiently. These factors have all combined to significantly raise the

[95] For example, public water systems often have 10–20 employees per 1000 connections, while efficient operations can operate with 1–2 (Haarmeyer and Mody 1997). State governments in Brazil own commercial banks that they force to lend to clients chosen by the government (World Bank 2000).

costs and reduce the quality of the goods produced by many SOEs.[96] As a result, private sector industries that rely on SOEs for inputs have faced higher costs and uncertain service, both of which have hindered investment and growth.

Political expediency has often meant that the prices charged by SOEs are held below cost.[97] In conjunction with the high costs of many SOE operations, this pricing policy has resulted in transfers to SOEs that often comprise a significant share of government spending in developing countries (Hemming 1991). For example, in low-income countries, the losses of SOEs averaged 2.3 percent of GDP between 1978 and 1991 (World Bank 1997).[98] Significant state resources, resources that could have gone into other public services, have been required to finance these losses (as well as to finance the equity invested in SOEs). Furthermore, a policy of pricing SOE goods below cost tends to be regressive since the rich are often larger consumers of state produced goods (such as water and electricity) than the poor.[99]

While some SOEs produce in sectors with little actual or potential private sector participation, in other cases, SOEs have displaced private producers. In some cases, legislation has prevented private participation by creating monopoly SOEs while, in other cases, state subsidies to SOEs have made it impossible for private firms to successfully compete against (even inefficient) state firms. While the exclusion of private firms could possibly be justified if the displaced private producers were likely to act as monopolies, in many cases SOEs that are producing essentially private goods have displaced private firms in industries that could potentially have

[96] For example, evidence indicates that the inefficient operation of state-owned public utilities in Uruguay and Argentina raised the costs of the services provided by these utilities by 30 percent (World Bank 1997). The four principal Egyptian ports operate as state monopolies and charge service fees that are three times their closest competitors. When private competition was introduced in Chilean and Mexican ports, shipping charges fell by up to 50 percent (World Bank 2000).

[97] In developing countries, municipal water companies typically collect revenues equal to only 35 percent of the cost of water (Haarmeyer and Mody 1997). According to Gupta et al. (1995), in most countries, electricity prices are significantly less than long-run marginal cost.

[98] In calculating SOE losses, the opportunity cost of government equity in SOEs is generally not included.

[99] Haarmeyer and Mody (1997) note that the poor sometimes pay 10 times more for water than the rich because the poor do not have access to subsidized municipal water and so must buy their water from private providers.

been competitive.[100] These include SOEs producing such products as steel, coal, textiles, construction services, chemicals and sugar as well as state monopoly import–export agencies and state monopoly marketing boards.[101] Not only did these investments have little economic rationale in many cases, they also frequently resulted in inefficient high cost production and overextended the fiscal capacity of the state.[102]

In conclusion, considerable state resources have gone to finance the operations of extremely inefficient SOEs. In addition to absorbing state resources, SOEs have hindered the development of a market economy by both raising the costs of private sector firms and displacing private firms from some industries. Given these problems, the allocation of state resources to these firms is unlikely to be justifiable in most cases. In particular, there is little justification for the state to be directly involved, as they are in many developing countries, in the production of essentially private goods. Spending on SOEs may also have regressive income distributional effects as many of the benefits of this spending are likely to go to workers in the state sector, or better-off consumers, rather than the rural poor. The continued allocation of state resources to SOEs must be carefully scrutinized to determine whether it is necessary for the state to be involved in the production of a particular good or service. The privatization or closure of SOEs, or the requirement that SOEs satisfy a hard budget constraint, may free up considerable resources that could then be used to provide more important public services.[103]

[100] Krueger (1990) notes that in many developing countries, the share of SOEs in manufacturing exceeded 50 percent.

[101] The inefficiency of marketing boards has meant that farmers received smaller incomes and, as a result, had less incentive to increase production (Krueger 1990).

[102] Examples include Korea's investment in chemical and heavy industries, Taiwan's "National Development Plan" of 1990, and the capital intensive investment program of industrial projects proposed in the Philippines during the mid-1980s (Rao 1998; World Bank 1997). The Korean and Taiwan plans had to be curtailed because they were fiscally unsustainable. However, Korea did initially make several successful investments in steel, fertilizer and petrochemicals (Westphal 1990; Rodrik 1997). These industries were chosen because they were providing necessary inputs to other sectors and the private sector did not appear to be ready to make the required investments. The Korean firms were managed at arms-length and were intended to be competitive and make profits. While India and Korea had similar shares of public enterprises in the nonagricultural sector, India's did not tend to be nearly as efficient (Datta-Chaudhuri 1990).

[103] The privatization of state-owned enterprises is not a panacea if it does not lead to more competition and efficient production. A private sector monopolist may not be any more efficient than a publicly owned noncompetitive firm. Some countries, such as China, Korea

Industrial Subsidies

In many developing countries, large quantities of state resources have been committed to industrial subsidies. Subsidies have been common for petroleum products, productive inputs (water, fertilizer and credit), agricultural outputs (through guaranteed prices), and the operation of state-owned firms (often utilities and banks). Four principal rationales have been used to justify these subsidies. First, by lowering firm costs, an input subsidy can assist new domestic industries in competing with established producers. Second, imperfect information with respect to the benefits of a new technology may impede its adoption by domestic risk-averse producers. A subsidy, by lowering the cost of the new technology, can encourage its more rapid adoption. For example, fertilizer subsidies have been justified as a way of encouraging farmers to adopt fertilizer-intensive production techniques (Mackenzie 1991b). Third, due to information asymmetries, or as a result of initial market size, the markets for some goods may not exist unless the government initially subsidizes production in these markets (Rodrik 1996). For example, rural credit markets often do not exist and so governments have often created subsidized credit agencies to provide credit in rural areas. Fourth, in the presence of inter-firm technological externalities, a subsidy would be necessary to induce firms to adopt the optimal level of investment in technology (Westphal 1990).[104] These rationales for industrial subsidies are predicated on several key assumptions: that governments know which emerging industries will succeed if they are subsidized, which markets that do not exist should exist, the technologies with significant externalities that have not been exploited optimally, and that governments have better information than producers with respect to the new technologies that will be economical and successful if adopted.

In practice, these assumptions are unlikely to hold. There is little reason to expect that governments, many of which have limited administrative capacity, will be able to identify potentially successful industries or new technologies better than private sector agents. Policies in the early 1960s

and Taiwan, have not privatized their SOEs, but rather have allowed the private sector to develop around the state sector (World Bank 1997). However, for this policy to be successful, it is necessary that state sector firms be relatively independent and face a hard budget constraint, and that the market be of sufficient size to accommodate multiple firms.

[104] Subsidies have also been introduced to counter externalities. For example, urban transit systems have been subsidized in order to cut pollution and congestion.

and 1970s, particularly in Africa, that promoted industrialization at the expense of agriculture, and import-substitution rather than export promotion, seem to have almost universally failed.[105] While there are many reasons why these policies failed, many states simply chose inappropriate sectors to support. Subsidies to support industries in which countries have no obvious comparative advantage, and subsidies to industries that required more private sector entrepreneurial and managerial capital than was available, have most often been unsuccessful. Although subsidies are frequently justified as short-term measures to support the establishment of new industries and disseminate new technology, in practice, they are rarely phased-out (unless there is a budgetary crisis).[106] As a result, firms become dependent on the subsidies and the subsidies, in turn, become a long-term drain on state resources. Given the history of the failure of most governments to successfully pick winning industrial policies, and the waste of resources and distortions that have resulted, it is necessary to be extremely critical of industrial subsidy programs.

In addition to committing large quantities of government resources to uneconomic purposes, subsidies may also introduce damaging distortions. Unless the social cost of an input is less than its private cost, subsidizing the use of the input will cause it to be used excessively (the social cost of the input will exceed its marginal benefit).[107] The use of production or input subsidies to support some sectors will encourage the expansion of these sectors and divert resources away from other sectors. This will inhibit growth in the nonsubsidized sectors and, by diverting inputs to the subsidized sectors, lead to the inefficient use of resources.[108] Furthermore,

[105] The case of the South East Asian "Tigers" is still a subject of intense debate about whether intervention actually helped or hindered development. Rodrik (1997) maintains that government subsidies for investment were key to the development success of both Korea and Taiwan, but that these policies may not transfer easily to other countries. Westphal (1990) makes similar arguments for Korea, but Borensztein and Lee (1999) provide evidence that suggests that subsidized credit in Korea was not allocated efficiently or with much positive effect.

[106] If a subsidy is introduced with a short-term justification, a schedule that indicates how the subsidy will be phased-out should be introduced at the same time. It may, however, be difficult for governments to commit to this schedule.

[107] Singapore encouraged the flow of foreign investment by providing tax incentives, subsidized infrastructure and worker training. Although Singapore was successful at marshalling savings and supporting investment, particularly by the private sector, some commentators believe it may have overinvested (Huff 1995).

[108] In order to promote export industries, East Asian governments provided access to foreign exchange and credit on the basis of export success. While this policy successfully

although input subsidies have been justified as redistributive devices, they are generally regressive because they benefit large producers who buy large quantities of the subsidized inputs (Gupta et al. 1995). For example, fertilizer subsidies tend to be regressive because they benefit large landowners more than smallholders (Mackenzie 1991b). Finally, firms that receive production or input subsidies need not be as efficient as other firms since they do not face the same competitive pressures. As a result, subsidies may encourage poor business practices that could hinder the ability of domestic industries to compete. Credit subsidies, for example, can lead to excessive borrowing and future debt problems.

Subsidies may also encourage excessive use of environmentally damaging inputs (pesticides, fertilizer) as well as the overexploitation of resources such as grazing lands, fish stocks and forests.[109] Fertilizer subsidies, a very common subsidy, are environmentally damaging because, by encouraging fertilizer use, they cause more pollution from fertilizer runoff and place extra demands on water supplies.[110] While irrigation subsidies have increased agricultural production, they have necessitated the flooding of land, increased the use of scarce water, and caused water logging and salinization (Gupta et al. 1995). Energy subsidies, another common subsidy, are an inefficient and environmentally damaging method of subsidizing industry as they reduce only the cost of the energy input and, thereby, promote energy-intensive industries and energy-intensive production techniques.

In summary, industrial subsidies have absorbed considerable resources in developing countries. Arguments in support of subsidies rely either on the identification of an externality or a missing market. In many cases, it is far from clear that subsidies are addressing a market failure. It is clear, however, that industrial subsidies are expensive, that they can significantly distort behavior, with adverse consequences, and that they are often regressive. Before resources are allocated to a subsidy program, the market failure being addressed by the subsidy should be clearly delineated, the

promoted exports, it tended to inhibit the development of domestic industries designed to serve domestic needs, particularly those that used imported goods (Westphal 1990).

[109] This can be done directly or indirectly by subsidizing a complementary input (i.e. a subsidy to irrigation may increase fertilizer use). For a discussion of the impact of government expenditure policies on the environment, see Gupta et al. (1995).

[110] Rosegrant et al. (1998) suggest that for Indonesia there would be a large increase in the output of food crops if the fertilizer subsidy was abandoned and the resulting savings invested in research, extension and irrigation.

direct resource cost of the subsidy should be estimated, and the distortions the subsidy will induce should be identified. In most cases, it is likely that the costs of a subsidy, both direct and indirect, will exceed its benefits and, as a result, state resources should not be allocated to the subsidy. Rather than subsidizing particular sectors or inputs, countries are likely to be much more successful if they provide the infrastructure and a policy environment that are conducive to investment.

Conclusion

Given the presence of severe measurement and data problems, it is not surprising that the cross-country empirical evidence on the impact of different patterns of sector-level spending on growth is often contradictory.[111] One major problem with these studies is that, even if relatively disaggregated data are available, differences in the efficiency and organization of spending programs are generally not observable, although these differences may have a significant impact on program results. While cross-country results are often ambiguous, the experiences of a large number of countries suggest several general principles that should guide inter-sectoral resource allocation decisions.

State intervention in the inter-sectoral allocation of resources can be justified as a response to market failure. Thus, before resources are allocated to a particular sector or sub-sector, the market failure the resources are intended to address should be identified, and some indication of the significance of the market failure should be provided. This determination would clarify the objective of the intervention, facilitate the design of an intervention strategy to meet this objective, and make the success or failure of the program easier to judge. Before implementing sector-level spending programs to provide a good that is not currently provided by the market, it is important to determine the factors that prevented private sector provision of the good, and the implications these factors are likely to have for the operation and success of the public program. Most state spending programs that allocate state resources to particular sectors induce changes in the behavior of economic agents, some of which may be undesirable. For example, programs that confer benefits on individuals or firms are likely to promote corruption and rent-seeking behavior. Thus, when determining the costs of a program designed to counteract a market

[111] Levine and Renelt (1992) discuss the fragility of these results.

failure, it is necessary to include the costs of the distortions the program will induce, any negative effects on other sectors, as well as any adverse effects on the distribution of income. Finally, some determination should be made of whether, given the magnitude of the market failure, the benefits of state intervention are likely to exceed the direct and indirect program costs (the marginal cost of funds, the cost of program-induced distortions and any adverse effects on the distribution of income).

While it may be possible to design a spending program to deal successfully with a market failure, the program may fail if the state administration does not have the capacity to implement the program. Spending programs should be prioritized so that only those programs within the capacity of the state are pursued. Attempting to implement a program for which the administrative capacity is not available is likely to result in a costly, inefficient and unsuccessful public program.

Many spending programs do not succeed, that is, they are high-cost, of poor quality and ineffective, because they have not been designed to provide incentives for administrators and beneficiaries to act in ways that are consistent with the program's goals. This shortcoming can be corrected to some extent by choosing programs for which it is easier to incorporate the correct incentives. Programs are likely to be more successful if program objectives are clear, if the program design provides incentives that induce the desired behavior, and if resources are allocated to monitoring both program inputs and outputs. If monitoring indicates that the allocation of resources to a sector has not resulted in improvements in output measures, it is important to determine the cause of this failure before allocating new resources to the sector.

Although it may be necessary for the state to organize and coordinate programs to address a market failure, in many cases, the private sector can serve as the actual provider of the necessary good or service. The use of private sector providers can reduce the magnitude of the administrative and capital resources the state must allocate to a sector and may, if there is adequate competition, increase efficiency. Even in the absence of competition, it is unclear whether a state monopoly will act any more efficiently, or require less monitoring, than a private monopoly.

By reducing demand and the share of costs borne by the state, user fees can reduce the quantity of state resources required to deliver public services. User fees are most relevant for government programs that yield large private benefits since, in most cases, the acquisition of these benefits should be paid for by the individual beneficiaries. If the appropriate mechanisms and incentives are in place, user fees may also be more successful at maintaining O&M. On the other hand, if the main beneficiaries of a program are the poor, user fees may not be appropriate due to their negative impact on the distribution of income.

The allocation of state resources to some sectors is more likely to have a positive impact on welfare and growth than the allocation of resources to other sectors. Types of state expenditures that are likely to have a positive benefit are those that address important market failures (public goods and spillovers), promote the efficient operation of government or the market, and improve the distribution of income. In particular, poorly functioning administrations are unlikely to respond effectively to market failures, and are unlikely to provide efficient and low-cost services, thus hindering the growth of the private sector. The operations of government can be improved by committing resources to increasing the efficiency and capacity of the administration. This is likely to involve aligning the wages of civil servants more closely with those in the private sector, while improving monitoring, accountability and training. In many countries, these types of changes must be combined with efforts to reduce the size of the civil service in order to control the total wage bill and improve civil service efficiency.

A number of sectors are critical to the efficient functioning of a market economy. For example, resources should be allocated to develop and maintain a legal system that is capable of protecting and enforcing property rights and contracts. Since a poorly functioning financial system is also likely to impede development, it is important to develop and implement a system of financial market regulations. The allocation of resources to the development of a transportation infrastructure can lower costs, promote the development of new markets and industries and increase competition. It may also be necessary for the state to provide other infrastructure, such as electricity, water and communications infrastructure, if this infrastructure is obviously in short supply and there is insufficient private capital to provide it. Sufficient resources should be devoted to the maintenance of basic infrastructure such as roads and electricity networks since, if these networks are in poor working order, they can hinder the operation and growth of the whole economy. Many public programs, particularly in the education and health sectors, suffer from both poor quality and inadequate funding of continuing operations. Resources should be allocated to improve incentives and program design in order to increase the quality and efficiency of spending in these sectors. Increases in spending, without careful monitoring and adequate incentives, are unlikely to be effective.

While some types of government-provided goods have large private consumption components, because they also have income distribution or spillover effects, governments have taken an active role in their provision. Examples include spending on primary education and basic health care (including water and sanitation), both of which may improve labor productivity, the quality of life, and the distribution of income. There may also be significant income distribution benefits from well-targeted redistribution programs as long as the costs of these programs can be kept at a reasonable level. As with many state services, health, education and redistribution programs often suffer from poor quality and high costs and should only be spending priorities if programs can be designed that address these problems.

There is likely to be little benefit from the allocation of state resources to some types of sector level programs, although considerable resources have been allocated to these programs in the past. The principal problems with these programs are that they produce goods that could be produced by the private sector, they do not address an explicit market failure, they are expensive and of poor quality, they introduce adverse incentives and distortions, they are not designed to meet their objectives, their effectiveness and cost-efficiency is not adequately monitored, and they have a regressive impact on the distribution of income. Examples of programs that should receive low spending priority include subsidies to SOEs that produce essentially private goods or that are high-cost inefficient producers, industrial subsidies and poorly targeted consumption subsidies, infrastructure development that could be undertaken by the private sector, large poorly conceived and operated capital projects, expensive social security programs, poorly targeted and administered income redistribution programs, university education (particularly in the humanities) in countries with poor primary education systems and low levels of development, hospital care when primary health care is of poor quality, military spending, and extensive regulation of the economy (which is costly to both governments and firms).

Although considerable state resources have been allocated inefficiently in the past, changes to these allocations are likely to occur very incrementally. Many programs and expenditures cannot be rapidly altered as this could cause acute social, political and economic disruption. In particular, political constraints must be considered in the design and phasing-in of any changes to sector-level resource allocations.

References

Ahmad, E., and R. Hemming. 1991. Poverty and Social Security. Chapter 19 in *Public Expenditure Handbook*, ed. Ke-young Chu and Richard Hemming. Washington, DC: International Monetary Fund: 130–138.

Arora, V., and T. Rayoumi. 1994. Reductions in World Military Expenditure: Who Stands to Gain? *Finance and Development* 31: 24–27.

Baffes, J., and A. Shah. 1998. Productivity of Public Spending, Sectoral Allocation Choices, and Economic Growth. *Economic Development and Cultural Change* 46 (2): 291–303.

Barro, Robert J. 1991. Economic Growth in a Cross Section of Countries. *Quarterly Journal of Economics* 106: 407–443.

———. 1997. *Determinants of Economic Growth: A Cross-Country Empirical Study*. Cambridge, MA: MIT Press.

Berman, Peter A. 1998. Rethinking Health Care Systems: Private Health Care Provision in India. *World Development* 26: 1463–1479.

Borensztein, E., and J.-W. Lee. 1999. *Credit Allocation and Financial Crisis in Korea*, Research Department. IMF Working Paper WP/99/20. Washington, DC: International Monetary Fund.

Burki, S.J., G.E. Perry, and W.R. Dillinger. 1999. *Beyond the Center: Decentralizing the State*. Washington, DC: The World Bank.

Cashin, P. 1995. Government Spending, Taxes and Economic Growth. *International Monetary Fund Staff Papers* 42: 237–269.

Collier, P., and J.W. Gunning. 1999. Why Has Africa Grown Slowly? *Journal of Economic Perspectives* 13: 3–22.

Crosby, B.L. 1996. Policy Implementation: The Organizational Challenge. *World Development* 24: 1403–1415.

Dailami, M., and M. Klein. 1997. *Government Support to Private Infrastructure Projects in Emerging Markets*. The World Bank. Mimeo.

Datta-Chaudhuri, M. 1990. Market Failure and Government Failure. *Journal of Economic Perspectives* 4: 25–39.

Devarajan, S., V. Swaroop, and H. Zou. 1996. The Composition of Public Expenditure and Economic Growth. *Journal of Monetary Economics* 37: 313–344.

Easterly, W., and R. Levine. 1997. Africa's Growth Tragedy: Policies and Ethnic Divisions. *Quarterly Journal of Economics* 112: 1203–1250.

Filmer, D., J. Hammer, and L. Pritchett. 1997. *Health Policy in Poor Countries: Weak Links in the Chain*. The World Bank. Mimeo.

Fischer, S., E. Hernández-Catá, and M.S. Khan. 1998. *Africa: Is This the Turning Point?* IMF Paper on Policy Analysis and Assessment PPAA/98/6. Washington, DC: International Monetary Fund.

Fogel, R.W. 1994. Economic Growth, Population Theory, and Physiology: The Bearing of Long-Term Processes on the Making of Economic Policy. *American Economic Review* 84: 369–395.

Gerson, P. 1998. *The Impact of Fiscal Policy Variables on Output Growth*, IMF Working Paper WP/98/1. Washington, DC: International Monetary Fund.

Glewwe, P. 1996. The Relevance of Standard Estimates of Rates of Return to Schooling for Education Policy: A Critical Assessment. *Journal of Development Economics* 51: 267–290.

Guasch, J.L., and R.W. Hahn. 1997. *The Costs and Benefits of Regulation: Some Implications for Developing Countries*. Background Paper for the 1997 World Development Report of the World Bank.

Gupta, S., K. Miranda, and I. Parry. 1995. Public Expenditure Policy and the Environment: A Review and Synthesis. *World Development* 23: 515–528.

Gupta, S., K. Honjo, and M. Verhoeven. 1997. *The Efficiency of Government Expenditure: Experiences from Africa*, IMF Working Paper WP/97/153. Washington, DC: International Monetary Fund.

Gupta, S., M. Verhoeven, and E. Tiongson. 1999. *Does Higher Government Spending Buy Better Results in Education and Health Care?* IMF Working Paper WP/99/21, Fiscal Affairs Department. Washington, DC: International Monetary Fund.

Haarmeyer, D., and A. Mody. 1997. Private Capital in Water and Sanitation. *Finance & Development* 34: 34–37.

Heller, P.S. 1991. Operations and Maintenance. Chapter 8 in *Public Expenditure Handbook*, ed. Ke-young Chu and Richard Hemming. Washington, DC: International Monetary Fund: 52–59.

Hemming, R. 1991. Transfers to Public Enterprises. Chapter 11 in *Public Expenditure Handbook*, ed. Ke-young Chu and Richard Hemming. Washington, DC: International Monetary Fund: 75–81.

Hemming, R., and D.P. Hewitt. 1991. Military Expenditure. Chapter 13 in *Public Expenditure Handbook*, ed. Ke-young Chu and Richard Hemming. Washington, DC: International Monetary Fund: 88–93.

Hemming, R., D.P. Hewitt, and G.A. Mackenzie. 1991. Public Expenditure Productivity. Chapter 4 in *Public Expenditure Handbook*, ed. Ke-young Chu and Richard Hemming. Washington, DC: International Monetary Fund: 26–31.

Huff, W.G. 1995. The Developmental State, Government, and Singapore's Economic Development Since 1960. *World Development* 23: 1421–1438.

Huther, J., S. Roberts, and A. Shah. 1997. *Public Expenditure Reform Under Adjustment Lending*, World Bank Discussion Paper No. 332. Washington, DC: The World Bank.

Jütting, J. 1999. *Strengthening Social Security Systems in Rural Areas of Developing Countries*, Discussion Paper on Development Policy Number 9. Bonn: Center for Development Research (ZEF), University of Bonn.

King, R.G., and R. Levine. 1993. Finance and Growth: Schumpeter Might Be Right. *Quarterly Journal of Economics* 108: 717–737.
Klitgaard, R. 1997. 'Unanticipated Consequences' in Anti-Poverty Programs. *World Development* 25: 1963–1972.
Kneller, R., M.F. Bleaney, and N. Gemmell. 1999. Fiscal Policy and Growth: Evidence from OECD Countries. *Journal of Public Economics* 74: 171–190.
Kochhar, K. 1991. Health. Chapter 15 in *Public Expenditure Handbook*, ed. Ke-young Chu and Richard Hemming. Washington, DC: International Monetary Fund: 103–106.
Krueger, Anne O. 1990. Government Failures in Development. *Journal of Economic Perspectives* 4: 9–23.
Krueger, Alan B., and M. Lindahl. 1998. *Education for Growth in Sweden and the World*, WP # 411. Princeton, NJ: Industrial Relations Section, Princeton University.
Levine, R. 1997. Financial Development and Economic Growth: Views and Agenda. *Journal of Economic Literature* 35: 688–726.
Levine, R., and D. Renelt. 1992. A Sensitivity Analysis of Cross-Country Growth Regressions. *American Economic Review* 82: 42–63.
Lienert, I., and J. Modi. 1997. *A Decade of Civil Service Reform in Sub-Saharan Africa*, IMF WP/97/179, Fiscal Affairs Department. Washington, DC: International Monetary Fund.
Lockheed, M.E., A.M. Verspoor, et al. 1991. *Improving Primary Education in Developing Countries*. New York: Oxford University Press for the World Bank.
Mackenzie, G.A. 1991a. Public Sector Employment. Chapter 6 in *Public Expenditure Handbook*, ed. Ke-young Chu and Richard Hemming. Washington, DC: International Monetary Fund: 41–45.
———. 1991b. Price Subsidies. Chapter 9 in *Public Expenditure Handbook*, ed. Ke-young Chu and Richard Hemming. Washington, DC: International Monetary Fund: 60–67.
———. 1991c. Education. Chapter 16 in *Public Expenditure Handbook*, ed. Ke-young Chu and Richard Hemming. Washington, DC: International Monetary Fund: 107–112.
Mackenzie, G.A., and J. Schiff. 1991. Public Sector Pay. Chapter 7 in *Public Expenditure Handbook*, ed. Ke-young Chu and Richard Hemming. Washington, DC: International Monetary Fund: 46–51.
Mingat, A. 1998. The Strategy Used by High-Performing Asian Economies in Education: Some Lessons for Developing Countries. *World Development* 26: 695–715.
Minten, B., and S. Kyle. 1999. The Effect of Distance and Road Quality on Food Collection, Marketing Margins, and Traders' Wages: Evidence from the Former Zaire. *Journal of Development Economics* 60: 467–495.

Nehru, V., E. Swanson, and A. Dubey. 1995. A New Database on Human Capital Stock in Developing and Industrial Countries: Sources, Methodology, and Results. *Journal of Development Economics* 46: 379–401.
Pennant-Rea, R., and I.G. Heggie. 1995. Commercializing Africa's Roads. *Finance & Development* 32: 30–32.
Psacharopoulos, G. 1994. Returns to Investment in Education: A Global Update. *World Development* 22: 1325–1343.
Rao, M.G. 1998. Accommodating Public Expenditure Policies: The Case of Fast Growing Asian Economies. *World Development* 26: 673–694.
Ravallion, M. 1999. Appraising Workfare. *The World Bank Research Observer* 14: 31–48.
Rodrik, D. 1996. Coordination Failures and Government Policy: A Model with Applications to East Asia and Eastern Europe. *Journal of International Economics* 40: 1–22.
———. 1997. The 'Paradoxes' of the Successful State. *European Economic Review* 41: 411–442.
Rosegrant, M.W., F. Kasryno, and N.D. Perez. 1998. Output Response to Prices and Public Investment in Agriculture: Indonesian Food Crops. *Journal of Development Economics* 55: 333–352.
Schultz, T.P. 1999. Health and Schooling Investments in Africa. *Journal of Economic Perspectives* 13: 67–88.
Schultz, T.P., and A. Tansel. 1997. Wage and Labor Supply Effects of Illness in Côte d'Ivoire and Ghana: Instrumental Variable Estimates for Days Disabled. *Journal of Development Economics* 53: 251–286.
Stiglitz, J.E. 1998. *More Instruments and Broader Goals: Moving Toward the Post-Washington Consensus*. The 1998 WIDER Annual Lecture, Helsinki, 7 January.
Temple, J. 1999. A Positive Effect of Human Capital on Growth. *Economics Letters* 65: 131–134.
van de Walle, D. 1998. Assessing the Welfare Impacts of Public Spending. *World Development* 26: 365–379.
Westphal, L.E. 1990. Industrial Policy in an Export-Propelled Economy: Lessons from South Korea's Experience. *Journal of Economic Perspectives* 4: 41–59.
World Bank. 1993. *World Development Report 1993: Investing in Health*. New York: Oxford University Press.
———. 1997. *World Development Report 1997: The State in a Changing World*. New York: Oxford University Press.
———. 1998. *World Development Report 1998: Knowledge for Development*. New York: Oxford University Press.
———. 2000. *World Development Report 1999/2000*. New York: Oxford University Press.
Wurgler, J. 1999. *Financial Markets and the Allocation of Capital*, School of Management. New Haven: Yale University.

CHAPTER 9

Evaluation of Decentralization Programs

Melville McMillan

Introduction

Governments are becoming more decentralized. Political power and public decision making in many countries around the world has, to varying degrees, shifted away from central governments, particularly over the past quarter century. This movement has been attributed to various forces; for example, the growing number of democracies, urbanization, increasing literacy, rising incomes, a growing middle class, and the failures of central governments. The World Bank has been involved in this transition. Many Bank studies and documents have addressed the role of decentralization in good governance and in economic development and Bank lending has often been for or linked to decentralization. Since 1987, 199 World Bank projects have been designated as decentralization projects.[1] Yet, as noted in the World Bank Development Report 1999/2000, "Decentralization is a work in progress. Many experiments are underway, and only limited evidence on the final outcomes is yet available" (World Bank 2000a, p. 124).

[1] Also see Litvack et al. (1998, ch. 1) which reports that 12 percent of Bank projects completed between 1993 and 1997 involved decentralizing responsibilities.

M. McMillan (✉)
Department of Economics, University of Alberta, Edmonton, AB, Canada
e-mail: melville.mcmillan@ualberta.ca

© The Author(s) 2020

A. Shah (ed.), *Policy, Program and Project Evaluation*,
https://doi.org/10.1007/978-3-030-48567-2_9

Given the extent of the movement occurring and the Bank's initiatives, there is a natural wish to assess the Bank's activities in regard to decentralization.[2] A comprehensive evaluation of the Bank's undertakings in this area creates the opportunity to understand better the potential for and limitations of decentralization, to identify the strengths and weaknesses of Bank activities and practices relating to decentralization, and to assist in refining Bank policies with respect to decentralization. Essentially, an evaluation is to generate information that will help the Bank's decentralization policies, programs, and practices be more successful.

This chapter outlines an approach to evaluating the Bank's decentralization initiatives. The basic methodology for evaluating individual decentralization projects is outlined initially. That basic sketch is elaborated upon in the two subsequent sections which outline components of decentralization and then steps to be taken in the evaluation. The method for extending the evaluation across many projects follows. The problem of selecting or sampling the projects to be evaluated is then discussed. Following that is a section focused on community-driven development. A section of thoughts on bringing the various analyses and the analysis of a rather diverse set of projects together and putting the results into perspective precedes the conclusion.

The Basic Methodology

"Decentralization entails the transfer of political, fiscal and administrative powers to ... autonomous elected subnational units of government capable of taking binding decisions in at least some policy areas. Decentralization may involve bringing such governments into existence. Or it may consist of expanding the resources and responsibilities of existing subnational governments."[3] While the definition of decentralization is helpful, a critical consideration is the purpose or objective of decentralization.

[2] To be included in the analysis of decentralization is community-driven development. Community-driven development is those projects and programs proposed by local communities with or without local government participation or sponsorship.

[3] World Bank (2000a, p. 108). Elaboration on the definition and meaning of decentralization and its variations (i.e., devolution, delegation, deconcentration, privatization) can be found in various sources; for example, Bird and Vaillancourt (1998, ch. 1), Burki et al. (1999, Prologue), Dillinger (1994), Litvack et al. (1998, ch. 2), and Manor (1999). Recall also, from the above footnote, that community-driven development is to be included in this analysis.

Decentralization is not an end in itself. Rather, decentralization is to make government, or more generally the public sector, work better by increasing subnational autonomy and accountability. Decentralization may aid political harmony but many of the benefits can be economic. Decentralization is a means of making government more politically and financially responsive to subnational needs and preferences while maintaining the benefits of the larger political and economic union. In short, decentralization is to enhance overall government performance and leave citizens more satisfied.

Keeping the goal of decentralization in mind, the object of this analysis is the evaluation of Bank undertakings having a focus on decentralization. The central questions are: (a) have these efforts been successful, unsuccessful, or had mixed results, and, at least equally important, (b) why those outcomes or why were the outcomes what they were? In seeking to address these problems, two further questions arise. First, how does one make, or go about, the evaluation? That is, what are the steps? Second, what is it that one evaluates when one evaluates decentralization; that is, what is it that one looks at and for in evaluating projects focused on decentralization?

The framework for addressing these questions and, indeed, the overall analysis is shown in Table 9.1. The columns there are the response to the first (i.e., the how to go about or what steps?) question. The rows are the response to the second (i.e., the what does one look at and look for?) question. Consider initially the columns in Table 9.1. There are five. Each is a stage of analysis or, if one likes, a step to be taken in analyzing decentralization projects. The five steps are: identifying the initial environment, describing the action taken, determining the outcomes, evaluating the outcomes plus assessing the reasons for those outcomes, and establishing the lessons to be learned from each project. Turning to the rows, note that there are circumstances making decentralization an attractive option and features that facilitate or hinder successful decentralization. World Bank and other experience and analysis have identified many of these circumstances and features. Projects that recognize and adopt those lessons have greater potential for success. Defined here are six major categories of circumstances and features that need attention. Call these the components of decentralization. The six components or categories are: government and political institutions, responsibilities and powers, resources, management authority, accountability, and beyond government factors.

The fundamental task of the evaluation effort is to complete the cells in the matrix of Table 9.1. That is, work through the steps of the analysis

Table 9.1 Decentralization components

	Environment	*Action*	*Outcomes*	*Assessment*	*Lessons*
	The initial situation	*Decentralization (and other) Recommendations and programs*	*Results of action*	*Reasons for the outcomes*	*Conclusions and implications*
Government and political institutions					
Responsibilities and powers					
Resources					
Management authority					
Accountability					
Beyond government					

Source: Author

with reference at each stage to the six components of decentralization giving close attention to the relevant circumstances and factors in each. This stepwise analysis of the components of decentralization will yield the evaluation. A concentration of attention on the roles and interactions of the components of decentralization and their elements plus the impacts of the project under review in its environment should reveal important reasons why decentralization projects achieved what they did. Thus, the main products of the exercise, beyond the important determination of project outcomes and relative success, are an understanding of the reasons for the outcomes realized, and the resulting lessons; that is, an evaluation of the decentralization project that will contribute to the evaluation of Bank decentralization practices, programs and policies.

Having outlined the basic approach, the following two sections elaborate upon the rows and columns of Table 9.1. Initially considered are the six categories of decentralization factors. That section is followed by discussion of the five steps in the analysis.

Components of Decentralization

This section reviews the six categories of factors important for successful decentralization. Those categories or components are: government and political institutions, responsibilities and powers, resources, management authority, accountability, and beyond government factors. These components recognize circumstances that make decentralization an appealing alternative and features that contribute to (or hinder) the success of decentralization.

The success of decentralization depends upon how well two major issues are addressed. One issue is the *assignment problem*. The other issue is the *institutional structure and arrangements*. The assignment problem has to do primarily with the allocation of responsibilities and with the allocation of resources among governments. The assignment problem is central to most discussions and studies of decentralization (and fiscal federalism).[4] Although sometimes given less attention, the institutional structures and arrangements are equally important to decentralization outcomes.[5] The term institutions refers to the laws, rules, arrangements, customs, conventions, practices, etc., in place and, given the assignments, there to guide the functioning and operations of the system.[6] Largely because they determine the incentives to which the participants respond, institutions influence greatly, whether the system works or does not work well. Institutions and assignments are not independent. Good institutions cannot offset a flawed assignment, nor will an ideal assignment be effective without suitable institutions. Strong performance requires quality in both.

The assignment and institution issues cannot be entirely segregated. The six topics noted for evaluation illustrate the interrelations. Five of those involve governmental arrangements; that is, government and political institutions, responsibilities and powers, resources, management authority, and accountability. The sixth is to include those other potential factors beyond government that may influence decentralization. The assignment problem is most closely associated with responsibilities and

[4] For an overview of the assignment problem, see, for example, Shah (1994).

[5] For perspectives offering a greater recognition of institutions, see, for example, Bird (2000), Burki et al. (1999), Dethier (2000), Litvack et al. (1998), Shah (2000) and United Nations (2000).

[6] Litvack et al. (1998, p. 16) define institutions as "... the rules of the game in society (or the incentives and constraints that influence human behavior) and the organizations and other means of enforcing them."

powers, resources, and management authority while institutions are linked most nearly to government and political institutions, accountability, and those factors beyond government. Yet the two overlap and interact considerably. For example, assignments will influence and be influenced by accountability and government and political institutions, while institutions impact on responsibilities and resource assignments and their success and institutions will change or be changed as a result of assignments. Keeping the overarching importance of the assignment question and the institutional context in mind, the six components noted seem a relatively comprehensive, convenient and logical framework for evaluating decentralization.

The discussion of these factors that follows has two objectives. One objective is to elaborate upon and so spell out the topic more extensively and, in doing so, to indicate the rationale for including the topic in the list of factors to consider in evaluation. The other purpose is to highlight, more for illustrative purposes than in any attempt at completeness, and to discuss briefly a variety of elements contributing to the topic which evaluators can watch for and may wish to consider in their analysis.

Government and Political Institutions

Democracy is central to decentralization. This link is clearly demonstrated in the definition of decentralization, which refers to the transfer of power to autonomous elected subnational governments.[7] The weaker the democratic system, the less likely is decentralization to succeed. The election of local political decision makers is at the heart of democratic local government. Central government appointment of major local officials (e.g., as, until recently, was the case for mayors and governors in much of Latin America) undermines local democracy. Central political party controls over candidate nominations, often even parallel party systems at the central and local levels, erode local autonomy. It should be relatively easy and inexpensive to run a viable campaign at the local level. This enhances the competitive nature of local politics and the potential for broadly representative local government and so reduces the potential for "capture" of local government by narrow interest groups or local elites.

Democracy is not complete with only elected representatives. A great deal of public participation is essential (e.g., World Bank 1996). Democratically elected officials want public input into the public decision-making process

[7] See Section "Summary and Conclusion".

and many members of the public want to contribute. There is a need for institutions to mobilize and harness civil society and provide an avenue for citizens to have an active rather than a passive role. The role of citizens individually or through community organizations and interest groups is to monitor, evaluate, advocate, reveal preferences, etc., and so, both as a client or consumer of public services and as an initiator, influence political processes and decision making.

A democratic system can only work well when it is transparent and citizens and representatives alike have information and can see what is happening. That is, the veil between government and the public is sheer. A relatively transparent political system enables timely, accurate information to be secured, processed and passed on to interested parties by the media, individuals, businesses, organizations, academics, etc. Good information allows voters to hold their elected representative accountable and civil society to function effectively.

Transparency in public affairs helps maintain the integrity of all the players. The goal is to have decisions made objectively in the public interest. Weak ethical standards and weak impediments to wrong doing in office promotes corruption, distorts public decision making and creates a threat to any public or private initiative. A vast difference exists in the potential for public programs (such as those undertaken by the Bank) depending upon whether the culture of the public sector, elected or appointed, is rent seeking or public service.

Attitudes toward decentralization, or the political climate of decentralization, are critical. This aspect involves the attitudes of the decentralizing government and those of the governments being decentralized to (i.e., the recipient governments). Call these the central and the local governments. The prospects for decentralization are probably best when both the central and the local governments have positive attitudes toward the planned decentralization. The prospects are likely the most dismal when the central government is positive but the local governments are resisting. This situation is most likely to occur with the central government forcing decentralization onto unwilling local authorities. Local governments are rarely in a position to force the central authority to decentralize. While the positions of the politicians are vital, bureaucrats must be cooperative if decentralization is to occur smoothly. Sometimes bureaucrats, especially at the central level and threatened with a loss of power, may resist. Citizens' attitudes also matter. Citizens are in the unique position of having both central and local interests. While preferring the arrangement that performs best for them, they may also be the most difficult group to inform about the consequences of change. Citizens' attitudes will reflect their relative trust in their governments. There should be concern, for example, if local politicians want decentralization but local citizens do not. Finally, decentralization is likely to proceed more smoothly and be more effective if it has credible and influential champions at both levels and among all groups.

The extent and nature of intergovernmental relations will impact on decentralization. Having and maintaining good relations among levels of government will have positive effects. Established and ongoing forums with true communication and discussion can help to transmit and share information, increase awareness and understanding, improve coordination, build consensus, and even create an element of trust between levels of government. General forums typically need to be supplemented with those focused on specific issues. Good intergovernmental relations typically require effective organizations of governments at the local (and, where they exist, at the state/provincial) level to help define common issues, positions, and agendas for discussion with the senior authority. In sum, openness and communication between levels of governments can lead to better and more workable intergovernmental arrangements initially and enable those arrangements to continue to operate better as conditions and circumstances evolve. The case for solid intergovernmental relations is essentially the idea that two heads are better than one when considering common problems.

Responsibilities and Powers

The assignment of expenditure responsibilities and other powers among a country's governments is one half of the assignment problem. (The assignment of taxation and other revenue generating powers is the other half.) Certain responsibilities are decentralized because subnational governments can be more aware of and more responsive to regional/local conditions and preferences and so capable of performing those functions more satisfactorily than the central government. Closely associated is the subsidiarity principle, which advocates assigning functions to the lowest level of government consistent with their effective performance. Other potential benefits of decentralization are that multiple providers of services expand choice, offer competition, stimulate innovation, and encourage political participation.

The principle of decentralization is clear but implementation often faces a variety of complications that can impose difficulties for decentralization in practice and especially for the transition to a more decentralized system. Decentralization works best if the decentralized function maps perfectly or corresponds exactly to the subnational jurisdiction to which it is assigned. That is, the whole subnational community is served, there are no spillovers of benefits or costs beyond the jurisdiction, economies of scale and scope are realized, and decision-making costs are low. While such situations are certainly approximated in some cases, very often this ideal is not fully realized or realizable and there are interjurisdictional externalities, realizable economies of scale and scope are not ideal, and, in the face of such complications, decision-making costs rise. That is, decentralization can be expected to involve some trade-offs.

The matching of implementing jurisdictions and benefit areas provides guidance for the assignment of the traditional broad areas of government activity; macroeconomic stabilization, distribution, and allocation. Typically, the impacts of stabilization and distributional policies are broad, commonly national, so these responsibilities are usually deemed appropriate for the central government. However, in geographically large countries, regional economies may not be coordinated, many provincial/state government stabilization policies have predominately regional impacts, preferences for distribution may vary somewhat and subnational distribution policies too may have limited effects beyond a state or province. Hence in large countries, there is often a case for some decentralization of certain stabilization and distribution responsibilities. Many allocative policies and programs, however, provide much more local benefits and can be determined and provided efficiently and effectively by small decentralized units of government. Hence, the provision of many public goods and services are the primary responsibilities of local and other subnational governments.

Subnational fiscal characteristics can introduce particular complications. A major benefit of a decentralized public sector is not only that the members of subnational jurisdictions decide on the services benefitting only them but do so knowing that they also pay the costs of those services. That is, there is a close and clear benefit–cost linkage that results in more efficient and better decisions. However, interjurisdictional variations in fiscal capacities can result in uneven provision (notably relative to uniform central services) sufficient to raise equity issues. Also, expenditure demands for some decentralized services may match poorly the revenue generating capacities of the tax bases well suited to subnational governments. These two factors may call for intergovernmental transfers to offset horizontal fiscal disparities and vertical fiscal gaps. Such transfers are by no means necessarily bad, indeed they are almost a standard feature of multitiered governments, but they do diminish the benefit–cost link that serves as a signal to taxpayer-voters and they must be carefully designed and employed to avoid introducing a soft budget constraint. But these are more resource issues to be addressed later. Further complications of decentralization (and the accompanying subnational finance) are the potential negative, as well as the positive, effects of government expenditure and tax competition and of interjurisdictional factor mobility.

Many public outputs are not purely national or local (to use a simple but useful dichotomy). Often, as in the case of schooling, while local production and local decision making are highly advantageous, there are broader (e.g., national) interests in the output for both economic and distributional reasons. Hence, for many important public services, responsibilities are shared among two or more levels of government. The variety of alternative arrangements is large. For example, there may be (a) largely separate but parallel, and somewhat coordinated, units operated by different governments servicing different parts of the "market" (e.g., national highways, provincial highways and local roads; state hospitals and local primarily health units), (b) a service supplied by only one level of government but with joint funding through grants (e.g., common with schooling), (c) one government providing the service but subject to at least some supervision and regulation by a senior government (not uncommon with health, schooling, water, and sanitation services), (d) a senior government simply monitoring and providing information about the performance of local governments' services (e.g., on schools and on local governments to local constituents). Other arrangements and variations of these exist. Sometimes, additional governments (such as regional or metropolitan governments) or single-purpose governments may be appropriate. Also, although it leans to deconcentration rather than decentralization, in some cases, senior governments may, de facto if not *de jure*, make subnational governments their agents for the purpose of delivering selected central services.

A move to decentralization implies that responsibilities and powers are now perceived as being too centralized. Excessive centralization may have resulted from an inappropriate initial or previous assignment that is now recognized as such, or because circumstances have changed that now make a more decentralized system possible and more attractive. While assignments need stability, they can evolve. Note, as suggested in the above paragraph, that decentralization typically does not eliminate central government responsibility but it does change its responsibility. Commonly, there will continue to be a shared (e.g., national) interest in decentralized responsibilities. Those shared interests may be reflected in cost sharing, regulation, monitoring, etc.

When there are overlapping interests in public services, there are many ways of governments sharing and unbundling responsibilities among the effected parties. The intergovernmental relationships may be complex because often the underlying economic and social relations are complicated. Hence, it should be no surprise if intergovernmental relations are not simple. Also, the apparent complexity is augmented by the fact that there typically is no single arrangement that operates best in all cases. A variety of workable solutions are often possible. One observes a great diversity of responsibility assignments and in intergovernmental arrangements. However, while alternative arrangements and solutions are feasible, that does not mean that all those observed are good examples or work well. In part, the prospects for better performance are enhanced if the lessons reflected in this discussion are considered.

Because the assignment of responsibilities and intergovernmental relations are often complicated, and can be especially difficult for citizens to discern, clarity of governments' mandates is essential, especially if governments are to be successfully held accountable. If omissions, duplications and conflicts are to be avoided, governments themselves must be clear about who is responsible for what and in what way and about what authority they have to meet those responsibilities. Clear definition of the responsibilities and authority of governments, especially when responsibilities are shared, is essential for successful accountability. In some cases—such as when there are grants to be provided, regulations and standards to be met, and contracts to be satisfied—accountability is from one government to another. Ultimately, in democratic systems, the accountability is to the citizen, the voter-taxpayer receiving and paying for services. Hence, it is essential that responsibilities be sufficiently clear and intergovernmental relations sufficiently transparent that citizens and civil society can be effective in holding public decision makers accountable.

Resources

The assignment of resources among governments is the other half of the assignment problem. Obviously, if the funds available are to meet the expenditure requirements, there must be a definite correspondence between the two. Three major sources of funds are possible; own-revenues from taxation, charges, operating surplus, fines, etc., transfers from other governments and debt. Each is reviewed in turn.

Taxes and Other Sources of Own Revenue

Recommendations for the assignment of revenue sources typically follow a number of principles. One that has already been suggested is that finance should follow function. That is, the greater the extent of the expenditure responsibilities that are assigned to a government, the greater should be the potential revenues from the revenue sources allocated to it. That is, more responsibilities, more available own funds.

The focus on expenditures and own revenues reveals a second principle, the benefit principle. That is, it is desirable that citizens see a clear linkage between the benefits that they vote for and the taxes, charges, etc., that they pay. A close linkage will improve decisions and efficiency by better relating willingness to pay to expenditures. For all levels of government, accountability and responsible decision making results when the benefits and costs are both confined to the respective constituents.

Despite the merits of the benefit principle, own revenues are typically less than the expenditures of subnational governments with intergovernmental transfers accounting for the difference. As noted below, there are various and quite legitimate reasons for such transfers. Decisions about the resource and expenditure assignments affect the magnitude of the gap to be met by transfers. A suggested guideline for that exercise is that if even the subnational governments with the greatest fiscal capacities are unable to meet expenditure requirements from own sources, this may be a signal that the gap between the assignment of revenue sources and expenditure responsibilities is too great and needs reassessment. Large gap closing transfers distort the benefit–cost linkage and may adversely influence subnational decision making. Also, unless well designed and administered, grants can unlatch the door to softened budget constraints.

Subnational governments should determine their own rates for the taxes, fees, etc. that they impose on their citizens and so determine their own revenues. If decentralized governments are to meet the tax and expenditure preferences of their constituents, they require the flexibility to generate locally determined levels of funds and spend them accordingly.[8]

[8]The freedom of subnational government to set tax rates may require some restriction in cases where, particularly taxes on business, tax exporting or harmful tax competition is possible.

Other features of a good own revenue assignment are adequacy of funds, stability, visibility, inability to shift or export the tax, ease of administration, and consider fair.

Analysis of the revenue assignment problem along these lines provides some guidelines in regard to which taxes are best suited for different levels of government. Just to highlight a few of the conclusions; property taxes fit well the circumstances of local governments, personal income taxes suit provincial and central governments, corporate income taxes the central government, VATs the central governments and retail sales taxes provincial although provincial piggybacking on a central VAT may be a manageable substitute. Revenues from natural resources are considered best suited for central governments. However, impacts of development are usually quite local, which calls for some sharing of revenues. Also resources are sometimes even owned by subnational governments, which can lead to wide fiscal disparities.[9] Charges and fees for government supplied goods and services are widely recommended as a first avenue for the generation of own revenues. If property designed, charges and fees can relate closely to benefits and so follow closely the benefit principle. If so, their use avoids more distorting and what may be no more equitable taxes.

Intergovernmental Transfers

Despite the recognized importance of own-source funding, intergovernmental transfers are typically important in subnational governments' budgets. The contribution of such grants varies widely but levels up to 50 percent are not uncommon. Given their prevalence and magnitudes, it is important that intergovernmental transfers effectively achieve legitimate objectives and not distort outcomes or misdirect funds.

Intergovernmental transfers are made for variety of reasons, both economic and political. Economic reasons are (a) to prevent resource misallocation due to interjurisdictional spillovers of benefits and costs, (b) to close fiscal gaps caused by unbalanced or mismatched revenue-raising and expenditure responsibilities, and (c) to equalize the abilities of governments to provide services despite dissimilar revenue generating capacities and expenditure requirements. Grants may be provided by senior

[9] Addressing the problems associated with natural resource revenues in those situations is often complicated by the failure to recognize that the revenues (or large parts of them) are really rents (i.e., returns to a collectively owned factor of production) and not tax revenue per se regardless of what called and how collected.

governments for other, political, reasons such as facilitating political cooperation and stability or strengthening frontier regions.

The purpose, notably the economic rationale, of a grant fundamentally determines its design and funding. Grants to correct for externalities provide compensation for the spillover benefits of locally produced public services. Schooling and transportation provide common examples. The funding is conditional (i.e., specific to the externality generating activity) and cost shared or matching (often with a limit) at a rate reflecting the extent of the externality.[10] Grants to close fiscal gaps arising from imbalances of revenue and expenditure responsibilities should be unconditional and the total amount of the transfer and its allocation should be based on estimates of expenditure requirements less revenue raising potential.[11] Often, however, both these total funding and distribution criteria are only imperfectly approached using some form of revenue sharing. Hence, even with revenue sharing, equalization grants are typically called for to offset to some degree serious interjurisdictional disparities in fiscal abilities to meet expenditure requirements and so facilitate more comparable service levels among subnational jurisdictions. Equalization grants need to be determined from objective estimates of the difference between expenditure requirements and revenue generating potential (not actual revenues).[12] An important issue is the standard for equalization. Equalization funds are unconditional grants, typically from senior governments. Having a clear purpose or objective defined and clear standards to meet resolves most of the grant design issues; that is, the amount of funding that is needed, the allocation of those funds, and the distribution.

Grants are also provided to meet political objectives. Political reasons include: promote cooperation, political stability, regional promotion, stretch the central budget, enhance visibility, and extend power or

[10] Sometimes one observes grants covering almost the total cost of a program supplied by a subnational government. In those cases, the arrangement is more of an intergovernmental contract than a grant.

[11] A large number of conditional grants covering the bulk of subnational activities suggests an excessive and inappropriate use of conditional funding and a need for general-purpose funding. Many countries have consolidated their conditional grant programs into a few specific-purpose programs consistent with national interest and/or substituted general-purpose, fiscal gap closing support.

[12] If the allocation of fiscal gap closing (e.g., revenue sharing) funds were on this basis, those transfers could be both gap closing and equalizing, negating any further need for equalization grants.

influence. Naturally, some of these objectives can influence the design of all grant programs.

Rarely are grant programs in practice so segregated by purpose. Rather, they tend to blend various economic as well as the political objectives. In addition, grant systems grow incrementally and are only infrequently reassessed. Hence, intergovernmental transfers are often complicated, even to governments, and this hampers accountability among governments and to citizens. Consequently, it is desirable to establish or refine as well as possible transfers meeting a number of desirable conditions. Characteristics of good grant programs are that they have a clear purpose, are allocated objectively (e.g., by formula), are relatively simple and transparent to all, ensure accountability both to donors and to beneficiaries, permit the autonomy and flexibility necessary for effective utilization, are stable, are adequate to cover needs, and provide some equalization. It is particularly important that grants not be negotiable and their magnitude not be determined by local decisions. Certainly at the margin, subnational jurisdictions should be spending their own money to realize local benefits. Grants should ease the demands on subnational budgets but not create a soft budget constraint.

Deficits and Debt

Deficits and debts are a potential source of finance for subnational governments. Debt finance is particularly appealing for financing infrastructure, a type of expenditure for which subnational governments, and especially local governments, commonly have a disproportionate responsibility. This situation raises a variety of interesting questions including the relative contributions of own funds, grants and debt; the appropriate role and the effects of capital grants; sources of borrowed funds; means of debt repayment (e.g., benefit-related charges or taxes), etc. However, the major new issue introduced by deficits and debt in a discussion of decentralization is the need for central government involvement through supervision and, potentially, bailouts.

In addressing deficits and debt, it is helpful to distinguish between operating and capital outlays and between regional (i.e., provincial or state) and local governments. Where regional governments are large, they may be able to have a legitimate stabilizing influence on regional economic activity. If so, there can be a case for running surpluses and deficits for regional stabilization purposes. The concern is that deficits intended or claimed for stabilization are not run to finance or mask overspending or to avoid or delay adjustments to long-term or permanently inferior economic conditions and so accumulate into burdensome debt. Possibly because of a stabilization role, and historical and political reasons, provincial and state governments often have some latitude in debt finance (e.g., Canada), although there may be self-imposed restrictions via state constitutions (e.g., the United States). In many instances, however, central controls exist (e.g., Australia). In contrast, deficits and debt of local governments are almost universally subject to controls by senior government. Typically, unlike for many provincial and state governments, a clear distinction is made between operating and capital accounts with deficits in operating accounts not permitted and debt only allowed for the finance of capital outlays.

Controls on subnational government debt arise from fear of fiscal irresponsibility and concern for potential macroeconomic management problems. While foreign debt may represent a special case, it is not obvious from the evidence that serious macroeconomic problems (need to) arise in the absence of central controls. Also, it could be that, left to their own devices and resources, subnational governments are no more irresponsible than their senior supervisors. The problems with subnational debt appear to emerge when inappropriate decisions and behavior are legitimized by central action. That is, if central governments (or supervising provincial or state governments in the case of some local governments) intervene in a debt crisis to resolve the problem with little or no cost to the borrower, debt problems will persist. Such actions create incentives to gain from a transfer of resources by defaulting on debt. Supervision and controls on debt financing by senior governments creates an implicit obligation on the supervising government, which many find hard to ignore should problems or default occur. While a case may be made for senior government assistance and possibly even advice in the case of new, naive and possibly small governments entering the capital market, if fiscal irresponsibility is to be avoided, the ultimate responsibility must rest on the borrower. That is, "your error, your cost." When aid extends to supervision, the allocation of the obligations becomes nebulous and potential difficulties emerge. Even if aid is provided, the cost to the assisted government should be sufficient to correct behavior. The full cost is the best reminder. The rules, however, need to be upfront; that is, known in advance of agreements.

Besides defining clear rules about fiscal responsibility, central governments make other decisions that can avoid financial problems for subnational governments. One consideration is to ensure that the assignment of expenditure responsibilities and revenue sources does not leave a debt-inducing gap or imbalance. Another is to ensure regular and accurate financial accounting by governments; that is, open and transparent public accounts.

Administrative Capacity

Deficiencies of administrative capacity at subnational, especially the local, levels are a frequently cited concern about decentralization.[13] Indeed, an excessive pace or volume of decentralization can cause problems. Decentralization does not change the amount of administrative capacity available within a country, although it changes the location of many decisions and, if action is not taken, may separate decision makers from administrative expertise. Presumably, if decisions are decentralized, at least some of the central expertise is redundant and programs could be put into place to get much of that to decentralized locations; for example, relocation, as advisors, as trainers, as consultants. Decision-making and administrative expertise also need to emerge at the local level.[14] With transparent procedures, citizen participation, and local accountability, the extent to which administrative capabilities can develop at the subnational level (especially when locally motivated) has been surprising. That is, local participation and the motivation of serving one's community can stimulate capacity development and performance. With nurturing and investment, a solid subnational administrative capacity can emerge. Ultimately, a competent, honest, motivated civil service at each level of government is needed if decentralization is to be successful.

Management Authority

If the potential advantages of decentralization are to be realized, SNGs must have the management authority and discretion to make the decisions about subnational matters. If central governments "decentralize" but then interfere by imposing numerous restrictions or continuing to micro-manage operations, decentralization has not actually occurred and there will be little opportunity to achieve benefits.

[13] The capacity for political decision making may also be a potential problem. Political capacity is largely built upon experience.

[14] Decentralization may require some augmentation of the country's administrative expertise in an area in response to greater efforts to meet local conditions. On the other hand, some economies may also be possible.

Taxation, or revenue generation generally, often provides examples of only partial decentralization. Once SNG revenue sources and tax bases have been established, SNGs should be free to set their own tax rates, charges, fees, etc. as required to meet their needs and to suit local services and circumstances. Often, however, uniform tax rates, fees, etc. are imposed by the central government. About the only legitimate case for central intervention in local taxes has to do with business taxes when undesirable local tax competition or tax exporting is a problem. In that situation, setting minimum and/or maximum rates for relevant business taxes may be appropriate.

Often, central governments are concerned about the spending, or the spending in certain areas, of decentralized governments. Hence, the central government may earmark certain revenues for expenditure on a specific service or the central government may mandate that the local government provide a particular service important to the central government. Such requirements reduce local autonomy and, by restricting parts of the budget, reduce flexibility. In addition, it is not obvious that either earmarking or mandating will result in the appropriate amount of designated services being provided or in them being supplied efficiently. Both mechanisms are crude instruments. As another form of lingering control, central governments sometimes decentralize specific programs (e.g., health, education) but then specify salary schedules and/or staffing levels. By doing so, the central government decreases substantially the management flexibility of the local authorities and, in so doing, reduces the opportunities for local management to realize economies or to improve services.

Occasionally, central governments require central approval of local budgets. Delays in budgets and local action often result. Such checks frequently get mired in details over which central authorities have little insight benefiting local residents. Requirements for central approval often reflect a lack of decentralized accountability to local citizens.

Decentralized governments need their own staff. In some places, those delivering the services for which local governments are responsible are actually central government, not local, employees. In such cases, those employees' respond to central authority and local decision makers have little control over the service for which they are supposed to be responsible. If subnational governments are to be able to manage local services, they require public servants accountable to them and not to others; that is, staff that they hire and, if necessary, fire. Closely related, local authorities should have the freedom to turn to private alternatives to supply part or all of their public provided services. Private contractors can be attractive, for example, in supplying garbage collection, road construction and/or maintenance, property value assessment for taxation, and selected health services.

Decentralization to SNGs involves making them responsible for planning, budgeting, and managing so that they deliver local services meeting local conditions and preferences. When the decentralized services are indeed "local", there should be no case for continued central intervention and the local authorities should have complete autonomy over expenditures and revenues. Problems are more likely to arise when central authorities see some broader or national interest in services for which SNGs have been given some authority. In such cases, two questions arise. First, is intervention necessary to meet national interests? Second, if so, what form of intervention the best? If left to make their own decisions, the services and service levels that local governments select may meet the central government's expectations and intervention would not be needed. However, if broader interests are not satisfied, the task is to see that those interests are met efficiently. Many central interventions impose input constraints while the central government is likely most interested in the outputs, or some of the outputs, from the local program. Improvements are likely if the central government created incentives for local decision makers to provide the missing outputs the central government wants. That would leave the decentralized authorities with the flexibility to achieve local and central objectives more efficiently. While it is important that legitimate national interests be recognized and met along with local priorities, a major potential gain from decentralization is that local authorities have the ability to manage to realize both those objectives effectively.

Accountability

Good government requires accountability. This statement is equally true for decentralized government. Indeed, for decentralized government, the relationships are typically more complex and so accountability may be more difficult to realize.

A decentralized government needs to be accountable to two major groups; those who benefit from its activities and those who pay for the services. Especially in the case of decentralized government, the two groups are not likely to coincide. Those who benefit are those who live within the jurisdiction (i.e., the citizens, voters, users of services) and possibly some outside the jurisdiction whose interests are usually represented by the central or senior government (although horizontal intergovernmental agreements are also not uncommon). Those who pay include those within the jurisdiction (primarily the local residents paying taxes, charges, etc.), the senior government (primarily through transfers), and lenders. Accountability to lenders is a well-understood obligation accepted as part of a financial transaction. The overlap of the residents in the beneficiary and payer groups is substantial and, even if somewhat uneven, well recognized. The presence of the central or senior government as a contributor and a "beneficiary" is what usually adds the extra complication to recognizing and defining the lines of accountability in decentralized government.

Information is essential for accountability. Information requirements include the lines and nature of responsibilities, budgeting and financial information, and information on performance. Accountability between levels of government works better when responsibilities are clearly defined and intergovernmental fiscal relations are carefully specified so there is little opportunity for confusion or obfuscation. Good information on local finances is important for budgeting and planning, for management and operational effectiveness, and for financial control. Such information is also critical for accountability. For accountability, however, that information must be also be transparent to those beyond government. That is, the information must be readily understandable, including explaining intergovernmental fiscal relations, to citizens and to the media that informs most of them. Financial information is more valuable if it can be related to performance. Performance indicators, even relatively simple ones, can be useful to public managers, public decision makers and to the public.

Many decentralized governments will strive to provide good information to their citizens in efforts to encourage public input and also to demonstrate good performance but not all need be so motivated. Information is most valuable if it is timely, complete, reliable/accurate, consistent, and transparent. Information for decentralized governments is more likely to approach these standards if organized and monitored by central governments. If done successfully, all parties will have access to meaningful data and the parties can debate the meaning and implications of the data rather than the data themselves. Ensuring good data on underlying governments is a valuable role for central government.[15] Indeed, it is an example of decentralization changing rather than eliminating central responsibilities.

Good information promotes good policy debates. Information is transmitted by, processed by, and further information and ideas are the products of the media, citizens, interest groups, think tanks, academics who evaluate, discuss, and debate and respond to politicians and bureaucrats (who rely on information themselves). A Russian visitor to Canada, at the end of a tour acquainting him with the public sector, referred to the "invisible college" comprised of the combination of and open interaction among these groups in many forums. In sum, it is very much a learning environment with a free exchange of ideas; a virtual college. Access to information and the freedom to use it, is input to policy development and to accountability.

There is another dimension to accountability that warrants mention again in this context. Decentralized governments need public servants that are accountable to them, not to senior level of government. That is, local (provincial) governments need their own local (provincial) civil servants.[16]

Accountability requires enforcement if it is to be effective. Normally, this includes the possibility that politicians can be voted out of office, government employees discharged, transfers withheld, loans not made. A weak enforcement mechanism, however, will undermine accountability and performance.[17]

Beyond Government

The preceding five topics have focused on the public sector and how public sector institutions, characteristics, decisions, etc. may contribute to or detract from the success of decentralization efforts. This section is a reminder that the development and transition of the public sector does not occur independently of the rest of the economy or the rest of society. That is not a novel idea and reference has already been made above to some of the (societal) interrelations but, here, the purpose is to introduce

[15] Senior governments should, of course, be an example and at least live up to the standards that they set for others.

[16] Note that this point does not suggest political appointees. Rather, it refers to which government a professional civil service should answer.

[17] Clearly, there is a connection between the factors discussed in the section on government and political institutions and this section on accountability.

some other linkages and reflect on some of those already mentioned in somewhat different ways.

What is the scope and capacity of the private sector of the economy, what drives it and how efficiently it operates will affect the role and shape of the public sector. For example, economies with well-developed private financial sectors can rely more on private institutions to fund and scrutinize public debt, possibly even that of local governments. Also, good capital markets in combination with large-scale corporate enterprises including engineering expertise may enable private operations to supply "public" utilities rather than rely on public ownership. The presence of a selection of competitive and reliable construction companies provides opportunities for tendering public projects. On the other hand, government can promote the development of private alternatives by opening projects to competitive bidding. In such cases, however, the difficult problem is to avoid favoritism in a limited market. Thus, the opportunities for pursuing private alternatives and the potential success of attempting to introduce private options depend on structure and capacity of the private sector.

The potential for employing private options depends also upon the capacity of the legal and regulatory system. Engaging private enterprises to provide services for government requires contracts and, particularly in the absence of competition, regulatory mechanisms. Successful programs require an effective legal system with knowledgable and quality staff on both the private and public side for negotiating contracts, regulating industry, and settling disputes.

Success with private alternatives will depend also upon the motivation of the private sector just as public sector success depends upon motivations there. If the private sector is competitive, innovative, entrepreneurial, and rewards merit, engaging the private sector is more likely to be rewarding. On the other hand, if it is instead rent seeking and lacks respect for the law, success is unlikely. The worst case is if both the private and public sector are rent seeking; the best case is both are competitive, innovative, entrepreneurial, and reward merit. Most likely is that both are somewhere in between with government having the weaker "entrepreneurial" motivations. Interaction of the two sectors and especially movement of people between the two can be expected to generate some cross-fertilization of ideas and opinions and harmonize thinking to some extent.

The presence of an evaluative mentality throughout society is positive. That is, people in all sectors assess situations, options, and actions. People look for improvement, expect results, and are performance oriented. At the same time, they expect ethical behavior. Basically, there is accountability throughout the economy and throughout the society. It is particularly important that there be a political culture to expect and accept public evaluation, criticism, and accountability plus the political freedom to permit and stimulate that thought.[18]

Finally, instability, be it economic, political, or social, complicate life and make transition, even to distinctly better states, difficult. Unfortunately, many countries considering or attempting steps toward decentralization face such unrest.

Concluding Note

This part of the chapter has outlined six components of decentralization. Drawing from the experience reflected in the considerable literature, features of these components have been sketched. In sum, the collection provides an overview of what analysts can look for in assessing the environment for decentralization and in assessing decentralization efforts. The main points are highlighted in the Appendix. While providing a broad perspective, this analysis need not be comprehensive.

Steps in Evaluating Decentralization Projects

The steps in evaluating decentralization projects consist of the columns in Table 9.1. Five steps are identified. These steps are: identifying the initial environment, describing the action taken, determining the outcomes, evaluating the outcomes and determining the reasons for those outcomes, and establishing the lessons to be learned from the project. Each of these is examined in turn.

Environment

The initial step is to establish the environment or the situation that the planners of the decentralization project faced and in which the decentralization project had to operate. Four main questions are to be answered from this review: (1) What is the problem? (2) Why is there a problem? (3) What are the constraints? (4) Where are the opportunities? That is, this

[18]The "invisible college" mentioned in the Accountability section above illustrates the evaluative environment.

analysis needs to identify the problem(s) the project sought to address, why it (they) existed, what factors constrained reaching a solution, and what created opportunities. Constraints can be binding or nonbinding. Hence, the constraints need to be looked at broadly as not only being the limitations (i.e., the negatives, weaknesses, cons) but also the assets (i.e., the positives, strengths, pros, advantages) that relax constraints. The "constraints" and the opportunities not only suggest the potential scope for solutions but can also indicate what may be critical constraints that programs might aim at softening. Defining the environment aims at identifying the problem(s) and the scope for and feasibility of short- and longer-term solutions. Reviewing the environment in the context of each of the six decentralization components, or at least those that are relevant, is an aid to a comprehensive assessment.

Reviewers will be particularly interested in the project's assessment of its environment. Project reports and inputs to the project will be central to defining that perception of the environment. The project's assessment of its environment must be carefully outlined.

Reviewers will also be watchful for oversights in the project's assessment of its environment. Reviewers will want to assess the consistency of the project's assessment of the situation that it faced with that indicated by previous Bank and other work. While it is unlikely that the project staff will have omitted or misinterpreted the initial situation based on the then available information, there may have been facts learned during the project or subsequently that would have been useful input at that time. Thus, more recent reports, country experts, or the reviewer may be aware of better information on the environment that would have been helpful to the project organizers. Thus, part of the exercise is to assess the quality of information on the project's environment that was available at the time as well as the project's utilization of that information.

Action

Action refers to the new policies, programs, or practices and to changes in policies, programs, or practices resulting from the project. All those actions relating to decentralization and any others that are relevant will need to be identified and carefully outlined. There may be a difference between those actions recommended and those actually adopted for implementation. If so, that distinction should be made and reasons for the gap recorded. Consideration needs to be given to the possibility that not all actions or outcomes may be immediate. Some recommendations may be acted upon immediately and be closely associated with a project. Others, however, may be deferred or even, seemingly, ignored. Part of the reasons for these delays may be that only so much change can be digested during a given time, or the conditions or the timing is not then suitable. Yet many recommendations, suggestions, etc. become seeds that eventually find fertile ground, sprout and grow. Others, for any of a variety of reasons (including, possibility, that they may be unsuitable, even bad, ideas) never mature. It is important to recognize that not all recommendations may see immediate results. Some may simply become a small piece of evidence contributing to the received wisdom. It is important to look also for those seeds that took root later, possibly even in a different country. Hence, when identifying the action resulting from a project, the perspective should not be too narrow. Clearly, the direct response will be especially important to catalogue and evaluate but the often longer-term and potentially more dispersed contributions should not be neglected. Bank documentation will likely follow the direct actions. The deferred and indirect actions will be more difficult to identify. Country and program experts may be best able to offer insights. Time, of course, provides opportunities for the eventual realization of recommendations initially set aside.

Recommended actions should be evaluated from the perspective of their consistency with the environment. That is, evaluate how consistent they are with the problem(s), reasons for the problem(s), the constraints, and the opportunities. Good recommendations take these factors into account. Recommendations that are implemented are expected to be those that are deemed most relevant at the time. Relevance is one of the Operations Evaluation Department's standard criteria.[19] Relevance is defined as "the extent which the project's objectives are consistent with the country's current development priorities and with current Bank country and sectoral assistance strategies and corporate goals."[20] Recommendations that are relevant to the country and the Bank are, rightfully, going to receive particular attention, take priority, and deserve special attention. However, others should not be neglected. Priorities, strategies, and goals change and recommendations that have long-term consistency, relevance, and appeal are valuable.

[19] See, e.g., Huther and Shah (1997, 2000) and OED (2000).

[20] Huther and Shah (2000, p. 8).

Outcomes

Outcomes are the results of the actions taken. Ideally, they would be what the new or changed policies, programs, and practices achieved but, definitely, they must include all that occurred as a consequence of the actions taken. Documenting outcomes is likely to be a significant task and one that may not easily be accomplished. The ease of the task will depend upon the extent of follow-up and, particularly, on subsequent evaluation of projects. When projects have been evaluated, the exercise is likely to be relatively simple. Where they have not been evaluated, information will need to be gleaned from subsequent studies, reports on related projects, reviews, etc. and from interviews with country and program authorities. That is, obtaining a complete record of a project's outcomes is likely to be the task of the reviewer, and require some initiative, not something that comes readily off-the-shelf or from a file.

Complicating the task of defining outcomes is the problem of time and the problem of indirect and delayed outcomes. It takes time for actions to result in outcomes. Attempting to identify and assess outcomes too early or too late makes the product more problematic. In the latter case, other events and other interventions have more opportunity to have both negative and positive effects. Many project outcomes may be unclear but, still, an indication of positive or negative prospects is helpful. Consequences of the direct or immediate actions are expected to be the most obvious and those of which people are most aware. But as noted above, many suggestions or recommendations may not be considered to be immediately relevant. Yet some of those may be acted upon over time as opportunities permit. The outcomes of those recommendations will be more difficult to identify and recent projects will have had less opportunity to reveal them. Still, efforts should be made to establish a comprehensive list.

Assessment

The assessment phase is central to the evaluation of decentralization projects. It has two major goals. One goal is to evaluate the outcomes in terms of what was accomplished. The second goal is to determine the reasons for those results.

The assessment relates closely to the preceding stages. For example, the success, failure, or intermediate result will depend upon (a) how well the initial situation was assessed (and whether there were unexpected intervening events), (b) how suitable were the actions recommended and implemented (and the implementation process itself), and (c) how closely outcomes matched those anticipated. There are really two dimensions to the evaluation that are expected to be of interest in most projects. First, there is a problem in the sense of an inferior social condition that the project is ultimately aimed at alleviating. Such problems could be poor (or limited access to) elementary schooling, lack of infrastructure, distorted budget allocations, etc. Second, some deficiency or failure in the (particularly) public system is seen as causing or contributing to the social problem and the project is also aimed at reforming the system to cause it to perform better. Programs to increase transparency of the budget system or to create a more effective intergovernmental transfer program are examples. In effect, the project aims at reducing a social problem by introducing some (in this case, decentralizing) changes to the (usually public) system. The two need to be distinguished and both need evaluation. That is, there is interest in both the effectiveness of the project in enhancing the social condition and in the effectiveness, contribution, and impact of the decentralizing reform to that (and other) development. For example, projects that successfully change practices but fail to improve the social condition (or reduce the cost of achieving the same condition) cannot be considered as successful as those realizing both.

OED evaluation criteria provide a useful and convenient methodology for the assessment of the outcomes.[21] These are highlighted as follows.

Relevance

Relevance is "the extent which the project's objectives are consistent with the country's current development priorities and with current Bank country and sectoral assistance strategies and corporate goals." Relevance has already been mentioned in the discussion of actions and the consistency of recommendations with the environment or the initial situation. While it is logical to assess relevance at that point, that assessment needs to be noted and summarized at the assessment step as well.

Efficacy

Efficacy is "the extent to which the project's objectives were achieved, or expected to be achieved, taking into account their relative importance." Assessing efficacy is an effort to determine the success in achieving stated goals. Obviously, efficacy is closely related to the discussion of project effectiveness in the proceeding paragraph. Care is warranted in this

[21] These follow Huther and Shah (2000).

analysis in that the stated objectives are neither too ambitious (i.e., unrealistic) nor too modest (i.e., too easily achieved and resulting in under accomplishment).

Sustainability

Sustainability is defined as "the resilience to risk of net benefit flows over time." In the context of decentralization programs, sustainability relates to the persistence of the project's programs in generating social improvements and of the decentralization reforms to have positive impacts over time. That is, will the benefits last? The OED notes that account needs to be taken of political, economic, financial, social, and external influences. This analysis, would add other considerations—for example, bureaucratic and other pressures—reflecting forces relating to the categories listed in Table 9.1.

Efficiency

Efficiency is "the extent to which the project achieved, or is expected to achieve, a higher return than the opportunity cost of capital and benefits at least compared to the alternatives." Because decentralization projects are largely focused on different ways of doing things and the benefits and costs are often not readily measured in financial terms (as could be the case with, for example, an infrastructure investment), efficiency is likely to be somewhat more difficult to grasp in many instances. Regardless, it is still an important consideration because the resources to effect change can be considerable and the potential benefits important.

Institutional Development

Institutional development is "the extent to which a project improves the ability of a country or region to make more efficient, equitable and sustainable use of its human, financial, and natural resources through: (a) better definition, stability, transparency, enforceability and predictability of institutional arrangements and/or (b) better alignment of the mission and capacity of an organization with its mandate, which derives from these institutional arrangements." Clearly, institutional development is a major consideration for the evaluation of decentralization projects. Indeed, much, potentially even most, of the analysis of the preceding criteria is directed at the institutional development aspects. Decentralization is oriented to changing the ways that things are done in order to enhance outcomes. Although decentralization projects may involve adding, shifting or reassigning resources, decentralization is largely institutional development.

Bank Performance

Bank performance is "the extent to which service provided by the Bank ensured quality at entry and supported implementation through appropriate supervision (including adequate transition arrangements for regular operation of the project)." This perspective is oriented to how well the Bank did its job in a project. Especially for decentralization projects, which are focused on institutional development, consideration should also be given to what the Bank has learned from the project that might be applied in the county or more widely.

Country (Borrower) Performance

Country performance includes the evaluation of the country's preparation, implementation, and compliance in regard to the project. Because decentralization typically affects practices significantly influenced by traditions and customs, country support (in combination with Bank sensitivity) is especially critical.

Considering these criteria will be helpful in achieving a complete assessment of a decentralization project. As indicated, some factors will be more important than others.

Understanding the reasons for the outcomes being what they were is as important as making an evaluation of the relative success of the outcomes according to relevant criteria. Whether results were good or bad is important to establish but determining the reason for those outcomes is critical for repeating successes and avoiding the repetition of failures. Assessing the environment, the action, and the outcomes systematically for each of the decentralization categories of Table 9.1 will assist in identifying factors that contributed to success or failure. Those categories are widely recognized as important components of decentralization and the elements of them highlighted in their discussion are also generally acknowledged as features that contribute to or hamper successful decentralization. Reference to those will aid reviewers of decentralization projects in identifying factors contributing to the evaluations assigned.

Many sources of information will need to be consulted. As already mentioned, project documentation and related Bank materials, especially country studies, will be valuable inputs. Especially subsequent works that will often offer some insights to outcomes will be useful. Complementary studies by other lender, donors, etc. may be excellent references. Again, country and program experts within and beyond the Bank can offer considerable insight. In addition, it could be useful to get assessments from those who directed or participated in the project. Their experience and hindsight could add a helpful dimension.

Lessons

The final step in the evaluation of each project is to determine and outline the lessons that have been learned from the study. That is, draw together the conclusions and implications for Bank policies, programs and practices. Considering that insights might be drawn from the several steps across the various categories, there could be a considerable number of conclusions and implications drawn from each project. It will be useful to document those but, also, it will be necessary to distil them down to a modest number of the most important lessons.

Methods of Analysis

The preceding parts of the paper have focused on the method for studying a single decentralization project. In this section, attention is directed to the methods for undertaking the study of the set of decentralization projects. That is, here one concentrates on the total package rather than the individual project. However, before committing entirely to the broad perspective, thought is given to adding a technique for evaluating individual projects that facilitates comparison of a project with many others. The already existing plan for analysis is to conduct a desk study of many decentralization projects followed by a very small number of country studies (i.e., the study of projects in a few countries). The second part of this section reviews that plan. The final part of the section suggests a variant that may provide additional insights.[22]

Comparing Evaluations Across Many Projects: Verbal and Quantitative Approaches

The objective of the analysis is to evaluate decentralization from an investigation of many decentralization projects. The number and diversity of those projects complicate comparison and assessment. Verbal analysis is essential but it can be difficult to summarize and possibly even through which to see all the relations. Quantitative analysis can be helpful but it

[22] The methods outlined below are intended to have broad application to the evaluation of decentralization. Note, however, that despite the overlap, community-driven development in the context of the projected study is addressed later in this chapter.

requires quantitative assessments of the variables in a situation where quantitative measurement is not implicit, potentially difficult, and possibly problematic. However, there is merit in considering both approaches.

The Verbal Approach

A method for investigating each project has been outlined above. It was projected as a verbal report with documentation. Because each project is input into the broader analysis of many projects, summary documentation is needed. Therefore, it is suggested that the report on each project should consist of (a) a summary outline, (b) an overview matrix highlighting the main points following the format of Table 9.1, and (c) the detailed analysis. The summary would be very short, providing:

- Identify project: country, region, dates
- Cost of project (i.e., resource inputs)
- Purpose of project
- Brief descriptions of:
  - Situation/environment
  - Actions taken
  - Results, outcomes
- Assessment of the project
  - Evaluation
  - Major reasons for success or failure
- Lessons

An overview matrix provides more detail by introducing the decentralization components. By permitting a more detailed perspective on each step in the evaluation process, reviewers can quickly obtain, or be reminded of, a more complete picture of the project and of each stage in the evaluation. Summary evaluations could also be extended here to the environment and action steps so as to understand better the reasons for the outcomes. The quality with which the project was undertaken is important. At the action stage, one consideration affecting outcomes is the "relevance" of the recommendations but a second is the quality of the implementation of the recommendations undertaken. Both can be evaluated.[23] The quality of the environmental assessment is another dimension

[23] Performance in conveying or selling the recommendations might be a further consideration but it is likely to be one that is more difficult to assess.

to the evaluation. In addition to the quality with which the project was undertaken, it may be that the circumstances also affect outcomes. That is, an assessment of how serious a situation is regarded to be as an impediment to development (or other objective) may also be useful input. Although it would overlap to some extent with the summary outline, it could be helpful to add an additional row to the matrix to provide the overall assessment in that context.

The summary outline and the overview matrix for each project are tools to facilitate the comparison and analysis of many projects. Supporting them is the detailed report from which they are derived.

A Quantitative Approach

A more quantitative evaluation may assist in identifying relationships and in determining results and understanding outcomes. As indicated above, much of the information, outcomes and analysis, does not lend itself to quantification. Yet, for example, evaluations of outcomes are required. A simple good or bad evaluation can be quantified; for example, Huther and Shah (2000) suggest four ratings for OED criteria; high, substantial, modest, and negligible. For example, for "relevance" they suggest:

- High; most of the major objectives were highly relevant.
- Substantial; most of the major objectives were at least substantially relevant.
- Modest; most of the major objectives were not highly or substantially relevant.
- Negligible; most of the major objectives were irrelevant or negligibly relevant.

And for "efficacy" they suggest:

- High; major objectives were fully met, or expected to be fully met, with no shortcomings.
- Substantial; major objectives were met, or expected to be met, with only minor shortcomings.
- Modest; major objectives were met, or expected to be met, with significant shortcomings.
- Negligible; major objectives were not met, or expected to be met, due to major shortcomings.

Such output ratings are applicable to the verbal evaluations but they can also be assigned numeric scores and made amenable to quantitative analysis. In their design paper for the evaluation of public expenditure reviews, Huther and Shah (1997) proposed scoring outputs on a 1–6 (high to low evaluation). They also suggested scoring the quality of the PERs evaluated on a 1–6 scale. Quality considerations included such factors as internalizing previous results, selection of relevant issues, and the rigor, consistency, and clarity of the analysis.

The scoring approach could be extended to the components of decentralization and used to rate the conditions for decentralization (i.e., the decentralization environments) and to rate the actions undertaken. That is, using environment as the example, for each one could assign scores for government and political institutions, for responsibilities and powers, etc. However, because these components are each composed of a number of separate factors (as summarized in the Appendix), those factors would need to be scored, or rated, as well. Thus, for example, government and political institutions includes democracy, participation, information and transparency, attitudes, and intergovernmental relations. For some of these and other components, indexes are available but their suitability will need review. For most, those undertaking the study (possibly with the analysts) will need to structure an index. The individual reviewers/analysts would need to determine the scores according to the indexes. While individual indexes might be useful, a composed composite index for each decentralization component may be preferred. Huther and Shah (1998) demonstrate a method for creating such indexes. Critical, of course, is the accuracy of the indexes components and the weight given each. Given the data and resource limitations, analysts may be called upon to use their knowledge, experience, and good judgment to determine a value along an agreed-upon scale for many (e.g., composite) indexes. Carefully considered assessments by knowledgeable persons may reflect well the situations and be good substitutes for those from more detailed investigations (perhaps the only substitute if the latter cannot be undertaken).

Indexes could be determined for each component of decentralization (and, as appropriate, the subcomponents) and scores assigned across cells in the matrix. Assuming reasonable indexes and scores can be established (and that may require careful consideration), relatively simple or even more sophisticated (e.g., regressions) quantitative analysis may yield interesting and helpful results in terms of identifying the policies and the underlying conditions that are most amenable to success. Thus, the verbal and quantitative analyses may effectively complement each other.

Desk and Country Analyses

Based on previous experience, the Bank plans that there will be an extensive set of desk studies of decentralization projects followed by intensive studies of a few selected countries. The focus here is primarily on the desk studies.

Desk Studies

The existing plan is that the desk analyses would cover a broad sample of the decentralization projects. Regional experts would be assigned to analyze all the decentralization projects associated with a region. There are six regions; East Asia and the Pacific, Europe and Central Asia, Latin American and the Caribbean, Middle East and North Africa, South Asia and sub-Saharan Africa.

A suggestion is that the Bank might consider two levels of desk studies. Given the number and the variety of potential projects to analyze, an overview level and a complete (in-depth) level of desk study would be helpful. The overview studies would cover all decentralization projects, provide an evaluation sufficient to make a reasonable overall assessment, and provide the insight necessary to determine the merits of further investigation. That is, the overview studies serve two purposes. One is to aid in the selection of projects for detailed study. The second purpose is that the census of overview studies provides a supplementary data set useful for backup analysis; that is, to serve as a check on and extension of the data from the detailed studies. The overview analysis might aim at completing (an initial round of) the summary outlines and, possibly even, the overview matrices mentioned above.[24]

There are considerable advantages to having regional experts reviewing projects undertaken in countries from their regions. However, decentralization projects cover a broad range of programs and it is unlikely that the regional experts will be uniformly well informed in all program areas.

[24]The need for the overview of all projects is based on the assumption that any standard OED evaluations of projects will not have covered all projects and/or not be sufficiently directed at the concerns here to serve the purpose without further investigation. Note too that this overview level of analysis is not recommended here for the proposed evaluation of community-driven development projects.

Hence, it is recommended that the desk studies of the projects, and especially the in-depth studies, be subject to dual reviews; once by a region/country expert and once by a program expert; as a form of cross-validation. Even if full-fledged program studies were not possible, it is recommended that program experts at least review the studies of decentralization projects in their areas. Beyond the two heads (with different but equally relevant expertise) are better than one logic, part of the rationale for dual analysis is that the second analyst provides a check for (in)consistency among the initial reviewers.[25] Looking at the list of decentralization projects provided in the Annex of Litvack et al. (1998), the projects appear to cluster in the following program areas: public expenditure reviews, macroeconomics/growth/stability, infrastructure, the social program areas of health, schooling and poverty, fiscal decentralization, and local government. Certainly there would be some overlapping here but relatively few program authorities could cover the vast majority and provide insight.

Country Studies

The countries to be studied and the projects/programs to be studied are expected to be largely a product of the desk analyses. The desk work in combination with the review and scrutiny of that by the analysts and the study directors will reveal to the group countries and projects that have been especially useful illustrations of decentralization efforts and for which additional intensive study is expected to be rewarding. Because many countries will have been involved in a large number of decentralization projects, not all projects undertaken in a country are likely to be selected for investigation in the country analysis. Rather, certainly in the case of some countries, attention will be restricted to a few or even to one project.

The country visits will be more intensive analyses than the desk studies. More time and effort can go into consulting the available documentation and in consulting with country, program, and other relevant experts. The main additional input will be country visits. The country visits allow consultations with a wide range of people. Meeting those personally acquainted with the project, ideally from initiation through to completion and operation, can yield valuable insights. Those contacted should include Bank staff, country representatives (politicians, bureaucrats), and others (e.g., other participants) and ideally include people across a range of

[25] Regardless, it is valuable to have the reviewers and the study directors gather and consult in an effort to ensure a high degree of uniformity in their methods and evaluation standards.

responsibilities and having a variety of perspectives. Also to be included are those delivering the newly decentralized services and their clients.

A Possible Extension

By studying World Bank decentralization projects, the analysis is limited to developing countries and to achieving a better understanding of the successes and failures of decentralization in that environment. Yet many developed countries are successful despite being quite centralized; for example, France and Australia. It would be interesting to study, at least review, a group of centralized developed countries in an effort to understand better their success (and possibility limitations to their success) under centralized conditions.[26] How do such countries differ from other successful developed countries that are less centralized? How do they differ from similarly centralized developing countries? What might developing countries, and the Bank, learn from the centralized developed countries? Such an investigation might offer interesting insights for decentralization in the developing world.[27]

Selection of the Projects for Analysis

There are many decentralization projects and reports that might be examined; far more than resources would permit detailed analysis. Choices will need to be made about which will be studied and at what level of intensity. Ultimately, those choices will need to be made by, or accepted by (if, e.g., randomly selected), those familiar with the work undertaken and the regions and countries involved. However, it is possible to reflect upon and illustrate some of the factors deserving consideration.

In-Depth Desk Study

The screening for the in-depth desk study is the most significant problem. Representation of the universe of cases is the prevailing objective for selecting those for closer examination. Numerous factors need to be taken into consideration. Regional representation is of major importance. The

[26] Studies of some aspects of decentralization in industrialized countries appear in work such as Ter-Minassian (1997).

[27] A review of problems with decentralization in still successful decentralized countries would also be interesting but is likely to be less relevant, partly because the lessons for decentralization have been fairly well established largely from the experience in industrialized countries even if the lessons are not always followed in each.

Bank uses six regions: sub-Saharan Africa, East Asia and Pacific, South Asia, Europe and Central Asia, Latin America and the Caribbean, and the Middle East and North Africa. Of the 199 decentralization projects over the fiscal years 1987–2001, most (over 60 percent) are in the sub-Saharan Africa and the Latin America and Caribbean regions while five went to the Middle East and North Africa. Financial significance may also matter. Over 40 percent of lending is directed to the Latin American and Caribbean region while the sub-Saharan Africa region received 13.9 percent. The average size project in the sub-Saharan Africa region was USD 37.3 million, less than half the overall average.

The 105 decentralization reports are more evenly distributed among the regions.[28] The largest number, about one-quarter of the total, were done for countries in the East Asia and Pacific region, and the smallest number, eight, for countries in the Middle East and North Africa region.

Besides regional representation, more attention is to be paid to cases in those countries to which the Bank has devoted more resources toward advisory reports. There are 16 emphasized countries. This contrasts to the 45 or more countries for which reports have been done. Note, in the East Asia and Pacific region, the Philippines had seven reports, which is comparable to those for Indonesia. Bangladesh, in South Asia, has had three, and Estonia, in Europe and Central Asia, has also had two.

Decentralization is directed to different levels. For example, in some cases, the effort is to shift from the central level to an intermediate state or provincial level. In others, decentralization goes to the local level from either the central or intermediate levels of government. Another area of interest is decentralization in the form of community-driven development; that is, initiatives from the local community level but not associated with any formal government. Thus, there are three categories of decentralization by level that it is also desirable to have represented.

Decentralization efforts typically have a program focus. That is, the intention is to seek improvement in a particular (program) area. The advisory reports are not uniformly distributed by program or region. There are areas of concentration. For example, infrastructure studies are almost entirely in only the East Asia and Pacific region and the sub-Saharan Africa region. Indeed, three regions have no such studies. In the Middle East and North Africa region, reports on local government predominate, while in

[28] Henceforth, "project" is used to refer to lending programs while "report" is used to refer to advisory programs of the Bank.

the Latin America and Caribbean area, reports on fiscal decentralization and on social programs dominate. Studies of social programs are widely distributed but are heavily concentrated in the Latin American and Caribbean region. Most of the 'fiscal decentralization' category studies were undertaken in the Latin America and Caribbean region and the East Asia and Pacific region. It appears that it may be difficult to always get regional balance while obtaining representative patterns. Given the focus on decentralization, the number and, to some degree, the distribution of reports, there could be a case for paying extra attention to studies addressing the fiscal decentralization, local government and social program areas. Given that public expenditure reviews have already been evaluated, there may be little need to include them (or similar broad-based studies) in the analysis.[29]

Other factors could be introduced for consideration in sample selection. The date when the decentralization project or report was done might be a factor. Decentralization is a relatively recent initiative and, presumably, there has been some learning by doing. Three possible periods might be considered; pre-1991, 1991–1995, and post-1995. The size or cost of the decentralization effort might be a consideration—for example, small, medium, large—but the potential importance of size may be questioned or it may be more relevant for lending than for advisory work. Selection of efforts for which the same people carried major responsibilities should probably be avoided. Finally, a representative balance of successful and unsuccessful efforts should be included.

How many cases should be sampled for in-depth analysis? The more factors that are considered relevant for obtaining representation, the greater is the desirable sample size. There are nine different factors and possibly over 48 different characteristics. Not all of those may be considered important, not all may be structured as outlined here,[30] and some overlap.[31] However, if there were to be a broad representation of even only the emphasized countries to represent regions, there could easily be in excess of 20 relevant characteristics (overlooking the specific countries).[32]

[29] This position assumes that the type of the analysis already completed of PERs suits sufficiently well the decentralization study requirements.

[30] For example, timing and size could each be made a single, continuous variable.

[31] Countries could be selected to represent all six regions.

[32] Given the patterns expected in the data, it is very likely that relatively few countries have sufficient (specifically) advisory reports to draw inferences for country performance even if all their cases were included in the sample.

What might this mean for the number selected for in-depth study? One way to look at this question is as if one were planning to do a quantitative, especially a regression, analysis of the data. If an index of success is assigned and used as a dependent variable, and relevant factor characteristics are handled as dummy (zero/one) variables, regression methods could be employed. In such a situation, it is reasonable to want, for example, 40 degrees of freedom, for the statistical analysis. Thus, if there are 20 relevant characteristics of interest, 60 observations (a sample of 20 + 40 = 60 cases) would be required. If more characteristics are of interest or if a finer degree of statistical confidence is sought, more observations are needed. Even if the analysis were to be only qualitative, larger numbers of studies increase the confidence in the observations made. It appears unlikely that fewer than 50 cases should be selected for in-depth study or that it would be necessary to exceed 100 which would amount to almost one-third of the total number of reports and projects.

Random selection of the designated number may generate a suitable sample.[33] However, outliers, or oddities, are always possible and they pose more of a potential problem the smaller the sample size. Various random samples might be drawn and each examined for potential outliers and also for their representation of the universe of possible observations.[34] One must be very cautious about deleting observations as "outliers" because legitimate information may be being discarded. The greater the picking and choosing, the less reliable the sample is of being representative.

There is also another potentially useful approach to selecting cases for in-depth study. That approach is to "match" observations (or subsets of observations) of, assuming that understanding the reasons for success or failure is an important objective, successful and unsuccessful cases and compare and contrast them. Certainly, there would still be reasons for having the matched observations be representative of the universe of cases. However, while no longer random sampling, the selection of studies made

[33] Because the number of projects and reports are in a ratio of approximately 2:1, consideration could be given to nonrandom sampling to provide a larger representation (e.g., 1:1) of the reports in the overall sample if the desired insight into the two types of Bank programs is equal.

[34] Examination of the sample could be done by the study directors with the country experts to be used as analysts/reviewers (and/or other knowledgeable persons). As noted in the methodological section, more informed opinions about the representativeness of observations would come after an initial overview desk-level study by the analysts of all potential projects and reports.

this way could be very useful. Such matching could also be a useful supplementary investigation to the analysis of the random sample.

Country Studies

Country studies are much more intensive again. There will be relatively few; four or six has been mentioned. Six would allow one country from each region to be included if complete regional representation were considered vital. Following further from the factors and characteristics noted above, six countries should make feasible a good selection of other features of interests. For example, six countries could allow all six program areas to be represented at least once (some more than once when at least some countries have multiple cases for analysis). In addition, it is conceivable to have at least two (or more) observations for each of the three levels of decentralization and, three (or more) observations on each of advising reports and lending projects. Six, appropriately selected countries (assuming a sufficient cross-country distribution of the various features of interest), could offer the potential for insight to the impact of various factors.

Presumably, countries selected for country studies will be selected for other reasons as well. One relevant consideration is how much more can be expected to be learned from a complete country study and how important are the anticipated results. For example, will further examination of decentralization in a particular country confirm or deny some important but questionable results? What is expected to be particularly relevant is which countries provide the best illustrations of what the overall decentralization study reveals; for example, the lessons learned. Countries for which there have been many reports or projects, those emphasized, may provide a fruitful group to consider but good alternatives may emerge elsewhere as well.

Bringing It All Together

For the lending and advisory decentralization projects, three levels of analysis are proposed for this study. The first is the review (or supplement the review) of the universe of cases available for analysis. Extending to this level of analysis may differ from past practice and go beyond initial expectations. The second level is the in-depth desk study of a sample from that universe. The third is the detailed country studies. The relative emphasis placed on these three levels depends, in part, on the relative importance of the answers to three broad questions: (a) Have the Bank's decentralization efforts been successful? (b) What conditions, initiatives, and/or actions predict successful/unsuccessful decentralization? (What works and when?) (c) Are there good illustrations of the experiences and the lessons learned and, in particular, are there countries that demonstrate these especially well?

To answer the first question, it is necessary to study a sufficiently large sample of decentralization efforts so as to have confidence in the results. To have that confidence, one must be confident of the representativeness of the sample and, to be confident of the sample, it is necessary to have a good grasp of the universe. Experts in the field may have that overall grasp but a systematic overview of the universe can provide a common perspective and a solid reference. This census need not be "in-depth" but it needs to be sufficiently rigorous to identify the main characteristics of each case and to rate the relative success with confidence. This information is important in identifying the important characteristics used that might be used in checking the representativeness of the sample selected for in-depth study and, possibly, in culling outliers or looking for replacements. In addition, that overview, especially if undertaken to completing the matrix of Table 9.1, can be a valuable input into supplementary analysis such as for confirming and cross-checking (even if that data is less refined and there is less confidence in it than in the in-depth data).

The in-depth desk analysis is directed toward answering the first two questions but is predicted to be particularly important for its contribution to the second question. While firming up the understanding of the results (outcomes) and the evaluation of the success of projects and reports, the deeper and more complete work is critical for sorting out reasons for the results. The conclusions reached from this analysis should, however, be consistent with that implied or suggested by the overview data which, if that is sufficiently available and organized, can be used as a check.

The comprehensive country analysis seems especially well suited to addressing the third question. The country analysis can and should provide analytical insights and clarifications of the individual cases or observations (which might require or allow refinement of some of the in-depth work or the analysis of that data). Also, it will provide the opportunity to look beyond the individual case and to see the commonalities, interactions, and interrelationships when a number of decentralization efforts have been undertaken in one country. However, detailed country analysis will be particularly useful for conveying the information and the lessons learned from the total exercise. It will "put meat on the bones" of the broader analysis and make the information more comprehensible and more palatable to many.

Conclusions from the full range of decentralization study need to be kept in perspective. In particular, conclusions about the successfulness of the Bank's decentralization efforts need to be put into perspective. If the relative success of decentralization is not to be over- or underrepresented with respect to other Bank initiatives, some comparison must be made between that of decentralization and those of other efforts. In doing so, comparisons of performance should be extended to separating components like lending, advisory and, especially these, to performance in regions or particular countries. Finally, some attention needs to be paid to the interaction between decentralization and other Bank, IMF, or donor efforts. Ideally, decentralization will have, at least in a long-term sense, aided other programs in reaching their objectives. However, even when itself successful, decentralization initiatives may have, at least temporarily, disrupted other activities.

Summary and Conclusion

Public decision making has become more decentralized in many countries. There is a widespread trend of central governments dispersing powers and responsibilities to intermediate and local governments and of community groups playing an increasing role. World Bank activities have paralleled, if not been at the forefront, of these movements. It has been advising governments on and lending to governments for decentralization. Decentralization and decentralization programs have been underway for some time and are still in progress. The Bank now wants to take stock of its decentralization activities; notably, evaluate their success and identify improvements to policies, programs, and practices. This chapter outlines an approach to evaluating the Bank's decentralization efforts.

A structure for examining decentralization activities was outlined (summarized in Table 9.1). It identifies a matrix of six components of decentralization needing analysis and five steps in the analysis and evaluation. The steps identify the initial environment, describe the actions taken, determine the outcomes, evaluate the outcomes plus the reasons for those results, and establish the lessons to be learned from each project. Six components of decentralization, each requiring assessment, are identified: government and political institutions, responsibilities and powers, resources, management authority, accountability, and factors beyond government. To aid the understanding and the analysis, the steps and components of the matrix were elaborated upon. The discussion of the components demonstrates the experience of and the lessons learned by the Bank and others working with decentralization. Existing Operations Evaluation Department evaluation criteria (i.e., relevance, efficacy, sustainability, efficiency, institutional development, bank performance, and country performance) provide an appropriate framework for assessment. Success with decentralization depends upon conditions and upon the quality of recommendations and implementation. Both need evaluation.

There are different types and different levels of analysis and evaluation. Verbal analysis and evaluation is essential. However, both vital characteristics and evaluations can be translated into quantitative form to facilitate summarization and numeric (and even) statistical analysis. The two methods are complementary and both methods are recommended. Based on successful prior experience, desk studies of numerous projects and a few intensive country studies are planned. Proposed here is to expand the desk analysis to two levels. One level would be the projected in-depth analysis of a sample of project, but potentially useful to add is an overview desk analysis covering all lending and advisory activities. The latter is to provide better supplementary information and data to increase confidence in the results. The in-depth evaluations are expected to be undertaken by regional experts. It is suggested that program experts also review those projects. This dual approach provides two important perspectives on the core data and also facilitates consistency in evaluations across evaluators.

A potentially interesting sidebar to the planned evaluations would be to study a number of successful but centralized developed countries to determine whether they provide lessons for relatively centralized developing countries that are an alternative to decentralization.

Selection of the countries for study is important. There is a trade-off in sample size between representativeness and economy. Consideration of some projects suggests a variety of potentially important attributes; for example, regions, emphasized countries, purpose of project, type of decentralization, date when initiated, size, success. If all these, and potentially other features, were important, a large sample could be required in order to have confidence in the results. For advisory and lending projects, a sample for in-depth analysis of 50–100 seems reasonable. Use of data from an overall survey could permit a smaller number; otherwise, a larger sample (estimated to be about one-third of the total projects) appears more appropriate.

A random sample might meet the needs of the study designers. On the other hand, some attributes of interest are concentrated so that a random sample could leave too few in the sample from which to draw conclusions (and could leave the results sensitive to outliers, which both the inclusion and exclusion of pose possible problems). Weighted sampling or selection among alternative random samples might solve this type of problem. Another option, more for the purpose of understanding the reasons for success or failure, would be to study a matched set of successful and unsuccessful projects. The sample should be scrutinized by the designers and the analysts as to its representativeness and its suitability for assessing priority issues. A serious overview of all projects aids in making these judgements.

Besides the overall perspective, intensive country studies are valuable. Of necessity, there must be few. Judicious selection can provide illustrative and insightful examples of the learning and lessons from the more broadly based work, part of which emerges from consideration of (likely) several projects within a common environment. Which countries best convey these messages, will need to emerge from the desk analysis and the combined judgment of the designers and the evaluators.

The evaluation of Bank decentralization activities seems directed primarily at three questions: (a) Have the Bank's decentralization efforts been successful?, (b) What conditions, initiatives, and/or actions predict successful/unsuccessful decentralization? (What works and when?) (c) Are there good illustrations of the experiences and the lessons learned and, in particular, are there countries that demonstrate these especially well? The approach outlined here for lending and advisory undertakings should go far toward answering these questions.

Appendix: Components of Decentralization and Factors Affecting the Potential Success of Decentralization

Government and Political Institutions

- Democracy and subnational democracy
- Public participation and civil society
- Information availability and its transparency
- Ethical standards
- Rent seeking
- Attitudes to decentralization and whose attitudes
- Intergovernmental relations

Responsibilities and Powers

- Subsidiarity
- Correspondence of political and economic jurisdictions (matching, mapping)
  - Benefit and cost spillovers
- Economies of public provision and decision making
  - Scale and scope
  - Decision making costs
- Benefit–cost linkage of public services
- Matching of service responsibilities and fiscal capacities
- Sharing responsibilities
  - Matching involvements with interests
- Unbundling responsibilities
  - Variety of solutions
  - Private options
- Continuity of central/senior government responsibilities
  - Senior government responsibilities not end with decentralization
- Clear mandates
- Stability of arrangements

Resources

— Taxes and own revenues

- Finance follows function; more responsibilities, more revenues
- The benefit principle (i.e., the benefit–cost linkage between services and levies)
  - charges and taxes
- Ability to set own tax rates and charges
- Adequacy of revenues
- Stability, visibility, administrative costs, fairness

— Transfers

- Justifiable on solid efficiency, equity or political grounds
  - Spillovers/externalities
  - Fiscal gap
    - Can richest subnational governments (SNG) satisfactorily meet responsibilities from own resources?
  - Equalization
  - Acceptable political reasons
- Adequacy
- Transparency
  - Rationale
  - Standards
  - Objective allocation
- Simplicity
- Stability
- Autonomy and flexibility in use of funds
- Nonnegotiable (not a soft budget constraint)

— Deficits and debts

- Responsibility/revenue match
- What stabilization role?, operating deficits
- Borrowing limited to capital only
- Central/senior government monitoring, supervision, and controls
- Senior government assistance with debt finance
- Clearly established rules; rules upfront

  - Borrower responsibility for repayment
  - Adherence to "your error, your cost"
  - Transparency of SNG accounts
  - A soft budget constraint?

— Administrative capacity

  - Decentralization does not change the national administrative capacity
  - Demand-driven vs. supply-driven capacity development
  - Potential for learning by doing
  - Responsiveness to local concern, transparency, citizen participation, accountability

Management Authority

- Scope of management authority and local discretion with
  - Decentralized responsibilities, expenditures and other
  - Own-revenue sources; taxes and charges
- Extent of mandate services and earmarking
- Staffing
  - Recruitment, rewards, removal
  - Civil service vs. political appointments
  - Private alternatives

Accountability

- To beneficiaries
  - Local citizens, taxpayers, voters
- To those who pay
  - Local taxpayers, pay fees, etc.
  - To those providing transfers, grants
  - To lenders
- Clear mandates
- Information availability and quality
  - Budget and planning
  - Management and operations
  - Financial control

- Reliable and uniform data
  - Senior government role
- Transparency of information beyond government
  Performance indicators
- Extent of policy debate; an "invisible college"?
- Of civil servants to the SNG

Beyond Government

- Size, scope, and capacity of the private sector
- Legal and regulatory system
- Justice system
- Motivations
  - Competitive, innovative, entrepreneurial, reward merit
  - Rent seeking, lack of respect for law
- Evaluative mentality, performance-oriented public and private sectors
- Political and economic stability

References

Bird, Richard M. 2000. *Intergovernmental Fiscal Relations: Universal Principles, Local Applications.* Working Paper 00–02, International Studies Program, School of Policy Studies, Georgia State University, April.

Bird, Richard M., and Francois Vaillancourt, eds. 1998. *Fiscal Decentralization in Developing Countries.* Cambridge, UK: Cambridge University Press.

Burki, Shahid Javed, Guillermo E. Perry, and William R. Dillinger. 1999. *Beyond the Center: Decentralizing the State*, World Bank Latin American and Caribbean Studies. Washington, DC: The World Bank.

Dethier, Jean-Jacques, ed. 2000. *Governance, Decentralization and Reform in China, India and Russia.* Dordecht: Kluwer Academic Publishers.

Dillinger, William. 1994. *Decentralization and Its Implications for Urban Service Delivery*, Urban Management Program. Washington, DC: The World Bank.

Huther, Jeff, and Anwar Shah. 1997. *A Design Paper on Evaluating the Impact of Public Expenditure Reviews*, Operations Evaluation Department. Washington, DC: World Bank.

———. 1998. *Applying a Simple Measure of Good Governance to the Debate on Fiscal Decentralization*, Operations Evaluation Department, Research Policy Working Paper 1894. Washington, DC: World Bank.

———. 2000. *Anti-Corruption Policies and Programs: A Framework for Evaluation.* World Bank Policy Research Working Paper No. 2501. Posted 2016.

Litvack, Jennie, Junaid Ahmad, and Richard Bird. 1998. *Rethinking Decentralization in Developing Countries*, PREM Sector Studies Series. Washington, DC: World Bank.

Manor, James. 1999. *The Political Economy of Democratic Decentralization.* Washington, DC: The World Bank.

Operations Evaluation Department (OED), World Bank. 2000. OED Methodology Syndicate – Evaluation Criteria Review, Draft, June 30.

Shah, Anwar. 1994. *The Reform of Intergovernmental Fiscal Relations in Developing and Emerging Market Economies*, Policy and Research Series, 23. Washington, DC: The World Bank.

———. 2000. *Governing for Results in a Globalized and Localized World.* Presented at the International Conference on Public Sector Financial Management: Fiscal Federalism and Decentralization, Madrid, June.

Ter-Minassian, Teresa, ed. 1997. *Fiscal Federalism in Theory and Practice.* Washington, DC: International Monetary Fund.

United Nations. 2000. *Decentralization: Conditions for Success – Lessons from Central and Eastern Europe and the Commonwealth of Independent States*, Economic and Social Affairs, Division of Public Economics and Public Administration. New York: United Nations.

World Bank. 1996. *World Bank Participation Sourcebook.* Washington, DC, February.

———. 2000a. *World Development Report, 1999/2000: Entering the 21st Century.* New York: Oxford University Press.

———. 2000b. *Lessons on Community Driven Development.* Lessons and Practices # 12, Operations Evaluation Department, Washington, DC, http://wbln0018.worldbank.org/oed/oeddoclib.nsf/3b01

CHAPTER 10

Evaluating the Conditionality of External Development Assistance Programs

Anwar Shah

Introduction

Development assistance, in this chapter, is more broadly defined to include grant and loan assistance within and across sovereign territorial limits by governmental and non-governmental actors and agencies. Such assistance is motivated by altruistic, economic, political, military and humanitarian considerations. It is used to advance wide-ranging objectives such as minimising risks for loan repayment, efficiency, equity of the public sector, overcoming infrastructure deficiencies, promoting growth, facilitating poverty alleviation and good governance, combating terrorism, support for a specific ideology, influence peddling, and economic and political

An earlier version of this chapter appeared as an OECD/EC working paper, "Development Assistance and Conditionality: Challenges in Design and Options for More Effective Assistance", May 2017, OECD, Paris. The author is grateful to OECD for financial support and to Dorothee Allain-Dupre, OECD for guiding his work on this paper. The author is also grateful to Peter Berkowitz of the European Commission (EC) for his comments.

A. Shah (✉)
Governance Studies, Brookings Institution, Washington, DC, USA

© The Author(s) 2020

A. Shah (ed.), *Policy, Program and Project Evaluation*,
https://doi.org/10.1007/978-3-030-48567-2_10

imperialism. The provision of such assistance is more often than not conditional as even unconditional assistance almost always carries some explicit preconditions and implicit conditions. Conditions are imposed as part of lending or grant assistance unilaterally or by mutual agreement of the donor and the recipient. These conditions form contractual terms of such assistance which bind the recipient to expected actions or results as a quid pro quo for receiving such financial assistance, and can vary from being very vague to extremely clear and precise. They may impose formal binding requirements or simply indicate informal non-binding expectations.

The conditions imposed may be *ex ante* (pre-requisites), *ex post* or both. *Ex ante* conditions are imposed to ensure that recipients have conditions in place to make effective and incorruptible use of funds and to achieve mutually agreed-upon goals. *Ex post* conditions are imposed to monitor that the interim performance of the assisted program is consistent with the expectations and to justify continuing assistance. *Ex post* conditions are also imposed to guide future assistance based upon past performance.

Conditions may be on consultations, transparency requirements related to project documents, procurement, reporting, and auditing requirements and associated procurement, accounting and auditing systems (process and financial management conditionality), the use of inputs, or expenditures on authorized functions and objects, intermediate inputs (input conditionality), outputs—service delivery results in terms of quality, quantity, and access (output conditionality)—or on outcomes (outcome conditionality) or impacts (impact conditionality). Process- and/or input-based conditionality is frequently practised—it undermines recipient autonomy but affords greater leverage and control to donors. Output-based conditionality is rarely practised but offers great potential for recipient autonomy with accountability for results. Outcome- and impact-based conditionality is occasionally used but dilutes recipient accountability to donors or citizens as many of the underlying factors would be beyond the control of public managers.

Conditions may also embody requirements for counterpart recipient funds to be eligible for donor assistance. Conditions may embody rewards for compliance and penalties for non-compliance. The conditions may relate to a geographic area, the whole-of-government, a level or branch of government, a sector, program activity or specific subject area targets (OECD 2013: 59). The conditions may relate to government processes such as the requirement for public consultation or having a participatory budgeting system or passing laws and regulations, or maybe concerned with substantive aspects of government operations.

Peter Berkowitz of the European Commission has suggested[1] that the conditions on substantive aspects of government operations could be broadly classified into five categories:

1. *Macro conditions*: These conditions provide targets for selective macroeconomic indicators such as growth rate, inflation, exchange rate, balance of payments, international reserves, monetary policy indicators, and debt and deficit limitations. IMF programs typically embody these conditions.
2. *Structural reforms conditions*: These conditions relate to reforms dealing with policies and programs and practices intended to help improve the working of the public sector to ensure efficiency and equity of revenue generation and public provisions. The conditions specify reform measures regarding the structure and organisation of government, civil service organisation, management and accountability, tax reform, public spending and regulatory reforms. World Bank and IMF lending and EU Structural Funds are replete with these conditions
3. *Governance and institutional reform conditions*: Governance is defined "as an exercise of authority and control to preserve and protect public interest and to enhance the quality of life enjoyed by citizens/residents" (Ivanyna and Shah 2011). Thus, it relates to both the governance environment (quality of institutions and processes) and governance outcomes. Governance indicators are now being used as tools for conducting development dialogue, allocating external assistance and influencing foreign direct investment. For example, the World Bank's International Association allocation—a window of subsidised lending to the developing world—and the United States Agency for International Development's Millennium Challenge Account use various governance indicators as criteria for allocating external assistance. The post-2015 development agenda on Sustainable Development Goals gives even more prominence to progress in governance. Governance and institutional reform conditions relate to institutions of accountability in governance such as the role of parliament, judiciary, media and civil society in holding

[1] Personal communications with the author.

the government to account; government's commitment to upholding the rule of law, human rights and citizen empowerment. In general, such conditions are intended to ensure FAIR (fair, accountable, incorruptible and responsive) public governance.

4. *Fiduciary/financial accountability conditions*: These conditions are intended to ensure integrity in the use of funds by recipients. Over time, donor emphasis has shifted from integrity in the use of assisted project funds to governmental systems, that is, overall integrity of government financial operations. Donors increasingly carry out detailed assessments of budgetary, accounting and auditing systems and impose conditions to improve the transparency and integrity of these systems. These conditions are commonplace in almost all donor programs.
5. *Results-based conditions such as public service delivery and access conditions*: Traditionally, donor emphasis has been on input-based conditionality to ensure that assistance funds were used for the intended purposes. This resulted in donor micromanagement of the use of funds and lack of autonomy in project design and operations by the recipient, but without any assurance in achieving agreed-upon objectives due to the possibility of fungibility of funds and also because the inefficiency in spending and inappropriateness in design may result in project failure. Recognising this, the European Commission initiated limited emphasis on output-based conditions. The World Bank followed suit as did other aid agencies, imposing results-based conditions; the record of these agencies in imposing readily monitorable output-based conditions, however, remains weak. Much confusion in aided projects remains on properly defining inputs, intermediate inputs, outputs, outcomes and impact and imposing conditions on outputs (service delivery performance), which are usually only within the control of a public manager.

The conditions discussed above have been a subject of controversy and debate (see Easterly 2005; Dijkstra 2002; Collier 1997; Klick et al. 1998; Koeberle et al. 2005; Stiglitz 1999; World Bank 1998, 1999). A prominent critic of such conditions notes that "*Why would a donor pay a recipient to do something that is anyway in his own interest? And if it is not in his own interest, why would the recipient do it anyway?*" (Streeten 1988 quoted in Martens et al. 2002: 12). This chapter explores the rationale and incentives/disincentives regimes fostered by such conditions. It will focus, however, only on the first three types of conditions, as the remaining two have already received exhaustive treatment in recent literature especially the OECD work. This focus is also justified as these three conditions are most relevant for discussions on effective delivery mechanisms of regional policy (particularly EU) in particular and development assistance in general.

Rationale for the Conditionality

Donors have advanced a number of rationales for imposing conditions on their assistance.

- *Safeguarding repayment of donor loans*: A case is often made that conditionality of assistance is required to ensure that the project is implemented as agreed to ensure that the donor gets repaid according to the terms of lending (IMF 2016). This is a weak argument as repayment of loans would depend critically upon a recipient's credit worthiness rather than any loan conditions. In addition, sovereign default on international borrowing has serious economic and fiscal consequences for the defaulter and as a result is relatively rare. International capital markets also exact a strong penalty for such defaults, thereby discouraging such perverse behaviour. Therefore, safeguarding repayment of donor loans may be a weak premise for imposing loan conditions (see also Collier et al. 1997).
- *Strengthening recipient ownership of the assisted programs.* Conditionality often forces a recipient to make political choices on reform options and to commit to specific policy prescription. In the absence of conditionality, such hard choices could not be made and policy makers may be inclined to simply kick the can down the road.
- *Ensuring integrity of donor-assisted operations.* This was traditionally done by having a special management unit run assisted operations and having appropriate budgeting, accounting and auditing of such operations. Such special arrangements impose significant additional costs for the recipient while limiting local autonomy and holding little assurance for the most effective use of donor funds. In view of this, in recent years donors have emphasised the reform of governmental systems to ensure integrity of operations rather than creating parallel systems. Minimum standards of transparency, integrity and

accountability of governmental systems should serve as a pre-requisite for such assistance rather than imposing specific loan conditions.

- *Influencing recipient priorities or as an inducement/incentive for reform.* In cases where there are serious conflicts among donor and recipient priorities, it makes sense to use loan funds as an inducement to influence local priorities. Loan conditions could be used to achieve this change. The success of such conditions, however, may be limited by the extent of the fungibility of funds. In the extreme case, when the recipient already spends more than the assisted funds and it is an area of low priority for the recipient, loan conditions may not have much impact in changing recipient priorities.
- *Paternalism*: The donor knows best what is good for the recipient. Donor conditions frequently embody an implicit judgement that the recipient lacks the knowledge to pursue economic policies that serve its best interest and donor agencies have better knowledge as to what would work best. The "Washington Consensus" and the "Modified Washington Consensus" are examples that shaped loan conditions in the 1980s and 1990s. Such policies, however, do not safeguard for aid dictum of "do no harm", as the consequences of failure of lending operations are only borne by the recipient.
- *Signaling* to safeguard the commitment to reform by the recipient. Conditionality is also advocated as an indication that the recipient is accepting conditionality and its associated possible adverse political consequences to demonstrate a commitment to reform. In practice, however, such signaling is typically done by recipients to shift blame to external actors to undertake domestically unpopular programs or to attribute failure of such programs.
- *Sustainability*: Loan conditions are sometimes advocated to sustain as assisted program over political cycles to overcome time inconsistency of commitment. The success of such conditions is, however, not assured as the new political administration may seek to renegotiate or suspend such operations.

The Conditionality and the Donor–Recipient Government Relationship[2]

Conditions the donor places on loans and grants are aimed at improving efficiency by reducing the distortions caused by political incentives. Conditions are required, in a large measure, because of the political costs of reallocating funds. Donor conditions make the shift of priorities more politically palatable for governments involved by shifting the responsibility for loss of political gains from government officials to the donor. The donor's ability to help a government reduce or remove the distortions on budgetary priorities depends on the political skills of the government's administrators. The challenge for administrators is to take credit for efficiency gains while placing blame for the accompanying political and personal losses on the donor.

Our discussion of donor-imposed conditions focuses on the incentives faced by a borrowing country's administrators and the donor's lending staff. The incentives of a country's administrators differ from those of the donor's staff because the conditions imposed on a loan also impose a political cost on a country's administrators. The important point to keep in mind when reviewing the effectiveness of donor-imposed conditions is that the willingness of a country's administrators to seek compliance with the donor's vision of reform depends on commonly shared development objectives. If there was a domestic commitment to conditions sought by the donor, then there would be no need for the conditions in the first place. Below we argue that inefficient use of public resources is the result of political incentives and that it is these political incentives which are the barriers to more efficient use of public resources. In this context, donor conditions are successful to the extent to which they acknowledge these incentives.

The donor's ability to attach conditions to loans is constrained by the political cost those conditions impose on country administrators. If the political cost of complying with loan conditions exceeds the political gain of obtaining the loan, country administrators will not comply with the conditions. On the other hand, if the cost of not complying with the conditions is greater than the cost of forgoing the loan, country administrators will not accept the loan. The effect of these constraints is that donor conditions generally require modest efficiency gains.

[2] This section is based on Huther and Shah (1996).

Table 10.1 Responses to donor conditions for reductions in public sector employment

Administrative action	*Political actions*
Comply with the conditions	Take credit for improving public sector efficiency Take credit for obtaining donor loans or grants Blame the donor for painful cuts
Ignore the conditions	Take credit for saving public sector jobs Take credit for obtaining donor loans or grants Blame the donor for unrealistic conditions Place the blame for non-compliance elsewhere
Forgo assistance	Take credit for maintaining independence from international lenders Blame the donor for attempting to interfere with domestic politics

Source: Huther and Shah (1996)

The political costs and benefits depend on the responsiveness of the government to political and public pressures, and the ability of the government to influence those pressures. Consider, for example, a donor condition that requires a government to reduce the number of its public sector employees. Reductions in public sector employment create a political loss in terms of a loss of patronage positions. Government administrators' willingness to accept and comply with this condition depends on their ability to minimise the political loss. This is accomplished by shifting the responsibility for the loss of jobs on the donor (Table 10.1) and by taking credit for the resulting efficiency gains.

The ability of administrators to take the actions listed in Table 10.1 depends on the political skills of the administrators and their opposition, and the severity of the conditions imposed by the donor. The severity of the conditions imposed by the donor will depend on how far the actual allocation of funds differs from the efficient allocation of funds. Unfortunately, the greater the political skills of administrators, the more likely it is that actual expenditure allocations differ significantly from the efficient allocation of expenditures.

Donor Influence Over Political Costs

The donor has influence over the political costs of conditions it imposes through the types of conditions imposed and through its influence over the public perceptions of those conditions. The types of conditions that the donor has imposed, and the political costs of those conditions, have varied substantially. The political cost of complying with a donor's condition depends on the level of flexibility administrators are given. The greater the flexibility, the more likely it is that administrators can reduce the political cost of compliance, but this flexibility may also lead to smaller efficiency gains if administrators can use flexibility to avoid compliance. Highly detailed, inflexible conditions are more easily monitored and, if complied with, are likely to generate the highest efficiency gains. However, these are also the types of conditions that are the most costly to comply with. The result is that donor lenders must assess the potential efficiency gains of compliance with potential political gains of non-compliance.

Public perceptions worsen the dilemma the donor faces with respect to the degree of detail and measurability it attaches to conditions. Although greater detail of conditions and more measurable conditions improve the potential for efficiency gains, they also create greater opportunity for attacks on the donor as unjustifiably interfering with domestic affairs. Measurable conditions also create the possibility that the donor will misjudge the appropriate level of fiscal adjustments. The result is that the donor must err on the side of insufficient adjustments since the political costs for the donor of imposing excessively severe conditions are significantly higher than the costs of imposing very lenient conditions.

Country Administrators' Influence Over Donor Conditions

Prior to the imposition of donor conditions, administrators have strong incentives to influence the severity of the conditions. If administrators can convince donor lenders to impose conditions which are politically painless to comply with, then the administrators can reap a political windfall. That is, administrators can take credit for obtaining donor loans or grants, creating donor-verified public sector improvements, and avoiding painful adjustments. Consequently, donor lenders are likely to be facing administrators who overstate the cost of compliance. Using the relationship in Table 10.1, donor lenders would like to increase the cost of complying up to the point where it is equal to the cost of ignoring the conditions. Government administrators, to the extent that they can influence donor conditions, would like to overstate the cost of not receiving assistance and the cost of complying, but understate the cost of ignoring the conditions.

Administrators are also aware of the political pressures facing donor lenders. The donor may face strong incentives to lend to politically or militarily powerful countries. Administrators of these countries know this and use this knowledge to avoid impositions of conditions on assistance. The result is a tendency by the donor to impose more severe conditions on assistance to countries that have less international influence. The top ten borrowers from the World Bank, for example, represent the most populous and most militarily powerful countries receiving World Bank assistance. Yet, these countries faced a very small percentage of World Bank conditions. For example, conditions have been imposed on Brazil, the World Bank's ninth highest borrower, in 6 areas on a single loan (mainly general conditions such as "reduce subsidies" and "correct monetary policy") whereas Uruguay faced conditions in 27 areas on 2 loans (including very specific conditions such as "tax increase of 0.3% of GDP" and "reduce structural deficit to 2% of GDP") (see Huther et al. 1997).

After donor staff have imposed conditions, they are open to "regulatory capture"—donor staff have a vested interest in acknowledging compliance with the conditions and defending the conditions imposed. In practice, this means donor staff are willing to overlook actions by country administrators to manipulate results to meet donor conditions either through favourable interpretations of events or through falsification of data or both. And, more subtly, donor staff seek favourable readings of results.

The rest of this chapter is organised as follows. The next section provides conceptual perspectives from game theory, public choice, fiscal federalism, political economy, new institutional economics and New Public Management literature on the design of external assistance and its potential impacts. The chapter then provides an overview of the historical evolution of perspectives on donor–recipient relations and on conditionality of external assistance. It highlights the developing consensus by the development assistance community on both the instruments of development finance and associated conditions. It also briefly notes progress, or lack thereof, for practice to conform to emerging consensus. The concluding section provides lessons on major issues in conditionality of development assistance.

Conceptual Perspectives

Program Design and the Conditionality: Conceptual Perspectives

This section will reinterpret the basic concepts from a wide body of theoretical and conceptual literature to draw implications for the conditionality of development assistance. Six major perspectives will be highlighted.

Game Theory[3]

The focus here is on the donor–recipient strategic choices in the presence of conditionality of assistance. Using the game theory approach this section will illustrate the perverse incentives faced by donor and recipient administrators that work to compromise the effectiveness of imposed conditions and thwarting the objectives of development assistance. The section will further highlight approaches to improve positive incentives for compliance and effectiveness of development assistance.

Placing Loan (Grant) Conditions in a Game Theory Framework

This section uses simple examples from game theory to illustrate the perverse incentives that virtually guarantee that loan conditions under the existing system will be non-binding or not complied with. It will begin with an example in which donor staff deal with a single group of country administrators to illustrate the technique. It will then consider a case where donor staff face two groups of administrators in a country: a progressive group and an entrenched bureaucracy. In both cases, a country's compliance or non-compliance with donor conditions is influenced by the donor's willingness to maintain loans in response to non-compliance.

Consider the case where the donor disburses a loan with a condition that will impose a political cost on the country's administrators. The donor staff benefit from the loan (it improves the country's welfare and enhances donor staff stature) and it benefits from the condition imposed if that condition is met (it improves the efficiency of provision of public services). The country's administrators benefit from the loan (they can take credit for the projects the money is used for) but the administrators face a political loss from complying with donor conditions (through losses of patronage positions, for example).

The donor's best possible outcome is that administrators comply with the condition and receive the loan (which generates two positive results). The administrator's best possible outcome is that the loan is made but the conditions are not complied with (which generates one positive result and no negative result).

The important point here is that country administrators know how the donor values each possible outcome. If the administrators do not comply with the condition, the donor's preferred result is that the loan is disbursed anyhow. The outcome is that country administrators do not

[3] This section is based upon Huther and Shah (1996).

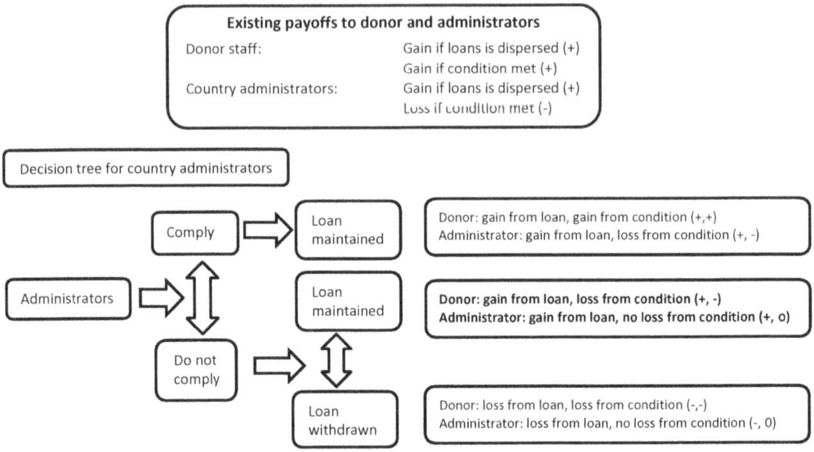

Fig. 10.1 Decision tree for country administrators. Note: Outcome in bold is the (Nash) equilibrium outcome. (Source: Huther and Shah 1996)

comply with conditions and the donor maintains the loans since it is preferable to withdrawing the loan. Given the existing incentive structure, neither donor nor country administrators can improve their outcome by changing their responses (see the decision tree for country administrators in Fig. 10.1).

The outcome of this process is clear from past aid evaluation results: donor officials tend to rate ongoing loans and grants as satisfactory (even when conditions are not being met) because they believe that disbursing the loan is preferable to acknowledging non-compliance (which would force a withdrawal of the loan). Once the project is completed, the incentives for over-estimating compliance are removed. Consequently, evaluations of completed projects generate lower assessments of satisfactory outcomes.

A Numerical Example

Suppose that the value to donor staff of disbursing a loan is 0.5 and the value of compliance with the loan is also 0.5. If the loan is complied with, the donor staff receive a payoff of 1. Also suppose that the value of a loan to country administrators is 0.5 but that the value of compliance is −0.5 (see payoff matrix in Table 10.2).

Table 10.2 Payoff matrix in a two-player game

Actions of donor administrators	*Actions of country administrators*	
	Compliance	*Non-compliance*
Loan maintained	(1, 0)	(0.5, 0.5)
Loan withdrawn	(0.5, −0.5)	(0, 0)

Source: Huther and Shah (1996)

Note: Nash equilibrium outcome is in bold

The order of payoffs in the matrix are (donor, country administrators). For example, if the condition is complied with, the payoffs from the upper left box are: donor staff benefit from the loan (+0.5) and benefit from compliance (+0.5), for a payoff of 1, country administrators benefit from the loan (+0.5) and lose from compliance (−0.5), for a payoff of 0.

In this example, donor staff receive a higher payoff from maintaining the loan regardless of the action taken by the country administrators. Country administrators have a higher payoff from non-compliance regardless of the action taken by the donor staff. The result is that the loan is maintained and the loan is not complied with.

A Three-Player Example

Now consider a slightly more complicated case where donor staff face two groups of administrators within a country with differing incentives. Progressive administrators may favour donor conditions as a method of encouraging more efficient use of public resources. Entrenched administrators may view donor conditions as politically costly in terms of reductions in patronage positions, reduced opportunities for corruption, or less support (political or financial) from enterprises benefiting from subsidies. In this case, the interests of the donor and progressive administrators coincide but compliance will depend on the outcome of a political battle between progressive and entrenched administrators.

If progressive administrators win the battle on compliance, the donor and progressive administrators benefit from the loan and from compliance while the entrenched administrators do not care about the loan but lose from compliance. If progressive administrators lose on compliance, the donor must decide whether to maintain or withdraw the loan. The donor, and the progressive administrators, are better-off if the loan is maintained even though the donor's condition is not complied with. Since the

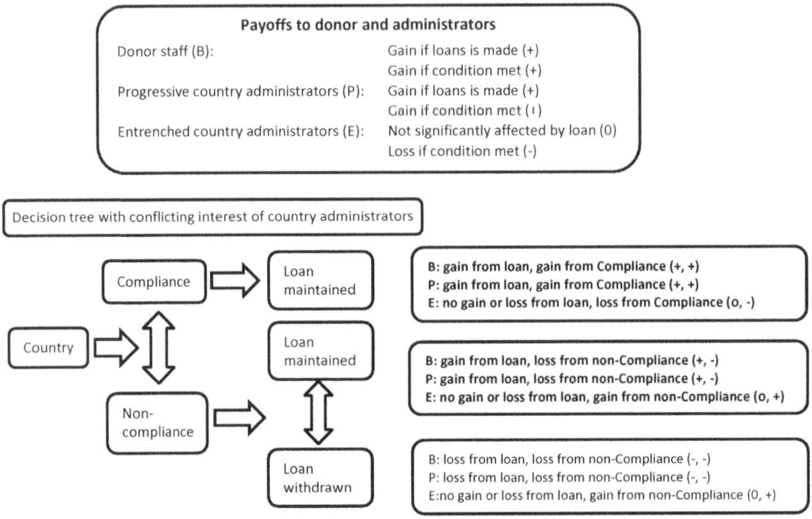

Fig. 10.2 Donor loan conditions for a country with conflicting administrative goals. Note: Both compliance and non-compliance with loan maintained are stable outcomes highlighted in bold (actual outcomes depend on domestic political battles). (Source: Huther and Shah 1996)

outcome of political battles usually depends on compromise, the entrenched administrators can use the donor's willingness to provide the loan as a means of discouraging compliance. The result is that the donor's desire to disburse the loan actually diminishes the likelihood of compliance (see Huther and Shah 1996; Huther et al. 1997).

There are two stable outcomes from this process (as illustrated in the decision tree in Fig. 10.2). If the progressive administrators win the domestic political battle, then the donor will disburse the loan and the country will comply with the condition. If the entrenched administrators win the domestic political battle, then the donor will maintain the loan even though the country does not comply with the condition. Since the outcome of most political battles is some form of compromise, the donor's known willingness to maintain loans despite non-compliance reduces the possibility of compliance.

Improvements in Donor-Imposed Conditions Suggested by Game Theory

There are two approaches suggested by the games outlined above that will lead to greater compliance with donor conditions. One approach is to increase the cost of non-compliance to country administrators. The other approach is to reduce the payoffs to donor staff of maintaining the loan when country administrators do not comply with the loan. This section describes potential applications of these approaches. The descriptions are meant to be illustrative examples rather than an exhaustive list of possible improvements (see Table 10.3).

Increasing the cost of non-compliance is a difficult subject in part because the citizens of countries seeking donor assistance would typically bear the burden of donor-imposed penalties. Other penalties face the same credibility problems that loan withdrawals face. Restrictions on future loans, for example, have the same incentive problems as current loans—country administrators know that the donor has an incentive to make the loans regardless of compliance. Additionally, country administrators may have short enough time horizons that they do not care about the existence or conditions of future loans.

One method of raising the cost of non-compliance would be to impose a higher level of administrative burden on donor loans to a non-complying country. The administrative burden could be increased through more frequent audits of the country's loan portfolio or requirements of additional background material to accompany future loan requests or adding an additional risk premium to the borrowing rate. Raising the administrative costs, however, is unlikely to influence compliance if country administrators have a sufficiently short time horizon or if the administrative burden is borne by politically weak groups within the government.

Table 10.3 Examples of approaches to improve incentives

Approach	*Method*	*New incentives*
Increase cost of non-compliance	Impose higher administrative burden for non-compliance	Comply or face greater oversight
Change donor staff incentives	Link promotion with compliance	Impose very lenient conditions
Change donor staff incentives	Link promotion with outputs improvements in service delivery quality and access	Impose conditions that service delivery quality and access indicators be improved

Source: Huther and Shah (1996)

The alternative to raising the cost of non-compliance is to reduce donor staff's incentives to disperse loans. One method of reducing incentives would be to issue a rule which links the promotion of task managers or division chiefs with the per cent of loan conditions that are complied with. This method would convince country administrators that their lack of compliance would lead to the loan being withdrawn. The drawback is that this rule creates incentives for donor staff to require very lenient conditions.

A method which would avoid the problem of excessive leniency is to reward donor staff based on improvements in service delivery quality and access and economic and quality-of-life indicators. This creates incentives for donor staff to design loan conditions that: (1) can and will be met; (2) focus on service delivery, economic and quality-of-life improvements; and (3) provide alternatives to status quo situations that are not generating improvements.

One outcome of a shift in focus to improvements in service delivery, quality-of-life indicators would be greater flexibility in the use of donor funds. Since many of the donor's projects are undertaken in conditions of uncertainty, it is inevitable that some of these projects will fail. If the focus for administrators is on the results of funding rather than the project itself, then both donor and country administrators will be more willing to discontinue unproductive projects.

Shifting donor staff incentives away from loan dispersal makes the threat of withdrawing loans credible. This is one of the useful paradoxes of game theory: the reduction of flexibility of donor staff to acquiesce to non-compliance strengthens the position of donor staff. Increased credibility of loan withdrawal, in turn, raises the cost of non-compliance to country administrators.

Limitations of the Examples Presented Here

The methods described in Table 10.3 are meant to represent simple examples rather than an exhaustive list of incentive improvements. Further, it should be noted that in the interest of simplicity, game theory approach presented here is static, while in practice development aid is a dynamic game with repeated interactions of multiple stakeholders. In the context of the EU, the game is even more complicated, since there is an additional dimension that the rules that govern the disbursement of aid are negotiated between donors and beneficiaries.

Game Theory Conclusion

While recognising these important limitations of this approach, our conclusion is that raising the cost of non-compliance is a less effective approach than reducing the payoffs to donor staff. The method that most effectively addresses the existing incentive problems is the one that shifts the goals of donor staff away from the technical and somewhat arbitrary questions of compliance with conditions towards a focus on results—measurable improvements in service delivery quality and access. The question that should be asked is how have country administrators used the donor loan to improve quality of life indicators or, more broadly, using a former World Bank President's direction, "has the loan made progress in 'putting a smile on a child's face'"?

The adversarial situation described above is one of a traditional borrower and lender. However, the donor's role is larger than that of a traditional lender since it has a stronger interest in the general well-being of the borrower than does a private sector lender. It is this larger interest that is interfering with the borrower–lender mechanisms that work in the private sector. The factor that has complicated the donor's incentive structure is that conditions are tied to loans that provide the potential for efficiency gains.

Success or failure of conditions must be measurable by a mutually agreed-upon method. Conditions are of little use if administrators can avoid compliance (through budget manipulation, for example). Once measures of success are agreed upon, administrators must be given complete flexibility to meet the conditions. This flexibility does not guarantee an efficient outcome—conditions imposing civil service cuts, for example, may lead to lower levels of basic services rather than fewer central administrators. This type of example suggests that conditions on expenditures should be abandoned in favour of conditions on the level of public goods or services provided.

Our suggestion is that the donors improve the incentives facing own staff by shifting the focus of conditions to results in terms of service delivery quality and access and quality-of-life indicators. Because many quality-of-life indicators change slowly, many conditions will need to be evaluated based on interim indicators. For example, if conditions are imposed that require a country to improve its literacy rates, an interim indicator would be increases in enrollment rates, graduation and dropout rates. If conditions are based on longevity, infant and child mortality rates would provide an interim indicator of the success or failure of conditions.

Public Choice Perspectives

Public choice literature focuses on the self-interested behaviour of actors (principals and agents) that defeats the public interest objectives of development assistance (see Dreher 2004).

Public choice literature distinguishes a broad spectrum of aid agencies that range from wholly motivated by altruism on the one extreme and those guided by economic and political imperialism. The first extreme is purely motivated by altruism, that is, to help disadvantaged individuals and nations overcome hunger, disease, deprivation, poverty and conflicts. At the opposite spectrum, external assistance serves as a tool to advance economic, political and military interests. In general, aid agencies will be distinguished by relative weights assigned to altruism versus self-interest and this emphasis will have profound implications for donor–recipient relations. The literature similarly places governments on a governance spectrum that ranges from those pursuing the doctrine of common good on the one extreme to those preserving the interests of governing elites. The latter type governments are subject to capture by dictators, bureaucrats or interest groups. Such governments may maximise economic rents for dominant interest groups (as in the leviathan model) or may advance compulsion or coercion. A leviathan government acts purely in its own self-interest relatively unconstrained by the voters. It usually is thought to be interested in maximising own size constrained only by its ability to extract tax revenues from the taxpayers or financial assistance from abroad (Boadway and Shah 2009: 28). Public choice literature in general endorses self-interest doctrine of government and argues that that various stakeholders involved in policy formulation and implementation are expected to use opportunities and resources to advance their self-interest.

To overcome donor failures, subjecting aid agencies to greater transparency, task specialisation, risk and reward sharing with recipient governments is expected to help restrain donor emphasis in advancing self-interest. To limit government failures, subjecting governments to competition within and beyond government, greater transparency and accountability to citizens can help restrain leviathan tendencies (Dollery and Wallis 2001). Therefore, donor conditionality should focus on fostering competitive public service delivery to ease supply constraints, sunshine provision and redress mechanisms, and enhancing voice and exit options for citizens' choice and holding government to account.

Limitations of the Approach

Public choice approach offers important clues to the lack of development effectiveness of external assistance. It also offers useful suggestions to overcome underlying constraints. However, some suggestions such as risk and reward sharing with recipients and exit and voice options for enhanced government accountability have proven difficult to achieve in practice.

Fiscal Federalism Perspective

Fiscal federalism literature is focused on safeguarding donor objectives while creating an incentive regime that respects local recipient autonomy but strengthens recipient accountability to overcome perverse fiscal behaviour of recipients. The literature highlights that the design of assistance must be consistent with its objectives and each assistance program must have a singular focus as combining multiple, often conflicting, objectives in a single program compromises the effectiveness of the entire program. This literature provides useful specific guidance on the design of the program and associated conditions to achieve the stipulated objective. The literature highlights fungibility of conditional assistance, flypaper effects (money sticks where it lands) and fiscal illusion (diminished local accountability associated with fragmented finance and resulting in leviathan governments) as discussed below.

A federal form of government has a multi-order governance structure, with all orders of government having some independent as well as shared decision-making responsibilities. Federal compact may entail both partnership and a principal–agent relationship. In decentralised federations, partnership principles dominate intergovernmental fiscal relations. Fiscal federalism principles therefore place a strong emphasis on strengthening partnership arrangements in the design of higher-level fiscal transfers. This is done by ensuring that higher-level general purpose assistance is non-intrusive and does not impair local autonomy and the design of specific purpose assistance should focus on creating incentives to accomplish partnership objectives while avoiding higher-level control and micromanagement. These principles also recognise real-life impact of these transfers on local fiscal behaviours. Table 10.4 provides a taxonomy of various type of fiscal transfers and potential impacts.

Table 10.4 shows that the choice of grant instrument must be based on its objectives. General purpose grants are more suitable for preserving local autonomy. Output-based conditionality is more desirable when the objective of the grant is to ensure improvement in service delivery

Table 10.4 Taxonomy of grants and their potential impacts: a stylised view

Grant type	*Grant (G) objectives*		
	Increase in spending on assisted service	*Results-based accountability*	*Recipient autonomy/ welfare*
General purpose (unconditional): lump-sum transfers			
Budget support	< G (amount of grant)	None/low	High
Budget support with pre-requisites	< G	None/low	Medium
Specific purpose (conditional): block, program or project transfers			
Non-matching with input or process conditionality	≤ G	None/low	Medium
Non-matching with output conditionality	≤ G	High	High
Open-ended matching (input conditions)	> G	Low/medium	Low
Closed-ended matching with binding constraint (input conditions)	≥ G	Low/medium	Low
Close-ended matching with non-binding constraint (input conditions)	≤ G	Low	Medium

Source: Shah (1994), Boadway and Shah (2009)

Notes: G: amount of grant funds; matching provision: requiring grant recipients to finance a specified percentage of expenditures using their own resources. This requirement serves to ensure local ownership and commitment to project goals; open-ended matching: the grantor matches whatever level of resources the recipient provides; closed-ended matching: the grantor matches recipient funds only up to a pre-specified limit

performance while respecting local autonomy. If stimulation of expenditure is the main objective then open-ended matching transfers would be desirable, but these grants impair local autonomy. The empirical literature shows that USD 1 received by the community in the form of general purpose transfers tends to increase local public spending by more than a USD 1 increase in residents' income (Rosen and Gayer 2005). Grant money tends to stick where it first lands, leaving a smaller than expected fraction available for tax relief, a phenomenon referred to as the "flypaper effect". The implication is that for political and bureaucratic reasons, grants to local governments tend to result in more local spending than they would have had the same transfers been made directly to local residents. An explanation for this impact is provided by the hypothesis that bureaucrats seek to maximise the size of their budgets, because doing so gives them greater power and influence in the community (Filimon et al. 1982). Another important observation noted by this literature is that specific purpose grants typically yield a smaller increase in spending on the assisted category than the size of the grant, with the remainder going to other public goods and service, and tax relief. This is the so-called fungibility effect of grants. The fungibility of conditional grants depends on both the level of spending on the assisted public service and the relative priority of such spending. For example, if the recipient's own financed expenditures on the assisted category exceed the amount of the conditional grant, the conditionality of the grant may or may not have any impact on the recipient's spending behaviour: all, some or none of the grant funds could go to the assisted function.

Why are conditional closed-ended matching grants common in industrial and developing countries when they seem ill-designed to solve problems and inefficiencies in the provision of public goods? The answer seems to be that correcting for inefficiencies is not the sole or perhaps even the primary objective. Instead, grants are employed to help local governments financially while promoting spending on activities given priority by the grantor. The conditional (selective) aspects of conditions on the spending are expected to ensure that the funds are directed toward an activity the grantor views as desirable. This, however, may be false comfort in view of the potential for fungibility of funds. The local matching or cost-sharing component affords the grantor a degree of control, requires a degree of accountability by the recipient and makes the cost known to the granting government.

Conditional closed-ended matching grants have advantages and disadvantages from the grantor's perspective. While such grants may result in a significant transfer of resources, they may distort outputs and cause inefficiencies, since the aid is often available only for a few activities, causing overspending on these functions while other functions are underfinanced. If capital outlays are subsidised while operating costs are not, grants may induce spending on capital-intensive alternatives and sometimes create white elephants—the projects that could not be sustained.

Conditional open-ended matching grants are the most suitable vehicles to induce lower-level governments to increase spending on the assisted function (Table 10.4). If the objective is simply to enhance the welfare of local residents, general purpose non-matching transfers are preferable, as they preserve local autonomy.

To ensure accountability for results, conditional non-matching output-based transfers are preferable to other types of transfers. Output-based transfers respect local autonomy and budgetary flexibility while providing incentives and citizen based accountability mechanisms to improve service delivery performance (see Table 10.5 for a comparative perspective on traditional versus output conditionality and Box 10.1 for an illustrative example).

Table 10.5 Traditional and output-based (performance-oriented) conditional grants

Criterion	*Traditional grant*	*Output-based grant*
Grant objectives	Spending levels	Quality and access to public services
Grant design and administration	Complex	Simple and transparent
Eligibility	Recipient government departments/agencies	Recipient government provides funds to all government and non-government providers
Conditions	Expenditures on authorised functions and objects	Outputs-service delivery results
Allocation criteria	Program or project proposals approvals with expenditure details	Demographic data on potential clients (service population)
Compliance verification	Higher-level inspections and audits	Client feedback and redress, comparison of baseline and post-grant data on quality and access
Penalties	Audit observations on financial compliance	Public censure, competitive pressures, voice and exit options for clients
Managerial flexibility	Little or none. No tolerance for risk and no accountability for failure	Absolute. Rewards for risks but penalties for persistent failure
Local government autonomy and budgetary flexibility	Little	Absolute
Transparency	Little	Absolute
Focus	Internal	External, competition, innovation and benchmarking
Accountability	Hierarchical and to higher level government, controls on inputs and process with little or no concern for results	Results-based, bottom-up, client-driven

Source: Shah (2007a)

Box 10.1 An Output-Based Transfer for School Finance: An Illustrative Example

Allocation basis to state/local governments: school-age population—population aged 5–17.

Distribution basis for service providers: equal per pupil to both government and non-government schools.

Conditions: universal access to primary and secondary education. Non-government school access to poor on merit. Improvement in achievement scores and graduation rates from baseline for each school. No conditions on the use of funds.

Penalties: public censure, reduction of grant funds and risk of termination with persistent non-compliance. Grant funds automatically decrease if parents pull their children out of non-performing schools.

Incentives: grant funds increase automatically as school attracts more students. Retention of savings for optional use from better management of resources.

Impact implications: encourages competition, innovation and accountability to citizens for improving quality and access. Automatic monitoring and enforcement provisions through parental choices of voting with their feet.

Fiscal federalism literature argues that the design of grants must be consistent with their objectives and it is desirable to have a singular focus—a single grant instrument for a single clearly specified objective. Further, the allocation criteria must be simple, objective, transparent and fair. Table 10.6 presents key objectives sought in these transfers and examples of design consistent with those objectives.

Summing up, the fiscal federalism literature provides the following guidance on instrument choice:

- Conditional non-matching output-based grants (no input conditionality but expectations regarding maintenance of agreed-upon standards and achieving expected results in service delivery) for merit goods such as education and health.
- Conditional matching grants for spillovers in some services such as transportation with matching rate consistent with benefit spill-outs.

Table 10.6 Principles and better practices in grant design

Grant objective	*Grant design*	*Examples of better practices*	*Examples of practices to avoid*
Bridge fiscal gap	Reassignment of responsibilities, tax abatement, tax base sharing	Tax abatement and tax base sharing (Canada)	Deficit grants, wage grants, tax by tax sharing (People's Republic of China, India)
Reduce regional fiscal disparities	General non-matching fiscal capacity equalisation transfers	Fiscal equalization with explicit standard that determines total pool as well as allocation (Canada, Denmark and Germany)	General revenue sharing with multiple factors (Brazil and India); fiscal equalisation with a fixed pool (Australia, People's Republic of China)
Compensate for benefit spillovers	Open-ended matching transfers with matching rate consistent with spill-out of benefits	Grant for teaching hospitals (South Africa)	Closed-ended matching grants
Set national minimum standards for merit public services	Conditional non-matching output-based block transfers with conditions on standards of service and access	Road maintenance and primary education grants (Indonesia before 2000); education transfers (Brazil, Canada, Chile, Colombia); health transfers (Brazil, Canada)	Conditional transfers with conditions on spending alone (most countries), pork barrel transfers, ad hoc grants
	Conditional planning-based capital grants to overcome identified infrastructure deficiencies based on a defined national standard, with matching rate that varies inversely with local fiscal capacity	Capital grant for school construction (Indonesia before 2000), highway construction matching grants to states (United States)	Formula-based capital grants. Capital grants with no matching and no future upkeep requirements, US federal grant for bridge to nowhere in Alaska, Indonesia DAK grants

(*continued*)

Table 10.6 (continued)

Grant objective	*Grant design*	*Examples of better practices*	*Examples of practices to avoid*
Influence local priorities in areas of high national but low local priority	Open-ended matching transfers (preferably with matching rate varying inversely with fiscal capacity)	Matching transfers for social assistance (Canada before 2004)	Ad hoc grants
To provide stabilization	Capital grants, provided maintenance possible	Capital grants with matching rates that vary inversely with local fiscal capacity	Stabilisation grants with no future upkeep requirements
Promote competition among local governments	Project or output grants using certification or tournament approaches	Albania, Russian Federation	

Source: Adapted from Boadway and Shah (2009)

Notes: Certification grants: the grantor promises assistance if certain pre-requisites specified by the grantor are fulfilled, for example, requiring appropriate systems of financial management and accountability being in place prior to release of grant tranche. Tournament grants: the grantor offers assistance to the top performers in a competitive grant program based upon pre-specified criteria for ranking performance

- Equalization grants to ensure that all local governments have the fiscal capacity to provide reasonably comparable levels of basic local services.
- Capital grants for infrastructure if low fiscal capacity.
- Capital market finance for income-generating infrastructure if higher fiscal capacity.
- Public–private partnerships for infrastructure finance if feasible, but keeping public ownership and control of strategic assets.

Beyond grant assistance, the fiscal federalism literature also provides guidance on debt desirability and affordability. It argues that the fiscal capacity of the recipient government and the type of investment are important criteria in deciding on the type of financing that may be desirable.

Table 10.7 highlights these choices. For fiscally poor recipient governments, bond finance would not in general be feasible. They would instead have to rely on grants for social infrastructure investments and in addition

Table 10.7 Sources of capital financing would differ by type of investment and fiscal capacity of the recipient government

Type of capital investment	*Fiscally poor government*	*Fiscally rich government*
Revenue-producing investment	Loans and grants	Loans and bonds
Social investment	Grants only	Loans and grants

Source: Petersen and Valadez (2004: 54)

on loan finance for revenue-producing investments. Richer local jurisdictions would have access to a wider array of financing instruments, including bond finance.

While much of the guidance from the fiscal federalism literature is cast in a multi-order governance framework within a nation, basic principles of this guidance are applicable to external development assistance. For example, this literature would argue against lending programs of external assistance for social investment and governance and institutional reform to fiscally poor developing countries. It also argues against input-based conditionality in both loan and grant assistance to support improved access to merit public services and for poverty alleviation and argues for output-based conditionality to meet such objectives (see also OECD 2013 and 2014 for guidance on the design and conditionality of assistance for regional development under multi-order governance to foster "mutual dependency" and overcome perverse incentives under principal–agent type of relationship).

Limitations of the Approach

In the international context, with multiple donors with conflicting interests, donor harmonisation is costly and difficult to achieve. Donor shopping could undermine incentives and accountability regimes created by following fiscal federalism. Further, in the international context, moral suasion and institutions of executive federalism are unlikely to work effectively. Nevertheless, the principles offered by the fiscal federalism approach, as adopted in international assistance, has the potential to make a significant positive impact on aid effectiveness.

New Public Management Perspectives

New Public Management (NPM) attributes failures of aid effectiveness primarily to the civil service regimes in aid agencies and recipient countries. These regimes support rigid rules-driven civil services with lifelong rotating appointments that discourage risk taking and task specialisation and have little accountability for results. Civil servants are incentivised to spend public and aid monies by following financial and procedural controls and are not held to account for failures in service delivery performance. Aid agency staff similarly face incentives to maximise aid flows whereas relatively less attention is paid to the effectiveness of such assistance. In any case, their career progression is directly linked with approval and disbursements of such assistance following complex procedures and is delinked from results on the ground. NPM brings a focus on the results-based chain in public management as illustrated in Chap. 2.

New Public Management approaches are concerned with creating a human resource management environment that affords public managers autonomy and flexibility and holds them to account for results—rewards them for success and punishes them for persistent failures (Table 10.8).

Such approaches are characterised as New Public Management and have the following common elements:

- Contracts or work program agreements based on pre-specified outputs, performance targets and budgetary allocations
- Managerial flexibility, coupled with accountability for results
- Use of subsidiarity principle in assigning responsibility to various orders of government
- Competitive public service provision

Table 10.8 On making the dog wag its tail: the NPM perspectives

Human resource culture in aid agencies and recipient governments	*New Public Management reform perspectives*
Rigid rules	Managerial flexibility
Input controls	Results matter
Top-down accountability	Top-down and bottom–up accountability
Low wages and high perks	Competitive wages but little else
Lifelong and rotating appointments	Contractual appointments
Focus on jack-of-all-trades staff	Task specialisation
Intolerance for risk/innovation	Freedom to succeed/fail. Ample rewards for success but persistent failure subject to separation

Source: Shah (2005)

Table 10.9 Comparison of two alternate results-based accountability approaches

Theoretical models	*Make managers manage*	*Let managers manage*
Strategies	Market-like arrangements	Managerial norms and competence
Mechanism	Contracts	Empowerment
Commonality	Give public managers the flexibility they need to improve performance	
Differences	Using specific, tightly written performance contracts that leave little room for trust Motivate improvements with extrinsic rewards	Implicitly trusting public managers to exercise their judgement intelligently Motivate primarily by the intrinsic rewards of public service
Examples	New Zealand	Australia, Sweden, United States

Source: Shah and Shen (2007)

There are two alternate approaches to results-based accountability that have been implemented by a selected group of countries, one relying on market-like arrangements and the other on managerial norms and competence (Table 10.9). The former strategy, "making managers manage", used by New Zealand, specifies contracts with budgetary allocations and competitive pressures. The latter approach, "letting managers manage", is practised in Australia and Sweden. Both strategies provide the flexibility public managers need to improve performance. The critical differences between them are the reliance on incentives and competitive spirit in the first and good will and trust in the latter. The two approaches take different perspectives on how to reward public servants. The performance-based contracts reward the chief executive financially if the organisation achieves its performance targets. The empowerment approach holds that public servants are more motivated by the intrinsic rewards of public service than material benefits. The contract-based approach relies on incentives and competitive market mechanisms to enforce the accountability of public managers. The empowerment approach simply hopes that managers will be ethically and professionally motivated for performance.

It is important to stress that managerial accountability must be based on outputs rather than outcomes, as outcomes are beyond mangers' direct control, difficult to define and quantify, and impossible to use as a costing basis. Major justifications for including output-based accountability are:

- It is difficult or implausible to link outcomes directly with managerial actions and decisions as outcomes are remote in time and space from what the program does and how it interacts with other factors. The extent of a manager's direct control over outputs is usually much more substantial than outcomes.
- Outcomes are immensely difficult to identify, and certainly difficult to quantify. The timescale for measuring outcomes normally spans sometime after the program intervention, and is generally not in sync with the same budgeting cycle.
- Calculating the cost of the effort to achieve outcomes can be more difficult than costing outputs (Kristensen et al. 2002: 16). Outcomes are typically achieved not just as the result of a single intervention by one program in isolation, but by the interaction of a number of different planned/unplanned factors and interventions. Hence, it is inappropriate and unrealistic to hold public managers accountable for outcomes. The focus on outputs as practised in Malaysia and New Zealand offers greater potential for accountability for results. Outcomes, however, should be monitored and could be the basis for cabinet accountability; an exclusive emphasis on quantitative output measures without a focus on at least some form on outcomes can distort attention in delivery agencies and run the risk of losing sight of the bigger picture of the impact of their programs on citizens and society.

On the way to fostering outputs-based accountability, it is essential to provide more managerial flexibility through relaxing central input controls. Relaxing central input controls operates at two levels: first, the consolidation of various budget lines into a single appropriation for all operating costs (salaries, travel, supplies, etc.); second, the relaxation of a variety of central management rules that inhibit managerial flexibility, particularly the personnel management function where most central rules exist. Personnel cost is generally the largest component of operating expenditures, and it makes little difference to consolidate budget lines if central rules in this area prevent any flexibility. Sweden's experience in dismantling central control over human resource management offers some interesting insights. Sweden gave full autonomy to line agencies to hire, fire, and set terms of employment and career development of their employees. Agencies were given full authority to manage personnel costs. The agencies made their employees contractual employees. This decentralised management of personnel and personnel costs resulted in major cost savings and performance improvements and also gave line agencies flexibility to meet changing demands for their services on a timely basis (Blondal 2003).

NPM influences are noticeable in recent emphasis on results-based accountability in donor–recipient relations (European Commission 2015). These perspectives, however, had little impact in reforming the human resource management framework in aid agencies and recipient country civil service regimes and the human resource regimes remain impermeable to newer views on incentives for results-based accountability.

Limitations of the Approach

The effectiveness of the NPM (results-based management) approach critically depends upon the public management paradigm in place in donor and government agencies. Unless these agencies embrace results-based management and evaluation as the human resource management paradigm, results-based accountability will have little impact on aid effectiveness.

Political Economy Perspectives

Political economy perspectives bring together an analysis of specific interests of economic and political actors and institutions and reflect upon timing, sequencing, consensus building for feasible and effective reform. Such perspectives are helpful in designing conditions of such assistance for forging recipient ownership and commitment to reform. For external assistance, political economy perspectives require analysis of stakeholders both on the donor and on the recipient side.

On the donor side, various principals and their agents with wide-ranging perspectives, objectives and approaches are involved. Various citizens' groups (principals) may have different perspectives on feasible reform options, the type and amount of assistance required, and may have concerns about the effectiveness of such assistance. Some groups may be committed to the status quo and may oppose all reforms. Donor political regimes (primary agent) may have own priorities in terms of targeting of country assistance. Donor agency staff (secondary agents) mediate government and citizen mandates. Various independent contractors and subcontractors (experts and consultants) may be involved in project implementation and monitoring of progress and results. Both the donor agency staff and contractors may have self-interest in maximising such assistance even when such assistance is deemed ineffective. Conditionality of such assistance may help donor agency staff get buy-in from the political and legislative regimes as well as citizens at large. Such an environment will be conducive to having soft conditions based on prior actions or during the period of assistance. The conditions will also depend on country ranking on donor priorities. Assistance from international or multinational agencies will also be guided by the interests and views of dominant shareholders.

On the recipient side, there is a complex web of stakeholders and their interests. These include political, executive, legislative, military and judicial institutions and associated stakeholders, civil society and special interest groups, experts and contractors, and citizens at large. Their perspectives and interests are often in conflict and change dynamically over time. Forging a consensus for externally assisted tasks is an uphill task and most countries may lack mediating institutions to develop even a rough consensus. This would be especially true when the institutions of accountability in governance are weak and citizens lack the empowerment to hold the government to account. Therefore, commitment to and ownership of such projects, which is critical to project success, may be in a flux. Even the potential beneficiaries of such projects may not be able to organise to present a unified platform. Under such circumstances, recipient governments typically have a short-term political horizon and may be willing to accept unrealistic conditions for assistance knowing fully well that those will not be fulfilled. Dictatorial regimes headed by military, feudal, political or bureaucratic regimes are often guided by short-term self-interest as opposed to public interest in negotiating external assistance. These regimes often seek to maximise such assistance to legitimise and perpetuate their dictatorial regimes.

An analysis of various stakeholders on both the donor and recipient sides can be helpful in designing conditions that would work in specific case study countries. Such conditions could play a critical role in changing the payoff matrix for various stakeholders to create a winning coalition for reform.

A vast literature has emerged on political economy of conditionality in aid programs (see, e.g. Alesina and Drazen 1991; Svensson 2000; Drazen 2002; Mayer and Mourmouras 2002; Joyce 2004). This literature concludes that in the absence of recipient country ownership, lack of credibility of sanction in the event of non-compliance undermines the effectiveness of conditionality. On the other hand, in the event the recipient fully owns the reform program, and is committed to donor conditionality, special interest groups may still undermine the success of such reforms. Therefore, design of assistance must develop mechanisms to deal with these important impediments to the success of the external assistance program (World Bank 2005).

Limitations of the Approach

The approach requires a deeper understanding of political and institutional malaise in the country and the relevance of various stakeholders to champion reforms. External donor agencies typically do not have such in-depth knowledge. In the event they do, due to the politically and culturally sensitive nature of these issues, donor views have the potential of being misused by interest groups opposed to serious reforms. In view of this, the utility of this approach in practice is significantly compromised.

New Institutional Economics Perspectives

New institutional economics (NIE) is concerned with minimising the transaction costs associated with donor–recipient interactions and holding both donors and recipient governments to account for results by their citizens as governors/principals. This framework offers helpful guidance in structuring donor–recipient interactions and the conditionality of such programs. It brings a heightened focus on facilitating network governance by local governments to foster competition and enhance the quality of and access to public services.

According to the NIE framework, on both the donor and the aid recipient side, various orders of governments (as agents) are created to initiative collective action to serve the interests of the citizens as governors/principals. The jurisdictional design should ensure that these agents serve the public interest while minimising the transaction costs for the principals.

The existing institutional framework does not permit such optimisation, because the principals have bounded rationality; that is, they make the best choices on the basis of the information at hand but are ill-informed about government operations. Enlarging the sphere of their knowledge entails high transaction costs, which citizens are not willing to incur. Those costs include participation and monitoring costs, legislative costs, executive decision-making costs, agency costs or costs incurred to induce compliance by agents with the compact, and uncertainty costs associated with unstable political regimes (Horn 1995; Shah 2007b). Agents (various orders of governments) are better informed about government operations than principals are, but they have an incentive to withhold information and to indulge in opportunistic behaviour or "self-interest seeking with guile" (Williamson 1985: 7). Thus, the principals have only incomplete contracts with their agents and have further imperfect knowledge about their activities and associated impacts. Such an environment fosters commitment problems because both the donor and the recipient's agents and contractors may not follow the compact.

The NIE literature identifies two types of problems in such an agency relationship. First, the agent may not follow the mandate from the principal and instead design programs to advance its own self-interest. For example, aid agency contractors may choose a project design that profits them most. This is termed the moral hazard of such an agency. On the recipient side, government may delay much needed reforms expecting future external financing. Second, the agent may manipulate the information he/she conveys to the principal to undermine the principal's interests. For example, aid agency contractors and/or evaluators may exaggerate the success of the project in reporting results to taxpayers in donor countries. This may lead to project selection bias in favour of projects where the results are easy to manipulate; for example, technocratic reform projects would be preferred over investment projects. This is recognised as the adverse selection problem in the literature. Note that both the moral hazard and the adverse selection problems also manifest themselves on the recipient side of aid as well. The challenge is to mitigate these problems by designing incentive regimes that encourage agents to be truthful to their principals (see also Martens et al. 2002). This challenge becomes even more formidable with external assistance programs that are aimed at governance and institutional reforms in developing countries as monitoring of the results-based chain becomes more difficult compared to investment projects. These problems are compounded by the trend away from investment projects and towards more aid for institutional reforms. Difficulties in measuring and monitoring results heighten moral hazard and adverse selection in external assistance for institutional reforms and make detection of non-compliance and enforcement more difficult. That is why most such assistance programs simply require passing of laws and regulations with little or no oversight on implementation and enforcement. In the end, one does not really know what the real impact of such assistance was although evaluation by objectives would term such projects successful. This suggests that strengthening the post-project independent evaluation function may not help to narrow the zone of ignorance by the principals. Multiple factors contribute to this difficulty: evaluation methodologies that focus on program objectives, moral hazard in donor financing of such evaluations and imperfect access to project knowledge by evaluators.

The situation is further complicated by three factors: weak or extant countervailing institutions, path dependency, and the interdependency of various actions. Countervailing institutions such as the judiciary, police, parliament and citizen activist groups, are usually weak and unable to restrain rent-seeking by politicians and bureaucrats. Historical and cultural factors and mental models by which people see little benefits to and high costs of activism prevent corrective action. Further empowering local councils to take actions on behalf of citizens often leads to loss of agency between voters and councils, because council members may interfere in executive decision making or may get co-opted in such operations while shirking their legislative responsibilities. The NIE framework stresses the need to use various elements of transaction costs in designing jurisdictions for various services and in evaluating choices between competing governance mechanisms.

Further complications on the recipient side arise from breakdown of vertical co-ordination with multiple orders of government and horizontal co-ordination among governmental agencies themselves and between beyond government agencies and groups. A structure of resource dependency vitiates against collective action in the interest of the common good because of the tragedy of commons associated with common pool resources. This scenario results in failures in vertical and horizontal co-ordination in a multi-organisation partnership (Dollery and Wallis 2001).

One possible solution is to introduce a market mechanism of governance, whereby a contract management agency enters into binding contracts with all partners. However, this solution is unworkable because the potential number of contingencies may simply be too large to be covered by such contracts. A second approach to overcoming horizontal co-ordination, the so-called hierarchical mechanism of governance, relies on institutional arrangements to clarify roles and responsibilities and to establish mechanisms for consultation, co-operation and co-ordination, as is done in some federal systems. Such institutional arrangements entail high transaction costs and are subject to a high degree of failure attributable to the conflicting interests of partners.

Given the high transaction costs and perceived infeasibility of market and hierarchical mechanisms of governance for partnerships of multiple organisations, a network mechanism of governance has been advanced as a possible mode of governance for such partnerships—the kind to be managed by local governments. The network form of governance relies on trust, loyalty and reciprocity between partners with no formal institutional safeguards. Networks formed on the basis of shared interests (interest-based networks) can provide a stable form of governance if membership is limited to partners that can make significant resource contributions and if there is a balance of powers among members. Members of such networks interact frequently and see co-operation in one area as contingent on co-operation in other areas. Repeated interaction among members builds trust. Hope-based networks are built on the shared sentiments and emotions of members. Members have shared beliefs in the worth and philosophy of the network goals and have the passion and commitment to achieve those goals. The stability of such networks is highly dependent on the commitment and style of their leadership (Dollery and Wallis 2001).

Local government has an opportunity to play a catalytic role in facilitating the roles of both interest-based and hope-based networks in improving social outcomes for local residents. To play such a role, local government must develop a strategic vision of how such partnerships can be formed and sustained. But then the local government requires a new local public management paradigm. Such a paradigm demands local government to separate policy advice from program implementation, assuming a role as a purchaser of public services but not necessarily as a provider of them. Local government may have to outsource services with higher provision costs and subject in-house providers to competitive pressures from outside providers to lower transaction costs for citizens. It also must actively seek the engagement of both interest-based and hope-based networks to supplant local services. It needs to develop the capacity to play a mediating role among various groups. In most recipient countries, local governments are hamstrung by the policy and legislative framework to play such a role.

By the NIE framework, the situation on the donor side is no different. Donor citizens as governors/principals have incomplete contracts with their agents (governments), who in turn have unenforceable contracts with their sub-agents (aid agencies) and who in turn have even more unenforceable contracts with their independent consultants and providers. Agents may not act in the public interest as political finance weakens this agency relationship and legislatures may not be able to exercise due oversight on the executive. Information asymmetries abound in citizens-legislature-executive-aid agency–contractors relationship. Only the aid agency staff and contractors have better knowledge about aid effectiveness and it is in their rational interest to withhold such information from governments, aid agencies and citizens so that support for such assistance does not wither away in the event non-effectiveness of such assistance gains currency in public opinion.

In donor-recipient relations the NIE framework argues for complete contracts with fully enforceable conditions. International organisations could play for-fee roles of contract management agencies on behalf of donors and recipients. However, as noted earlier, potential contingencies in practice may be too large to make such contracts unworkable and unenforceable. A network form of governance where the recipient country or an international agency co-ordinates the activities of all donors offers some potential, but may not work due to high transaction costs associated with such co-ordination and lack of loyalty, trust and reciprocity in an international setting. A network form of governance may, however, be worth trying for expanding access to clearly defined global public goods.

Limitations of the Approach

As noted earlier, the NIE framework emphasises citizen empowerment and governments acting as agents of people fulfilling contractual mandates. Complete contracts, however, remain infeasible and agency problems at best could be mitigated to some extent with absolute transparency, home rule, strengthening counter-veiling institutions, and accountability and redress mechanisms, but could never be overcome completely.

A Synthesis of Conceptual Perspectives

Various conceptual approaches briefly sketched in the previous section highlight the following issues in external development assistance and associated conditions.

- *Donor–recipient relations:* The approaches highlight the complexity of such relations and conflicting interests of various stakeholders on either side and offer predictions as to the final outcome of such interactions. All approaches predict sub-optimal outcomes unless the design of such assistance addresses to mitigate the perverse incentives faced by various stakeholders in these repeated interactions. Individual approaches differ on the underlying critical factors guiding such relationships and the means to overcome those constraints (see Table 10.9).

- *Multiplicity of donor and recipient stakeholders:* All approaches with the partial exception of game theory recognise multiplicity of stakeholders on both sides of the equation. While there may be confluence of interests by principals on both sides, principal–agent conflicts on either side dominate and guide donor–recipient relations. The approaches recognise the possibility of collusion by agents of the donor and the recipient to maximise aid flows without worrying about the effectiveness of such assistance.
- *Role of citizens on both sides:* With the sole exception of the NIE approach, the role of citizens as governors/principals is not sufficiently recognised by various conceptual approaches discussed here.
- *Improving aid effectiveness:* Various conceptual approaches provide differing perspectives on improving aid effectiveness. Game theory emphasises that improving donor agency incentives and accountability mechanisms and credibility of sanctions and imposing higher administrative costs for assistance in the event of non-compliance will represent a welfare-improving proposition for both the donor and the recipients. Public choice theory argues for greater competition and voice and exit options. Fiscal federalism literature emphasises better design of such assistance to promote partnership within and beyond governments. It further argues that there should be singular focus in each grant instrument. Grant design should be consistent with its objective, respect autonomy but enforce accountability for results. It encourages use of lending instruments for income-producing physical investments but discourages their use for governance and institutional reforms. It also emphasises a strong role of executive and legislative federalism within the nation for horizontal and vertical co-ordination. Political economy perspectives suggest taking a closer look at recipient country institutions and building effective coalitions for reform. NPM emphasises reforming the bureaucratic culture of aid agencies and recipient governments to embrace results-based management and evaluations. The NIE argues for citizen empowerment through localisation, direct democracy provisions, letting the sunshine on government operations

through transparency requirements and lowering the transaction costs for citizens to hold government to account.

- *Implications for conditionality of assistance:* All approaches argue for the conditionality of external assistance but argue against input-based conditionality. However, various approaches differ as to the type of conditions to be imposed.
  - Game theory suggests conditions should assure that both the donor and the recipient share both the rewards of success and the consequences of failure. For example, for a failed loan-financed project, the donor must also bear partial financial consequences of the failure. This is intended to mitigate somewhat the adverse consequences of "loan approval and disbursement culture" with no attention to results.
  - Fiscal federalism literature argues against input- and process-based conditionality that undermines recipient autonomy and instead advocates output-based conditionality to enforce results-based accountability. It favours the golden rule of borrowing, that is, borrowing for capital investments only and no borrowing to finance operating expenditures (e.g. expenditures associated with institutional and governance reforms). It discourages general budget support if the aim is to finance merit public services.
  - NPM argues for conditions that help monitor the results-based chain but for holding the recipient to account for service delivery performance (output accountability).
  - The NIE advocates contractually enforceable conditions on both the donor and the recipient for specific results to be achieved and having the requisite governance environment to hold the aid agency and recipient government to account for direct democracy and sunshine provisions, observance of the subsidiarity rule and lowering the transaction costs to hold various agencies and government to account (Table 10.10).

Table 10.10 Implications of conceptual perspectives for loan/grant conditions: a synthesis

Features	*Alternative conceptual approaches*					
	Game theory	*Public choice*	*Fiscal federalism*	*Political economy*	*New Public Management*	*New institutional economics*
Donor-recipient relations	Non-cooperative strategic behaviours by donor and recipients lead to sub-optimal results	Donor and recipient collusive behaviour to the detriment of public interest	Partners with shared objectives but varying perspectives on how to achieve them. Conflicting interests mediated through higher-order incentives	Collaboration to build domestic consensus for reform	Human resource incentives in both aid agencies and government work to undermine aid effectiveness	Conflicting interests and values of principals and agents on both sides. Principals on both sides have incomplete contracts and imperfect knowledge about agents' behaviours and activities. Agents on both sides disconnected from their citizens (principals/governors)
Multiplicity of donor stakeholders	Partially recognized	Recognised	Recognised	Recognised	Recognised	Recognised
Multiplicity of recipient stakeholders	Partially recognised	Recognised	Recognised	Recognised	Recognised	Recognised

(*continued*)

Table 10.10 (continued)

Features	*Alternative conceptual approaches*					
	Game theory	*Public choice*	*Fiscal federalism*	*Political economy*	*New Public Management*	*New institutional economics*
Role of citizens on both sides	Not addressed	Limited role	Limited recognition	Modest recognition	Modest recognition	Strong emphasis on citizens as governors but role circumvented on both sides
Improving aid effectiveness	Address donor agency incentives and accountability and impose higher administrative costs for future assistance in the event of non-compliance	Greater competition, voice and exit options	Making design consistent with objectives. Singular focus. Respecting recipient autonomy but having accountability for results. Institutions of executive and legislative federalism	Focus on recipient country institutions	Focus on reforming civil service culture and introducing results-based management and accountability	Citizen empowerment through home rule, bill of rights, direct democracy provisions such as referenda and recall; redress mechanisms, and letting the sun shine on government operations and reducing transaction costs to hold government to account

Implications for conditionality	Ensure that both donor and recipient share both the rewards of success and risks of failure	Focus on the governing environment as a pre-requisite of assistance	Input- and process-based conditionality impairs recipient autonomy and may create white elephants. Output-based conditionality respects autonomy and enhances accountability for results General budget support less desirable to ensure minimum standards of merit services. Borrowing not desirable for operating expenditures	Detailed analysis of country's political, economic and social institutions should be a pre-requisite for assistance. Conditions should facilitate coalition building for reform	Monitoring of results-based chain but output-based accountability for both donors and recipients	Contractually enforceable conditions on both donor and recipient to emphasise specific results to be achieved, sunshine provisions, citizen empowerment and lowering transaction costs to hold both parties to account for contract performance. Local government to be given an enhanced role in service delivery and oversight of higher-level government's activities in local area

(*continued*)

Table 10.10 (continued)

Features	*Alternative conceptual approaches*					
	Game theory	*Public choice*	*Fiscal federalism*	*Political economy*	*New Public Management*	*New institutional economics*
Should conditionality be dispensed with altogether	No	No	No	No	No	No

Source: Author

Evolving Institutional Perspectives on the Conditionality

International Development Assistance: Evolving Perspectives on the Conditionality of Assistance

Conditionality of international development assistance has been a subject of perennial controversy and debate. This debate had a significant impact on the design and delivery of external development assistance with a trend away from donor-imposed design and conditionality to somewhat participatory approaches to the same with recipients given significant opportunity to influence donor-driven program design and conditionality. Annex A provides an overview of such evolution by individual multilateral institutions. This section traces the evolution of this thinking both in loan and grant assistance and provides a discussion of outstanding issues.

Evolving Landscape on the Conditionality of Development Assistance

Loan Conditions

IMF, World Bank and European Investment Bank lending instruments and conditionality have evolved over time. Until the early 1980s, IMF loan conditions focused on macroeconomic policies and IMF staff had a free hand carrying out the diagnostics and developing conditions that a borrower must accept. In the ensuing two decades, the demand for IMF lending softened and the IMF carved out a growing role in competition with the World Bank, the Asian Development Bank, the Inter-American Development Bank among others in lending assistance for structural reforms. This led to an explosive growth in IMF conditions with an average of 17 conditions per program per year. However, various evaluation studies suggested that these conditions had little structural depth and weak compliance (IMF 2007). The international financial crisis of 2008 led to an explosive demand for the IMF's stabilisation assistance program. This helped the IMF to streamline its conditionality in 2009 and have a greater focus on areas of its competency. The requirement that all conditionality must be macro-critical—that it is critical to the achievement of macroeconomic program goals—was reinforced. More recently, income inequality and unemployment concerns led the IMF to emphasise "macro-social" criticality of its loan conditions. Recent guidelines (IMF 2010, 2012, 2014, 2016) also emphasise recipient country inputs on loan design and conditionality. The overall thrust of the new guidelines is to have greater parsimony in conditions (now about five or less per program per year) and greater flexibility in program implementation provided there is assurance of achievement of program objectives.

World Bank loan instruments and conditions have also significantly evolved over time. Prior to the 1980s, World Bank lending assistance was focused on physical and social infrastructure projects with conditionality on procurement, implementation monitoring and auditing.

The effectiveness of these loans was measured by project outcomes and by pre- and post-project rates of return. Compliance record with these conditions was good and a large majority of these projects had "successful" outcomes, but about a third of such "successful" operations were not sustainable. The project rates of return, however, appeared less useful as they showed a consistent over-optimism in *ex ante* rates of return. However, in the World Bank's judgement, these projects could not address the broader policy and institutional malaise that hindered development. In the early 1980s, the World Bank brought a greater emphasis to policy and institutional reform through policy-based lending programs. Policy-based lending brought a newer kind of conditionality in lending that emphasised broader policy reforms through legislative and executive actions. These conditions varied in terms of specificity, clarity, monitorability, enforceability and difficulty in implementation. Conditions also varied by the economic and political clout of the borrowing countries. Large upper middle-income borrowers typically faced softer conditions, whereas small low-income countries were subjected to a degree of detail that could be misconstrued as micromanagement by an external aid agency. The conditions typically embodied the so-called Washington Consensus on policy reform and emphasised trade liberalisation, privatisation, public enterprise reforms, and fiscal policy and tax administration reforms.

The conditionality of World Bank lending accompanied by newer windows such as enhanced assistance from China for infrastructure assistance contributed to a softening of the demand for World Bank lending during the period 2001–2005. Subsequent World Bank internal management reviews of adjustment lending (World Bank 2005) stated that changed economic circumstances in recipient countries called for a move from adjustment lending to programmatic lending to have a sharper focus on governance and institutional reforms. Program lending through development policy and sectoral development loans would provide opportunities to develop comprehensive medium- to long-term reforms. Loan

Table 10.11 Good practice principles for development policy lending by the World Bank

Ownership	*Reinforce country ownership*
Harmonisation	Agree upfront with the government and other financial partners on a co-ordinated accountability framework
Customisation	Customise the accountability framework and modalities of World Bank support to country circumstances
Criticality	Choose only actions critical for achieving results as conditions for disbursement
Transparency and predictability	Conduct transparent progress reviews conducive to predictable and performance-based financial support

Source: World Bank (2007), "Conditionality in development policy lending", p.i, http://siteresources.worldbank.org/PROJECTS/Resources/40940-1114615847489/Conditionalityfinalreport120407.pdf

conditions for such programs are intended to emphasise country ownership and sustained commitments to reform and strict compliance with loan conditions would be de-emphasised provided the client is on track in achieving mutually agreed reform objectives. Table 10.11 highlights the principles adopted by the World Bank for development policy lending.

In conclusion, both World Bank lending instruments and associated loan conditions have undergone profound changes over the last 50 years. It should be noted nevertheless that while instituting this new shift in emphasis on results in development policy lending, the World Bank continues to follow traditional conditionality in its investment project assistance. There has been greater flexibility in lending instruments and associated conditions for development policy in recent years. A significant part of lending simply provides general budget support. Lending emphasis have shifted from the "Bank knows best" to joint learning and a greater focus on an enabling environment for better economic and social outcomes. There is a greater emphasis now on local ownership. Still, there are residual concerns with the mutual accountability framework as donor agency staff are incentivised to approve and disburse loans with little accountability in the event of failure. The system of frequent rotating appointments shields individual World Bank staff from accountability for failure while taking credit for loan approval and disbursement. The burden of failure rests solely on the recipient's shoulders with no adverse consequences for the World Bank as the World Bank being the prime creditor would almost always be repaid. This contrasts with private bank lending where loan failures have consequences both for the lender and the borrower. These perverse incentives are at the heart of the problem of limiting development effectiveness of loan conditions.

Grant Conditions

EU member states and the European Commission provide development assistance in the form of grants. Together, they constitute the largest donor of such assistance.

EU/EC policies on conditionality have evolved over time. Traditional conditionality with unilateral input- or process-based donor conditions with little harmonisation across member states and the EC dominated the EU aid regime in the late twentieth century. The EU also imposes political conditionality relating to democratisation and human rights in recipient countries. Non-compliance with these conditions led to inconsistent sanction responses across countries (see Del Biondo 2011). EU aid programs suffered from excessive concerns with input-related tasks and financial and procedural controls and insufficient attention to project quality and almost no attention to results (see Seabright 2002; Martens et al. 2002). Martens et al. note:

> ... policy and program objectives will tend to be broader, vaguer and less well defined, taking into account the views and opinions of a wide range of parties and making implementation more difficult and less efficient. The absence of majority voting for most decisions in the Council makes the situation even worse. Furthermore, member states compete with each other to get the largest possible share of the EC's aid contracts cake. They provide political support for their own private aid services suppliers in this competition. National and service suppliers actively lobby their political representatives in Brussels for that purpose; national representatives in EC foreign aid decision making communities spend a considerable part of their time exploring and pursuing contract opportunities for national suppliers. This focuses attention very much on inputs and procurement procedures (budgets, contracts, tenders, etc.), thereby further tilting the bias in favour of inputs and away from outputs and performance. Because of the lack of single political ownership at EC level and intensive competition between member states, input bias in EC aid is likely to be stronger than in bilateral aid programs. (p. 31)

However, with the dawn of the twenty-first century, the EU has actively pursued to improve aid effectiveness by playing an active role in important international agreements that aim to reform the delivery of economic assistance. These include the 2005 Paris Declaration, the 2008 Accra Agenda for Action, the 2011 Busan Outcome document, the 2014 Mexico Commitment, the 2015 Addis Ababa Action Agenda for the implementation of the Sustainable Development Goals and the 2016 Brussels 2030 Agenda for Sustainable Development. The overall thrust of these agreements is to reform donor–recipient relations using the following principles (European Commission 2015):

- Focus on country ownership
- Transparency and mutual accountability
- Unconditional assistance
- Focus on results
- Focus on forging partnerships for development
- Predictability of assistance
- Focus on inclusive and sustainable development.

In recent years, EU members and the European Commission have made modest progress in bringing aid programs in conformity with the above principles (European Union 2016). The European Commission adopted a results framework in 2015 that emphasises developing a results-based chain for assurance that program activities and inputs are consistent with the objectives to be achieved (European Commission 2009, 2015). Significant progress has been made on country ownership and focus on inclusive development. Modest progress has been made on unconditional assistance and partnership principles. Transparency and mutual accountability goals remain elusive. There have been reversals on aid predictability (European Commission 2011) by member countries and the results focus still seems on intermediate inputs (Adam et al. 2004); mutual accountability remains a distant dream as country systems are rarely used by donor agencies (European Union 2015, 2016).

Emerging Consensus on the New Model of Conditionality and Current Practice

Multilateral development agencies are gradually moving away from traditional conditionality that emphasised input-based conditions as a tool for leverage and control ensuring that assistance funds were used for the intended purposes following processes laid out by the donor agencies. These agencies have come to recognise that while the traditional conditionality was intrusive, it also undermined the effectiveness of their assistance by reducing flexibility in program design to meet local conditions by the recipients. The new view is that the conditionality should be specifically tailored to the special circumstances of each recipient and focus on an agreed framework that will facilitate monitoring progress to achieve jointly shared objectives. The conditionality therefore should be seen as a tool of mutual accountability and due diligence rather than of financial leverage and input controls. The new conditionality also emphasises country ownership as the key to the success of the project/program and sees sustained dialogue as key to strengthening recipient ownership as well as meeting fiduciary due diligence requirements. The new conditionality also sees outcome-based results focus as a means to enhance development effectiveness. There is also an emphasis on having fewer conditions that are critical to the project's success and have the necessary buy-in of the recipient government. Multilateral agencies also emphasise placing a greater emphasis on general budget support and rewarding reforming countries for prior actions taken.

In practice, multilateral agencies continue to practice input-based conditionality for traditional investment projects. For structural and institutional reforms, much confusion remains among outcome, output and intermediate inputs conditionality. In many cases, multilateral agencies impose conditions on intermediate inputs but construe these as outputs or outcomes. Notwithstanding the results focus in international aid dialogues, it should also be noted that bilateral grant assistance that dominates overall aid flows has not seen much transformation and this assistance primarily flows through project assistance with input-based conditionality (see Box 10.2 for selected examples of failure of such assistance).

Box 10.2 Selected Examples of Development Assistance That Did Not Work as Intended

While donors and recipients can point out numerous examples of success of development assistance, this box highlights a few illustrative cases that worked as predicted by the theoretical literature on aid effectiveness.

(*continued*)

Box 10.2 (continued)

Soft conditions by the donor to ensure project success: The World Bank provided a fast disbursing structural adjustment loan (P066867) of USD 606 million to Mexico with no counterpart financing in 2001 to advance decentralization reforms. The overall objective of the loan was greater transparency of federal transfers and subjecting local borrowing to market discipline. To advance these objectives, the loan imposed two conditions: (1) federal transfers must be published as part of the federal budget; (2) two credit-rating agencies be established to develop and monitor state and municipal credit ratings. These conditions were immediately complied with by Mexico and the loan was fully disbursed within six months of approval. But the loan overlooked some important facts: (1) the statistical annex to the President's report to the congress— a more widely circulated document than the federal budget—had a long tradition of publishing the details on federal transfers; (2) a credit-rating agency was already doing credit ratings for subnational governments long before the dialogue on the Decentralization SAL began (see World Bank 2003; ICR Review Report No. ICRR 10974).

Project approval culture with little attention to project success: In 1991, after the fall of the Ceaucescu regime, Romania sought World Bank emergency assistance for critical imports due to a shortage of tyres for commercial vehicles. The World Bank provided fast-track approval of this loan in June 1991. However, under World Bank rules, Romania had to follow a competitive international bidding process to procure the needed commercial tires. As the Romanians were unaware of such procurement practices, the World Bank offered a training program. It took Romania three years to comply with the procurement process and by the time the tyres were imported, they were no longer needed as the market had already filled the gap. As a result, five years later, the tyres were still sitting in government warehouses while the government frantically searched for a solution to get rid of the surplus tyres (see World Bank 1996).

Repeated nash equilibrium in IMF stabilization assistance to Pakistan with no learning: Pakistan, from its formation in 1947 to the present day, has been an on-again off-again recipient of IMF

(*continued*)

Box 10.2 (continued)

stabilization assistance. The objectives of these programs were almost identical from the 1950s to the 2010s. Pakistan complies with IMF conditions for about two years and then goes off-track. A couple of years later it enters into a new stabilization program and the game continues to be repeated ad infinitum until the present time with no end in sight to this vicious cycle of debt trap (see McCartney 2012).

Delayed reforms in anticipation of foreign assistance: In early 1992, Pakistan was isolated internationally due to its nuclear experiments and the government adopted a comprehensive fast-track program of structural reforms recommended by an independent Economy Commission with wider political support. This program was to be implemented in the fall of 1992. However, in the early fall the international development assistance community resumed its aid relations to Pakistan. The Pakistani government immediately shelved its deeper structural reform program and was successful in obtaining external assistance for cosmetic reforms.

Technocratic solutions ill-suited to local conditions: Indonesia received multi-donor external assistance led by the IMF/World Bank to achieve better financing of subnational governments and improved monitoring of local service delivery performance as part of support for decentralization reforms in 2000. Following external advice, it revamped its home-designed subnational transfers program that had served its objectives well and substituted it with a highly complex, yet inefficient and inequitable, system of fiscal transfers. It also imposed complex, laborious data collection and reporting requirements unrelated to local service delivery performance, for example, providing data on the Gini coefficients and human development indexes on a quarterly basis. Local governments face high compliance costs yet receive no feedback on these reports from the central government (see Shah 2012, 2014). Another example of "ill-suited" advice comes from World Bank decentralization operations where the World Bank recommended setting up UK-type local audit commissions for local governments to a large number of countries. This experiment imposed high costs in the United Kingdom and was abandoned in 2010, but developing countries that set up similar institutions at substantial costs may not have such an option if they faced a situation similar to the one in the United Kingdom.

(*continued*)

Box 10.2 (continued)

Another important example of failures of technocratic solutions favoured by the development assistance community comes from contrasting experience with privatization reforms in the Czech Republic and Romania. Contrary to World Bank/IMF advice, the Czech Republic adopted a program of rapid privatization, leaving the restructuring of the enterprises to the new owners. This program of mass privatization with two short waves each conducted over less than a year was remarkably successful and the centrally planned economy was completely transformed into a private market economy in record time. Romania, on the other hand, followed World Bank/IMF advice to restructure state enterprises and make them profitable prior to their sale and its privatization program was derailed as public managers organized to oppose privatization by keeping the enterprises in a loss-making position (see World Bank 1996, 1997).

Outstanding Issues and Views

This section highlights the key outstanding issues and current views on how to address these challenges. The reader is well advised also to consult World Bank (2005, 2007) for a comprehensive treatment and synthesis of the wide-ranging issues under discussion by the development assistance community.

Policy-Based Lending

Several factors contributed to the popularity of policy-based lending by multilateral agencies in the late 1990s (see Williamson 2005). These included: an urgent need for fast disbursing assistance to deal with the oil and debt crisis; growing recognition of the importance of the policy environment for effectiveness of development assistance; growing realisation of the importance of fungibility of foreign assistance—recipients' ability to put their best projects forward for external financing and to use the financing to finance other pet expenditures, for example, military expenditures; shrinking demand for multilateral conditionality ridden project assistance. The preferred tool for policy-based lending was programmatic lending, where donors provided general budget support to carry out wide-ranging policy reforms. In many cases, the donor went shopping looking for recent reforms already undertaken to shower their assistance. Such assistance mostly went to higher middle-income countries. Initially, there was pervasive political conditionality mostly for legislative and executive actions, for example, presenting draft legislation to parliament, issuing regulations, etc. As the record of non-compliance with these conditions piled up, lenders embraced a change towards consensual conditions and country selectivity-favouring reforming countries. There was general support for the view that the reforming countries should develop a long-term plan and get donors to buy in to elements of this program for external financing—the so-called common pool approach (Kanbur and Sandler 1999). However, in practice such a co-ordinated view of country assistance could not be implemented.

While there seems to be a broad-based donor consensus on policy-based lending, the conceptual literature presented earlier does not support such a perspective. This is because most of the support goes to general budget support for the government with the expectation that it will implement policy reforms the net fiscal cost of which in most cases is zero or even negative (say tax reforms). Thus, such lending violates the cardinal rule of fiscal prudence—the golden rule for borrowing—and enhances the indebtedness of highly indebted countries. Furthermore, country selectivity criteria is of little help to fragile and low-income countries in dire straits that lack the basic institutions of good governance or do not have in-home policy expertise. General budget support for non-democratic regimes could perpetuate non-inclusive elite services or go towards wasteful military and civilian expenditures. Financing prior actions when they were not part of the agreed-upon program have the potential to reward countries for political reasons and also diverts assistance to higher income countries while depriving assistance to countries in greater need.

Minimum International Standards

An emerging donor consensus is to use in the future country systems rather than donor-mandated processes to ensure integrity in the use of donor funds. To this end, donors increasingly rely on public expenditure and financial accountability assessments to form a considered view of country systems. Setting up minimum international standards, however, remains an area of debate. Some worry that a higher standard would exclude some countries deserving of aid while a lower standard may create inertia for some countries not to strive for higher standards. These concerns can be overcome by the design suggestions presented below.

Minimum international standards of fiscal and financial management and accountability are a useful construct. These standards could usefully serve as pre-requisites for receiving external assistance and would possibly circumvent the need for special project implementation units and donor-specific procurement rules and project and financial reporting requirements. These standards, however, need to be carefully constructed for a various class of countries based on their public expenditure and financial accountability assessments and other relevant country-specific circumstances. Certification grants could be a useful tool for encouraging countries to graduate to the next higher classification of minimum standards. This is an area requiring donor attention as not much progress has been made yet in the use of country systems and unharmonised donor systems impose significant costs for the recipients.

Minimum international standards for basic public services along the lines of the Millennium/Sustainable Development Goals could be a useful tool in determining external aid priorities, eligibility for various types of assistance and monitoring progress. These minimum international standards could also vary by country classes (e.g. fragile, low-income, middle-income and upper middle-income) and affordability issues but a universal class of minimum standards in basic public services would apply to all countries and a rights-based approach may be used to assure universal access to such standards.

Mutual Accountability

While there is consensus on the need for mutual accountability, very few practical ideas have emerged to make it happen. A results-based focus is seen as the primary tool for advancing this objective. The results-based focus, however, will bring to light a more informed perspective on project/program achievements but would have a limited impact on mutual accountability. In the event the aid recipient diverts aid resources to non-assisted functions, there is hardly any remedy available to the donor. Alternately, if there is lack of integrity or waste in the use of funds, the donor has options for future assistance but the consequences of donor actions may not affect the regime but may have a greater impact on the impoverished members of the society if, in fact, they received some benefits from aid flows. On the other side, there are presently not any significant consequences for a lender for a bad loan or bad advice that leaves the recipient in greater debt and more impoverished conditions. While practical options for risk and reward sharing are available, the development assistance community has not shown any interest in examining such options for future adoption.

Country Ownership and Conditionality: Some Tensions

An emerging consensus in the development assistance community is the importance of country ownership for project success. This is being proposed as an important criterion for selectivity of assistance. It is argued that if country ownership is confirmed by the donor, then a donor may provide such a country assistance for prior actions, unconditional assistance and budget support to finance its reform program. There are nevertheless risks with such a strategy. The ownership by an elite government may not imply legislative buy-in or citizens' ownership of government programs. Further, lending assistance may not be appropriate for institutional reforms with net fiscal costs being zero or less. Also, selectivity may lead to greater assistance for countries in lesser need of assistance than for countries in greater need. Selectivity may also be based upon donor criteria that may implicitly incorporate value judgments, for example, the World Bank Governance Indicators are based mostly on the perceptions of a handful of foreign experts mostly based on Western media reports about other countries rather than in-depth knowledge about the governance environment in specific countries. Such perceptions can be shown to be wrong in many instances and may be in conflict with citizens' perceptions. Similarly, the World Bank's Country Performance and Institutional Assessment indicators are developed by World Bank staff with direct responsibility for assistance to the same countries and therefore hold no assurance of an unbiased perspective.

Current State of Partnership for Development Assistance

Recent discussions on the effectiveness of development assistance has also emphasised multi-donor partnership under the country leadership to finance development. Various reforms are proposed as a way to develop such a partnership. These include the country taking the lead in donor co-ordination, harmonisation of donor requirements and conditionality, donors' use of country systems in place of own requirements, the country developing a development plan in consultation with internal and external stakeholders, and donors making a commitment to finance a slice of the program on a long-term basis, and the use of conditions simply for mutual accountability and monitoring progress and not as a source of donor leverage and control. Consensus on these principles, however, has not resulted in much progress on the ground. Impediments to progress include both the capability and willingness to bear the transaction costs of such ambitious undertaking by the recipient countries, especially low-income and fragile countries; conflicting agendas and interests of bilateral donors and reluctance to give up control for fear of abuse of funds, financial and fiscal crisis limiting predictability and stability of donor financing, and a changing political landscape and policy priorities in donor countries. In general, major progress on this front in the near future seems uncertain. There is also a view that the partnership approach is less workable to deal with fiscal, financial and humanitarian crises or natural disasters, as these require urgent responses through quick consultations of the donor with the central agencies directly responsible to deal with such crises.

Lessons on the Conditionality of Development Assistance

This section draws lessons from conceptual underpinnings and practical experiences with the use of conditionality in development assistance.

Instrument choice and the conditionality must be consistent with reform objectives.

Macroeconomic Stabilisation Goals The conditions on key macroeconomic indicators that are critical to the achievement of stabilisation goals and are within the control of recipient government policy makers are appropriate both for grant and loan finance. For loan finance, care must be taken to ensure that with stabilisation, the debt is affordable and repayable by the country in the short to intermediate run. Also, while hard conditions on major macro indicators, for example, debt and deficit limitation, are desirable, the escape clause must be linked to a decline in GDP, a major recession, or civil strife or catastrophe to afford flexibility in the event of a crisis and not to cut off aid to a country when it needs it the most. Another useful alternative to the escape clause is the IMF-type joint program reviews to take into account unexpected exogenous factors and readjust the program accordingly as escape clauses cannot take all unexpected factors into account.

Structural Reform Goals Results—(output-based) rather than process—and input-based conditionality would be desirable for structural reforms. Grant financing is appropriate but care must be taken in providing loan finance. Loan finance would not be desirable for fiscally poor countries that may not have the potential to repay such loans over a reasonably long-term horizon.

Governance and Institutional Reform Goals Output conditionality based on a clearly articulated results-based chain is desirable for grant finance. Care must be taken in designing such output conditions to mitigate moral hazard. Certification-based grants where implementation of governance and institutional reforms are treated as pre-requisites for rewarding reforming governments, are appropriate for this purpose. Note that this differs from rewarding countries for prior actions as used by multilateral development agencies. Pre-requisites in a certification program are part of the agreed-upon phased assistance program whereas prior actions simply reward governments for having already taken reform steps to the liking of the donor. Certification grants therefore serve as an inducement to reform whereas prior actions in most cases lack any incentives for reform and simply provide windfall gains to the recipient. However, prior actions that are implemented as part of the conditions for approval of a program would be justified for the first disbursement. Loan finance may not be appropriate for fiscally poor countries. Loan finance as a general budget support for governance reforms is particularly questionable as it violates the golden rule for borrowing and contributes to imprudent fiscal management. Of course, if the governance reform program has a long-lived investment component, borrowing would be justified for that component only. Ruling elites with a short time horizon may use such borrowing to perpetuate their regimes. Untied aid (unconditional assistance) also would not provide any assurance for the achievement of the reform goals. Unconditional assistance is only appropriate if the donor's objective is simply to augment the fiscal capacity of the recipient to follow its own priorities.

Government ownership in the absence of citizen-centric governance holds no assurance of country ownership.

"Country ownership" is considered critical to a project's success as confirmed by various evaluation reports. Most of this literature, however, equates "country ownership" with "government or ruling regime" ownership. But government ownership in the absence of citizen-centric governance or strong citizen empowerment holds no assurance that broader development effectiveness objectives cherished by donors would be fulfilled even if the project was successful. Therefore, program design using a results-based chain must pay close attention to the reach (see Chap. 2, Fig. 2.1) or winners and losers associated with each program. This emphasis is a missing link in aid deliberations including the EC Results Framework. In the absence of such attention, the so-called country ownership is a necessary but not a sufficient condition to ensure equity in public services provision and the feasibility and sustainability of the program.

The conditionality of assistance can be an important tool for positive inducement for commitment and ownership.

World Bank (2005) observes the following regarding conditionality and country ownership: "The main lesson learned from the literature is that conditionality can be useful in helping identify and implement necessary reforms but it is only when there is 'ownership' of the policy that conditionality can succeed, Conditionality helps when it supports governments already strongly committed to reform". (p. i, para 4).

The survey of conceptual literature presented earlier contradicts the above observation. Especially for structural and institutional reforms, conditional assistance is a means to provide a positive inducement for commitment and ownership to reform, failing which there will be financial consequences for the recipient. If the country already had ownership of and commitment to such reforms, it may only need external technical assistance for most governance and institutional reforms and conditionality would be irrelevant and financial assistance in most non-crisis cases probably not necessary.

The conditions and associated indicators should be mission critical, parsimonious, objectively and accurately measurable, timely, meaningful and understandable, firmly grounded in the results-based chain, administratively simple (cost-effective), comparable, well-documented, facilitate streamlined reporting, well-publicised for public scrutiny, and could be verifiable by ordinary citizens or independent scholars and think tanks.

To ease administrative burden, to the extent possible, indicators chosen should be based on data that are already being collected. Further, the indicators chosen must avoid unintended perverse incentives as often "what gets measured is what gets done". No conditions should be imposed on input allocation, spending levels, program and process design. However, transparency of the results-based chain should permit citizens and independent experts to monitor the entire chain. Monitoring of performance by the donor must be linked to timely feedback to the recipient on his performance. Compliance failures should have credible and significant consequences both for the recipient government as well as the aid agency. Incentives for staff career progression in the aid agency and government should be linked to the development effectiveness of such assistance. An independent rating agency may be encouraged to rate both the donor and the recipient for development effectiveness of their aid-financed programs. Administrative costs of external finance should reflect these ratings just as country credit ratings have implications for capital market access and risk premiums by individual countries.

Program design must attempt to mitigate the unintended negative consequences of the conditionality. Unco-ordinated cross conditionality should be avoided in the interest of better policy and program implementation by designating a donor institution with the lead agency role.

We have already noted that external assistance poses many moral hazards for recipients. These include: positive incentives for delaying reforms and getting rewarded for late implementation by fulfilling donor conditions; putting the best project forward to donors for which domestic financing was assured in order to avail the opportunity to have unproductive pet public expenditures financed by donor resources; the opportunity for bureaucratic and political elite to receive private gains, including employment opportunities for relatives and kin in donor institutions; profit from procurement processes and rules; perpetuating the rule of unpopular regimes; improved fiscal position contributing to postponement or abandonment of fundamental reforms. On the aid agency side, moral hazard arises from aid agency contractors choosing project design options that maximise their profits. They may also face positive incentives in reporting results leading to project selection (so-called adverse selection problem) that may not be in the best interests of the principal. Aid agencies themselves may have incentives to maximise aid flows to build their dream bureaucratic empires or to ensure long-term existence through mission creep. There are no easy solutions to mitigate these moral hazards.

Whereas soft conditionality can be easily ignored, hard, strictly enforced sanction-based conditions such as fiscal rules on deficit and debt limitations, while desirable, may in some cases have negative long-term consequences for countries requiring fiscal stimulus to overcome recession. These negative externalities, however, can be mitigated by suitable design options, for example, having a review clause empowering either party to initiate a request for a joint just-in-time program review or providing an automatic escape clause from debt and deficit limitations that are linked to the decline in the growth rate of GDP as done by the Brazil's Fiscal Responsibility Law, 2000. A review clause may be a better option than an escape clause when data such as GDP becomes available with a significant time lag and preliminary data could be manipulated by a country to trigger an escape clause.

The unco-ordinated myriad conditions, at times conflicting, set by different donor agencies adversely affect policy and program implementation and place a heavy burden on recipient countries. These can be avoided by bringing all concerned institutions and donors under one specific program umbrella. Such a suggestion is difficult to implement in the current circumstances in view of the presence of a myriad of aid agencies with overlapping and conflicting mandates. If aid agencies can come to an agreement to designate a lead agency role for various tasks to various institutions, then it may be feasible for the designated lead agency to develop a critical set key conditions acceptable to all donors and the recipient.

Use country systems to minimise administrative burdens of recipient performance and compliance monitoring.

Strong trade-offs between effectiveness, ownership and administrative burdens emerge when donor conditions are unco-ordinated and are on inputs, processes and activities with donor-specific reporting, accounting and auditing requirements. The existing development assistance regimes are replete with such trade-offs, which undermine recipient ownership, impose huge administrative burdens to meet donor reporting requirements and by shifting focus on inputs and processes undermine results-based accountability and effectiveness of development assistance. These trade-offs are mitigated by output conditionality subject to wider citizen-based monitoring and evaluation and citizen empowerment for oversight on government operations and wider civil society/citizenry support for externally assisted programs. Donor monitoring should be based on the use of country systems rather than specialised reporting through project implementation units.

Results-based (output) conditionality helps mitigate strategic game theoretic responses from the recipient and donor agency staff and furthers the development effectiveness of external assistance.

Output conditionality promotes responsibility and autonomy with accountability for results. Such an approach empowers citizens to hold the government and aid agencies to account and is helpful in mutual accountability. Such conditionality is also less burdensome administratively.

For results-based mutual accountability to work, human resource management frameworks in aid agencies and government must embody results-based management and evaluation. The reform of executive boards of multilateral institutions may also be critical.

For results-based accountability to work, human resource management frameworks in both donor and recipient agencies must embody results-based management and evaluation to ensure that internal organisational incentives are aligned with the organisation's objectives. There has not been any progress in changing the culture and incentives of staff in aid agencies and in executive agencies of the recipient governments. Staff incentives continue to be in harmony with the aid maximisation culture. The executive boards of the multilateral development institutions have full-time, in-residence members with dual mandates to advance the interests of home countries, that is, maximising assistance and procurement and career interests of home country stakeholders, as well as providing oversight on the executive. These conflicting mandates undermine executive oversight and limit development effectiveness of external assistance. A part-time, non-resident board comprising government and civil society members would be more effective in its oversight role.

Fragmentation and non-predictability of external development assistance and non-credibility of conditions compromise development effectiveness.

Fragmentation and non-predictability of external development assistance also compromise development effectiveness. Credibility of non-compliance sanctions is unworkable in such an environment as donors compete against each other to benefit their own contractors/suppliers in multilateral assistance. In bilateral aid relations, political considerations undermine the sanctity of fiscal relations. Bilateral assistance often lacks a long-term perspective. This is compounded by recurring fiscal and financial crises in industrial countries. As a result, aid flows have become more unpredictable in recent years. Short time horizons and unpredictability of aid flows work to the detriment of having a long-term perspective on development finance.

Fragmentation of assistance could be overcome by reaching consensus on an overarching policy framework for the country supported by multilateral and bilateral donors and the recipient. This was the original idea behind the IMF's Country Policy Framework and the World Bank's Country Assistance Strategy and Poverty Reduction Strategy papers. These were conceptually sound initiatives but did not yield the expected results due to high transaction costs and only pro-forma commitment by some stakeholders. Renewed efforts at least at the sectoral level by using a lead agency concept may be worth trying to overcome fragmentation of assistance and restore the credibility of non-compliance sanctions.

Aid conditionality should facilitate network governance and partnership for development.

The delivery of external finance can be used as tool for forging international and domestic partnerships for development. On the international front, a single purpose aid agency/organisation could serve as the catalyst for co-ordinating and harmonising the assistance of all donors with the same focus. At the domestic front, it requires that the government act as a purchaser and financier but a competitive provider of public services and all public and non-public providers receive at-par public financing consistent with the population served. This role would be best played by local governments acting as catalysts for developing network governance by bringing together all providers—public, private for-profit, non-profit, good samaritans, self-help groups, hope-based groups and interest-based groups to form a network for local development. Thus, it would be desirable for external assistance to flow directly to local governments willing and able to forge such network governance. Aid conditionality could facilitate development of such networks.

Donor conditions can help advance inclusive and sustainable development by encouraging greater transparency, results-based accountability and citizen empowerment through direct democracy and rights-based approaches to basic public services.

While there is a consensus on inclusive and sustainable development in the development assistance community, the goal of inclusive and sustainable development remains an elusive dream. This is because the tax systems in the developing world are proportional at best and public spending lacks a pro-poor bias. External development assistance is only of modest help as donors lack basic information on the reach (winners and losers) and fiscal incidence of their programs of assistance and the poor do not figure prominently in recipient government political calculus. Recent trends towards greater transparency, results-based accountability and citizen empowerment through direct democracy and rights-based approaches to merit public services can help. Donor conditionality potentially has important role to play here.

A broken information feedback loop is better overcome by higher standards of transparency and results-based management and accountability rather than aid agency self-financed "independent" formal evaluations.

There is a large body of literature making a case for more spending by multilateral and bilateral aid agencies on formal evaluations in the interest of aid effectiveness. Martens et al. (2002) makes an interesting case for higher spending on formal evaluations as a means to enhance the information feedback mechanism. He argues that in donor countries there are two constituencies for aid with conflicting objectives—taxpayers with altruism who genuinely seek to help impoverished human beings elsewhere and suppliers of aid services who are guided by self-interest to maximise their own profits to work as intermediaries. In view of the broken feedback loop and the moral hazard posed by the aid suppliers, Martens argues that taxpayers will be kept in the dark about the beneficiaries and the effectiveness of such assistance. Formal evaluations by aid agencies can help to overcome this problem by introducing an explicit information feedback mechanism on aid effectiveness. Martens, however, recognises that such evaluations by aid agencies are subject to manipulation by aid suppliers as they are the best informed about how aid works. International experience with aid evaluations further suggests that such evaluations are typically dated and not timely for use in improving current operations and are subject to strong moral hazard influences, especially if these are financed by aid agencies, regardless of whether the evaluation office has a significant degree of independence from the management.

An interesting example is presented by the Independent Evaluation Group (IEG), which reports directly to the Executive Board of the World Bank. The staff, however, are assured career mobility within the World Bank. The career interests and ambitions of IEG staff, therefore, place a limit on their independence. Full-time, in-residence executive board members with a focus on advancing home country interests are in a weak position to safeguard the independence and integrity of such evaluations. Further, the IEG evaluates the World Bank's and country's performance based on the objectives giving little weight to their relevance. This "evaluation by objectives" methodology places a premium on defining objectives modestly and overachieving these for a highly successful outcome. In addition, the evaluation separates outcome ratings from sustainability rating. A project may be declared highly successful while it may be unsustainable. This happens for nearly one-third of so-called successful projects. This introduces an upward bias in successful project/program outcomes. A more objective evaluation methodology would use "theory-based evaluations", which establish backward linkages of outcomes to inputs in a results-based chain without worrying about specified objectives. Also, the outcome is all-inclusive of sustainable results.

In view of the moral hazard associated with aid agency financed evaluations, the information feedback loop is better established through greater transparency of aid and aid delivery mechanisms and making full information on the results-based chain made public so that independent scholars, citizens/taxpayers and think tanks can conduct their own evaluations and/or form their own views on aid effectiveness. Therefore, rather than requiring aid agencies to spend more on evaluations, they should be encouraged to disseminate objective data on the project/program more widely. Further, if the aid agencies embrace results-based management and evaluation as the human resource management paradigm, there would not be any need for in-house "independent" evaluations, as the program managers would be accountable for results and therefore incentivised to have continuing evaluations to deliver improved program performance. The resources saved from "in-house independent" or aid agency financed evaluations could be used to further transparency objectives. This would further encourage more arm's-length civil society and think tank evaluations with greater social benefits. Of course, this does not obviate the need for the aid agency's own evaluations to ensure the efficiency, equity and integrity of its operations.

References

Adam, C., et al. 2004. Performance Based Conditionality: A European Perspective. *World Development* 32 (6): 1059–1070. https://doi.org/10.1016/j.worlddev.2004.01.004.

Alesina, A., and A. Drazen. 1991. Why Are Stabilizations Delayed? *The American Economic Review* 81 (5): 1170–1189. www.jstor.org/stable/2006912.

Blondal, J.R. 2003. Budget Reform in OECD Member Countries: Common Trends. *OECD Journal of Budgeting* 2 (4): 7–25. https://doi.org/10.1787/budget-v2-art20-en.

Boadway, R., and A. Shah. 2009. *Fiscal Federalism: Principles and Practice of Multi-order Governance*. London: Cambridge University Press.

Collier, P., 1997. "The Failure of Conditionality," in C. Gwin and J. Nelson, eds., Perspectives on Aid and Development. Washington, DC: Overseas Development Council.

Collier, P., et al. 1997. Redesigning Conditionality. *World Development* 25 (9): 1399–1407. https://doi.org/10.1016/S0305-750X(97)00053-3.

Del Biondo, K. 2011. EU Aid Conditionality in ACP Countries: Explaining Inconsistency. *Journal of Contemporary European Research* 7 (3): 380–395. https://www.jcer.net/index.php/jcer/article/view/294.

Dijkstra, A.G. 2002. The Effectiveness of Policy Conditionality: Eight Country Experiences. *Development and Change* 33 (2): 307–334. https://doi.org/10.1111/1467-7660.00256.

Dollery, B., and J. Wallis. 2001. *The Political Economy of Local Government*. Cheltenham: Edward Elgar.

Drazen, A. 2002. Conditionality and Ownership in IMF Lending: A Political Economy Approach. IMF Staff Papers, No. 49, Special Issue, International Monetary Fund, Washington, DC. https://www.imf.org/external/pubs/ft/staffp/2001/00-00/pdf/ad.pdf

Dreher, A. 2004. A Public Choice Perspective of IMF and World Bank Lending and Conditionality. *Public Choice* 119: 445–464.

Easterly, W. 2005. What Did Structural Adjustment Adjust? The Association of Policies and Growth with Repeated IMF and World Bank Adjustment Loans. *Journal of Development Economics* 76 (1): 1–22.

European Commission. 2009. Aid Effectiveness After Accra: Where Does the EU Stand and What More Do We Need to Do? Commission Staff Working Paper. SEC(2009) 443. Brussels, 8.4.2009.

———. 2011. EU Common Position for the Fourth High Level Forum on Aid Effectiveness. Busan, 29 November–1 December.

———. 2015. Launching the EU International Cooperation and Development Results Framework. Staff Working Document, SWD(2015)80 final, European Commission, Brussels, https://ec.europa.eu/europeaid/staff-working-document-launching-eu-international-cooperation-and-development-results-framework_en

European Union. 2015. A Global Partnership for Poverty Eradication and Sustainable Development After 2015. Communication from the Commission to the European Parliament, the Council, the European Economic and Social Committee and the Committee of the Regions, European Commission, Brussels, https://ec.europa.eu/europeaid/sites/devco/files/com-2015-44-final-5-2-2015_en.pdf

———. 2016. Effective Development Cooperation: Has the European Union Delivered? Comprehensive Study. European Union, Brussels. https://ec.europa.eu/europeaid/effective-development-cooperation-has-european-union-delivered_en

Filimon, R., T. Romer, and H. Rosenthal. 1982. Asymmetric Information and Agenda Control: The Bases of Monopoly Power and Public Spending. *Journal of Public Economics* 17 (1): 51–70. https://doi.org/10.1016/0047-2727(82)90025-1.

Horn, M.J. 1995. *The Political Economy of Public Administration*. London: Cambridge University Press.

Huther, J., and A. Shah. 1996. World Bank Lending and Conditionality: A Game Theory Perspective on the Bank-Country Relations. Unpublished Background Paper for Huther, Roberts and Shah (1997), *op. cit.*

Huther, J., S. Roberts, and A. Shah. 1997. *Public Expenditure Reform Under Adjustment Lending: Lessons from World Bank Experiences*, World Bank Discussion Paper, No. 382. Washington, DC: World Bank. http://documents.worldbank.org/curated/en/914451468741582621/pdf/multi-page.pdf

IMF. 2007. *Structural Conditionality in IMF-Supported Programs*. Evaluation Report, Independent Evaluation Office of the International Monetary Fund, Washington, DC. www.ieo-imf.org/ieo/files/completedevaluations/01032008SC_main_report.pdf

———. 2010. Application of Structural Conditionality – 2009 Annual Report. Strategy Policy and Review Department, March 09.

———. 2012. 2011 Review of Conditionality. Strategy, Policy and Review Department, June 19.

———. 2014. *Revised Operational Guidance to IMF Staff on the 2002 Conditionality Guidelines*. Washington, DC: International Monetary Fund. https://www.imf.org/external/np/pp/eng/2014/072314.pdf

———. 2016. *International Monetary Fund Factsheet: IMF Conditionality*. Washington, DC: International Monetary Fund.

Ivanyna, M., and A. Shah. 2011. Citizen-Centric Governance Indicators: Measuring and Monitoring Governance by Listening to the People. *CESifo Forum* 1: 59–71. www.cesifo-group.de/DocDL/forum1-11-special2.pdf

Joyce, J.P. 2004. Adoption, Implementation and Impact of IMF Programs: A Review of the Issues and Evidence. *Comparative Economic Studies* 46 (2): 451–467. https://doi.org/10.1057/palgrave.ces.8100052.

Kanbur, R., and T. Sandler. 1999. *The Future of Development Assistance: Common Pools and International Public Goods*, Overseas Development Council.

Klick, R., R. Gunatilaka, and A. Marr. 1998. *Aid and the Political Economy of Policy Change*, Overseas Development Institute. London: Routledge.

Koeberle, S., et al. eds. 2005. *Conditionality Revisited, Concepts, Experience and Lessons*. Washington, DC: World Bank. http://documents.worldbank.org/curated/en/524471468320048931/pdf/32524a.pdf

Kristensen, J., W. Groszyk, and B. Bühler. 2002. Outcome Focused Management and Budgeting. *OECD Journal of Budgeting* 1 (4): 7–34. https://doi.org/10.1787/budget-v1-art20-en.

Martens, B., et al. 2002. *The Institutional Economics of Foreign Aid*. London: Cambridge University Press.

Mayer, W., and A. Mourmouras. 2002. IMF Conditionality and the Theory of Special Interest Politics. *Comparative Economic Studies* 46 (3): 400–422. https://doi.org/10.1057/palgrave.ces.8100064.

McCartney, M. 2012. Competitiveness and Pakistan: A Dangerous, Distorting and Dead End Obsession. *The Lahore Journal of Economics* 17: 213–241.

OECD. 2013. *Investing Together: Working Effectively Across Levels of Government*. Paris: OECD Publishing. https://doi.org/10.1787/9789264197022-en.

———. 2014. *Recommendation of the Council on Effective Public Investment Across Levels of Government*. Paris: OECD. www.oecd.org/effective-public-investment-toolkit/recommendation-effective-public-investment-across-levels-of-government.htm

Petersen, John, and Miguel Valadez. 2004. Borrowing Instruments and Restrictions on Their Use. In *Subnational Capital Markets in Developing Countries*, Sectiin II, eds., M. Freire, John Petersen with Marcela Huertas and Miguel Valadez, 47–110. Washington, DC: World Bank.

Rosen, H.S., and T. Gayer. 2005. *Public Finance*. Boston: McGraw Hill-Irwin.

Seabright, P. 2002. Conflict of Objectives and Task Allocation in Aid Agencies: General Issues and Application to the European Union. Chapter 2. In *The Institutional Economics of Foreign Aid*, ed. B. Martens et al., 34–68. London: Cambridge University Press.

Shah, A. 1994. *The Reform of Intergovernmental Fiscal Relations in Developing and Emerging Market Economies*, Policy and Research Series No.23. Washington, DC: World Bank.

———. 2005. On Getting the Giant to Kneel: Approaches to a Change in the Bureaucratic Culture. In *Fiscal Management*, Public Sector Governance and Accountability Series, ed. A. Shah, 211–228. Washington, DC: World Bank.

———. 2007a. A Practitioner's Guide to Intergovernmental Fiscal Transfers. Chapter 1. In *Intergovernmental Fiscal Transfers*, ed. R. Boadway and A. Shah, 1–54. Washington, DC: World Bank.

———. 2007b. Institutional Arrangements for Intergovernmental Fiscal Transfers and a Framework for Evaluation. Chapter 10. In *Intergovernmental Fiscal Transfers*, ed. A. Shah, 293–318. Washington, DC: World Bank.

———. 2012. Options for Financing Sub-national Governments in Indonesia. Chapter 13. In *Fiscal Decentralization in Indonesia: A Decade After Big Bang*, ed. Ministry of Finance Indonesia, 222–254. Jakarta: University of Indonesia Press.

———. 2014. Responsibility with Accountability: A FAIR Governance Framework for Performance Accountability of Local Governments. *Journal of Economics and Business* (Zbornik radova Ekonomskog fakulteta u Rijeci: časopis za ekonomsku teoriju i praksu/Proceedings of Rijeka Faculty of Economics) 32 (2): 343–377. https://hrcak.srce.hr/file/194351

Shah, A., and C. Shen. 2007. A Primer on Performance Budgeting. Chapter 5. In *Budgeting and Budgetary Institutions*, ed. A. Shah. Washington, DC: World Bank.

Stiglitz, J.E. 1999. The World Bank at the Millenium. *Economic Journal* 109: F577–F597.

Streeten, P. 1988. Conditionality: A Double Paradox. In *North-South Cooperation in Retrospect and Prospect*. London: Routledge.

Svensson, J. 2000. When Is Foreign Policy Credible? Aid Dependence and Conditionality. *Journal of Development Economics* 61 (1): 61–84. https://doi.org/10.1016/S0304-3878(99)00061-9.

Williamson, O.E. 1985. *The Economic Institutions of Capitalism*. New York: Free Press.

———. 2005. Transaction Cost Economics. Chapter 3. In *Handbook of New Institutional Economics*, ed. Claude Maynard and Mary Shirley, 41–65. New York: Springer.

World Bank. 1996. *Performance Audit Report: Romania: Technical Assistance/Critical Imports Loan and the SAL*, Report No. 15791.

———. 1997. *Performance Audit Report: Czech and Slovak Republics – Structural Adjustment Loan*, Report No. 16804. OED.

———. 1998. *Assessing Aid: What Works, What Doesn't and Why?* World Bank Policy Research Report. New York: Oxford University Press.

———. 1999. *Annual Review of Development Effectiveness*. Washington, DC: World Bank.

———. 2003. *Programmatic Adjustment Lending Retrospective*. Washington, DC: World Bank.

———. 2005. *Review of World Bank Conditionality. The Theory and Practice of Conditionality: A Literature Review*. Washington, DC: World Bank.

———. 2007. *Conditionality in Development Policy Lending*. Washington, DC: World Bank. http://siteresources.worldbank.org/PROJECTS/Resources/40940-1114615847489/Conditionalityfinalreport120407.pdf

Author Index[1]

[1] Note: Page numbers followed by 'n' refer to notes.

© The Author(s) 2020

A. Shah (ed.), *Policy, Program and Project Evaluation*,
https://doi.org/10.1007/978-3-030-48567-2

Subject Index[1]

[1] Note: Page numbers followed by 'n' refer to notes.

© The Author(s) 2020

A. Shah (ed.), *Policy, Program and Project Evaluation*,
https://doi.org/10.1007/978-3-030-48567-2

The manufacturer's authorised representative in the EU is Springer Nature Customer Service Centre GmbH, Europaplatz 3, 69115 Heidelberg, Germany. If you have any concerns regarding our products, please contact ProductSafety@springernature.com

Printed and bound by CPI Group (UK) Ltd, Croydon, CR0 4YY

05/10/2026

02228125-0015